THE FIFTEEN

ALSO BY WILLIAM GEROUX

The Ghost Ships of Archangel

The Mathews Men

THE FIFTEEN

× × × × × × × × × × × × × × × ×

MURDER, RETRIBUTION,

AND THE FORGOTTEN STORY

OF NAZI POWS IN AMERICA

× × × × × × × × × × × × × × ×

WILLIAM GEROUX

CROWN
NEW YORK

Published in the United States by Crown, an imprint of the Crown Publishing Group, a division of Penguin Random House LLC, New York.
crownpublishing.com

CROWN and the Crown colophon are registered trademarks of Penguin Random House LLC.

Maps on pages x to xi and on page xiii copyright © 2024 by Gene Thorp. Based on maps by the University of Wisconsin Cartographic Lab, printed in Carlson, Lewis H. *We Were Each Other's Prisoners: An Oral History of World War II American and German Prisoners of War.* New York: Basic Books, 1997.

Library of Congress Cataloging-in-Publication Data
Names: Geroux, William, author. Title: The fifteen: murder, retribution, and the forgotten story of Nazi POWs in America / William Geroux. Other titles: Murder, retribution, and the forgotten story of Nazi POWs in America. Description: First edition. | New York: Crown, [2025] | Includes bibliographical references and index. | Identifiers: LCCN 2024033251 (print) | LCCN 2024033252 (ebook) | ISBN 9780593594254 (hardcover) | ISBN 9780593594261 (ebook) Subjects: LCSH: Prisoner-of-war camps—United States—History—20th century. | World War, 1939-1945—Prisoners and prisons, American. | Prisoners of war—Germany—History—20th century. | Germans—United States—History—20th century. | Murder—United States—History—20th century.
Classification: LCC D805.U5 G467 2025 (print) | LCC D805.U5 (ebook) | DDC 940.54/7273—dc23/eng/20241129
LC record available at https://lccn.loc.gov/2024033251
LC ebook record available at https://lccn.loc.gov/2024033252

Hardcover ISBN 978-0-593-59425-4
Ebook ISBN 978-0-593-59426-1

Printed in the United States of America on acid-free paper

Editor: Paul Whitlatch
Editorial assistant: Katie Berry
Production editor: Patricia Shaw
Text designer: Aubrey Khan
Production manager: Heather Williamson
Copy editor: Elisabeth Magnus
Proofreaders: Andrea Peabbles and Lawrence Krauser
Indexer: Cathy Dorsey
Publicist: Josie McRoberts
Marketer: Chantelle Walker

9 8 7 6 5 4 3 2 1

First Edition

For my father, Raymond H. Geroux,

and for Paul R. Tyler Jr.

Contents

PART II

In German Hands

PART III

Wartime Justice

PART IV
Hostage Diplomacy

Main POW Camps for Germans in the United States

HUNDREDS OF SMALLER "BRANCH" CAMPS ARE NOT SHOWN

POW camps marked with white pull-out boxes were the scenes of
political killings by German POWs in World War II. Fort Leavenworth,
Kansas, marked in black, is where the convicted killers were held on
death row to await hanging.

MAINE
Camp Stark

VT.

N.H.

MASS.

CONN. — R.I.

NEW YORK

WISCONSIN

MICHIGAN

NESOTA

IOWA

PENNSYLVANIA   N.J.

Fort Leavenworth

OHIO

INDIANA

ILLINOIS

WEST VIRGINIA

MD. DEL.

D.C.

VIRGINIA

MISSOURI

KENTUCKY

NORTH CAROLINA

amp Gruber

Camp Chaffee

TENNESSEE

Camp Aiken

SOUTH CAROLINA

ARKANSAS

Camp Gordon

Camp Gordon

ALABAMA

GEORGIA

Atlantic

Ocean

MISSISSIPPI

Camp ntsville

LOUISIANA

ouston

FLORIDA

Gulf of

Mexico

Map by Gene Thorp

Main German Camps for Allied POWs

North Sea

SWEDEN

Copenhagen

DENMARK

EAST PRUSSIA (GER.)

Baltic Sea

DANZIG

Barth
(Stalag Luft I)

Neubrandenburg
(Stalag 2-A)

Schubin
(Oflag 64)

Elbe

Luckenwalde
(Stalag 3-A)

Berlin

Lt. Col. William Schaefer's journey as a POW

POLAND

GERMANY

Weser

Lt. James Schmitz's long winter march in 1945

NETHERLANDS

Rhine

BEL.

Colditz Castle
(Oflag 4-C)

Prague

LUX.

Luxembourg

Main

Hammelburg
(Stalag 13-C)

CZECHOSLOVAKIA

FRANCE

Danube

Vienna

SWITZ.

AUSTRIA

HUNGARY

Mauthausen
(SS labor and
death camp)

ITALY

N
W   E
S

100 Miles
100 Kilometers

Adriatic Sea

Lt. Col. **William Schaefer** was held at Oflag 64 in Poland and then transferred to Oflag 4-C at Colditz Castle in Germany.

Lt. **James Schmitz** was held at Oflag 64 in Poland and then marched in winter to Stalag 13-C at Hammelburg, Germany.

Col. **Henry Spicer** was interrogated at Stalag 3-A in Luckenwalde, Germany, and then held at Stalag Luft I in Barth, Germany.

OSS Agent Cpl. **Louis Biagioni** was held at the Mauthausen concentration camp in Austria.

Map by Gene Thorp

Cast of Characters

In Washington, D.C.

Secretary of War **HENRY STIMSON**—Supported the German POWs' murder convictions and death sentences; came around slowly to the idea of exchanging the condemned Germans for American prisoners.

Secretary of State **EDWARD STETTINIUS JR.**—His office pressed for an exchange of condemned prisoners.

President **FRANKLIN D. ROOSEVELT**—Approved several of the Germans' death sentences before his death in April 1945 forced his successor to review the sentences.

President **HARRY S. TRUMAN**— Roosevelt's death left him to decide the fates of the condemned Germans.

Army Provost Marshal General **ARCHER LERCH**—Pushed for the condemned Germans to be executed as soon as Germany surrendered.

GERMANS

Camp Tonkawa, Oklahoma

Victim

Cpl. **JOHANN KUNZE**—beaten to death on November 4, 1943

Accused killers

- 1st Sgt. **WALTER BEYER**
- Tech. Sgt. **BERTHOLD SEIDEL**
- Sgt. **HANS DEMME**
- Cpl. **HANS SCHOMER**
- Cpl. **WILLI SCHOLZ**

Camp Papago Park, Arizona

Victim

U-boat man **WERNER DRESCHLER**—hanged in the shower room on March 12, 1944

Accused killers (all U-boat crewmen)

- ROLF WIZUY
- OTTO STENGEL
- FRITZ FRANKE
- HELMUT FISCHER
- GUENTHER KUELSEN
- HEINRICH LUDWIG
- BERNHARD REYAK

Camp Chaffee, Arkansas

Victim

Luftwaffe Paratrooper HANS GELLER, fatally beaten on March 23, 1944

Accused killer

- Sgt. EDGAR MENSCHNER

Camp Aiken, South Carolina

Victim

Pvt. HORST GUENTHER—hanged on April 5, 1944, in a tent at a branch camp

Accused killers

- Sgt. ERICH GAUSS
- Pvt. RUDOLF STRAUB

Camp Hearne, Texas

Victim

HUGO KRAUSS—a native of the United States who had joined the Hitler Youth and then the Afrika Korps, fatally beaten on December 17, 1943

Accused killers

- Cpl. GUENTHER MEISEL
- Sgt. ANTON BOEHMER
- Cpl. HEINRICH BRAUN
- Cpl. ERICH VON DER HEYDT

- Sgt. HELMUT MEYER
- Cpl. WERNER HOSSANN
- Cpl. WERNER JASCHKO

Camp Concordia, Kansas

Victims

Capt. FELIX TROPSCHUH—Forced to commit suicide in his quarters on October 19, 1943

Cpl. FRANZ KETTNER—Driven to suicide on January 11, 1944

Author's Note

One October morning in 2018, I returned some books to my local library, the Meyera E. Oberndorf Central Library in Virginia Beach, and noticed a new state historical marker planted in the ground near the front entrance. It said the library was built on the site of a World War II prisoner of war camp. More than six thousand captured soldiers of Nazi Germany had been confined at POW Camp Ashby between 1944 and 1946. The marker said the camp had been part of a network of more than five hundred camps holding nearly four hundred thousand German prisoners in the United States.

I was surprised and a little embarrassed not to have known this. I have had a lifelong fascination with World War II, in which my father fought as a member of the Eighty-Second Airborne. I've read countless books about the war and written two books about it myself. How could I not have heard about all those German POW camps, including one just a few miles from my home? I went into the library and scoured the shelves in vain for a book on the subject. Then I drove through the former site of the camp, which the historical marker showed on a map. I saw no trace of Camp Ashby. In its place stood not only the library but a furniture store, an Applebee's, a strip shopping center (with my favorite Thai restaurant), and blocks of brick ranchers and two-story homes. I asked a guy on the street if he knew anything about the old POW camp. "Nope," he replied.

I went home, logged onto my computer, and plunged down an internet "rabbit hole." I found information about German POW camps all across America. Much of it consisted of surprisingly positive recollections by former prisoners of their days in the camps, and by Americans for whom the prisoners had worked. But a few of the links suggested a darker side to importing so many of Adolf Hitler's soldiers onto American soil. I began to wonder if a great story might be hidden in the camps.

I hunted down out-of-print books, starting with Arnold Krammer's seminal study, *Nazi Prisoners of War in America*. Other books had been published by small presses and university presses. I read some lively tales of escapes, but the escapes never really amounted to anything. What caught my attention was an outbreak of brutal political murders in the POW camps. Who were the victims, and why were they murdered?

None of the murders had occurred in Virginia Beach, but the conditions that spawned them had existed at Camp Ashby. A 1944 story in a local newspaper reported the camp was rife with hard-core Nazis from the Germans' famous Afrika Korps who, despite being captured, "retain all of their arrogance, of their insufferable conceit" and regarded Americans as "soft" and "inferior." A group of those Nazis had held a raucous celebration of Hitler's birthday, April 20, 1945, even as the Third Reich was disintegrating. A POW who rejected Nazism had criticized the celebrants, and they had responded by attacking him in the middle of the night. He and his friends had fought off the Nazis with two-by-fours and baseball bats, which they kept by their bunks for just such an emergency. The Nazis at Camp Ashby apparently had caused no further trouble. But, I discovered, the problem had not been so easily solved at other camps in the United States. Nazi prisoners and their followers had engaged in a campaign of deadly violence against fellow prisoners who were turning away from Hitler. The killings and their aftermath had reverberated through the highest levels of government in Washington and Berlin, and had turned American POWs in Germany into hostages.

The principal figures in the story were dead. But I found a huge trove of information about the camps and the killings at National Archives II at College Park, Maryland. I pored over the trial records and transcripts of the POW murder cases at the National Archives regional office in St. Louis and the University of California-Davis. I reviewed the personal papers of Stephen M. Farrand, a key figure in the POW camp operations, at the Hoover Institution Library and Archives at Stanford University in Palo Alto, California; and the personal papers of Leon Jaworski, who investigated and prosecuted two of the POW murder cases, in the Texas Collection at the Baylor University Library in Waco, Texas. I accessed the wartime diary of U.S. secretary of war Henry Stimson, which is held at the Yale University Library in New Haven, Connecticut. I visited hole-in-the-wall museums at former POW camp sites in the Midwest and Southwest.

Official documents only go so far in telling human stories, and I found family members of some of the American POWs who were gracious enough to speak with me. I also found hundreds of oral histories and transcribed interviews with now-deceased German POWs, camp guards, and American citizens living near the camps. The fact that so many of those accounts have survived is a tribute to local historians, both amateur and professional, who had the forethought to collect them while the men and women who lived them were still alive. Authors who write about World War II and other American history from now on will owe those people a debt.

To me, the murders touched on the most fascinating aspects of the camps—the brutal, volatile nature of Nazism; America's lack of understanding of the enemy we were detaining; and the U.S. government struggling to do the right thing under intense pressure. The story of the murders in the camps and the aftermath was unlike any war story I had heard. I have set out to tell it.

Prologue

The farmers of Cloud County, Kansas, got up before sunrise on October 19, 1943, to milk their cows and feed their chickens, hogs, and cattle, just as their parents and grandparents had done every morning for years. Change had always come gradually to Cloud County. But lately it had arrived seemingly overnight. While the farmers set about their chores, some new neighbors in the remote Kansas wheatfields were performing a very different morning ritual. Four thousand captured soldiers of Adolf Hitler's elite Afrika Korps were lining up in formation for a head count in a barbed-wire enclosure just off State Route 81. The U.S. Army was counting the German prisoners of war to make sure none had escaped overnight from a hastily built installation named POW Camp Concordia.

The camp was carved into the gently rolling hills about two and a half miles north of the town of Concordia, whose population was not much larger than the camp's. Camp Concordia, built in the course of three months between February and May of 1943, was one of hundreds of POW camps scattered across the United States and holding hundreds of thousands of German prisoners. Every day except Sunday, the Germans were led out of the camps under armed guard to work at local farms and businesses. Every night they were led back inside the camps' two concentric nine-foot fences, monitored from towers by guards with rifles, .30 caliber machine guns, and search-lights. Escapes were rare, and the head counts tended to be unevent-ful. But on the unseasonably warm and stormy morning of October 19, the count at Camp Concordia came up one man short.

The guards began calling out each prisoner by name. Miscounts were common with so many prisoners, and sometimes the Germans ducked in and out of formation to skew the count and annoy the Americans. But this time a prisoner really was missing. Capt. Felix Tropschuh, a thirty-year-old combat engineer, did not respond to re-peated calls. None of the other Germans seemed to know where he was. A contingent of guards set out for his quarters, hurrying along the camp's gravel walkways past rows of cheaply built, wood-framed barracks. Had Tropschuh simply overslept? Or was something sinister going on?

The camp had been on edge. Three days before, a guard had fatally shot a young German prisoner for chasing a soccer ball too close to the perimeter fence. The killing had nearly provoked a riot. The Ger-mans had poured out of their barracks and marched and shouted and sung martial songs for hours. They eventually had returned to their barracks, but they had erected a makeshift memorial to the dead soc-cer player, whom they insisted had been murdered. They still refused to work. Now a German officer was missing from the head count.

The guards entered Tropschuh's small, Spartan quarters, which he shared with two other officers. Tropschuh's bed was empty. He had not overslept. He was dead. His body dangled from a noose at the end of a clothesline secured to a rafter. A chair was overturned beneath his feet. A short, handwritten note lay near his body: "I voluntarily take leave of my life."

At first, the American camp commander, U.S. Army Col. Thomas Sterling, saw no reason to suspect foul play. It seemed plausible to him that Tropschuh had committed suicide. The men of the Afrika Korps had fallen far from their glory days as an elite unit of the Ger-man army under the leadership of Field Marshal Erwin Rommel. After a series of defeats, starved for supplies and ammunition, they had been forced into a mass surrender and shipped five thousand miles to sit out the rest of the war on the Kansas prairie. To some Germans, Concordia felt like an alien land. The distances between towns and even farmhouses were immense. The wind never stopped blowing, "hotter than heck in the summer and colder than heck in the winter," a guard said. One POW awakened in a panic whenever a ferocious Midwest thunderstorm struck in the middle of the night, fearing he was under a Russian artillery barrage. Prisoners worried about their loved ones in Germany, with good reason. Letters from home took months to arrive or just stopped coming. By the time Tropschuh's body was found, several despondent Germans already had taken their lives at POW camps in the United States, including one at Camp Concordia.

Still, something about Tropschuh's death did not add up. When the army made plans to dig his grave next to the graves of two Germans who previously had died at Concordia, the highest-ranking German officer in the camp, Col. Alfred Koester, bristled. Koester, who acted as spokesman for all POWs at the camp, declared Tropschuh had dishonored Germany by killing himself. Therefore, he must not be allowed to share the same ground with the two "honorable" Germans who had died before him. That made no sense to the Americans because one of those "honorable" Germans also had committed suicide. But the camp commander, Colonel Sterling, did not argue. He may have been trying to reduce the tension at Concordia. He agreed to bury Tropschuh in an outlying, unused part of the camp cemetery. Colonel Sterling offered to provide fabric for the Germans to fashion a flag with a swastika to drape over the coffin, as with the two previous cases. But Colonel Koester would not accept the fabric. He refused to have anything to do with Tropschuh. A detail of U.S. Army guards lowered the bare coffin into the grave with military honors—a rifle salute and the playing of "Taps"—as required by the Geneva Convention, an international treaty governing the treatment of POWs. None of the four thousand Germans at Concordia attended the burial ceremony. The Americans had to wonder.

No sooner had Tropschuh been laid in the ground than German

informants told army authorities what had really happened. Trop-schuh had not wanted to kill himself, they said. The ardent Nazis in the camp had orchestrated his suicide. They had handed him a chair and a clothesline and ordered him to take his own life. Behind the scenes, the Nazis ran Camp Concordia. They secretly ran other camps in the United States too. They were growing bolder, and Tropschuh would not be their last victim. The next killing was less than two weeks away, in Oklahoma. The killers would not bother making this one look like a suicide.

PART I

Life and Death
in the Fritz Ritz

1

From *Afrika* and the Sea

T ry as he might, Ernie Pyle could not get inside the heads of the
German prisoners. He was not accustomed to such difficulty. Pyle,
a frail-looking, chain-smoking, Indiana-born war correspondent, had
a gift for communicating with common soldiers. His popular newspaper column, syndicated in newspapers across the United States, offered readers a grunt's-eye view of World War II that revealed more
about the war's terror, confusion, and boredom than did the official
reports of generals and politicians. In November 1942—a year before
Tropschuh's suicide at Camp Concordia—Pyle had followed the first
American troops into combat against the Germans after Operation
Torch, the Allied invasion of North Africa. At the age of forty-two, he
crossed the Sahara Desert with infantrymen young enough to be his
sons. He pitched his pup tent among theirs and shared their meals,
bull sessions, and battles with the German Afrika Korps. Pyle understood what American soldiers cared about, what they thought of the
war, what made them tick. But his interviews with the captured Afrika Korps men left him baffled. The Germans seemed utterly divorced
from reality.

The reality that stared them and Pyle in the face was the utter defeat of the Afrika Korps on May 13, 1943. More than 170,000 captured

Germans lined the dusty roads or camped in fields under the blazing sun in the Tunisian capital of Tunis. "Today you saw Germans walking alone along highways," Pyle wrote. "You saw them riding, stacked up in our jeeps, with one lone American driver. You saw them by the hundreds, crammed as in a subway in their own trucks, with their own drivers." The Germans were hungry, thirsty, and exhausted. Their tanks and armored vehicles, bearing the Afrika Korps emblem of a swastika and a palm tree, lay abandoned, wrecked, and smoldering on the desert floor. In addition to the huge haul of prisoners, the British and American troops captured twelve German generals and "vast quantities of guns and war material of all kinds, including guns and aircraft in serviceable condition." American and British troops were astonished by the sheer number of prisoners and the acres and acres of captured equipment. For many Allied soldiers, however, the prevailing feeling was relief, "as if one has been holding one's breath, and you have just let it go for the first time," a British captain wrote to his father. American GIs kept asking Ernie Pyle if he knew when they could expect to go home.

The defeat of the Afrika Korps was not just a military disaster for Germany but a public relations one. Three years earlier, Adolf Hitler, at the height of his power, had dispatched the desert expeditionary force to Africa to bail out Germany's feckless ally, Italy, which had tried to establish a colony in Africa but was being driven off the continent by the British. The British had been fighting World War II for two years before America was thrust into the war by the Japanese attack on Pearl Harbor in December 1941. Although the United States had joined the battle against the Japanese immediately after Pearl Harbor, it had waited for almost another year before sending its armies against the Germans, in North Africa. At first, the Afrika Korps had enjoyed success under its celebrated leader, Field Marshal Erwin Rommel, the "Desert Fox." It bloodied inexperienced American troops at Kasserine Pass in Tunisia and captured the supposedly impregnable British fortress of Tobruk in Libya.

The Afrika Korps captured the public imagination too, partly because of its distinctive gear—sand-colored uniforms, long-billed caps, goggles, and long dusters. Even the British declared Rommel a genius. But Rommel had relied heavily on stolen Allied secrets, and he often outran his supply lines. When his intel and supplies ran out, he was relieved of command in Africa and sent back to Europe sick and exhausted. The Allies gained control of the Mediterranean Sea and the skies over North Africa, and cut off the Afrika Korps' food, fuel, ammunition, and reinforcements. The Germans were forced to retreat into encirclement at Tunis and then to surrender.

The Allied victory in North Africa was in some ways a poor substitute for a victory in western Europe, which Nazi Germany still held in a vise grip. But it gave American troops experience and confidence, and a base from which to invade Sicily and Italy. The Afrika Korps surrender had come only three months after Germany's catastrophic defeat by the Russians at Stalingrad, which had changed the course of World War II. Pyle, with the aid of an interpreter, set out to hear what the captured Afrika Korps men thought of it all.

To his surprise, many of them seemed more defiant than defeated. "You seldom find a prisoner who has any doubt that Germany will win the war," Pyle wrote in a column dated May 20. "They say they lost here because we finally got more stuff into Tunisia than they had." They laughed when Pyle suggested the Allies might next invade Nazi-occupied Europe. They felt certain Germany would bring America to heel instead. They did not understand why America had gotten involved in the war. The more Germans Pyle interviewed, the more puzzled he became. "Whether from deliberate Nazi propaganda or mere natural rumor, I don't know," he wrote, "but the prisoners have a lot of false news in their heads." Some of them insisted Japan was driving the Russians out of Siberia, when in fact Japan was not even at war with Russia. One prisoner declared that the Luftwaffe—the German air force—had bombed New York City. When Pyle told him that was ridiculous, "he said he didn't see himself how it was possible."

Beneath the Germans' laughable misconceptions, Pyle found a disturbing truth: although the Germans seemed pleasant at first, "if you talk to them long enough you find in them the very thing we are fighting this war about—their superior-race complex, their smug belief in their divine right to run this part of the world." An American photographer captured an image of a "super-arrogant" German prisoner contemptuously refusing a loaf of bread. Pyle concluded that if American soldiers got the chance to speak with the Germans as he had, "they would come out of it madder than ever before at their enemy." The *Washington Star* newspaper printed Pyle's column under the headline "Nazi Prisoners Bare Superior-Race Complex and Other Screwy Ideas."

Not all the German prisoners felt the same, as their American captors would discover. But the soldiers at the heart of the Afrika Korps, particularly the officers and noncommissioned sergeants and corporals, were true believers in the Third Reich. Many had grown up in the Hitler Youth. Once in the German army, they had become even more certain of Nazi superiority by the ease with which the Wehrmacht had overrun western Europe. They were so confident that they brushed aside any development that challenged their beliefs. Their capture was just a short-lived setback on the road to conquest. Their faith in Hitler and Nazism was frozen in time. One angry Afrika Korps lieutenant, Willy Wulf, wrote to his wife: "After a victorious end to this war, retaliation for this will be taken. We have to suffer badly here, but nothing can break our morale."

The Afrika Korps' defiance was personified by its leader, Col. Gen. Hans-Jürgen von Arnim, who had replaced Rommel in Africa. Von Arnim was an aristocrat, descended from a long line of Prussian military officers, and a fiercely committed Nazi. He was a decorated veteran of World War I and had seen World War II at its most savage, commanding a Panzer tank corps against the Russians on the Eastern Front before being transferred to North Africa. In Africa, he had rounded up Jewish civilians for the hot, exhausting labor of building fortifications. Von Arnim initially had shared command of German forces in Africa with Rommel and sometimes had clashed with him, at one point withholding tanks from a planned offensive. After Rommel's departure, von Arnim fumed over Hitler's broken promises to send supplies and ammunition to Africa. When his superiors criticized him for "squinting over your shoulder"—for worrying about

Allied attacks—von Arnim shot back that he had been "squinting at the horizon" for promised supplies that never arrived. Hitler ordered him to fight to the last man, but von Arnim reported fighting "to the last cartridge." He ordered his remaining tanks destroyed, and surrendered. He was livid. The surrender was one of many examples of troops being captured or killed in great numbers because dictators like Hitler and Joseph Stalin of the Soviet Union demanded they hold territory that no longer was defensible.

To his captors, von Arnim came across as arrogant, haughty. "Standing in the moonlit British headquarters after a hot supper last night, von Arnim's only comments were about his baggage," a United Press reporter wrote. The British treated von Arnim with deference because of his rank, but the Americans seemed to go out of their way not to. Von Arnim was indignant when Gen. Dwight D. Eisenhower refused to meet with him and sent subordinates to accept his surrender. (Eisenhower made it his policy not to meet with any German general until Germany surrendered.) Von Arnim turned out for his formal surrender in a long-waisted tunic and gleaming riding boots. When ordered to hand over his automatic pistol and knife, he threw them down. He refused to sign the formal terms of surrender, but Allied authorities said it did not matter. He rode into captivity standing up in his staff car, passing long columns of his former troops on the dusty roads. They gave him the straight-armed "Heil Hitler" salute and chanted his name as he went by.

Von Arnim was a prize catch for Allied interrogators. The British installed him in temporary lodgings at the palace of the governor of Gibraltar and then shipped him to a manicured estate in England, where he could be questioned in comfort and at leisure. Most of his troops, however, were bound much farther away. They would be shipped across the Atlantic Ocean—into a vast network of POW camps that was being hastily built for them in the United States.

There was nowhere else to put the Germans but in America. The British already were detaining more than half a million German and Italian prisoners in temporary pens. Britain, a tiny island nation, had no room to house tens of thousands of Afrika Korps men on a long-term basis. It had no spare troops to guard them and no surplus food to feed them. The United States had all of those in abundance. President Franklin D. Roosevelt pointed out that America could compel the prisoners to work on American farms. But bringing so many German soldiers to American soil raised "the specter of thousands of escaped Nazi prisoners sabotaging and raping their way across the United States," as the historian Arnold Krammer put it.

The U.S. homeland had not been entirely unscathed. After the Pearl Harbor attack, a Japanese submarine had fired on an oil refinery in Santa Barbara, California; another sub had launched a miniature float plane and dropped incendiary bombs to start forest fires in the Pacific Northwest.* German U-boats attacked Allied cargo ships all along the U.S. East and Gulf Coasts, sometimes torpedoing them before the eyes of startled beachgoers. Germany had conducted sabotage operations in America in both world wars. During World War I, German agents had detonated a cache of explosives at a rail yard on Black Tom Island at the tip of Lower Manhattan, causing a thunderous explosion that killed four people including a baby and pockmarked the Statue of Liberty with shrapnel. And in June 1942—eleven months before the Afrika Korps surrender at Tunis—German U-boats had landed two four-man teams of saboteurs on beaches in New York and Florida with orders to strike at power plants, aluminum plants, the locks of the Ohio River, and the New York City water supply. The mission quickly fell apart when its leader lost his nerve and turned himself in to the FBI. All eight Germans were convicted of espionage and sentenced to death; six died in the electric chair in the Washington, D.C., jail, while two who had given evidence against the others received long prison terms. The Roosevelt administration touted the foiled sabotage plot as proof of the government's vigilance.

While Germany and Japan searched constantly for ways to strike

---

* Later in the war, the Japanese launched thousands of large hydrogen balloons carrying incendiary bombs across the Pacific toward the United States on the easterly winds. One balloon killed five people in Oregon; another set a garage on fire near Chicago; still another momentarily cut the power to a facility in eastern Washington State where plutonium was being produced for the atomic bomb.

Americans where they lived, most communities in the United States were a world away from the battlefields. For families with no loved ones overseas, the home front war mostly amounted to following the war news and coping with the rationing of foods such as sugar, meat, coffee, and butter, as well as rubber and gasoline (whose shortages prompted restrictions on "pleasure driving"). Hundreds of thousands of American men and women went to work in factories and shipyards to mass-produce the tools of war. The automaker Chrysler built tanks and antiaircraft guns. Its competitor Ford manufactured B-24 bombers. The industrialist Henry Kaiser developed shipyards capable of churning out cargo vessels, called Liberty ships, in thirty days or less. Smaller factories produced everything from radios to parachutes to mosquito netting. It was those vital home front industries that the U.S. government hoped to protect from escaped POWs.

At first, the United States agreed to accept only "an emergency batch" of 50,000 German prisoners, reasoning that any larger number would pose an unacceptable security risk. But that worry quickly gave way to sheer necessity. The United States agreed to take an additional 55,000 Afrika Korps men, and then 30,000 more. The total of 135,000 was more soldiers than America had had in uniform when it entered World War II. The German POWs were "a white elephant on our hands," Ernie Pyle wrote from North Africa. "And yet . . . what we want is about 50 or more white elephants just like this one."

The U.S. government intended to treat the Germans well in the United States, for reasons both moral and calculating. America had signed on to the 1929 Geneva Convention, an international treaty that outlined requirements for the humane treatment of POWs. All the major powers in World War II had signed except for Japan and the Soviet Union. The Convention said prisoners must be treated as soldiers loyal to their countries of origin, not as civilians or war criminals. They could retain their citizenship, their military ranks, and their chains of command. They were to be housed and fed just like American soldiers based in the United States. They were allowed regular contact with their families, the German government, the Swiss, the International Red Cross, and other agencies.

Neutral Switzerland accepted the difficult role as "Protecting Power" under the Geneva Convention. The Swiss were tasked with inspecting both German and Allied POW camps and acting as a go-between in disputes about the treatment of prisoners. Warring nations had engaged neutral third nations to mediate such matters since at least the sixteenth century. The United States had served as "protecting power" for several of the countries fighting World War I until America entered the war and its "protecting power" duties were divided among the Swiss, Dutch, and Spanish. The Geneva Convention made engaging a "protecting power" optional. Most of the combatants in World War II nonetheless chose the Swiss for that role.

The Geneva Convention's requirements for the treatment of POWs struck some Americans as dated and overly generous—"an outworn code of military chivalry instituted when war was still the sport of gentlemen," one newspaper columnist wrote. To others, treating prisoners well was simply the right thing for a great nation to do. "We ought to be humane and generous," *Collier's* magazine declared, "because we are Americans and because we believe as a nation in decency, humanity, humaneness and a break for the underdog, which prisoners certainly are."

The United States also had a purely selfish motive for adhering closely to the Geneva Convention: by treating enemy prisoners well, America might encourage its enemies to treat captured American soldiers well. Humane treatment of POWs was not a given in World War II. In the Pacific, the Japanese frequently abused and killed prisoners. On the Eastern Front in Europe, the Germans and Soviets executed and enslaved each other's captured soldiers. The Germans seemed to have tried to abide by the Geneva Convention in their treatment of British and Canadian prisoners, and to have extended that approach to American POWs after the United States entered the war. But what would Hitler do when he became desperate? Harrowing reports of the organized killing of Jews showed what the Nazis were capable of. The Germans already had captured thousands of American soldiers in North Africa and would capture tens of thousands more in Europe. For the time being, all the American government could do to protect them was to treat German prisoners well and hope Germany reciprocated. The U.S. House Military Affairs Committee declared that America must follow the Geneva Convention to the letter, "since the slightest deviation therefrom on our part would instantly result in more than retaliatory measures on the part of our enemies against American prisoners of war in their hands. Such a contingency must not be overlooked for a single instant."

×　　×　　×

After their capture at Tunis, the Afrika Korps men were held for weeks in pup tent cities in the North African desert, where they queued up in long lines for turns at the water tank. They were plagued by mosquitoes, extreme temperature changes, and the ever-present threat of abuse by vengeful Arabs and French guards. Then they were packed like sardines into boxcars and cattle cars, with no latrines or sufficient water, and carried by rail for more than five hundred miles to the ports of Oran in Algeria and Casablanca in Morocco. Those ports were the delivery points for convoys of Allied cargo ships hauling supplies and reinforcements across the Atlantic from the U.S. East Coast. Most of the vessels were Liberty ships, newly built American freighters whose cavernous cargo holds could accommodate nine thousand tons of supplies. Once the cargo was unloaded in North Africa, the prisoners were loaded into the ships' empty holds for the return voyages to the United States. There were so many German POWs that even luxury ocean liners were pressed into service to carry them to America. British prime minister Winston Churchill was surprised to discover he was sailing with German prisoners aboard the RMS *Queen Mary* on his way to meet with Roosevelt in June 1943.

Many of the POW ships were hopelessly overcrowded. Heino Erichsen and his fellow Germans slept on the steel deck in the cargo hold, wrapped in blankets the ship's captain had provided. Erichsen witnessed fierce political arguments on the ship that "convinced me that the Nazis still felt powerful, not only in Germany but in our midst." The ardent Nazis on another POW transport ship gave American merchant mariner Jim Greer the creeps. They glared at the American crew and spoke only among themselves, in low tones. "They always looked like they were scheming," Greer recalled. On a different transport ship, a U.S. Army nurse, 2nd Lt. Yvonne Humphrey, found some of the German officers openly hostile: "You felt rather than saw the great loathing inside them for all things democratic and American."

The voyage from North Africa to America took from six days to three weeks, depending on the weather and the level of U-boat activity. In one of the war's many ironies, German POWs sailed to America under constant threat from their own submarines, which stalked the North Atlantic convoys in wolfpacks. A captured U-boat crewman on his way to America, Rüdiger von Wechmar, found the voyage particularly frightening because "I know what torpedoes do to ships." At one point in the trip, the captain announced over the ship's loudspeaker that U-boats had been detected ahead and that all the prisoners should put on their life vests. Von Wechmar knew the vests would be little help if the ship was sunk in midocean. There were nowhere near enough lifeboats for all the prisoners, and no other ship would stop to pick up survivors and risk becoming the U-boats' next victim. The captain tried to reassure the prisoners by telling them he had radioed the Red Cross to warn the U-boat commanders not to kill their own comrades. Von Wechmar thought to himself, "Well, that will never work."*

Von Wechmar was one of a growing number of U-boat men being captured by the Allies. By the middle of 1943, advances in Allied antisubmarine tactics and technology had transformed the U-boats from the hunters into the hunted. U-boats were being sunk as never before, but the outgunned submariners rarely gave up without a fight. The U-615, for example, was stalking Allied tankers in the Caribbean Sea in August 1943 when an Allied bomb disabled its diving mechanism.

---

* Despite numerous U-boat sightings, no Allied vessel transporting German prisoners to the United States was ever sunk by a U-boat. But in the Pacific on July 1, 1942, an American sub in the South China Sea sank a Japanese merchant ship, the *Montevideo Maru,* that was carrying more than 1,000 Allied prisoners, including 850 Australians. It was Australia's largest loss of life at sea during the war.

That left the sub a sitting duck on the water's surface four thousand miles from home. Instead of surrendering, the crew manned the sub's antiaircraft guns and fought a weeklong running battle with Allied warplanes. The U-615 shot down one plane and damaged two others. But the planes' bombs and machine guns took a toll. On the morning of August 7, the submarine commander ordered the surviving crewmen to abandon ship. Then he took the U-boat to the bottom himself to keep the Allies from capturing it. The forty-three survivors swam to a British rescue ship, where an interrogator found their morale high. A young German named Rolf Wizuy stood out for his sheer arrogance. "Here is an oyster of the Nazi school who can be opened only with the greatest difficulty," his interrogator wrote of him. "This fanatic refuses to disclose even the most innocent facts." Wizuy and his boatmates, like their comrades in the Afrika Korps, would carry the spirit of Nazi Germany into the POW camps in the United States.

As the prisoner transport ships approached New York Harbor, some of the Germans stared at the New York City skyline. It showed no sign of the bomb damage that Nazi propagandists had insisted the Luftwaffe was inflicting on the United States. The dedicated Nazi POWs insisted the propaganda was true: the ships surely were being routed away from the bombed-out areas. When the liner *Queen Mary* docked in New York Harbor in June 1943 with thousands of prisoners, eight Germans squeezed through a porthole and plunged into the water. A sentry on the docks saw the splashes and fired a warning shot, which brought a rush of police and contingents of the U.S. Marines, Navy, and Coast Guard. Patrol boats beamed searchlights on the swimmers and the marines jumped in after them. "Some of the Germans were overtaken and after desperate battles were captured and dragged ashore," the Associated Press reported. "All were soon captured with the exception of a submarine officer who was found hiding beneath an Army truck."

Day after day, the ships landed thousands of Germans in New York, Boston, and Newport News, Virginia. Once on U.S. soil, the prisoners were fingerprinted and given numbers. They were deloused with insecticide sprayed over their heads and into "every hairy area," a prisoner wrote. They were issued clean new denim uniforms with "PW" stenciled on the backsides, sleeves, and pant legs. "High-value" prisoners such as senior officers and U-boat crewmen were taken to a secret interrogation center at Fort Hunt, Virginia, outside Washington, D.C. But the vast majority of incoming prisoners were put on passenger trains for the final legs of their journeys to their assigned camps. The Germans rode in surplus Pullman coaches with upholstered seats. They were amazed; the German army had always traveled in boxcars. "There were immediate shouts of 'Man, oh, man!' and 'How about that!' when we followed orders to board the coaches," wrote one prisoner.

As the trains carrying the Germans rumbled along a web of rail lines connecting the East Coast to the South, Midwest, and beyond, the U.S. Army was scrambling to get ready for them. The army built some camps from scratch in only three months. The typical camp was a one-square-mile, self-contained cluster of crude, wood-framed barracks, surrounded by barbed-wire fences and guard towers. The train rides to camps in the Midwest took three full days without any stops, and the Germans marveled at America's sheer size. "We traveled . . . through huge areas, incredible distances for a German," prisoner Heinz Richter wrote to his family. "Our Germany is not much larger than one of the American states." Karl Gassman noticed that America seemed untouched by the war: "No blackout at night, streets and parking lots in front of the factories filled with cars, everything full of energy and efficiency," he wrote. "We began to understand that this powerful and resourceful land couldn't be overcome." Some prisoners also were struck by America's natural beauty—herons gliding through the marshes of Houma, Louisiana, where gray strings of Spanish moss hung from the trees "like a veil." A U-boat man found "a weird, compelling beauty" in the Sonoran Desert in Arizona that reminded him of the sea.

The train rides failed to impress the Nazi true believers. Two were killed leaping from moving trains, and a third was fatally shot when he fled along a station platform toward a crowd of civilians. Dietrich Koll stayed on his train but made a list of every town it passed so that he could find his way back to the coast when he escaped. His list started with the port of Newport News, Virginia, and tailed off with the Nebraska towns of Chadron, Whitney, and Crawford. Some of the Nazis insisted the trains were being driven in circles to make America look bigger and more formidable than it was. One Afrika Korps sergeant watched the green Midwest prairie roll past and remarked, "Many fields, good earth, many automobiles—that all will be our colony at some time." It would take more than barbed wire and guard towers to deal with some of these men.

2

"I Just Didn't Lose"

Leonidas "Leon" Jaworski was born in Waco, Texas, in 1905, the son of immigrants who came to Texas from Germany seeking opportunities for their children. His Polish-born father, Joseph, had emigrated to Germany as a young man in order to study at universities and a seminary, from which he had emerged as an evangelical Presbyterian minister. But Joseph considered Europe "a continent dominated by royalty, a land in which one's life seemed regimented by birth," whereas in America "every man was free to seek his own destiny and worship God as he chose." Joseph spoke several languages fluently and was fascinated by ancient history. He named Leonidas after the Spartan king who had defended the pass at Thermopylae against the Persians in 480 B.C.; one of Leon's brothers was named Hannibal.

Only two years after Leon's birth, his Austrian-born mother, Mira, became ill, and her doctor recommended a more restful environment than the bustling young city of Waco. Joseph took a job as pastor of a small church in the German immigrant enclave of Geronimo in Guadalupe County. He drove a horse-drawn buckboard wagon between tiny, far-flung churches, preaching in German to fellow immigrants in a deep baritone. Leon worried anytime his father had not returned by nightfall. "The nearest neighbor lived over a mile away," he wrote. "Night winds moaned in the cedars in the front yard, and I would shiver at the wail of the coyotes in the mesquite grove that stretched endlessly outside our bedroom window."

The move to Geronimo did not help Leon's mother, who died only a year later, when Leon was three years old. She was buried on the Texas prairie beneath a granite cross with the German inscription *Die Liebe Höret Nimmer Auf*—"Love Never Ends." Leon had barely known her. But his father, "a dark-haired man with a black moustache and burning brown eyes," provided plenty of inspiration and guidance. Joseph took the boy along with him when he baptized babies and delivered stern sermons about the wages of sin. He instilled in Leon a deep faith in God's love and his laws. For the rest of his life, Leon would pray before every significant choice or challenge. Joseph also taught him to stand up for what he believed, even if it cost him dearly, as it had cost his namesake at Thermopylae. Joseph insisted his children work hard and be ambitious. They had to take full advantage of the opportunities for which their parents had crossed the ocean on a steamship. Joseph's teachings formed the bedrock of Leon's life.

After Joseph remarried, the family moved in 1914 back to Waco. The city had grown into a center of the cotton and insurance industries, with a population of about thirty-five thousand. Nine-year-old Leon was awestruck by the traffic and long blocks of buildings, including what was then the tallest building in Texas. Waco was a city of churches—the "buckle on the Bible Belt"—and dominated by the spires of Baylor University, a Baptist school. But the city also had a pioneering, rough-and-tumble spirit that tested Leon from the day he returned.

The family had always spoken German around the house in Geronimo, and Leon arrived in Waco with a thick German accent that his classmates mocked. At first, he struggled to read English-language textbooks. He was slight of build with a "muffin face"—a square head with a bulbous nose—that made him look younger than he was. Adjusting to life in Waco became even harder when America entered

World War I in 1917. Anti-German and anti-immigrant sentiment swirled through the city. Streets that had been named for Beethoven and Wagner were renamed for General Pershing, President Woodrow Wilson, and other American leaders. Sauerkraut, a staple of German Americans' diet, was renamed "liberty cabbage." Sometimes the taunts intensified into confrontations. A stranger strode up to Leon's father on the street, called him a "dirty Hun," and punched him in the face. A federal agent visited Joseph's new church in Waco after a passerby reported hearing the flock of mostly German immigrants chanting support for the Imperial German Army. In fact, the congregation had been singing "A Mighty Fortress Is Our God" in German.

Leon finally found acceptance among his peers through his talent for debate. He won a high school debating championship as a junior, and again as a senior. That success prompted him to abandon his childhood dream of becoming a doctor, like his brother Hannibal, and decide to become a lawyer. The law "offered an opportunity halfway between medicine and the ministry," he decided. "Some kind of idealism is essential to the lawyer's fulfillment of his duties." At the age of sixteen, Leon enrolled at Baylor, working in his professors' offices to help pay tuition. That same year, he was shocked when a small-town Texas sheriff in the nearby town of Lorena was shot and wounded while trying to stop an illegal Ku Klux Klan march. Leon was appalled that some of the most prominent men in Lorena, as well as in Waco, hid beneath hoods and robes in order to terrorize immigrants. Most of those Klansmen were churchgoers who regarded themselves as God-fearing men. As disturbing as those revelations were, Jaworski wrote, they served him well in the coming years: "I better understood the news stories on the rapid spread of Nazism."

After a year as an undergraduate at Baylor, Jaworski applied to its law school. The dean rejected him for being too young, so he presented his sterling academic record to the school president, who admitted him. He graduated from the law school at the age of nineteen, becoming the youngest lawyer in Texas history. He earned a Master of Court degree at George Washington University in Washington, D.C., while working part-time for Texas U.S. senator Thomas Connally. At night after classes, Jaworski sometimes traveled to small churches in Maryland to preach so that the regular pastors could take a night off.

Jaworski returned to Texas and immersed himself in the practice of law. He was a driven man with little time for pleasant distractions. "I have no patience with minutia," he wrote in his autobiography. "I have spent my life cutting through trivia, getting to the core of a story. Maybe this is why I have read, from beginning to end, only two long novels in my lifetime: *Gone with the Wind* and *Dr. Zhivago*." He prepared exhaustively for cases, but his forte was arguing them in court. He had a gift for reading people on the witness stand and in the jury box. He cut his teeth as a criminal defense lawyer, representing moonshiners and bootleggers. In 1929, he was appointed by a judge to defend an illiterate Black tenant farmer accused of fatally shooting a White couple. Jaworski believed the farmer's claims of innocence. His client had no hope of being acquitted by an all-White jury in small-town Texas. Jaworski tried to spare him from the electric chair.

The case exposed ugliness beneath Waco's surface. Jaworski received obscene phone calls and anonymous death threats, which reminded him of his family's experiences during World War I. But he never considered quitting the case. The jury convicted the farmer. Jaworski won him a new trial. Then he discovered his client was guilty; he had killed the two victims in a robbery. Jaworski kept defending him but could not prevent him from being convicted a second time and executed. Jaworski never lost another client to the electric chair. In one capital case, he wrote, he told the jurors that if they were considering sentencing his client to death, they might as well just stab him to death in the courtroom. Jaworski drew a stiletto from his pocket and offered it to the jury foreman, who blanched and refused to take it. Jaworski would change his views about the death penalty several times over the course of his life.

One day in 1929, friends introduced Jaworski to a lawyer from Houston, who offered him a job as his associate. Jaworski hesitated to leave familiar Waco, despite the dark side it sometimes showed him. Houston was the biggest city in Texas, "a whiskey and trombone town . . . short on culture but long on credit and faith and ambition."

He asked his father, Joseph, who advised him to pray. That night, Jaworski wrote, "I sank to my knees by my bed and opened my soul to God. His answer came the next day in a clear, unmistakable conviction within me. I *knew* I should go to Houston." Jaworski admitted that earthly considerations also played a part in his decision: "Ambition, a characteristic my father sought to instill in all his children, may have influenced me." In Houston, Jaworski's clients were no longer murderers or moonshiners but wealthy families and businesses. The civil cases he tried were not usually as dramatic, but they were more complex and they paid better. Jaworski threw himself into his work but always returned to Waco on holidays. On Christmas night in 1930, he proposed to Jeannette Adam, a pretty brunette who played the organ in his father's church.

Soon after returning to Houston, Jaworski encountered John H. Freeman, a partner in the up-and-coming Houston law firm of Fulbright, Crooker, Freeman, and Bates. Jaworski had surprised Freeman by besting him in a case months before. Freeman offered him a job that was too attractive to refuse. Jaworski's clients were now big corporations and the oilmen who were transforming Texas. The latter included Glenn Herbert McCarthy, a brash, go-for-broke wildcatter who would inspire the character of Jett Rink, portrayed by the actor James Dean in the movie version of Edna Ferber's novel *Giant*. Jaworski worked harder than ever. "You can't name a lawsuit I didn't try," he recalled. "And . . . I didn't lose a lawsuit. You see, my trials were mostly jury trials, and I just won 'em. I worked like a son of a bitch. I worked at nights. I got my cases prepared. I knew what I was doing. And the reason I [got ahead] as I did is because I just didn't lose any cases." By the time America entered World War II, Jaworski had earned a reputation as a first-rate litigator and a rising star. Then in 1943 he shocked everyone he knew by announcing he was joining the army.

×   ×   ×

Jaworski was thirty-six years old and the sole breadwinner for his wife and three children. He was in no danger of being drafted. Nor did he thirst for "planetary adventure," as he put it. He joined the army because "I believed seriously in the debt I owed this country, which had embraced my parents as immigrants from Europe," he wrote. His mother's native Austria had been annexed and Nazified by Hitler, with the aim of uniting ethnic Germans; his father's native Poland had been brutally subjugated to provide food and "living space" for an expanding Germany. Jeannette Jaworski did not stand in her husband's way, but she privately worried about him leaving home to engage in "a young man's war." Jaworski set his sights on an officer's commission in the Judge Advocate General's (JAG) Office, the army's legal arm. While other prominent men used their connections to stay out of military service, Jaworski used his to get in. He pestered Senator Connally to fast-track his paperwork. He coaxed letters of recommendation out of military officers, lawyers, and judges. When a high blood pressure reading threatened to disqualify him from serving, he blamed it on a tense jury trial and asked for a retest, which produced an acceptable reading.

On June 16, 1943—a month after the mass surrender of the Afrika Korps in North Africa—the army commissioned Jaworski as a captain. He reported to Washington, D.C., for a crash course in the laws, rules, and procedures of the military justice system, about which he knew nothing. His superiors wanted to give him a desk job in Washington, but he asked to be sent into the field. They accommodated him and assigned him to the JAG office at the Eighth Service Command in Texas. He would handle criminal cases in military courts on the home front. The number of those cases was climbing as the wartime army grew into a force of more than nine million. In 1944 alone, eighteen thousand American soldiers would be convicted in general courts-martial of crimes ranging from larceny to rape to murder.

Jaworski's job mostly involved prosecuting American GIs, but he also would be responsible for prosecuting prisoners in POW camps in the United States. Escaping from a camp was not a crime; under the Geneva Convention, every prisoner had the right to escape. But the Convention allowed prisoners to be prosecuted under U.S. law for any crimes they committed in American camps, or after they had escaped, such as stealing cars. Despite Jaworski's deep German roots, he had no sympathy for captured soldiers of Nazi Germany. He saw the Allies' war against Hitler as nothing less than a struggle of good versus evil. He assumed he would be serving on the periphery. To his surprise, he soon would meet the enemy face to face, in the unlikeliest of places.

3

Incoming

The first trainload of four hundred Afrika Korps prisoners arrived at the station in Concordia, Kansas, on the steaming hot afternoon of July 3, 1943. The army tried to keep their arrival a secret, but the word got out, and a large crowd of locals showed up to watch the Germans disembark from the Pullman coaches into a formation of armed guards. The citizens, by and large, were disappointed. Hitler's supermen looked like kids—their average age was twenty-two—and they were bedraggled and weary. "They were wearing heavy uniforms and were sweating clear through," observed Chester Erickson, a local truck driver. "You could smell them a half block away." Erickson felt sorry for them. No one thought they looked particularly dangerous. Mothers of teenage girls in Concordia worried more about the American guards who drifted into town in the evenings on leave looking for a little fun. The Germans marched obediently from the train station up Highway 81 toward Camp Concordia, two and a half miles away. But the day was so hot that after a while the army sent trucks to carry the prisoners and their guards the rest of the way.

Similar scenes were playing out that summer in small communities across America. The Germans' arrival in slow-paced Hearne, Texas, south of Waco, "was the greatest thing since popcorn," a guard said.

Army authorities blocked the roads around newly built Camp Hearne, but the townspeople trekked through fields to get a glimpse. At Mexia in the Texas Hill Country, the arrival of 3,250 Afrika Korps men increased the town's population by half. In Crossville, Tennessee, Beverly Smith, a writer for *American Magazine,* watched German and Italian POWs disembark from a train and tried to imagine how it felt to them to pass from their world of fire and blood into the world of small-town America: "They glance about with a puzzled expression. For them, the Axis glory trail has led to Main Street, USA, opposite the Last Chance Café, the filling station, Cole's Cash Store, and 'New and Used Shoe Repairs While U Wait.'"

The experience was entirely new for America too. Nothing in the nation's 167-year history had prepared it for detaining large numbers of Germans in World War II. Never before had the United States brought so many captured enemy soldiers to its shores. Before World War II, America had ad-libbed its handling of relatively small numbers of POWs. It had used prisoners mainly for exchanges, ransom, or recruitment. During the American Revolution, the undermanned Continental Army released British prisoners into the colonies to find their own food, lodging, and work if they gave their word not to rejoin the fight. The British treated some American prisoners as criminals, insisting the war was merely civil unrest. In 1775, Gen. George Washington warned British lieutenant general Thomas Gage, "My duty now makes it necessary to apprize you, that for the future I shall regulate my Conduct toward [British prisoners] exactly by the Rule you shall observe toward those of ours, now in your Custody." After the British surrendered, more than five thousand Hessians—German mercenaries fighting for Britain—stayed and settled in the United States. It's entirely possible that some of their descendants employed and befriended German POWs in America during World War II.

During the Civil War, neither side had been ready for the flood of prisoners. Thousands of wounded prisoners on both sides died for want of medical attention. Overcrowded camps became breeding grounds for disease. More than fifty thousand POWs on both sides died in captivity, including thirteen thousand Union prisoners in the notorious Confederate camp at Andersonville, Georgia. Union general Ulysses S. Grant halted prisoner exchanges because he was defeating the Rebel armies by attrition. Still, thousands of prisoners were exchanged during the course of the war. After the surrender at Appomattox, more than 174,000 Confederate prisoners were allowed to return to their homes with their weapons in exchange for promises to stop fighting. Many of them went on to fight a guerrilla war against newly enfranchised Black voters and thwart Reconstruction in the postwar South.

The Spanish-American War in 1898 prompted the first organized plan by U.S. authorities to use POWs as labor, to build roads to carry American troops through undeveloped country. But the war lasted only three months, and the prisoners were released before doing any significant work. Nineteen years later, when America entered World War I in 1917, some congressmen and newspaper editors called for German prisoners to be shipped to the United States to pick crops, build highways, and serve as hostages if captured Americans were threatened. But Gen. John J. Pershing, the commander of the American Expeditionary Forces in Europe, wanted the POWs to stay in France and work for him. Only 1,336 German prisoners ended up in the United States.

Given America's scant experience with POWs in World War I, the U.S. government had no blueprint for handling an influx of prisoners in World War II. The care and feeding of POWs in the United States was a far lower priority than training American GIs to fight overseas and producing the weapons they needed. On the day the Afrika Korps surrendered in Tunis, the United States held only about 380 enemy prisoners on American soil. Most of them were German and Italian merchant seamen whose cargo ships had been docked at U.S. ports when Hitler declared war on America four days after Pearl Harbor. By the time the Allies prevailed in North Africa in May 1943, American troops had been fighting the Japanese in the Pacific for seventeen months, but few Japanese POWs had come to the United States. The Pacific battlefields were too far away, and many Japanese soldiers fought to the death rather than surrender, which they had been taught was dishonorable. The total number of POWs in America in the spring of 1943 did not include the nearly 120,000 men, women, and children of Japanese heritage whom U.S. authorities uprooted from their homes on the West Coast and interned in dusty, remote, primitive camps, on the chance they might be disloyal.

U.S. authorities did not begin seriously planning to detain German POWs until September 1942, a month before the invasion of North Africa. Even then, they anticipated a relatively small number of prisoners. No one in Washington imagined that nearly four hundred thousand German POWs would end up in America. The task of running POW camps in the United States was assigned to the U.S. Army's newly created Provost Marshal General's Office, which also was tasked with staffing the camps with guards and protecting potential sabotage targets. The first POW camps in the United States were set up in places that could be repurposed easily for that role: old, vacant Civilian Conservation Corps camps and unused parts of existing U.S. military bases, including Fort Bliss, Texas; Fort Bragg, North Carolina; Fort Devens, Massachusetts; Fort Meade, Maryland; Camp Shelby, Mississippi; and Fort Sill, Oklahoma. By September 1942, the army had seven camps ready for prisoners and was building nine others. It already was clear, however, that those camps would not be nearly enough. In December, Congress readily gave the army $50 million— roughly $1 billion in today's dollars—to build scores of additional POW camps from scratch.

The army's initial criteria for siting new camps were national security and cost. The ideal camp would be built in a rural area, far from population centers, national borders, navigable waterways, and factories involved in the war effort. It would be located along a rail line for easy transport of prisoners and supplies. And it would be built in the South or Southwest, where land and labor were cheap and the mild climate would reduce the cost of insulation. But events soon would compel the army to relax its criteria and build camps in almost every corner of the continental United States. It would end up building more than 600 of them, including 155 large, "main" camps for 1,000 to 4,000 prisoners, and 450 smaller "branch" camps, for between 150 and 400 prisoners. It would build at least one camp in each of the then-forty-eight states except North Dakota. The camps would be concentrated in the South and Southwest, as the army originally had intended. Texas would house the most camps with thirty-three, followed by Arkansas with seventeen and Oklahoma with fifteen. But New York State would have fourteen camps; California and Nebraska, eleven; and Michigan, ten. By 1944, tens of millions of Americans would have German prisoners as neighbors, although many of them would not know it.

The army either bought or leased the parcels for large, "main" camps it chose to build in areas with no suitable federally owned property. It hired contractors to build the camps as quickly and cheaply as possible, to a simple, uniform design: a one-square-mile parcel of land with a cluster of barracks and support buildings at its core. That core was surrounded by two parallel chain-link fences, each of them nine feet tall and topped with barbed wire. Guard towers stood at intervals along the fences, manned around the clock by GIs with rifles, .30 caliber machine guns, and searchlights. The barracks were rows of crude, wood-framed, single-story buildings, covered with tar paper or corrugated tin for insulation, and resting on bricks or concrete slabs. In each barracks, rows of cots and footlockers surrounded one or more potbellied stoves, which provided the only heat. Each camp was divided into three or four POW compounds, each separated from the others by fences. Each compound had its own barracks; mess hall; latrine with toilets, showers, and hot and cold running water; infirmary; parade ground for daily head counts; recreation field for soccer and other sports; workshop; and canteen where prisoners could relax and buy small items.

The American guards occupied a separate section of the camp with the same layout and facilities as the German sections, as well as a headquarters building, a post office, a chapel, an officers' club, warehouses, and a water tower, which usually was the tallest structure for miles around. The Geneva Convention required that guards and POWs live in similar conditions. The army took that requirement so seriously that at times when overcrowding temporarily forced some

POWs to sleep in tents, their guards had to pitch tents too. Smaller "branch" camps radiated out from the main camps, like forward operating bases in combat zones, bringing prisoners closer to farms and businesses where they worked. Some branch camps were little more than tent cities encircled by barbed wire.

Camp Concordia in north-central Kansas met all the army's criteria for an ideal "main" camp. The property was near the geographic center of the United States. It was remote even by the standards of the rural Midwest. In order to clear the property, workers had had to chop down a profusion of wild sunflowers that towered over the barracks buildings. The only nearby border to Concordia was Nebraska's. The nearest community of any size was the town of Concordia (population 5,647), which lay two and a half miles to the southeast. The site was close enough to the Red River to dump its untreated sewage into the water, in the custom of the day. The army bought the 660 acres for the camp for $27,800 from three local farmers, who complained they were not getting fair value for their property. The Army Corps of Engineers developed the plan for the camp and hired contractors from Nebraska to build it quickly, in time for the prisoners to arrive.

Local politicians and businessmen welcomed Camp Concordia for the jobs, revenue, and POW labor. The region was still recovering from the Great Depression, and farmers in Kansas and throughout the United States were desperate for laborers. By the spring of 1943, American farms, ranches, canneries, and other businesses had lost more than three million workers to the military and the booming war industries. In Kansas alone, 195,000 men had left farm jobs. Schools dismissed children early so they could work longer hours in the fields. Kansas congressman Clifford R. Hope introduced a letter from one of his constituents:

> I am a widow 56 years of age, and my son and I are alone on a farm of 200 acres. I am not able to do the farm work, but I keep the home and take care of the chickens and the garden while he farms the land, raises hogs, and milks cows. We have our

farm machinery and have a good deal of livestock, and we will have a lot of fall pigs to take care of. My son does all the farming, but he has now been ordered to the hospital for examination, and if he is called into the Army, I do not know what in the world to do.

But some citizens feared the prospect of Hitler's soldiers moving into their isolated communities. "I never felt comfortable having the Germans so near," wrote Rachel Forsberg of Concordia. After the Board of Commissioners of Butler County, Kansas, voted to pursue a branch camp, opponents of the project gathered 1,053 signatures on a petition asking the board to reconsider: "These unsocial and fanatic soldiers of Adolph Hitler are ill prepared to be thrust upon the citizenry of Butler County and are desperate characters when given a chance to escape." A coalition of farmers and stockmen persuaded the commission to stand by its vote. After a camp was proposed for Ottawa, Kansas, a woman wrote a letter to the *Ottawa Herald* asking, "Are the people of Ottawa so soft that they can't get along without the help of a Nazi? . . . My husband is out there on a ship in the Pacific fighting for you and me. The servicemen are working twenty-four hours a day—Can't we work a little harder ourselves and not have a prison camp in our fair city?" In the end, economic need usually trumped all other considerations. The Germans came to rural America.

Some of the Germans were just glad to be anywhere other than North Africa. "We were tired, exhausted soldiers who were hunted in the last days in Tunisia like hares," Alfred Arens wrote. At his POW camp at Fort McClellan, Alabama, he was issued a comfortable cot with clean sheets, blankets, and quilts, and a new set of clothes in addition to his Afrika Korps uniform: two pairs of shoes, three pairs of pants, a wool jacket, five pairs of socks, four pairs of underwear, four undershirts, a raincoat, a pair of gloves, and some handkerchiefs. The American camp commander promised to treat Arens and his fellow POWs in strict accordance with the Geneva Convention and never to go out of his way to make their lives harder. The Germans were allowed to choose their own leaders, including an overall camp spokesman to serve as their main point of contact with the Americans, the Swiss, the International Red Cross, and various POW assistance groups. Arens rejoiced when his first day in camp ended with "a meal of turkeys big like eagles served by men in white jackets; we thought we had arrived in paradise."

The quantity and quality of the food in the camps amazed the Germans. "Here we eat more in a single day than during a whole week at home," one prisoner wrote to his family. Another felt guilty about using flour to line the POW soccer field while some people in Germany went hungry. The army even adjusted its menus in order to serve food the Germans liked, so long as their preferences did not raise costs. When it became clear that most Germans hated white bread, the army provided German cooks with the ingredients for denser German black bread. The camps quit serving corn after discovering the Germans regarded it as fit only for swine. A prisoner at Camp Trinidad in eastern Colorado wrote to his mother:

> Don't you worry anymore. You would be surprised at our food. For breakfast we have coffee, white bread, scrambled eggs with bacon and fruit. At noon, coffee, potatoes, salad, bread and butter. We also get plenty of milk. . . . Therefore, mother dear, it is as though we were on a vacation.

To the dedicated Nazis, every hearty meal and comfortable bunk was further proof of America's weakness. "If you give us good bread, it is only to coax us, to corrupt us," one Afrika Korps man declared. "If you are treating us so well, it is only because you are afraid of losing the war." The Nazis hated everything about the United States. A POW at Camp Trinidad in southern Colorado wrote: "The Americans seem to have dragged me to this place on purpose, as there can be nothing worse than this. The heat is so intense that one dares not venture outside. . . . This section of the country is fit for Indians and not for white men." A Nazi at Camp Huntsville in Texas called the

Lone Star State "a place where the devil would fight his own grand-mother." The Nazis did not intend to let the Americans lull them or their comrades into soft acquiescence. A prisoner at Camp Chaffee in Arkansas wrote to his family in Germany: "The Americans hope to destroy our Nazi convictions. How these poor devils deceived themselves. They really do not know us at all."

4

The Fritz Ritz

Having made a name for himself in Texas legal circles, Lt. Col. Leon Jaworski quickly discovered he would have to climb the career ladder all over again in the army. His new boss at the Eighth Service Command in Texas, Col. Julien C. Hyer, knew nothing about Jaworski's experience trying high-profile cases in Waco and Houston. Hyer assigned Jaworski to work on transferring criminal cases against American soldiers from civilian courts into military courts. The job was mostly paperwork, and Jaworski yearned for important cases and courts-martial, the military equivalents of trials. He did not complain or try to use his connections, he wrote after the war. "Army life was still strange to me. I would not have attempted to pull any strings even if I had known how." Then, "quite by accident," Hyer bumped into a Houston lawyer who told him about Jaworski's background. Hyer immediately shifted Jaworski into courtroom work.

Jaworski's early cases were routine. He prosecuted American soldiers at U.S. Army bases in the West and South for a wide range of offenses: going AWOL, sleeping on guard duty, failing to pay alimony, being drunk in uniform, smuggling liquor over the Mexican border, making improper advances to women, and writing bad checks. He prosecuted one young recruit for chopping off his fingers in order to get out of the army. Jaworski did not understand why anyone thought men in uniform deserved lighter treatment for their crimes. "Soldiers, like law officers and politicians, are figures of authority whose actions are essential to the public order," he wrote in a book after the war. "They must be held accountable, swiftly and fully, for their misdeeds." He practiced that philosophy as he graduated to more serious cases, including those of German POWs.

×   ×   ×

The thousands of German POWs arriving at camps across the United States were given a short time to adjust to their new surroundings. Then they were put to work. The Geneva Convention stipulated that all enlisted prisoners could be compelled to work, so long as the jobs were not unduly hazardous and did not directly aid the enemy's war effort. Prisoners could be made to produce gas masks, for instance, but not guns. The prisoners were nominally paid the same wages as American civilians, but most of their pay went to the U.S. Treasury for the upkeep of the camps. The prisoners were allowed to keep eighty cents a day in the form of scrip to spend at the camp canteens, which sold toiletries, cigarettes, newspapers, magazines, and—when available—even 3.2 beer. Army Provost Marshal General Archer Lerch thought the average German "works better if he knows he can buy a glass of beer at night." Lerch liked to quote Confederate general Thomas "Stonewall" Jackson about the treatment of prisoners: "It is easier to feed them than to fight them."

Noncommissioned POW officers were not required to work at all, although many did as supervisors. Lieutenants still were paid twenty dollars a week, captains thirty dollars, and field grade officers forty dollars. The German High Command in Berlin issued a statement encouraging all prisoners to work because "work offers opportunity of finding diversion necessary for the maintenance of physical and mental health." Despite occasional strikes and work slowdowns, the Germans generally followed the High Command's directive. Farmers and business owners contracted with the army for prisoner labor.

They had to submit applications with the U.S. Manpower Commission showing they needed workers badly to fill in for those in uniform overseas. They flooded the commission with applications. The army would decide first if a camp was feasible in an area, and then if enough POWs were available to fill one. The demand for prisoner labor often exceeded the supply. In Camp Scottsbluff in western Nebraska, the army reported, requests for prisoners to work "are running between six or seven times the number available." Politicians from coast to coast lobbied for new camps in their districts the way they lobbied for new bridges and highways. In the fall of 1943, the army made it official: the highest priority for locating new camps was no longer national security. It was the level of need for labor.

German POWs herded cattle, cut pulpwood, cooked meals, canned fish, mopped floors, translated documents, and emptied bedpans. They shoveled snow on the northern plains, cleared hurricane debris in Florida, and filled sandbags to hold back Mississippi River floods in Missouri and Louisiana. They cut timber in New Hampshire and Maine, packed kosher meat in New Jersey, and stuffed olives in Texas. Mostly they labored on farms. They harvested wheat in Kansas, tobacco in North Carolina, vegetables in New York, asparagus in Illinois, spinach in Oklahoma, beets in Idaho, fruit in California, pecans in Georgia, oranges in Florida, sugarcane in Louisiana, and cotton all over the Deep South. Between October and December 1943, German prisoners picked 6.5 million pounds of seed cotton in Mississippi alone. Some POWs were moved from camp to camp like migrant workers as different crops ripened for harvest. The Germans were credited with saving the sugarcane crop in Florida, the apple crop in New Hampshire, and the potato crop in Maine because they harvested them when no one else was available.

On some farms in the Midwest, German American families welcomed the prisoners like members of an extended family. Some families actually had cousins in the camps. Many families had at least some members who spoke German. Hard work in a time of need forged a bond. Bill Strauss of Junction City, Kansas, who was eighteen years old in 1943, kept reminding himself the Germans were the enemy, "but how could you work with them without becoming friends?" Some farm wives insisted the prisoners and guards join them around the family dinner table when the day's work was done—a flagrant violation of army regulations, which prohibited prisoners from entering homes. A Nebraska farmer recalled a German prisoner goose-stepping playfully through the fields with the farmer's laughing eight-year-old son on his shoulders. "It was a thrill for our little boy that he still remembers to this day." Ernest Blecha of Belleville, Kansas, said a prisoner kept looking at his infant daughter in her crib and finally asked if he could hold her. Blecha let him, and "pretty soon he had tears on his cheeks. He said he had one like that at home." Some POWs were deeply affected by the unexpected kindness of everyday Americans they met on work details. Guenther Oswald wrote home to his family from Camp Trinidad in Colorado that he felt his worldview shifting:

> Growing up under the Nazis we were brainwashed. We considered it perfectly all right to sacrifice ourselves—even our lives—for the Fatherland. I began to change my attitude toward Hitler and National Socialism when I . . . met the common American people. They were friendly and open and didn't hesitate to express themselves. They were not filled with hatred toward us. In Nazi Germany, we would never have been allowed to talk and act the way Americans did. Our parents couldn't educate us in the right way because it was too dangerous for them. So what I saw in American civilian society made me think about German society, and what I wanted to do with my life.

The Germans were not just welcomed in the Midwest. In Bulloch County, Georgia, a farmer drove five hours to Florida to buy extra cigarettes for his POW workers, who had agreed to exceed their contract quotas at harvest time. The local newspaper, the *Bulloch Times*, reflected in September 1943 that "the people of Bulloch County—especially those who are engaged in agriculture—are finding themselves growing more tolerant of those foreign elements whom we may have heretofore regarded merely as monsters."

Because so many of the camps were located in the South, the Germans got a close look at the racism of the Jim Crow era. From the trains, they saw Black families living in soot-covered shacks along the railroad tracks. "Even Russia was better than this," one prisoner remarked. The POWs picked peanuts and cotton alongside Black laborers and saw how little they had. German prisoner Peter Spoden stole shoes from the warehouse at Camp Hearne to give to a Black coworker whose shoes were falling apart. At times, the Germans got caught up in the Jim Crow system. An escapee from Camp Como in Mississippi gave himself away by sitting in the back of a bus under a "Colored People Only" sign he could not read. Two other German prisoners made the same mistake on steamboats. In 1944, the celebrated Black singer and actress Lena Horne was forced to travel in a segregated train car to sing to the troops at Camp Robinson in Little Rock, Arkansas. After the concert, she asked why no Black soldiers had attended and was told they had not been informed she was coming. Horne insisted a piano be brought to the Black soldiers' mess tent so that she could sing for them, but she stormed off in midperformance when German POWs began crowding into the tent, "to the annoyance of the colored soldiers." Horne later wrote, "I don't think I have ever been more furious in my life."

On many occasions, German POWs ate and drank in restaurants in the South that refused to serve Black GIs, including the POWs' guards. One guard recalled wedging his foot in the door of a Whites-only public restroom to try to ensure that a German prisoner who had been allowed inside did not try to escape through a window. *Yank* magazine printed a letter from a Black U.S. Army corporal, Rupert Trimmingham, who was forced to eat in the kitchen at a Louisiana train station while two dozen Germans, in transit between camps, ate in the dining room. They "sat at the tables, had their meals served, talked, smoked, in fact had quite a swell time," Trimmingham wrote. "I stood on the outside looking on, and I could not help ask myself . . . Are these men sworn enemies of this country? . . . Then why are they treated better than we are? . . . Why does the Government allow such things to go on?"

× × ×

Typically, German prisoners began their days with reveille at 5:30 a.m. Guards clumped through the barracks blowing whistles. Prisoners dressed and ate breakfast at the mess hall, then had an hour to shower, wash, shave, and don work uniforms with "PW" stenciled on the sleeves, legs, and backsides. By 7:30 a.m. they were on their way on foot or by truck to their work sites. They were allowed a thirty-minute lunch break around noon and then went back to work until 5 p.m., when they were brought back to the camp for dinner. Between dinner and 10 p.m. when the lights were turned out, the Germans were free to take advantage of the camp's many leisure opportunities. They could relax with friends at the canteen; pay to see an American movie; play soccer or board games; take classes in English, history, geography, and other subjects; tinker in the workshop; paint, sculpt, or play music; or perform on stage. A newspaper reporter visiting a Colorado camp was surprised to see a POW production of Johann Wolfgang von Goethe's play *Faust,* complete with a chorus and a lighting system. Prisoners could send and receive mail from home. Enlisted men and noncoms could write two twenty-four-line letters and one postcard per week, while officers got five of each per week. POWs were allowed to receive gifts and even visits from relatives living in the United States. A prisoner at Camp Hearne, Texas, reunited with a brother from Kansas he had not seen for twenty-five years. All in all, life in camps in the United States was far better than most of the Germans had imagined. It was nothing like being a prisoner of the Russians, who abused and murdered German POWs. Stalin humiliated captured German generals by forcing them to march in public through the streets of Moscow.

Inevitably, reports of German POWs living the good life in captivity reached the American public. Newspaper columnists Walter Winchell, Drew Pearson, and other influential commentators vilified the army for isolated, egregious incidents, such as when Louisiana rice farmers thanked their POW workers with beer and a seafood feast and, at least in one account, the services of prostitutes. Parents of men fighting in Europe, whose views carried a special emotional and political weight in the United States, wrote angry letters calling for harsh treatment of German POWs. "Put them in Death Valley, chuck in a side of beef, and let them starve to death," one writer suggested. Others demanded the army stop "coddling" the Germans, or the "Fritzes," as the Germans sometimes were called because Fritz was a nickname for the common German name of Friedrich. Some critics dubbed the army's network of POW camps "the Fritz Ritz."

Army authorities answered the criticism by citing the Geneva Convention and the need to encourage Nazi Germany to treat American POWs well. The army could fall back on the fact that the camps generally were functioning well. They were providing precious labor to thousands of American farms and businesses while posing no real threat to American citizens. The U.S. government's early fears of widespread escapes and sabotage were proving unfounded.

×   ×   ×

It was easy enough for a German POW to sneak away from a camp, and especially from a work detail. His problem was what to do next. In Europe, an escaped POW might avoid capture long enough to find protection with a Resistance group or to slip across the border into neutral Sweden or Switzerland. But an escaped German prisoner in the United States had to find his way across hundreds or thousands of miles of unfamiliar territory just to reach the ocean or the border of Canada or Mexico—both of which were at war with Germany. He could expect no sympathetic Americans to offer him food or shelter during his flight. He would have to hide in daylight and travel at night, foraging or stealing food. He would be hunted by the army, local sheriffs, state police, and possibly the FBI. Any small mistake could give him away, and not even the cleverest prisoner could anticipate every possible pitfall. One resourceful Luftwaffe pilot walked away from a camp in Canada, stole a boat and paddled across the U.S. border to Detroit, and set out for Mexico by buses and trains. He got all the way to San Antonio before he betrayed himself when he could not figure out how much money to give the waitress at a diner.

Over the course of World War II, 1,073 German prisoners escaped from camps in the United States. Roughly half of them were caught within twenty-four hours, and almost all were caught within three days. Only one ever made it back to Germany to rejoin the war, walking away from a camp in Oklahoma; hitchhiking to Baltimore; talking his way onto the crew of a freighter bound for Lisbon; and then traveling across Portugal and Italy to Germany. He was recaptured shortly after Germany's surrender. Two other German POWs escaped from Camp Scottsbluff in Nebraska and roamed the United States and Canada for four months before the FBI caught them trying to stow away on a freighter docked in Philadelphia.

On rare occasions, escapees were aided by sympathetic Americans. Two prisoners in a Michigan camp escaped with the help of a pro-Nazi guard, who joined them in a futile run for the Mexican border. In Colorado, three Nisei Japanese sisters—American born to Japanese parents—offered a ride and civilian clothes to two young Afrika Korps escapees from Camp Trinidad. The sisters were essentially prisoners themselves, having been uprooted by the army from their homes in San Francisco and confined to an internment camp. An investigation showed they had helped the escapees in pursuit of a romantic fling. The Germans ultimately were apprehended getting drunk in a tavern. But federal prosecutors set out to make examples of the "little Benedict Arnolds in skirts." A jury convicted the sisters of conspiracy and sentenced them to two years in prison. The escapees faced no charges and ended up testifying against the sisters.

Most German POWs who escaped did so out of boredom rather than patriotic fervor. An SS man took "a vacation trip" from a camp in Florida and spent several days "swimming at Miami Beach and looking for employment" before he was caught sleeping in an unlocked truck. Other prisoners fled their camps to woo American women, some of whom found the young, fit, blond Germans irresistible. A camp in Minnesota erected a fence, citing the need to "protect the prisoners from predatory females and other wild animals."

Perhaps the most unusual escapee was Franz Bacher, an aspiring artist who walked away from Camp Stark in New Hampshire, where he was cutting pulpwood. He left a note saying that he feared he might accidentally mutilate his hands and that if he could no longer paint, he could not bear to live. He caught a bus to New York City, set up an easel in Central Park, and sold landscape paintings to passersby. He made enough money to rent a flat in the East Village. He was enjoying his new life until he bumped into one of his guards on furlough in Manhattan. Some paintings said to be Bacher's are still for sale online.

The largest and most audacious escape took place at Camp Papago Park near Phoenix, Arizona, just before Christmas 1944. Twenty-five U-boat men crawled one by one through a 178-foot tunnel they had spent months digging through the dry, rocky desert soil. The escapees scattered and ran for Mexico, pursued by the FBI and native American scouts. *The Phoenix Gazette* printed mug shots of the Germans and reminded its readers of the government's reward of twenty-five dollars per man. In the Sonoran Desert, the U-boat men shivered in cold, wet weather in an unforgiving landscape of cacti, sand ridges, and arroyos. Within two weeks, most were captured or gave up. Three got within forty miles from the Mexican border. The last escapee to remain at large, an ardent Nazi U-boat commander, finally gave up and trudged into Phoenix. He dined at a restaurant and slept in a hotel lobby. Early the next morning, he struck up a conversation with a city street-cleaning crew, gave himself away, and was arrested—a month and a day after emerging from the tunnel.

For all the excitement, the mass escape from Papago Park only underscored the futility of trying to get out of Stalag America. The vast majority of German POWs never even tried. The most dangerous men in the camps were not the relative few who escaped but those who chose to carry on the war against America from inside the barbed wire.

5

Little Germanies

The last thing German prisoner Carl Amery expected when he arrived at Camp Hood in Texas in the summer of 1943 was that his new life in captivity would feel like his old life in the Afrika Korps. But it did. "The first thing that struck me was there was, basically, a situation favorable to the Nazis in the camp," Amery wrote to his family in Germany. "The Afrika Korps was a disciplined force where everybody obeyed as one man, and since the Americans respected the Geneva Convention, they let us develop right away a parallel hierarchy. . . . German discipline immediately was recreated, with its orders, its cries, its howls." To the twenty-one-year-old Amery, Camp Hood felt like home. Though not all the POWs were ardent Nazis, Amery was pleased that a shard of the Afrika Korps had crossed the Atlantic virtually intact and embedded itself in the heart of the United States.

This dynamic was in no way unique to Fort Hood. At Camp Como, a camp for German officers in Mississippi, "the Nazi fanatics terrorized everyone," wrote German POW Josef Krumbachner, who described himself as a political moderate. At Camp Trinidad in Colorado, new arrival Luca Felix Müller was warned never to suggest that Germany might be defeated. "Here, we hold the spirit of Rommel alive," an Afrika Korps veteran told him. "After the war is won in

Europe, we pour out of these POW camps and roll over America."
Müller had defected from the German army and thought he would be
safe in America. Now, he wrote, "in this land of the free we were to be
ruled by Nazis."

The tension in the camps was rooted in a reality that U.S. authorities had failed to recognize in North Africa: the average German soldier was not a Nazi fanatic. Many of them did not belong to Hitler's
National Socialist Party or care much about its politics. They followed
their Nazi leaders out of fear, nationalist fervor, or the belief, rein-
forced by years of propaganda, that Hitler would lead Germany to a
rightful place of dominance in the world. The German army was a
mixture of ardent Nazis, professional soldiers, conscripts from the
draft, and former soldiers of nations conquered by Nazi Germany
who had been "recruited" into the Wehrmacht at the point of a gun.
The latter group included Poles, Czechs, Yugoslavs, Luxembourgers,
and Russians. The Afrika Korps also included the 999th Probation
Division, a catchall collection of communists, political prisoners,
criminals, and troublemakers. They had been organized into a combat unit to serve as human cannon fodder on hazardous missions such
as clearing mines or assaulting entrenched enemies.

On the battlefield, German officers held the various factions together through strict discipline, shared danger, and the threat of death
for disobedience. But in the POW camps, thousands of miles from the
center of Nazi power and propaganda, that formula did not work as
well. Prisoners felt freer to think and act for themselves, but the Nazis
in the camps had other ideas. American authorities would regret not
giving more thought to the differences among the Germans they were
cramming into the camps.

The U.S. Army, in its haste to process tens of thousands of prisoners in North Africa, had ignored the British example of carefully
screening the captured men to gauge the extremity of their political
views. It simply lumped them all together as Nazis. "We never had a
theory of segregating Nazis from anti-Nazis," acknowledged Maj.
Maxwell McKnight, the administrative chief of the POW camps. "We
could do it on the basis of color, but on the basis of ideology? This

never occurred to us." Army authorities did try to identify members of the SS, Hitler's elite personal army, by inspecting prisoners' armpits. SS men had their blood types marked in dime-sized tattoos under their left arms to ensure they were first in line for transfusions if blood was scarce. Despite the army's efforts, numerous SS men and Gestapo agents passed through the screenings unnoticed among the ordinary prisoners.

The rules of the Geneva Convention helped the Nazis establish dominance in the camps. Since the POWs had the right to choose their own leaders, the Afrika Korps men predictably chose the officers and noncoms who had led them in North Africa. Those men almost always were dedicated Nazis, and they and their supporters were the best organized and most forceful bloc of prisoners. They simply transferred the Nazi power structure from the battlefield to the camps. And because the Afrika Korps men were the first POWs in the camps, they set the standard for prisoner behavior in many camps. The War Department unintentionally helped them by allowing them to maintain traditions that were not required by the Geneva Convention, such as the straight-armed salute and the draping of swastika flags over coffins during burials. It was little wonder that Carl Amery felt at home at Camp Hood.

The quality of the American guards in the camps also helped the Nazis. Most of the guards had been kept on the home front because they were considered physically or psychologically unfit for combat overseas. Many camp officers were aging veterans who had been called up from retirement, or younger men with poor service records. Although many fine soldiers ended up serving in the camps, the demand was so great that "we were pretty much dredging the bottom of the barrel," said Major McKnight, the POW camp operations chief. "We had all kinds of kooks and crazy people." Guards were hurried through training. Some resented their home front assignments and "easily become disgusted and often slipshod and unmilitary as a result," an army inspector wrote. An army circular reminded guards to maintain a military bearing at all times to show the Germans "that a democracy is not a sleepy and lackadaisical place but that it is alert—quick—and on its toes!" Most guards labored under the enormous disadvantage of being unable to speak German. The army had shipped most of its fluent German speakers to Europe. The guards were left to wonder what the POWs were saying to them and to each other. "All we could do was to stand back, listen, and try to look intelligent as though we knew what they were talking about—just in case they were talking about us," recalled a guard at Camp Hearne in Texas. The American commander of Camp Breckinridge, Kentucky, led a large group of prisoners to church one morning, thinking they were singing a hymn in German. In fact they were singing the Horst Wessel Song, a Nazi anthem whose lyrics included: "The street is free for the storm troopers / Millions full of hope, look at our swastika." Many German POWs regarded their captors as clueless. A former prisoner at Camp Concordia in Kansas compared some of his guards to the clownish German guards in the postwar American TV sitcom *Hogan's Heroes*.

Some American camp commanders and guards openly admired the Nazis' soldierly professionalism. U.S. Army Sgt. Richard Staff, who served at Camp Hearne in Texas and Camp Robinson in Nebraska, acknowledged his respect for how his prisoners carried themselves: "Damn! They were a well-disciplined bunch of guys—physically healthy, well-trained and excellent soldiers. They still maintained the dignity and discipline that they had learned in the German army, and I—we all—respected them for it."

The anti-Nazi POWs lacked the Nazis' efficiency, particularly on work details. The guards found them lazy and argumentative, especially the communists, whose disdain for the United States ran as deep as the Nazis'. "Our officers don't like the anti-Nazis," one camp commander told *Collier's* magazine. "I have heard them called Hitler's scum." POW Heino Erichsen wrote that the Americans' love of efficiency "led to a disastrous strengthening of German militarism and Nazism inside the camps."

Behind the scenes, the Nazis controlled their fellow prisoners through the same tactics they employed at home in Germany. They monitored conversations for any hint of disloyalty or doubt. They rifled through diaries and letters. They took note if a prisoner worked harder than necessary or accepted a job that brought him into close contact with the Americans, such as interpreter. They watched how prisoners reacted to news about the war, particularly when German news dispatches conflicted with American and British reports. One POW was taken into protective custody after the Nazis in his camp overheard him tell a friend, "I'm afraid Hitler made a mistake by invading Russia." At Camp Mexia in Texas, Nazi leaders required all prisoners to attend regular lectures on Nazi doctrine and readings from Hitler's autobiography, *Mein Kampf*. POW Luca Müller wrote that he "enjoyed more political freedom in the traditional German army than I would in an American camp."

When the Nazis wanted to bring a prisoner back into line, they might threaten to send coded messages to Germany, either in letters or inside the bandages of wounded German POWs being sent home, to sic the SS or Gestapo on their families. No one who had lived under Nazi rule could easily dismiss such a threat, because they had been "indoctrinated into believing the SS to be practically omniscient," an informant named "Karl P." told army investigators at Camp Trinidad in Colorado. An anti-Nazi prisoner at Fort Sam Houston in Texas brushed aside the Nazis' threats, only to learn later that his family in Austria had been persecuted for his beliefs.

More serious offenses to Nazi order might be punished in clandestine "courts of honor," convened at night after the guards had withdrawn from the German sections of the camps. These kangaroo courts might sentence a POW to confinement in his quarters or order his fellow prisoners to shun him—a severe penalty in a place so far from home. Or they might arrange for a gang of men to assault him. The attackers usually struck in the dead of night. The victims awoke in their cots to feel pillowcases being forced over their heads to prevent them from identifying their attackers. The Germans called the pillowcase attacks "visits" from *Der Heilig Geist*—the Holy Ghost, the invisible third member of the Christian Holy Trinity. The beatings often were severe. A *Heilig Geist* visit at Camp Huntsville injured anti-Nazi POW Hans Wilfinger so badly that he spent weeks in a hospital. The pillowcases at least suggested the victims were meant to survive. But not all the gangs brought pillowcases.

Some prisoners slept with clubs by their beds, as well as buckets so they could piss at night without risking a walk across the yard to the latrine in the dark. "You were walking a knife's edge all the time," wrote Fritz Haus, a prisoner at Camp Hearne, Texas. "You looked over your shoulder, even in church, you could never be absolutely frank." James H. Powers, the foreign editor of *The Boston Globe,* wrote that the Nazis were a secret police force in many of the camps and that "the effect of their rule is a little Germany, where persecution of the anti-Nazis is thorough and violent."

By July 1943, with reports of violent incidents in the camps piling up, the army acknowledged that Nazis were terrorizing some of their fellow prisoners. It directed camp commanders to weed out all "Nazi leaders, Gestapo agents and extremists" and transfer them to Camp Alva, a newly designated camp for incorrigible Nazis in the remote hills of north-central Oklahoma. But the army left the task of identifying the Nazis to the camp commanders, who lacked the knowledge and training. Arrogant, outspoken Nazis were easy to identify, but the shrewder ones concealed their views. The most dangerous men often were not even members of the Nazi Party but battle-hardened soldiers who followed orders without hesitation. The army urged camp commanders to try to gain the trust of anti-Nazi prisoners who could point out the worst Nazis. But the army warned camp commanders in a pamphlet that many prisoners who claimed to be anti-Nazis had been Nazis until they were captured: "Unfortunately, after more than 11 years of Nazi education, there are very few 'good' Germans left."

The extent of Nazi influence in the U.S. camps is hard to quantify. Not all of the POW camp records have survived. At the height of the war, the army concluded that roughly 40 percent of the 371,000 German prisoners in the United States were "pro-Nazi." Of those, 10 percent were "rabid Nazis" and the other 30 percent "deeply sympathetic" to the Nazi cause. Another 40 percent of the prisoners were apolitical but "heavily propagandized." The true anti-Nazis, who outspokenly opposed the Nazis, represented less than 10 percent. A postwar army survey listed 211 violent incidents at German POW camps in the United States. In 1979, historian Arnold Krammer found incidents of political violence at more than two hundred camps. Later studies and the author's research suggest that few camps were entirely free of problems with aggressive Nazis. The severity of those problems varied widely from camp to camp, and even from week to week as prisoners were transferred in and out. A speaker at a conference of camp commanders admitted: "About the only way to distinguish a Nazi from an anti-Nazi is when you see a man being pursued by a crowd of fifty others who are howling for murder, you can be sure that the man who is running is an anti-Nazi."

At Camp Ellis in Illinois, "15 Nazis so unmercifully assaulted a Polish prisoner that he required hospital treatment for several days," an army inspector reported. At Camp Huntsville in Texas, Nazis and anti-Nazis fought constantly with improvised weapons. "They would go into the latrines and tear the boards apart and beat each other with the boards with the nails in the ends of the boards," recalled guard Tex Geyser. "They were rough." At Camp Crossville in Tennessee, a guard fatally stabbed a prisoner who seized the camp commander during a riot. In August 1943, a crowd of Nazis at Camp Hearne in Texas attacked a smaller group of anti-Nazis, setting their barracks on fire and severely beating several of them. The anti-Nazis fought back with chains and clubs spiked with razor blades. It was only a matter of time before someone was killed.

×　　×　　×

Camp Concordia had been simmering. Ever since its establishment in May 1943, the camp in the remote Kansas wheatfields had been loosely run by its commander, Col. Thomas Sterling, a World War I veteran called out of retirement. Sterling may have been too lenient by nature. Or he may not have relished the assignment of containing four thousand Afrika Korps veterans in a cage on the Kansas prairie. In any case, under his leadership, "things were shortly out of hand at Concordia," according to an army history of the camp. "The Germans seem to have seized the initiative from the beginning." The camp had a strong Nazi presence, from its ranking officer and camp spokesman, Col. Alfred Koester, to a lowly private who worked as a janitor in the U.S. Army headquarters building. The janitor would startle the civilian office staff with vehement outbursts against Jews. "You didn't dare say anything to him about Jews or he would go into a rage," a female clerk recalled. "Something was mentioned one time and he took his broom and pushed my chair clear across the room."

The guards at Concordia sensed a growing defiance in the prisoners. In September 1943, the camp transferred to pro-Nazi Camp Alva "a Gestapo agent working, undercover, to create dissatisfaction and to break down the morale of the other prisoners" and guards. During a POW soccer match on October 16, the Germans kept booting balls over a waist-high fence—the "deadline"—marking the border of a forbidden zone within fifteen feet of the camp's main stockade fences. Guards in the towers kept shouting to the Germans to stay on their side of the deadline, but the prisoners kept kicking balls over it and retrieving them. The guards decided they were being tested. A guard in the nearest tower asked his superiors how he should respond. He was told, unhelpfully, to use his own judgment. A young Afrika Korps corporal named Adolph Huebner jumped over the deadline and chased a ball. The guard warned him to stop, in German and in English. Huebner kept going. The guard raised his rifle and shot him between the eyes.

Every one of the four thousand Germans at Camp Concordia rushed out of the barracks. The prisoners formed marching columns, shouting, and singing martial songs whose words the guards could not understand. A few POWs threw rocks. The camp's emergency sirens wailed. The sound carried through the surrounding hills. Harriet Fahlstrom, whose family lived one and a half miles away, recalled "screaming and yelling like you never heard." Colonel Sterling called out every available guard and canceled all leaves. As darkness fell, guard Carl Stangel feared a riot was imminent. The Germans out-numbered the guards by a ratio of 4 to 1. But after a few hours, the Germans returned to their barracks. Stangel felt enormous relief. The next day, however, the Germans planted a cross in the ground near the site of the shooting with the inscription, "This cross marks the spot where Adolph Huebner was murdered by the Americans." The Ger-mans refused to go on work details. Then, three days after the shoot-ing, on the morning of October 19, the guards discovered the body of German army captain Felix Tropschuh hanging from a makeshift noose in his quarters.

At first, Colonel Sterling was content to classify Tropschuh's death as a suicide. An army source told the local *Concordia Blade-Empire* newspaper that Tropschuh suffered from "a chronic disease of such a nature as to cause despondency." A suicide note had been found near the body; another prisoner at Concordia already had killed himself out of despair. Even after the Germans shunned the dead man—boycotting Tropschuh's burial service after insisting he be buried apart from "honorable" Germans who had died at the camp previously—Colonel Sterling let sleeping Dobermans lie.

Immediately after the funeral, however, more than a half dozen German informants, including three lieutenants, told the Americans the truth. Colonel Koester and the other ardent Nazis at Concordia had forced Tropschuh to commit suicide. The Nazis had long been suspicious of Tropschuh. Rumors had followed him from North Af-rica that he had warned the British of an escape plot. At Concordia, Tropschuh had never criticized Nazism or Hitler in public, but Koes-ter found him slow to obey orders. On the morning of October 18, two days after Adolph Huebner was shot to death and with emotions still raw in the camp, one of Tropschuh's roommates rifled through his belongings and stole his diary. In it, Tropschuh had written that Nazism would be Germany's ruin. The thief gave the diary to Koester.

After the Americans had withdrawn from the German barracks that night, Koester called a meeting of the POWs in the camp's main square. He confronted Tropschuh with the diary and accused him of "treason to the Fatherland." Tropschuh feared he would be killed. He bolted for the camp's main gate, where an army truck was passing. The driver slowed but then sped off as Tropschuh approached with a crowd of prisoners at his heels. Tropschuh quickly was overtaken, beaten, and dragged back to his barracks. A prisoner who quietly shared Tropschuh's political views sought out Colonel Sterling and asked him to place Tropschuh in protective custody. The prisoner may not have told Sterling about the night's events. Sterling rejected the idea that Tropschuh would be harmed, saying, "We have Democrats and Republicans in America but we don't kill each other."

Later that night, the informants said, Koester convened a clandestine "honor court," which sentenced Tropschuh to die by his own hand. If he refused, he was told, the Nazis would get word back to Germany to kill his wife, Teressa, in his place. Tropschuh was forced to sign the suicide note written by another officer. He was handed a chair and a clothesline and sent to his quarters. Two Nazis stood guard by his door. Others pressed their faces against a window to watch. Tropschuh paced the floor for more than an hour. One informant said an "executioner" finally helped him decide. Tropschuh's former comrades left him to hang until the next morning's head count, when he did not appear and the guards went to look for him. The cruelty of the forced suicide disturbed even some of the prisoners who had been getting along with the Nazis. "This brutality, forcing a suicide and, worse yet, watching it from an outside window, shocked the majority of us and made us feel ashamed of some of our officer comrades," wrote Karl Gassman. Tropschuh's friend and fellow prisoner Willi Lelle thought, "I might be next." Lelle and other secret anti-Nazis had been too afraid to attend Tropschuh's burial service.

An army investigation in the following weeks did not confirm all the details of the informants' accounts, but it concluded that Tropschuh had been subjected to "very great mental pressure equivalent to murder." The army did not charge anyone with the killing, but it transferred Koester and one of his burly enforcers to Camp Alva, the special camp for hardcore Nazis in Oklahoma. U.S. Army Cpl. Albert Purdy helped escort the two Germans on the four-hour ride to Camp

Alva. Purdy could hardly wait to rid himself of the "very arrogant colonel" and the "large German sergeant." In the days that followed, Willi Lelle and a half dozen other prisoners at Camp Concordia requested transfers to camps where they would be safe from the Nazis. Those requests would be hard for the army to fulfill. The killings in the camps had just begun.

6

"No Place for a Priest"

Sixteen days after Felix Tropschuh's death in Kansas, German first sergeant Walter Beyer called a mass meeting of the two hundred prisoners in his company of POWs at Camp Tonkawa in rural Oklahoma. He waited until late at night, after the guards had withdrawn from the German sections of the camp as they did every night. Beyer wanted to make sure the Americans did not intervene, as they surely would have. He was calling the meeting to accuse a fellow prisoner of betraying Nazi Germany. Camp Tonkawa was a little over two hundred miles south of Camp Concordia; it's possible but not likely that word of Tropschuh's death had reached the Germans at Tonkawa through a transferred prisoner.

Beyer was the highest-ranking prisoner at Tonkawa and the camp spokesman. He had a rigid military bearing and steel-blue eyes. An Afrika Korps comrade described him as "a nervous man . . . a good man with discipline, but hot-tempered. When he gives an order, it is carried out immediately." Beyer and his second-in-command, a rugged technical sergeant named Berthold Seidel, called the two hundred prisoners to the mess hall without telling them why. The room was abuzz. Beyer commanded his men into silence. Then he revealed his stunning news in a calm, even voice: "Comrades, I am sorry, and it

hurts me in my soul to tell you this. Bad as it may seem, we have a traitor in our company!"

The men stared at him and then at one another. Beyer let his words
sink in. Then he continued. He said he had come into possession of a
note that a prisoner had intended to pass to an American contact at
the camp hospital. The note suggested targets for Allied bombers in
the German port city of Hamburg. Beyer read parts of the note aloud:
"Hamburg: The main railroad station was camouflaged as a house-
block with dummies and paint. Through the center a light strip was
marked like a street."

The writer of the note also identified a newly arrived prisoner at
Camp Tonkawa as "a thorough Nazi" and another as an anti-Nazi
who should be interviewed by army intelligence officers. The writer
asked to be allowed to send additional notes through the camp hospital "whenever there is something to report."

Beyer did not mention to the POWs in the mess hall that his wife
and three children lived in Hamburg, which already had been devastated by British bombs three months earlier, in a raid that started a
firestorm that left twenty thousand people dead and almost a million homeless. By the time Beyer finished reading from the note, his
men were in an uproar. Beyer called again for silence. He said the
note bore no signature but he had matched the handwriting to the
writing on a letter written by a soldier in the company. As camp
spokesman, Beyer handled all the prisoners' mail. Beyer did not
name the writer of the note. But the other prisoners noticed that a
young corporal, Johann Kunze, was fidgeting and sweating pro-
fusely. Beyer called Kunze forward and told him to compare the
handwriting on the note and the letter. The mess hall fell silent
again as Kunze examined what would be his final letter to his wife.
"Dear Erna," it began, "I am well, I am getting older and slower, in
playing football I am not quite able to keep up anymore. The days
go by in thinking, every once in a while a game of chess, some English lessons, also French. I do not bother with the sequence of the
days of the week or the date. The companionship of the [other pris-
oners] is good."

The crowd in the mess hall grew impatient as Kunze examined the letter. Men jostled him and demanded he say whether he had written the note. One prisoner thought he heard Kunze shout, "Comrades! It was not me!" But it was difficult to hear anything amid the din. Beyer said something to the effect that the men should not hurt Kunze or "we will have the Americans on our backs." But he had struck a spark. His right-hand man, Sergeant Seidel, who also had family in Hamburg, seized Kunze and punched him in the face. Blood flew from Kunze's nose. Seidel kept striking Kunze until he knocked him down. Then he yanked him to his feet for others to take a turn. The Germans engulfed Kunze, hitting and kicking him. Men on the periphery who could not reach him climbed up on tables in the mess hall and hurled cups and plates at him. The guards in their own barracks were too far away to hear the racket.

Kunze was strong. He broke free of his attackers and ran into the kitchen. A prisoner tackled him and knocked him to the floor in a shower of shattering crockery. Kunze ran back into the mess hall, leaving a trail of blood. The men converged on him again. A prisoner who was studying to be a Catholic priest got up on a bench and called on the men to stop. A few of them glared at him, and Sergeant Beyer warned him, "This is no place for a priest." Beyer shouted again for the men to quit beating Kunze, but they ignored him. Kunze broke free again and staggered out the door of the mess hall. The mob caught up with him, and this time he would not get away. They pummeled him. They lifted him and hurled him against the concrete foundation of the mess hall. Kunze no longer offered any resistance, but they kept picking him up and throwing his limp body against the building. Finally they dispersed, leaving Kunze in a pool of his own blood. No one called the guards. The prisoners went back to the mess hall and made a futile effort to clean up. Then they returned to their barracks and waited for the sun to rise.

The guards discovered Kunze's body on their morning rounds and summoned their superiors. No one mistook this death for a suicide. The commanding officer of Camp Tonkawa examined the mess hall inside and out. His report captured the savagery of the killing:

We found blood stains on the eastern side of the mess hall, a milk bottle covered with blood, bloodstains on the door leading into the mess hall. In the storeroom, blood was found on the walls, floor and potato sacks. Going into the kitchen, we found a shovel which had been used to scrape blood stains from the wall. There was blood on the floor, ice chest and sink. We also found a bushel basket full of broken, bloody dishes, including a set of broken false teeth. . . . Continuing on, we found blood stains on the dishes stacked in their proper places on the mess table, and numerous blood stains on the floor.

The camp physician theorized that Kunze had been attacked with a meat cleaver, which prompted a fruitless search for one in the mess hall. An autopsy revealed that Kunze had died of multiple blows to the head that had fractured his skull and driven splinters of bone into his brain.

To a man, the POWs denied any knowledge of the killing. Camp Tonkawa's chief of security, Capt. Theodore Maffitt, ordered the guards to line up every prisoner in the company and check them for signs of a struggle. Thirteen had what appeared to be fresh blood on their clothes. Maffitt ordered those men confined to solitary cells. He commandeered a small room adjoining the camp's officers' club and opened a formal, three-man board of inquiry. He began interrogating the prisoners one by one through a translator. Maffitt assumed they all knew what had happened to Kunze. Every prisoner at Camp Tonkawa seemed to know. They showed their contempt for Kunze in the same way their counterparts at Camp Concordia had showed their contempt for Capt. Felix Tropschuh. They refused to provide a German flag for Kunze's coffin or attend his brief burial service. While a Lutheran minister spoke over the grave in a drizzling rain, some of the Germans started a raucous soccer match in an adjacent field.

At the U.S. Army Eighth Service Command's JAG office in Dallas, Leon Jaworski had been promoted to lieutenant colonel, but his advancement in rank did not reflect how far he had risen in his short time as an army prosecutor. No longer mired in paperwork or routine cases, Jaworski was excelling in the kind of high-profile courtroom work that had made him a success as a civilian lawyer in Waco and Houston. He had become a roving troubleshooter for the army, traveling across the South and Southwest to try cases that were too complex or sensitive for less experienced prosecutors. Those cases included assault, manslaughter, and murder. In July 1943, Jaworski had won convictions against three Black GIs at Camp Claiborne in Louisiana for raping a young White woman. The defense team, which included future Supreme Court justice Thurgood Marshall, representing the NAACP Legal Defense Fund, argued that the GIs had paid the woman for consensual sex. The all-White jury had sentenced all three defendants to hang. (After Jaworski moved on to other cases, Marshall got the men's sentences commuted to life imprisonment, and all three were freed on parole in 1947.) The only kind of cases in which Jaworski still lacked much experience in 1943 involved POWs. He had prosecuted only one German prisoner, for stealing a car during a short-lived escape attempt.

The Camp Tonkawa murder caught the attention of the War Department in Washington, which informed Maj. Gen. Richard Donovan of the Eighth Service Command that the case was "a test case" that could have broader ramifications. General Donovan passed that word to Colonel Hyer, Jaworski's boss in Dallas. Hyer immediately assigned the case to Jaworski with the instructions to "go all out." Jaworski knew about the political tension in the camps, but he had never imagined a Nazi gang committing a brutal murder in the green hills of Oklahoma. He was glad the army was not just writing off the murder as a case of bad guys killing bad guys. "Crimes committed by one prisoner against another are easy enough to ignore," he wrote, but allowing Johann Kunze's murder to go unpunished "would have been equivalent to licensing the Nazi subgovernments that operated in every camp."

Jaworski canceled his Thanksgiving plans with his family, signed out a vehicle from the army motor pool in Dallas, and set out for Camp Tonkawa. The camp was about three hundred miles north of Dallas, a short distance from the town of Tonkawa. The town sat along the Salt Fork of the Arkansas River on land once roamed by the Tonkawa and Nez Perce tribes. Since its settlement by White farmers in 1893, Tonkawa had flourished briefly as a railroad town and experienced an even briefer oil boom. By the 1940s, its population had leveled off to around three thousand people. The POW camp boosted the local economy. The first prisoners arrived in August 1943 and were put to work on local farms and ranches and in an alfalfa-drying plant.

The drive to Tonkawa took Jaworski nearly five hours, mostly on two-lane blacktops bisecting empty prairie. Snow flurries danced across the road. Jaworski had time to think about the challenge ahead. His fluency in German would be a great advantage; it would help him use his talent for reading people. But murders by mobs were not easy cases. You could not charge a group of people collectively with a killing. You needed names to attach to specific acts. The German POWs, bound by loyalty and fear, would not willingly provide them.

While Jaworski was en route, Captain Maffitt already was discovering how difficult the investigation would be. The first prisoner he interrogated told him, "If I talk to you, I'm a dead man." After Maffitt promised to protect him, he disclosed that Sergeants Beyer and Seidel had called a mass meeting at which Kunze had been labeled a traitor. The prisoner insisted he could not identify a single POW who had assaulted Kunze. He clearly was lying but would say no more. Maffitt told the guards to bring Beyer and Seidel to him.

Beyer answered Maffitt's questions coolly and precisely. He admitted calling the meeting in the mess hall, reading the unsigned note, and pointing the finger at Kunze. Beyer said he thought the prisoners might beat Kunze but not kill him. "It is the understanding among German soldiers that a traitor should be killed, but not in an enemy internment camp," he explained. Beyer said he had tried to stop the beating but the men were too angry. Who were those men? Maffitt asked. Beyer said he could not identify any of them—"There were so many men running around that I couldn't get a good view of anything." Maffitt scoffed. "You know every man in your company," he told Beyer. "Do you think we believe you when you tell us you watched the progress of a fight within five feet of you, and you cannot think of the name of a single man who hit Kunze that night?" Beyer replied, "I could not recognize any of them. . . . I cannot just look up in the air and pick out a name." Beyer added that whoever had killed Kunze should be tried by a German court "because we are Germans, and this is an act among the Germans." Maffitt told him the Geneva Convention allowed POWs to be tried under U.S. law. Beyer replied, "I do not see the right of it." Maffitt sent for Seidel.

Sgt. Berthold Seidel was not a Nazi—he had been a Social Democrat before Hitler outlawed his party—but he was dedicated to the Third Reich. Before being captured with the Afrika Korps, he had fought in Norway, Belgium, France, Holland, and Russia, where, he added cryptically, the Russians had taught the Germans that "small things matter." Since being captured in North Africa, Seidel had escaped twice from the British and once from the French before being shipped to America. He admitted to Maffitt that he had been among the first to hit Kunze, and possibly *the* first. "I am not a boxer, but I struck his nose and blood came at the first blow," he added with pride. Seidel claimed that he had spent his anger by landing five or six hard punches and that he then had left the mess hall to wash Kunze's blood off his hands in the latrine. He emerged from the latrine to see a mob throwing Kunze's body against the base of the mess hall with "loud thuds." Maffitt asked Seidel why he had not stopped them. Seidel said he might have been killed if he had tried. Besides, he wanted to see Kunze hurt. He tried to make Maffitt understand:

SEIDEL: I was very much excited. My company Fuehrer had read a letter. This letter was from Kunze, and in this letter was a little piece about Hamburg. And I think of my family, my father, mother and sister in Hamburg, and Kunze is giving in this letter a description of Hamburg, and therefore I was very much excited.

MAFFITT: We can understand that, Seidel, but we do not understand why you took a man out and killed him, and then think that we would do nothing about it.

SEIDEL: You cannot understand why I wish to kill him?

MAFFITT: Yes, we understand that, but you do not think we should do anything about it?

SEIDEL: I do not know what would happen to an American soldier in Germany if the situation were reversed. There would have been many American soldiers who would say that the man was no good.

Seidel had a point. One of the most popular American movies about World War II, *Stalag 17,* dramatized the efforts of Allied prisoners in a POW camp in Germany to unmask a traitor in their midst. They finally identify him, and after tying clattering tin cans to his legs, they throw him out of the barracks at night, knowing the German guards will shoot him. The traitor's death drew cheers from American theater audiences when the movie was released in 1953.

Seidel said he could not identify any of the other men who had assaulted Kunze—"I have seen many soldiers, but it was dark." Maffitt asked him if he was afraid to name the killers. "I am a long time a soldier," Seidel replied. "I have no fear."

Maffitt was growing frustrated by the Germans' bland, obvious lies. During a break between interrogations, he startled his staff by blurting out, "Those Nazi sons of bitches killed a man down there, and the bastards think they can get away with it!"

Maffitt was in the middle of a new interrogation when Jaworski slid unobtrusively into a seat next to him. Jaworski listened. He quickly concluded that Maffitt knew what he was doing, and sent word to Dallas that he did not need another investigator. Jaworski's arrival made an instant impression on Wilma Parnell, a civilian court reporter at the camp who was recording the proceedings in shorthand. "Jaworski's quiet confidence was a quick restorative," Parnell wrote. His "steady eyes and calm, unassuming manner were reassuring. Physically, he made a spit-and-polish impression—his officer's pinks and blouse were elegantly tailored, and his close-cropped, wavy hair contained threads of silver—but there was nothing flamboyant about him. When he spoke, he looked at you squarely, and the intelligence behind the steady eyes was shrewdly cool and deliberate." Parnell also noticed that Jaworski was a keen observer. During a lunch break, he picked up her drinking glass, held it up to the light, and commented, "Look at that set of fingerprints. Perfect impressions." Parnell suggested the reason was that the glass was cold and her fingers were somewhat greasy. "Not necessarily," Jaworski replied. "You have whorls that print well."

Until the interrogations, Parnell had half-believed the image of the Afrika Korps fighters as "mythic heroes with sun-streaked hair, dauntless desert warriors with ice-blue eyes, given to song and battle." Now, however, she had seen who the Germans really were: "It was the hysteria and the brutish savagery of the Kunze killing that shocked us, the clotted blood on the walls and the broken dentures swept into the trash basket."

Jaworski was determined to cut through the lies and find the killers. He reviewed Parnell's transcripts of the interrogations he had missed. He asked that Beyer, Seidel, and others be called back for additional questions. Jaworski got a sense that two of the prisoners would tell what they knew if they felt protected. He had them moved to a nearby hospital where he could question them at length without their comrades' knowledge. One of the two was a Polish giant, Josef Heidutzek, who had been given the choice of fighting for Germany or being executed. The other was German corporal Georg Persons, who hoped to leverage his testimony into a travel visa to Argentina. Heidutzek and Persons described Beyer's and Seidel's actions in more detail. They also named three other Afrika Korps soldiers who had taken part in the attack. Jaworski and Maffitt summoned those men for questioning. All three admitted minor roles.

Twenty-two-year-old corporal Willi Scholz said he had hit Kunze "three or four" times in the mess hall. Scholz acknowledged he was a member of the Nazi Party. He said he was angry over the note about the bombing targets. Like Sergeant Seidel, he said he had felt satisfied after landing several blows and had left the mess hall when Kunze was still on his feet.

Hans Demme, a baby-faced twenty-three-year-old sergeant, told Jaworski he had launched his 108-pound frame at the muscular Kunze after the latter fled from the mess hall into the kitchen. "I wound up my fist and thundered him one in the face, then I grabbed him around the hips," Demme boasted. Kunze then lost his balance, hitting his head on a table full of dishes, and, in Demme's telling, crashed to the floor as crockery shattered around him. Kunze got up and ran from the kitchen. Demme said he had not touched him again. Jaworski asked Demme if he thought he had helped to kill Kunze. "Yes, I think so," Demme replied. He said he hated Kunze for suggesting targets for Allied bombers, which had destroyed his family farm in Germany. Like many of the Germans who would commit the POW camp murders, Demme complained bitterly of his personal losses in the war but seemed oblivious to the losses inflicted by Nazi Germany.

Hans Schomer, a twenty-seven-year-old cook, said he had never touched Kunze but had thrown two cups at him, missing both times. Schomer said he had gotten out of a sickbed to investigate the commotion in the mess hall and had climbed up on a bench in the kitchen to see over the crowd. He saw Kunze trying to fight off the mob. Some men near Schomer were throwing cups and plates at Kunze, so Schomer grabbed two cups and threw them. One cup hit another prisoner in the back, he said, and the other missed everyone. Schomer said he had returned to bed while Kunze was still fighting back. Jaworski asked if he thought Kunze had deserved to die. Schomer replied, "Yes. It was hard punishment, but it was right." Neither Scholz, Schomer, nor Demme named any other prisoners who had taken part in the attack.

On December 3, nearly a month after the killing, Jaworski decided to charge Beyer, Seidel, Scholz, Demme, and Schomer with rioting and premeditated murder, which carried a penalty of death by hanging. Military law did not require a grand jury to indict the Germans, but Jaworski explained to Colonel Hyer why he had charged each of the five: Beyer had not touched Kunze but had called the mass meeting to expose him as a traitor; Seidel had started the beating, although he apparently had quit after several punches; Scholz and Schomer had struck Kunze before the attack turned deadly; and Demme had thrown two cups at Kunze without hitting him. Jaworski was well aware that the men who actually had struck the fatal blows—who had hurled the helpless Kunze against the base of the mess hall—were getting away. The only men he had been able to charge were those who were either too naive or too confident of the rightness of their actions to keep their mouths shut. "We can't get all of the men that were guilty," Jaworski later would argue in court. "You never do when you have a mob. But we have gotten a number of them, and it isn't our fault . . . that more were not gotten."

Violent incidents at POW camps were spreading to other states. Jaworski was temporarily distracted from the Camp Tonkawa case by a riot at Camp Huntsville, north of Houston. On November 25, a gang of Nazis with clubs and nail-studded boards attacked anti-Nazis on the camp's main street, while a second group of Nazis formed a human cordon to block the guards from intervening. One prisoner tried to escape in the chaos and was fatally shot by a guard. Another guard shot and wounded a prisoner who ambushed him and knocked him to the ground with a club. While the guards were busy with the street fight, a third group of Nazis subjected the camp's Catholic priest to a severe *Heilig Geist* beating. The army said the priest suffered "unmentionable brutalism and tortures." After a stay in the hospital, he was transferred out of Camp Huntsville. Why the priest had been attacked was not clear. Jaworski apparently did not rush to Camp Huntsville to join the investigation, but he would end up prosecuting two POWs for their roles in the street fight.

At Camp Tonkawa, Jaworski managed to persuade all five of the defendants to write sworn statements summarizing what they had told their interrogators. The Germans undoubtedly saw it as a chance to cast their actions in a better light, but their statements amounted to confessions to murder. They would serve as Jaworski's chief evidence against them. On December 3, Jaworski summoned the defendants one at a time to the interrogation room to hear a formal reading of the charges. A dance was under way in the adjoining officer's club, with an orchestra playing "White Christmas" and "Don't Sit under the Apple Tree (with Anyone Else but Me)." The music filled the little interrogation room every time a prisoner passed through the door. Walter Beyer, who had called the mass meeting to expose Kunze, objected to being charged with premeditated murder, saying, "I cannot see how that accusation can be justified."

Some of the army's lawyers shared Beyer's skepticism about the charges. Jaworski's work on the case had been impressive, but were his conclusions justified? Col. James E. Morrisette, the assistant judge advocate general in Dallas, questioned whether all five of the POWs had intended to kill Kunze. Morrissette considered the evidence against Beyer "obviously weak" and "far short of establishing his participation in murder." He thought Beyer had committed no worse offense than rioting. He suggested General Donovan closely review the case before letting it proceed. Jaworski took the criticism seriously enough to seek advice from the JAG office in Washington. In a letter, he described each of the five Germans' actions in detail and asked if they could be considered principals in the murder. A prosecutor from Washington wrote back that Jaworski was on firm legal ground and referred him to the legal definition of a "principal" in federal criminal law: "Whoever directly commits any act constituting an offense defined in any law of the United States, or aids, abets, counsels, commands, induces or procures its commission, is a principal." Jaworski pressed on with the five murder charges.

Although the Geneva Convention allowed the POWs to be tried under the laws of the United States, it did not specify exactly how. The War Department decided to bypass the civilian courts, which were slow and unpredictable. It also bypassed the regular military courts. The Germans would be court-martialed before a military tribunal of eleven U.S. Army officers, selected by General Donovan of the Eighth Service Command. Various forms of military tribunals had been used to try enemy nationals in wartime in America since 1780, when a tribunal ordered by Gen. George Washington convicted British major John André of spying and sentenced him to hang, in retribution for the British hanging of the American spy Nathan Hale. Much more recently, the case of the U-boat saboteurs in 1942 had set a precedent for special military courts on the home front.

Trying the German POWs by military tribunal would enable the army to deal with the case quickly and secretly. Jaworski noted that there was virtually no red tape in a court-martial. The prosecution laid out all the evidence it possessed; the defense "was not permitted to resort to some stratagems used in civil trials." Camp Tonkawa had no courtroom, so the court-martial would be held at the closest military base that did: Camp Gruber in eastern Oklahoma, 165 miles away. General Donovan scheduled the court-martial to begin on January 17, 1944—five weeks after the charges were filed. By that time, more German POWs would be dead and the violence in the camps would be spreading.

7

Secret Verdicts

Just as Jaworski was starting to prepare his case at Camp Tonkawa, word arrived that a second German POW had been beaten to death not far from Jaworski's boyhood home. Camp Hearne, Texas, was located only sixty-five miles southeast of Waco, in the fertile bottomland of the Brazos River. The camp lay just west of the town of Hearne, population 3,500, a former stagecoach stop that now boasted two cotton gins and two railroad lines. The victim, twenty-four-year-old corporal Hugo Krauss, had been lying in his cot in his barracks on the night of December 17 when a group of six to ten men slipped in from another part of the camp. They surrounded Krauss and beat him with fists, clubs, and a lead pipe. Krauss screamed but none of the men in his barracks intervened. The attack lasted only a minute or two but left Krauss with two broken arms and bruises all over his face and body. He remained semiconscious, and some fellow POWs helped him walk to the camp hospital. They assumed he would recover. But Krauss's skull had been fractured. He lapsed into a coma and died six days later.

Krauss was an unusual prisoner of war. Born in Germany, he had immigrated to New York at age nine with his parents, who, like Jaworski's parents, had sought opportunity in the United States. The family settled in Manhattan, in the German American enclave of Yorkville. In 1939, when Krauss was nineteen years old, the pro-Nazi German American Bund organization paid his way to visit relatives in Germany. Krauss was surprised to be drafted into the German army after the invasion of Poland. He initially avoided serving by claiming to be an American citizen, but he later reconsidered and enlisted. It's unclear what was going on in the young man's head at that point. Krauss fought with the Wehrmacht in Russia before being captured with the Afrika Korps at Tunis. Less than four years after leaving the United States, he was back as a German POW. At Camp Hearne, where most prisoners picked cotton or worked in a shop that repaired raincoats, Krauss, who spoke fluent German and English, worked as an interpreter. He seemed to go out of his way to infuriate his fellow prisoners. He told them he had no intention of going back to Germany, which he said was certain to lose the war. He said he would stay in America with his parents, who still lived in New York. They visited him at Camp Hearne and bought him a transistor radio. Krauss listened only to American music and war news. He talked about getting a furlough from the camp at Christmas and joining the U.S. Army. He "was very much disliked and was considered a traitor to Germany, especially by the younger prisoners of war who were devout Hitlerites," an army report concluded. A week before he was attacked, Krauss tipped off the guards that several German sergeants were orchestrating a work slowdown. The sergeants were transferred, but from that day on, Krauss was a marked man.

After his death, investigators at Camp Hearne questioned forty-five of his fellow prisoners but failed to identify a single suspect. The murder investigation went nowhere. Even though Camp Hearne was in Jaworski's territory, neither he nor any other outside investigator was called in to help with the case. Most likely, Jaworski's superiors wanted him to stay focused as much as possible on the fast-approaching Camp Tonkawa "test case."

×   ×   ×

The Tonkawa court-martial began as scheduled on the morning of January 17, 1944, at Camp Gruber. Wilma Parnell, the civilian court reporter from Tonkawa, was called as a prosecution witness. She assumed the proceedings would be open to the public and press. But instead of a gaggle of reporters and onlookers at Camp Gruber, she found tight security and absolute secrecy. She was cautioned not to divulge anything about the case to anyone. The Geneva Convention allowed POWs' trials to be conducted in secret if "the safety of the State" was at stake. Parnell wrote that she was told by a highly placed source—probably Jaworski—that the army feared "the incendiary effect the trial publicity might have on prisoner-of-war camps throughout the country." Jaworski wrote that the army did not want to be accused of turning the trials into public spectacles or using them for propaganda purposes. Nor was the army "anxious to publicize the whereabouts of the German POWs."

Even as the violent incidents multiplied, the American public knew little about what was happening in the camps, or even about the camps' existence. Most Americans had no idea that a nationwide network of camps held nearly four hundred thousand German POWs—enough Germans to constitute four armies, or to equal the 1944 population of Denver, Seattle, or Jersey City. Americans might know a little about a camp near them, if there was one, but they had no sense of the scope. They were focused on the war overseas, where their friends and loved ones were fighting and dying. The front pages of local newspapers were dominated by reports of local men shipping out, being promoted, going missing, or getting captured, wounded, or killed. The POW camps were mostly out of sight and out of mind. The army took pains to limit journalists' access to them. Occasionally, reporters the army considered friendly were given tours of camps. The resulting stories usually focused on the prisoners' contributions to the local economy. The papers also chronicled POW escapes and recaptures. But the American public would have been surprised to learn that five German prisoners in rural Oklahoma were being court-martialed for beating one of their comrades to death.

The military tribunal at Camp Gruber comprised eleven army

officers between the ranks of captain and colonel. Col. Elmer C.
Desobry, a West Point graduate with thirty-five years of army service,
acted as president, much like a judge. An army lawyer, Maj. Arnold
Davis, served as the panel's law member, or legal adviser. They and
nine other officers acted as jurors. Jaworski was the trial judge advocate, or head prosecutor, assisted by Maj. John L. Fuller, the regular
army prosecutor at Camp Gruber. Fuller did not object to working
under Jaworski, whom he described in his Oklahoma drawl as "a
crackin' good trial lawyer." The chief defense lawyer was Lt. Col. Alfred P. C. Petsch, an army lawyer from Camp Robinson, Arkansas,
assisted by Maj. Murray B. Jones from Camp Gruber. Neither of the
defense lawyers had any experience in such cases; they usually defended American POWs. And they had little time to prepare for this
one. They had showed up at Camp Tonkawa to interview potential
witnesses only five days before the trial. Also in the courtroom were a
German POW lawyer whom the defendants had requested to help
with the case; and Werner Weingaertner, chief of the Division of
German Interests of the Swiss Legation in Washington. Weingaertner's job as a representative of the Swiss "Protecting Power" was to
observe the court-martial and report on it to the government of Nazi
Germany.

Jaworski passed up the chance to make an opening statement. Instead, he began the prosecution's case with a grim procession of witnesses who described the scene of Johann Kunze's murder. "His head
was busted open," testified Army Capt. Joe Robinette. "Busted wide
open?" he was asked. "Yes sir," Robinette replied. "You could see his
brains." Other witnesses described the trail of blood Kunze had left in
his flight from the mess hall to the kitchen to a storage room and then
back through the mess hall into the yard. One witness said a splotch
on the concrete base of the mess hall appeared to mark a spot where
Kunze's head had struck. Jaworski pointed out that Kunze had suffered several skull fractures. He suggested the fatal blow could have
been struck in the mess hall and that Kunze merely had staggered outside to die.

Jaworski showed the tribunal the anonymous note that had led to

Kunze's killing. He revealed that the information in the note about possible bombing targets in Hamburg and elsewhere was no military secret. It had come straight from an article in a 1941 issue of *Life* magazine, which most likely had been donated to the camp. Jaworski argued that Kunze may not even have written the note: he might have been framed by Beyer, who hated Kunze for refusing to obey his orders at Camp Tonkawa. Kunze used to infuriate Beyer by reminding him, "We are not in Germany anymore."

Jaworski argued that the most powerful evidence was the Germans' own statements. While the POWs had written them to try to help themselves, "they tell a story of cruelty and barbarity that I know is shocking to this court." He skillfully mixed a workmanlike presentation of the evidence and the law with dramatic verbal flourishes and slang. He said Beyer surely had known when he called the mass meeting that the men might kill Kunze. He called Seidel's jackhammer punching of Kunze "a keg of dynamite set off." Jaworski acknowledged that the three other defendants had admitted only minor roles in the attack but said that under the law they were all principals in the killing. Schomer, who had thrown the cups, was not innocent just because he "isn't a baseball pitcher and didn't hit Kunze in the head," Jaworski said. "It isn't the actual striking of a man under those circumstances; it is the participation in those acts the accumulation of which lead to the death of the victim. He was there. He threw two cups. . . . He just missed his aim, that's all."

Jaworski did not ask the tribunal to sentence the five Germans to death. But if they asked for sympathy, Jaworski thundered, the tribunal members should ask themselves, "What sympathy was extended by these accused to the little wife and three children of the deceased living in Germany? They didn't extend Johannes Kunze any sympathy and they are not in a position to ask for any sympathy."

The defense attorneys faced a daunting challenge. Going up against Jaworski would have been difficult under the best of circumstances. But defending a bitter enemy in the heat of war before a hand-picked jury of U.S. military officers was a nearly impossible task. They called the five Germans to the witness stand to give unsworn statements.

(The Germans declared they were duty-bound not to give sworn statements to a foreign court.) Each defendant insisted that while Kunze was a traitor, they had not meant for him to die. Possibly at the urging of the German POW lawyer, the defense introduced testimony that both translators at the Camp Tonkawa board of inquiry had been Jewish. The president of the tribunal quickly cut off that testimony as irrelevant and scolded the defense.

In closing arguments, Major Jones, the assistant defense attorney, pointed out that no one knew who had inflicted the fatal injuries. There was no evidence that any of the five men on trial had helped throw Kunze against the base of the mess hall. Petsch, the chief defense lawyer, argued that the Germans had not committed murder; they simply had done their duty as soldiers and "killed a traitor to prevent him from committing a further act of treason." Petsch asked the officers on the tribunal to imagine a group of American soldiers in a German POW camp discovering that one of their number was betraying them. "What do you think the American soldiers would have done?" Petsch asked. "What do you think they should have done? On the battlefields in the theaters of operation they have a way of taking care of that situation in any army, I am told." Petsch added that his clients feared that if they failed to stop Kunze, they would be charged with dereliction of duty when they returned to Germany after the war. The arguments and testimony were translated for the Germans. Despite their lawyers' vigorous arguments on their behalf, they seemed puzzled by the court procedures and the courtroom atmosphere in general. It bothered them to see their lawyers chatting pleasantly with Jaworski during breaks. "Does not this Colonel represent the enemy of the Third Reich?" one asked.

After both sides had finished their closing arguments, the tribunal adjourned to deliberate. The Germans were taken back to temporary holding cells at Camp Gruber. After two and a half hours, at 5:21 p.m. on January 25, the tribunal returned its verdicts. The eleven officers unanimously convicted all five Germans of rioting and murder and sentenced them "to be hanged by the neck until dead." While the State of Oklahoma used the electric chair for executions, the army used the gallows. The verdicts and death sentences were even more secret than the trial. By prior order from the Provost Marshal General's Office in Washington, they were disclosed only to the prosecutors, the defense lawyers, and their chain of command. Petsch, the lead defense attorney, was ordered not to tell his clients they had been sentenced to die until some unspecified date after they had been transported to their place of execution, the U.S. Army Disciplinary Barracks at Fort Leavenworth, Kansas. The Geneva Convention did not address when and how the condemned men were to be informed of the verdicts. The Germans sat in their cells at Fort Gruber, waiting and wondering.

The War Department disclosed the verdicts to the State Department, which informed the Swiss. The Swiss then notified the German government, as required by Article 66 of the Geneva Convention: "If the death penalty is pronounced against a prisoner of war, a communication setting forth in detail the nature and circumstances of the offense shall be sent as soon as possible to the representative of the Protecting Power for transmission to the Power in whose armies the prisoner served. The sentence shall not be executed before the expiration of at least three months after this communication."

The Geneva Convention did not provide any formal process by which the government of Germany could appeal or protest the verdicts. The German government merely had to be told about them.

×   ×   ×

Jaworski had known from the start that the Camp Tonkawa "test case" would receive unusual scrutiny. The verdicts and death sentences would be reviewed by General Donovan at the Eighth Service Command in Dallas; army review boards in Dallas and Washington; the Judge Advocate General's Office; the secretary of war; and the president of the United States. But the toughest critic was certain to be the government of Nazi Germany.

Jaworski wanted to believe that the Germans would see that the court-martial had been conducted fairly. He had tried to do everything by the book. As the trial was winding down, he had perfumed the court record with praise for the fairness of the proceedings. "I have never appeared before a court anywhere in which as much consideration to the facts of the case were given as in this case," he began one rhetorical flourish. Even the defense attorneys, who had been forced to scramble to interview witnesses, joined in the praise. Even so, Jaworski knew that sentencing five German POWs to death would cause a stir in Berlin. "We knew how carefully the German authorities would study the trial record," he wrote. "If they had been able to find any flaw in our proceedings, we knew it would be ammunition in their propaganda war against us." Even worse, the Germans were holding American POWs, Jaworski wrote, "and the risk of reprisal troubled us to no end." Defense attorney Petsch warned that the U.S. government was playing with fire. In his appeal of the verdicts, he wrote that the Germans would not view the Tonkawa prosecution as legitimate. They would see it as America using its legal system "to kill five German soldiers whose lives were spared by American soldiers on the battlefield." And they were certain to respond by sentencing American POWs to death.

Petsch would prove prophetic. Jaworski's fears of reprisal would be realized. The murders in the POW camps in the United States, starting at Camp Tonkawa, would turn fifteen American POWs in Germany into hostages. The first of those fifteen already was in German hands. He was a big, imposing U.S. Army infantry officer known to his men as "King Kong."

PART II

In German Hands

8

King Kong in a Cage

William Herbert Schaefer was born on June 30, 1900, in Wabash County, Illinois, in a tiny farming community named Kitchen's Bridge, which was named for an actual bridge over muddy, winding Bonpas Creek near the Indiana border. Schaefer was the youngest of six children of German immigrants, who probably settled in that remote corner of Illinois because it was already an enclave of German Americans. Kitchen's Bridge was little more than a cluster of homes and a one-room schoolhouse with a single teacher. Schaefer's father, who spoke six languages, worked as a foreman in a packing house. He died when Schaefer was only four and a half years old. Schaefer's mother died when he was six. The boy spent most of his tumultuous early years living in Pittsburgh with an uncle, whom he remembered as brilliant but strict. The uncle made Schaefer study French, Spanish, and German for an hour after school every day, and for two hours on days when school was out. It paid off. By the time Schaefer was halfway through elementary school, he spoke French and German fluently.

After graduating from high school near Kitchen's Bridge, Schaefer enlisted in the U.S. Army. He saw action on the front lines in France during World War I. He got hooked on the army. It became his family. He stayed in uniform after the war and applied to West Point—an unusual step for a man who already had served as an enlisted soldier. He was accepted, and excelled in his classes while also wrestling and playing varsity football. After graduating in 1924, Schaefer served in the Far East, including an assignment in the Philippines. Then in the spring of 1942 the army called him home to help prepare for Operation Torch, the Allied invasion of North Africa—the opening of America's ground war against Germany. Lieutenant Colonel Schaefer was given command of the First Battalion of the 180th Infantry Division, a collection of more than eight hundred green recruits, and was told to get them ready to fight the Nazis.

Schaefer had grown into an imposing figure, dark-haired, broadshouldered, and thick chested. At six foot four, he somehow gave the appearance of being short and stocky. One of his men observed that Schaefer had "a square face and a personality to match. He was gruff, not courteous. Stubborn, authoritative, and industrious." Schaefer did not suffer fools or anyone else gladly. He exuded a confidence bordering on arrogance. He cared little for the opinions of men of lower rank and held a particular disdain for the "citizen-soldiers" whom the war had catapulted almost straight out of civilian life into the officer corps. But there was no denying Schaefer's energy and intellect. Men could not help but look up to him. He was old enough to be a father figure. One junior officer called Schaefer one of the finest leaders he had ever known: "What a man he was!" Another officer described Schaefer as "a brilliant tactician who knew von Clausewitz from cover to cover."* Behind Schaefer's broad back, the enlisted men called him by a nickname that suggested an irresistible force of nature: "King Kong."

Schaefer called his men his "knot heads." He prepared them for mountain warfare in West Virginia and for amphibious landings on the shores of Chesapeake Bay and Cape Cod. Schaefer found some of the army's training programs lacking. At one point, his battalion was assigned to practice hand-to-hand combat in a field overgrown with

---

* Carl von Clausewitz was a nineteenth-century Prussian general and military thinker whose book *On War* is widely regarded as a classic on military strategy.

poison ivy. Three hundred of his men became so itchy that jugs of calamine lotion had to be rushed to them from a nearby camp hospital and their training was disrupted for three days. Schaefer angrily pulled rank on the training staff, chewed them out, and took over his unit's training. As a final training exercise on Cape Cod, Schaefer's battalion "subdued the island of Martha's Vineyard" with the help of paratroopers. The training concluded with a formal review by Secretary of War Henry Stimson and other Pentagon brass, followed by promotions for the training officers whom Schaefer had found so incompetent. Schaefer stewed over those promotions.

After all the training, Schaefer and his battalion ended up seeing no real action in North Africa. But their turn came in July 1943 in the invasion of Sicily. After defeating the Afrika Korps in North Africa, the Allies had chosen the Italian island as their next target. From Sicily, they could cross to the Italian mainland and fight their way north to Rome. Allied planners regarded Italy as the soft underbelly of Nazi-held Europe. They knew they eventually would have to launch an amphibious invasion of France in order to carry the fight into Germany. But in the summer of 1943, they still did not think their forces were ready to assault the German fortifications along the French coast—Hitler's so-called Atlantic Wall. So the Allies settled for invading Sicily.

The invasion of Sicily on July 9, 1943, was the largest amphibious landing in World War II—larger than the D-Day invasion of France. Schaefer's battalion was in the first wave. He was assigned to lead a landing team to seize control of the mouth of the Acate River on Sicily's southern coast. A few weeks before the invasion, Schaefer seriously injured his right leg when he fell into a landing craft during a practice landing at Oran, a port city in Algeria. He could not walk without crutches and did not see how he could lead his men ashore in that condition. But his superiors pointed out that he was the only man in the battalion who had ever been under enemy fire, albeit in a previous world war; his inexperienced men might need his leadership if the fighting got heavy. "I felt complimented and did not want to miss the action in any case," Schaefer recalled later. So he hobbled into combat.

The First Battalion rode toward Sicily from North Africa aboard the U.S. Navy assault ship USS *Calvert,* which carried small landing craft. As the *Calvert* ploughed through heavy seas toward the landing zone, officers gave inspirational speeches over the loudspeaker. Schaefer found the speeches annoying. He grew angry when a chaplain told the soldiers not to fear dying for a righteous cause. Schaefer told his men to forget about the hereafter and focus on staying alive. He also reminded them to do everything they could to avoid being captured, "because captives can't fight." After dark, Schaefer and his men boarded their landing craft on the *Calvert* and were released into the rough water. Several times big waves lifted the little boat and slammed it into the side of the *Calvert.* The landing craft's coxswain had trouble starting its engine. Finally the boat headed toward the beach. German machine-gun bullets spattered against its side "like gravel thrown against a tin surface" but did not injure anyone. The coxswain landed them at the mouth of the Acate River, right where they were supposed to be. But other craft that were to have landed with them were driven off course by the currents; a few turned back for reasons Schaefer did not understand. He and his men were left on the beach virtually alone, without mortars or a radio. They were pinned down briefly by machine-gun fire, but the gun mysteriously fell silent, and they advanced up the beach. Schaefer, struggling on his crutches, fell over a small clay cliff, aggravating his leg injury.

Accompanying Schaefer's battalion onto the beach was a navy sailor named Francis Carpenter. He told Schaefer he was a stage actor and had ridden a horse along the same stretch of beach before the war. He and a second man volunteered to scout the area on foot. Schaefer told the men it was dangerous and they were under no obligation to go. A short distance along, the second man stepped on a German land mine that killed him and threw Carpenter into the air. Carpenter got up and kept going, taking note of all the roads near the landing beaches. He found an Italian family cowering in a cornfield. He assured them the Americans were their friends, and put them at ease by singing "La donna è mobile" from the opera *Rigoletto.* The family pointed out all the German land mines in the area.

After a couple of hours on the beach, Schaefer and his men made their way through sand dunes into a rolling grassy area dotted with cottages and one-story houses. An Italian civilian offered the Americans wine, which Schaefer tasted and found "superior." Then an Italian army officer approached, waving his hands frantically. He told Schaefer he wanted to surrender two entire companies of Italian soldiers who had no desire to fight. Schaefer accepted on the condition they give up their weapons and remove any land mines in the area. The Italian officer agreed but protested that the mines had been laid by the Germans, who had since departed. The Germans had not gone far, however. Before the end of the day they mounted a counterattack. Panzer tanks raced through the groves of olives and grapes with German infantry riding on top. Schaefer had received a few reinforcements, but the Americans still were outnumbered and outgunned. A mortar shell killed a GI near Schaefer. Another shell sent a hot shard of shrapnel into his injured right leg. One of his men panicked, got up and ran, and was shot. Schaefer wondered if his own troops were attacking him by mistake. In the confusion, with night falling, he and five other soldiers became separated from the rest of the battalion.

Schaefer tried to lead the group back to the battalion in the darkness. Germans seemed to be all around them. The Americans hid in thigh-high grass. Machine-gun rounds passed over their heads, followed by a shower of grenades. A grenade glanced off Schaefer's helmet and fell to the ground next to where he lay. He saw the blue light of its fuse, a blinding flash, and then lost consciousness. A sergeant woke him and Schaefer warned him to lie still and silent. Two columns of German infantry marched by, so close that "I could have slapped the legs of both columns as they passed," he wrote later. The Americans stayed hidden in the high grass. The night dragged on. At one point, Schaefer had to piss so badly that he rolled onto his side and did it, worrying that the sound would give him away. The first faint light of dawn revealed Germans in front of and behind him. But soon after sunrise, they started to withdraw. "We lay still in the grass until I thought they must be all gone," Schaefer wrote. "I should have had more patience. As I rose out of the grass . . . a German lieutenant

with an orderly and armed with a machine rifle almost fell over me."
A little over twenty-four hours had passed since Schaefer had landed
on the beach. He felt mortified at being captured after having lectured
his men not to let themselves be captured. When the Germans allowed
him to send a note to his superior officers, Schaefer wrote sheepishly,
"I'm sorry I got captured."

The Germans thought Schaefer was a paratrooper because of a
Thunderbird shoulder patch on his uniform. He did not immediately
reveal that he spoke German. An interrogator peppered him with
questions in English about U.S. airborne units and drop zones. Finally,
a German intelligence officer consulted an issue of *National Geographic* magazine and saw that the Thunderbird was the insignia for
the U.S. Army's Forty-Fifth Infantry Division. Schaefer's rank of lieutenant colonel still made him a potentially valuable prisoner, and he
was assigned a personal guard with a machine pistol. He and several
other POWs were sent to sleep outdoors on the ground. The night was
cold, and Schaefer had no warm clothes. He curled up in a ball to
conserve his body heat. A German soldier paced back and forth past
the prisoners, grumbling about having to stay out in the cold to guard
the American "swine" and "subhumans." Schaefer understood his
every word. Then, to Schaefer's surprise, the guard muttered, "*Aber
sie sind auch Menschen*" (But they are people too). The guard took off
his overcoat and covered Schaefer with it. Schaefer pretended to be
asleep, but he was moved by the gesture of kindness. The guard's
comment stuck with him. He later would entitle a book on his POW
experiences *People Too*.

Schaefer's capture notwithstanding, the Allied invasion of Sicily
was a success. American and British troops conquered the island in
thirty-eight days, reclaiming their first piece of European soil from
Hitler. The victory reopened the Mediterranean Sea to Allied shipping. It gave the American and British armies a jumping-off point for
the invasion of mainland Italy in September. The Allies' only serious
mistake was allowing more than one hundred thousand German
troops to evacuate from Sicily across the narrow Strait of Messina to
the Italian mainland, where they would keep fighting. The invasion of

Sicily cost the Germans nearly 30,000 men killed or wounded and 140,000 captured. Most of the captured were shipped across the Atlantic to POW camps in the United States to join the captured soldiers of the Afrika Korps. The British lost 2,717 dead and 10,122 wounded and captured. The American casualties included 2,237 dead and 6,544 wounded or captured, including Schaefer.

The Germans moved Schaefer by rail through Italy toward their network of POW camps in Germany and Poland, as they did with most of their prisoners (although thousands of POWs were held in camps in Italy before the Allies drove the Germans out). Schaefer rode through Italy mostly in passenger cars as comfortable as the Pullmans that carried German prisoners across the United States. The Italian passenger cars had big glass windows and—a true luxury—bathrooms at either end. But the trip through Italy was slow and extremely dangerous. One of Schaefer's trains passed through Salerno just as Allied planes were bombing and strafing a nearby airfield, and the pilots noticed the train and attacked it too. "Fifty caliber bullets made a shambles of the glass of the train," Schaefer wrote. Bombs began to fall. The train halted. Its crew and most of its passengers fled for their lives. Schaefer's guard ran across a field but fell before he could reach the cover of some woods. Schaefer could not run so he crawled and rolled. A piece of shrapnel from a bomb lodged in his back. Dozens of American prisoners escaped in the chaos, but Schaefer could not move fast enough. After the planes flew off, he got back on the train with the Germans and the remaining prisoners. The attack had killed five POWs. As the train resumed its journey north, a German sergeant asked Schaefer if the prisoners included any doctors. A dozen German guards had been severely wounded in the air attack, and the sergeant had been given charge of them despite having no medical training and no medicine. Schaefer followed him to a boxcar where the wounded Germans lay. Some obviously were dying. All Schaefer could do was to persuade some British prisoners on the train to give up their spare morphine pills to take away their dying enemies' pain.

At the next stop, a foul prison camp at Capua in the Campania region of southern Italy, the grateful German sergeant arranged for

Schaefer to be moved to the camp hospital, where doctors removed the shrapnel from his body and set his injured leg. One doctor told Schaefer to stay off the leg or he might never regain full use of it. Life in the hospital was hard. Schaefer caught pneumonia and was treated with leeches. One day an Allied bomb landed close enough to throw him from his bed and knock him unconscious. Later, some British POWs asked Schaefer to visit a mortally wounded American prisoner in another part of the hospital. The dying GI explained to Schaefer that although the British and Italians had treated him well, he wanted to be with an American officer when he died. Schaefer recited the Twenty-Third Psalm, which contains the lines "Yea, though I walk through the valley of the shadow of death, I will fear no evil; for thou art with me; thy rod and thy staff they comfort me." The soldier thanked him and died.

After Schaefer had healed enough to travel again, he rode in a boxcar with other POWs on the final leg of his trip into Germany. As the train neared the German border, Schaefer helped conceal the escape of three fellow prisoners who had broken a hole in the floor of the boxcar. He sat over the hole whenever the guards entered the boxcar, and moved around during head counts to make the Germans think all the prisoners were still there. The guards were furious when they finally discovered the truth. Schaefer suggested that no prisoners actually had escaped: the guards had been given an inaccurate list of prisoners from the start. The guards knew better, but as Schaefer had expected, they enthusiastically embraced the lie because it absolved them of blame.

The boxcar journey was hard on Schaefer, who still needed a crutch to walk. He had lost his crutches during his capture, but a fellow prisoner had somehow gotten hold of some wood and nails and fashioned a replacement for him. Schaefer had lost so much weight from the meager POW rations that "my pants would go halfway around me a second time." A young German officer told him, not unkindly, that he was too old to be fighting a war against men "young and quick like me." Schaefer finally arrived on German soil for the first time in his life in November 1943—about the time the killings in the POW camps in the United States began. Allied troops were struggling to advance through southern Italy. The British had started bombing Berlin but were suffering heavy losses.

Schaefer was sent to an interrogation center at Luckenwalde, near Berlin, where all captured U.S. Army officers were questioned about the activities of their fighting units and Allied war strategy in general. MIS-X, or Military Intelligence Service-X, a secret branch of the U.S. government helping Americans behind enemy lines, described Luckenwalde as a harsh prison with "starvation rations and prolonged periods of solitary confinement." The Germans excused those blatant violations of the Geneva Convention by insisting that all captured officers had to be considered possible spies until they proved otherwise. The only way for them to do that was to reveal details of the combat units in which they served.

Schaefer was placed in a tiny isolation cell, which he described as about three and a half feet wide and eight feet long, with stone walls that were perfectly smooth. The only furnishings were a crude bench, a stool, a table, a gunnysack full of wood shavings for a mattress, and a smaller gunnysack with wood shavings for a pillow. He had nothing but his crutch and the clothes he was wearing. Once a day, he was taken from his cell to relieve himself in front of a guard. Occasionally, without warning, he was summoned for interrogation. The Germans seemed to think he was more important than he was. They asked him how many atomic bombs America possessed. He knew nothing about the Manhattan Project, of course—not even Vice President Harry Truman knew about it—but Schaefer tried to give the impression that he did. His interrogators noted his German name and offered to make him a general commanding a brigade of German American soldiers fighting for Hitler. Schaefer declined. He told the Germans they never would be able to raise such a brigade. That comment ended Schaefer's solicitous treatment. He was sent back to his cell.

A month passed and the isolation began getting to Schaefer. The only light in his cell came from a painted-over window high on the wall opposite the door. In the perpetual half light, he could tell day from night but little more. "Try it sometime," he wrote in *People Too*:

"You are in a kind of eternity. Your only resources are your body, your brain, your mind, your Soul, our God, your knowledge, your beliefs if any (and they will be tested) and your past experience. You are face to face with yourself and nothing else day after day." Schaefer was determined to keep his mind sharp. He recited the Declaration of Independence over and over. He analyzed Shakespeare's plays for modern lessons. He concocted complex math problems and military problems to solve. He designed imaginary bridges, septic tanks, and drainage systems.

One day, hoping he was not being watched, he balanced the stool atop the bench, climbed up to the painted-over window, and scratched a pinhole just large enough to allow a point of light to strike the opposite wall. He watched the point move across the wall as the sun tracked across the sky. Then he scratched faint marks on the wall to create a rudimentary sundial. It helped. "Part of eternity was broken," he wrote. "I had TIME . . ."

Schaefer also figured out how to open a peephole on his cell door from the inside, which enabled him to see into the corridor adjoining his cell. That proved a mixed blessing. One day he heard shouting, peered through the peephole, and saw a fellow prisoner being dragged along the corridor by guards. The man kept screaming words to the effect of "You promised! You said if I told you what you wanted, you would not put me back in there! You promised!" Although Schaefer rarely saw prisoners beaten, the Germans took every opportunity to humiliate them. "You were told that you were lower than the lowest German soldier," he wrote afterwards. "German privates were sent into your room to sit until you went to bed. Mixed in with this, there were speeches by the craziest people. Weird propaganda. Near starvation and bitter cold."

If Schaefer thought it could get no worse, he would learn otherwise.

9

Wrong Side of the River

Though the fates of "King Kong" Schaefer and U.S. Army Lt. James R. Schmitz would entwine, the two officers could not have been more different. While Schaefer was curt and intimidating, Jimmy Schmitz was friendly and approachable. Schmitz was thirteen years younger. He stood five foot six and was slightly pudgy, with short blond hair, a fair complexion, deep-set blue eyes, and a ready smile. A fellow officer described him as "friendly, always trying to please. . . . His personality was that of a rural politician." That was exactly who Schmitz was.

Schmitz was born on May 11, 1913, in the small city of Ottawa, Illinois, in La Salle County about sixty miles southwest of Chicago. One thing he did have in common with Schaefer was losing his father at a young age. Schmitz's father, a railroad brakeman, was crushed between two electric rail cars. His two older brothers worked to pay the bills while he finished high school. Then he worked in a local factory and as sports editor of the *Ottawa Republican-Times* newspaper. In 1938, he was hired by LaSalle County treasurer Fred J. Hart, a savvy politico who became his mentor.

Schmitz proved a natural at politics. He could talk to anybody. He was equally comfortable at campaign rallies and in the proverbial smoke-filled backrooms where the real decisions were made. La Salle County politics was rough-and-tumble. During the Prohibition era, the county had so many links to organized crime in Chicago that a book on the area's history is entitled *Capone's Cornfields*. Schmitz was elected president of the LaSalle County Young Republican Club and chairman of the Ottawa Republican Party. He was promoted to regional supervisor for the Illinois Tax Commission. He seemed like a young man on the rise, but he kept a secret that threatened his ambitions: He was attracted to men.

Had the army known of Schmitz's sexual orientation, it would have turned him away when he showed up at the local enlistment office in July 1942 at the age of twenty-nine. Instead, the army gained a capable officer who spoke fluent German and who stood up for his men at the risk of his life. Schmitz graduated from the infantry school at Fort Benning, Georgia, as a second lieutenant. He was one of the "citizen soldiers" whom Schaefer dismissed as amateurs. Schmitz was sent overseas in October 1942 to take part in the invasion of North Africa.

Schmitz saw no action there, nor did he take part in the Allied invasion of Sicily. But he and his regiment were transported to Sicily because it was the departure point for the Allied invasion of mainland Italy. They were among the first U.S. combat units to set foot on the Italian mainland, landing at Salerno on September 9, 1943.

Allied troops poured into Salerno and other ports at the southern end of Italy, which the Germans had mostly abandoned and booby-trapped. American and British armies turned northwest to fight their way up the Italian "boot" to Rome. Fighting the Germans in the rugged mountains of Italy proved more difficult than expected. "The country was shockingly beautiful, and just as shockingly hard to capture from the enemy," wrote the war correspondent Ernie Pyle, who accompanied the U.S. troops. "The hills rose to high ridges of almost solid rock. We couldn't go around them through the flat peaceful valleys, because the Germans were up there looking down on us, and they would have let us have it. So we had to go up and over. A mere platoon of Germans, well dug-in on a high rock-spined hill, could hold out for a long time against tremendous onslaughts." Winter brought weeks of heavy rain, reducing the already-poor roads and airfields to mud. Snow piled up in twenty-foot drifts on the high peaks where the outposts stood. Field hospitals filled with victims of exposure, frostbite, and "trench foot." By the last days of 1943, the Allied drive up the Italian "boot" had ground to a miserable, costly stalemate.

To that point, Schmitz had seen little action in Italy. He had been promoted to first lieutenant and given command of a seventy-five-man mortar platoon in the 143rd Infantry Regiment, Thirty-Sixth Infantry Division. But the platoon had not yet been sent into combat. Schmitz even had found time to relax. A fellow soldier from Ottawa, Illinois, wrote that he and Schmitz had dined together twice, including a meal on Christmas Eve where they were "served by men in tuxedos." On January 11, 1944, however, Schmitz wrote to his sister in Ottawa that he was "going into the hills to fight." The "hills" were the rugged mountains along the Winter Line, or Gustav Line, a German defensive front that extended through the city of Cassino and the valley of the Rapido River, which American soldiers called "the Valley of the Purple Heart" because so many men were wounded there. Schmitz's mortar platoon was deployed to a high ridge overlooking Cassino and the river valley from the south. The Germans occupied a similarly high ridge on the opposite side of the narrow valley. Each side could see the other's every movement in daylight, so all attacks took place at night. The Allies kept striking at the Winter Line and getting driven back with heavy losses.

On January 21, American lieutenant general Mark W. Clark ordered a new attack on the Winter Line. It would be led by Schmitz and his mortar platoon. Their regiment and a second regiment would row small rubber boats across the Gari River, a fast-flowing tributary of the Rapido, and establish a foothold on the German side. Then more troops would follow them across the river. Schmitz thought the plan very risky. If the first men across did not break through the German defenses, they would be trapped with their backs to the river. The attack may have been no more than a diversion to pull German troops away from the Anzio area, where an Allied amphibious force was to land the next day. In any case, Schmitz had his orders. After dark on the twenty-first, he and his men clambered into rubber boats on the south bank of the Gari and rowed toward the German side.

The crossing was eerily quiet. As the boats carrying Schmitz and his men neared the opposite shore, they encountered a minefield and had to slow. When the men landed, the Germans on the high ground in front of them began raining artillery shells and mortar rounds on them. Then German infantry attacked with small arms, grenades, and bazookas. The Germans sank the Americans' boats and blew up the only bridge on that stretch of the river. The attack was stopped only three hundred yards from the riverbank. General Clark sent no more troops across. Schmitz had been right about the danger. By the next afternoon, most of the men in his mortar platoon had been killed or wounded. The Germans launched a new attack against the trapped American regiments, and Schmitz and one hundred others chose being captured over being killed.

The Germans could not evacuate the prisoners quickly from the battle zone, and Schmitz spent his first hours of captivity under a terrifying barrage from the American artillery across the Gari River. Both sides had suffered so many casualties that they agreed to a two-hour ceasefire to retrieve the dead and wounded from no-man's-land. Schmitz had not been alone in thinking the attack was risky. Another American officer was captured with a note in his pocket saying the attack seemed foolhardy and he feared becoming a casualty. The Germans used the note in a piece of propaganda entitled "American Major Has Great Fear of the German Army." But what the major had feared was his leaders' battle plan. The disastrous river crossing drew some German troops away from the Anzio area, but not nearly enough. The Allied invasion force at Anzio was bottled up on the beach. Allied planners blamed one another for the setbacks. Those repercussions were lost on Schmitz, whose war appeared over.

×   ×   ×

Like "King Kong" Schaefer, Schmitz endured an arduous journey as a POW through Italy on his way to Germany. He was marched for three days with little to eat or drink. The Germans said every well in the area was contaminated. They finally reached a small town, where Schmitz was questioned. His interrogators said a man like him with a German name should fight for the Fatherland. Schmitz replied that his great-great-grandfather was German but that his family had long since placed its loyalty with the United States. His great-grandfather had fought for America in the War of 1812; his grandfather had fought for the Union in the Civil War; and his father had fought for the United States in World War I—against Germany. Schmitz would not break that tradition.

He and other prisoners were loaded into boxcars and taken across the German border to a huge POW camp at Mühlburg, where they took showers and were sprayed for lice by Russian prisoners who had been captured on the Eastern Front. The Russians told them in hushed voices that the Germans were committing terrible atrocities in nearby concentration camps. Their descriptions were so horrific that Schmitz thought they must be lies: "It was difficult to believe that civilized people could do such things." The Americans got back into the boxcars for the final, 120-mile leg of the journey to a POW camp in Poland. "We saw eastern Germany and western Poland as a cow being sent to market would see it," a prisoner wrote. Their train kept being shunted onto sidetracks to let German troop trains thunder past on the main line. No signs marked the Polish border. The Germans had destroyed them. They were trying to erase Poland as a nation. Schmitz's train passed from farmland into rolling hills and stopped at the Polish town of Schubin. The Germans had renamed the town "Alterburgund"— "Old Burgundy"—and its cobblestoned main street "Adolph Hitler Strasse." The guards marched Schmitz and the other Americans down the street to the main gate of Oflag 64, a POW camp for American officers.*

Oflag 64 occupied the grounds of a Polish boys' school, with two

---

* The name Oflag was short for *Offizierlager,* a German term for an army officers' camp. A Stalag housed enlisted prisoners; a Marlag held naval prisoners; and a Stalag Luft was a camp for aviators, operated by the Luftwaffe. Each branch of the German armed forces ran its own camps.

large manor houses and several trees. The manor houses contained senior officers' quarters and the camp infirmary. The ten-acre campus was surrounded by two concentric barbed-wire fences, with coils of old, rusted barbed wire in the spaces between the fences. There were guard towers with machine guns and searchlights. Most of Oflag 64 was laid out like the camps in the United States, with rows of rough, newly built, wooden barracks. Each bunk came with two blankets, a "mattress" consisting of an onion sack stuffed with wood shavings, and a smaller onion sack of shavings for a pillow. Oflag 64 was a far cry from the "Fritz Ritz" camps in the United States, but it met the basic requirements of the Geneva Convention.

The Germans allowed the prisoners at Oflag 64 and other camps to choose their own leaders and to let those leaders run day-to-day life in the American sections of the camps unless someone stepped out of line. That was the same approach the U.S. Army had tried in its camps in America, only to have the Nazis take power. The German army was an extension of a ruthless dictatorship that was breaking apart. The cracks were visible to the prisoners at Oflag 64. The camp commandant, Col. Fritz Schneider, was a proud career German army officer who did everything by the book. He confided to senior American officers that he was not a Nazi and did not subscribe to National Socialist views. But Schneider had to share power in the camp with its well-connected Nazi security officer, Capt. G. Zimmerman.

Zimmerman was an ardent and arrogant Nazi from Bayreuth "who took great delight in making life unbearable for the American prisoners by constantly belittling them," a prisoner wrote. Zimmerman "had the reputation of killing without provocation and in a way that seldom if ever brought any kind of investigation," wrote POW Clarence Ferguson, and everyone who crossed paths with Zimmerman was "justly terrified when dealing with this man." Zimmerman probably lived in terror too. His predecessor at Oflag 64, a Czech Nazi, had been sent to the Russian front after thirty-six prisoners escaped from the camp, even though none of the escapees made it to Allied lines. Zimmerman took no chances. He doubled Oflag 64's perimeter guard at night and ordered sentries to patrol outside the wire with dogs. He warned the guards that if they did not run a strict camp, the SS would take it over.

Schmitz resolved not to do anything to attract Zimmerman's attention. Schmitz worked as an assistant adjutant, processing American prisoners' paperwork. He also served as a point of contact between the senior American POWs and the Germans. Because of his fluent German, he got to know many of the guards. A guard who was about to be transferred to the battlefront asked Schmitz to write him a note in English saying, "I give up." He planned to hand the note to the first American soldier he saw and hope he was sent to the United States. Schmitz wrote the note. He was well liked by both the Americans and the Germans.

There is no indication that Schmitz revealed to anyone at Oflag 64 that he was gay. Doing so might have cost him friends, or worse. At the time, the army tried to screen out homosexuals on the ground that they suffered from a mental illness. A homosexual discovered in uniform might be ousted with a "blue discharge" without veterans benefits. The army also court-martialed soldiers for sodomy. Leon Jaworski had prosecuted a GI in Texas for having sexual relations with a man. The Nazis persecuted and imprisoned homosexuals, and German guards in some POW camps beat prisoners for homosexual acts or even for behaving in what they considered an effeminate manner. For Schmitz, keeping his secret surely came with a cost, said his nephew, James Schmitz. "I've always thought he must have felt like he was in a prison inside a prison."

Still, Schmitz felt fortunate, he wrote later, to have been sent to Oflag 64 rather than a harsher camp. He was certain the Allies would win the war without further help from him, and he saw no point in risking his life trying to escape. He was determined to get home alive to Ottawa, Illinois. His mother already had lost her husband to a rail car accident and her youngest son to a drowning. Schmitz's needless death surely would break her heart. Schmitz did his job and kept his head down. He never took part in the constant escape planning and tunnel digging that went on at Oflag 64. And he never went out of his way to antagonize the Germans the way he saw "King Kong" Schaefer do.

Schaefer had arrived at Oflag 64 several weeks after Schmitz. Six weeks of interrogation and solitary confinement at Luckenwalde had left Schaefer exhausted, filthy, and half-starved. Oflag 64 was different. Schaefer was allowed to shower and shave. He was issued clean clothes. A POW tailor even fitted him for a new U.S. Army uniform. His rank of lieutenant colonel made him second-in-command of the American prisoners at the camp. For the first time in weeks, he had plenty to eat, thanks to the twice-weekly packages from the Red Cross, which contained such foods as Spam, canned roast or corned beef, tuna fish, cheese, raisins, prunes, dates, sugar, coffee, crackers, and margarine. Schaefer had to admit, "After all I had experienced to date, I found Oflag 64 quite nice."

But Schaefer, unlike Schmitz, could not just settle comfortably into captivity and wait to be freed. His bad leg made escape unlikely, but despite his age and poor health, Schaefer considered it his duty to make life hard for his captors—to show "pure cussedness," as Civil War prisoners called it. Schaefer constantly protested the camp's food and living conditions. He carried around a dogeared copy of the Geneva Convention and challenged the legality of German orders. He got loud. Schaefer "had a reputation for being ornery at the best of times," a fellow prisoner wrote, "and he never lost an opportunity to bait the Germans." Schaefer even weaponized his false teeth, another POW recalled. If a guard "shouted at him or bothered him in some way, Schaefer would swiftly pull out his set of false teeth, point them at the German offender and snap those teeth with amazing ferocity and speed."

Schaefer knew that some of the Germans "hated my guts." None of them hated him more than Captain Zimmerman, the vindictive Nazi security officer. Zimmerman would turn Schaefer and Schmitz into hostages of Nazi Germany.

10

The Bastards Get Lucky

While "King Kong" Schaefer and James Schmitz languished at the Oflag 64 POW camp in Poland, Col. Henry R. Spicer of the U.S. Army Air Forces was trying desperately to get into the war.

Spicer was born in 1909 in Colorado Springs, Colorado. His father, Carroll Atchison Spicer, was a farmer who decided to try construction contracting. Money was tight at first, and the family lived in a rooming house. But Carroll soon moved his family to Los Angeles and built a prosperous business. He helped build the Coolidge Dam on the Gila River near Globe, Arizona, and the Grand Central air terminal in Glendale, California. His son Henry worked part-time at the air terminal in high school and fell in love with flying. He graduated from the University of Arizona in 1932 with a degree in economics while participating in the NROTC training program and the Cavalry Reserve. An expert horseman, he played on the college's polo team, which was so good that it toured the country challenging other schools. The team called itself "the Horseless Wonders" because it left its own horses in Arizona and played on whatever horses its opponents provided.

But Spicer wanted to fly, not ride. To his surprise, he failed the army air forces physical on his first try. He spent the next year toughening himself up by panning for gold in the Arizona desert. He passed the physical on his second try. He graduated from flight school in 1934. His superiors wanted to make him a bomber pilot, but he wanted to fly fighters. He served in fighter squadrons in California and at Pearl Harbor before the Japanese attack. His senior officers were so impressed by his flying skills that they put him in charge of the Advanced Flying School at Randolph Field and Moore Field near Mission, Texas. Spicer was a hearty, squarely built man with blue-gray eyes he often focused into a penetrating gaze. He had a bristling handlebar moustache and a briar pipe always clenched in his teeth. He was also a memorable instructor. When a trainee passed his final test in the air, Spicer would radio him, "Okay, mister, I've got it," and then put his own plane through a series of impressive acrobatic maneuvers. When a trainee failed the test, Spicer just landed his plane.

Spicer married a Texas woman, Louise Leonard, and became a father. In 1943, at the age of thirty-four, he was promoted to lieutenant colonel. He was prominent in the community. "As much a fixture at Moore Field as the loudly painted water tower is the black pipe of Lt. Col. Henry R. Spicer," *The McAllen (Tex.) Monitor* declared in May 1943. "He probably smokes it while he shaves. . . . When he tries his hand at poker, the pipe burns furiously." But Spicer puffed partly in frustration. He had logged more than four thousand hours of flying time and was tired of teaching other, younger men to fight. He kept asking to be sent to England, the takeoff point for bombing raids on Germany and Nazi-held Europe. Finally in February 1944, the army gave him everything he had asked for and more: the command of a fighter group of forty-six P-51 Mustangs, a new plane that was changing the air war over Europe.

For most of 1943, American bombers had flown missions in daylight while the British flew them at night. The British had stopped flying daylight missions because of heavy losses. So had the Germans. But the U.S. Army Air Forces thought its heavily armed B-17 "Flying Fortresses" could defend themselves even if the Germans could see them. The bombers often were escorted by American and British fighters to fend off the German fighters. But the early Allied fighters, including the iconic British Spitfire, lacked the range to fly the entire 560 miles from England to Berlin and back. They had to turn around 50 miles short of Berlin, leaving the bombers to fend for themselves on the most critical leg of their mission. The Germans learned to wait until the Allied fighters had turned back to send up their own fighters. American bombers suffered breathtaking losses. In October 1943, the United States lost 148 bombers in seven days over Germany, including 60 in a single raid on a ball-bearing factory in Bavaria.

When the P-51 Mustang debuted in Europe in December 1943, it shifted the balance. It was a fast, nimble fighter that could easily fly to Berlin and back in four to five hours, thanks to an efficient, liquid-cooled Rolls-Royce Merlin engine and extra fuel tanks on its exterior that could be jettisoned when empty. The Mustang had six machine guns, including two .50 calibers mounted on the nose and two .30 calibers on each wing. It could outperform all the German fighters in dogfights. P-51 pilots were encouraged to leave formation to pursue enemy planes all the way down to the treetops—"down to the deck"—to destroy them. By the end of the war, P-51s would shoot down 4,950 enemy aircraft and play an outsized role in the destruction of the Luftwaffe. A U.S. Senate committee analyzing the American war effort called the P-51 "the most aerodynamically perfect pursuit plane in existence."

Spicer arrived in Britain in early February. The war was going well but slowly. The fighting in Italy was hard. The Allies were planning an elaborate ruse to make the Germans think the invasion of France would take place near Calais rather than at Normandy, where D-Day was secretly scheduled for the summer. On the Eastern Front, the Soviet Red Army had broken the German siege of Leningrad/St. Petersburg, where more than eight hundred thousand Russians had died of starvation, exposure, and disease. In the Pacific, the Japanese were in retreat. But neither they nor the Germans showed any sign of giving up. So Allied bombers kept taking off day and night from the British coast, and so did their fighter escorts.

Spicer was assigned to the British air base at Leiston, three miles from the coast of the North Sea. British and American airmen both operated from the British bases, essentially attacking the Nazis in shifts. Many damaged bombers and fighters had straggled home to Leiston or had failed to return there. Spicer was given command of the 357th Fighter Group and a P-51 Mustang he named "Tony Boy" for his young son Tony. Other planes in the group were named "Hurry Home Honey," "Daddy Rabbit," "Speedball Alice," "American Girl," and "Billy's Bitch." The fighters' main mission was to protect Allied bombers on raids over Germany and France. The pilots dueled in mid-air with German fighter pilots who rose to meet the bombers. The German fighters included Focke-Wulf 190s and 200s and Messer-schmitt 109s and 110s. None of them could perform like the Mustang, but they were all dangerous.

In addition to watching for German fighters, the P-51 pilots had to cope with flak, the common term for antiaircraft fire. Flak, an abbre-viation of the German *Flugabwehrkanone* or "air-defense cannon," was a collective term for projectiles fired skyward by fearsome-looking 88mm cannons. The rounds were set to burst at a certain height. From a distance, the explosions looked like puffs of black or white smoke, but each one sprayed jagged fragments for one hundred feet in every direction. A sky abloom with flak was an unforgettable sight. Fighter pilots often engaged in dogfights with flak bursting around them. Other threats included friendly fire, the fickle winter weather, exhaus-tion from long hours in a loud, vibrating cockpit, and the P-51 itself. The new plane had a few significant bugs. Engines cut off without warning; guns jammed in the thick of dogfights.

×　　×　　×

Spicer had never flown a P-51 before arriving in England. He had never been in combat. But he was well aware of the dangers and could hardly wait to face them. On February 19, 1944, he put "Tony Boy" through its paces in a practice flight. The next day he flew in a long bombing raid on Leipzig. Asked by a fellow officer if he needed more time to get used to the plane, Spicer replied, "Well, it's a long way to enemy territory. I'll have time to feel her out on the way." He led his group of forty-six fighters on its next mission, a bombing raid on the German city of Stuttgart. His pilots shot down two German fighters, but one of the pilots did not make it back to Leiston. He was listed as missing in action. Two more of Spicer's men were lost on the next mission, a bombing raid on a ball-bearing plant in Schweinfurt, Germany. Spicer's fliers reported destroying seven enemy fighters, and Spicer was credited with downing a Messerschmitt 109. Spicer's "kill" was recorded in the traditional way: a small black swastika in a white circle was painted on "Tony Boy's" fuselage just below the cockpit.

Spicer led the group on missions every day the weather was sufficiently clear. The cockpit was heated by warm air from the coolant radiator. On February 24, while escorting bombers over Erfurt, Germany, Spicer shot down two more German planes. In a report, he described pursuing one of them, a German Junkers 88 fighter bomber equipped with a rocket:

We went down fast, losing altitude in a steep spiral. At 3,000 feet I turned tight inside of him and he obligingly straightened out, allowing me to do the same, so I closed in straight down the alley and opened fire at about 600 yards in an effort to discourage the tail gunner. Steady fire was held until he burst into flames. I overran him rapidly [and circled back] to watch the fun. The whole airplane was coming unbuttoned. . . . It continued straight ahead, diving at an angle of about 40 degrees until contact with Mother Earth was made, which caused the usual splendid spectacle of smoke and flame.

The two German crewmen parachuted to safety—"bad shooting on my part," Spicer wrote in his report. Soon after downing the Junkers 88, he chased down a Messerschmitt 110 and sprayed it with machine-gun fire until one of its engines burst into flame. Spicer wrote that he saw the German pilot preparing to bail out—"He was dressed in brown and had streaming yellow hair (the handsome devil)."

Spicer was confident, even cocky. He fit right in with the dashing

British fighter pilots and even picked up some of their expressions, calling his men "lad" and "laddie" in his Texas drawl. On long missions he would call his pilots on the radio just to ask, "Are you all right, laddie?" By the first week of March, Spicer had flown fourteen missions and had three little swastikas painted near his cockpit. He seemed to be in his element, making up for lost time. "I'll always remember Col. Spicer as the most heroic figure of WWII [that] I ever had the privilege of knowing," recalled Lem Henslee, the fighter group's adjutant. "He really turned our group around, from a bunch of scared kids to a really hot outfit, not afraid of anything."

Spicer's confidence came with a daredevil streak that worried his wingmen. Their job was to fly close to the group leader and protect him, and Spicer did not make that easy. One of his wingmen was Chuck Yeager, a sharp-eyed, twenty-one-year-old lieutenant who would go on to become a peerless test pilot and the personification of "the right stuff." Even Yeager thought Spicer took too many chances. He wrote that Spicer "was fearless [and] loved to dogfight without concern for personal risk or his wingman's, apparently." On flights home from bombing runs, Yeager wrote, Spicer always dropped down below twelve thousand feet so he could take off his oxygen mask and smoke his pipe. As Spicer's wingman, Yeager had to fly just as low. One day, Spicer "dropped down right over Paris," Yeager wrote. "German flak guns were pounding at us, but I could see Spicer in his cockpit tamping his tobacco and lighting his Zippo. We were barely over rooftops as tracers flashed by my canopy. I wasn't happy & finally spoke up: 'Christ, Col. Spicer, we're gonna get shot down!'" Spicer "chuckled through a cloud of pipe smoke, and said, 'Laddie, those bastards couldn't hit a billboard.'"

On March 5, Spicer led forty-six P-51s on a mission escorting bombers to Bordeaux, France. German fighters rose in force. The dogfighting was unusually intense. One of Spicer's pilots was almost knocked out of the sky by a flying chunk of a German plane disintegrating in midair, he wrote: "Large pieces of the enemy aircraft damaged my wingman's airplane, and something large went past me though I don't know what it was." Spicer attacked a Focke-Wulf 190 but veered off, saying "something was wrong with his guns." His fellow pilots ended up claiming seven kills and four enemy planes damaged. On the return flight to Leiston, Spicer dropped down low when he crossed the Loire River. Yeager, who was not his wingman that day,* speculated Spicer was "trying to light that damned pipe." He probably was right. Another pilot who accompanied Spicer that day recalled that he and Spicer's wingman, Lt. John F. Pugh, thought flying so low was risky, "but we wouldn't dare tell a full colonel and group commander what to do."

All went well until the planes neared the French city of Caen. Then a burst of white flak suddenly struck "Tony Boy." Spicer was unhurt but knew immediately that his plane was too badly damaged to make it home to England. He radioed Pugh that he intended to fly as far as he could and then ditch the plane in the English Channel if necessary. "Tony Boy" caught fire just as it passed over the French coast around 2 p.m. Spicer calmly reminded Pugh to take a fix on his position and to keep sending Mayday calls. Then he bailed out.

The plane splashed into the Channel about ten miles off the French coast. Spicer parachuted into the frigid water after it. He managed to inflate a small raft from his emergency kit and struggle into it. Overhead, Lieutenant Pugh saw Spicer's chute open and his raft inflate. Pugh was low on fuel and had to hurry to the nearest British air base. The Royal Air Force launched Hawker Typhoon search planes. Searches for downed pilots were common but often unsuccessful. Thousands of aviators on both sides, including an estimated two thousand Americans, went missing in the cold waters of the English Channel and the North Sea during World War II. From the air, Spicer's raft was just a tiny dot in the Channel, and the British could not find it. They finally broadcast Spicer's name, hometown, and last known position on an international radio band, hoping that at least the Germans would find him in time to save his life.

---

* Yeager's P-51 was shot down the same day as Spicer's. But Yeager managed to get back to Allied lines with the help of a French Resistance group. He went on to record twelve and a half kills in his P-51s—second only to Emil "Bud" Anderson's sixteen and a quarter. A fraction of a kill meant the pilot shared credit for the kill with other pilots.

×   ×   ×

Spicer was soaked and the air was cold. He tried to paddle the raft in the direction of England, but currents and tides kept pushing him back to France. He drifted for almost two days. His hands and feet became frostbitten. He began to worry he would die of exposure. On the morning of March 7, a German patrol found him lying on a beach at Cherbourg, France, near his raft. He was shivering, exhausted, and unable to walk. The Germans quickly identified Spicer as an aviator and sent him by train to a Luftwaffe interrogation camp at Oberursel, near Frankfurt.

Back in San Antonio, Spicer's wife, Louise, first learned he had been shot down from postcards sent to her by several volunteers at shortwave listening stations on the East and West Coasts. They had heard the international radio broadcast. Spicer's name had been indistinct on the broadcast, but his hometown of San Antonio had come through clearly. A few days later Louise received the official notice that her husband was missing in action. Stories about Spicer appeared in newspapers in Texas, Colorado, and California, including the *Los Angeles Times.*

At the interrogation center, Spicer was turned over to the Luftwaffe's master interrogator, Hanns Joachim Scharff. Scharff was the opposite of the stereotypical German interrogator. He disdained beatings and threats and offered his subjects respect, empathy, and occasional kindnesses. "He was a very smart questioner who used low-key methods to extract information, no matter how insignificant," wrote Mozart Kaufman, an American fighter pilot whom he interrogated.

> He tried to talk to me about home and family, anything to pick up bits of information that could be useful when the next pilot came through from my outfit. With the next man, he could then casually mention things I had talked about to show that such conversations were all right. Then he would start fishing for the [information] he really wanted. He kept jabbing at me from

different directions and questions and general conversation to draw me around for the things he really wanted to find out. I was very careful to keep a poker face so that when he hit a sensitive point, I didn't show any surprise in my expression. It was a real cat and mouse game, even though a deadly one.

Scharff interrogated roughly five hundred Allied aviators and estimated that he drew helpful information from all but twenty. One of those twenty, he admitted, was Spicer. When Spicer first arrived at the interrogation center, exhausted and half-frozen, Scharff thought him "a pitiful sight." But he found Spicer engaging and likable. "I gave him as much freedom as possible," Scharff wrote, "and he took advantage of it." Spicer wrote that he once talked Scharff into drinking an entire bottle of scotch with him in an attempt to loosen Spicer's tongue. At times, Spicer would tell the guards he needed to speak with Scharff immediately. But rather than offer information, Spicer would ask Scharff for food or favors. "I doubt if this had ever been heard of before in all German war history," Scharff wrote. "You would probably call Russ Spicer a character." Spicer was the highest-ranking officer Scharff had interrogated up to that point, and "Spicer made a fool of me, good and solid, teaching me a lesson." Scharff found Spicer's way of dodging questions amusing:

Whenever he did not want to answer a query, he would beg me for the mustache clipper I kept in my desk drawer. He knew where it was and knew I would not refuse him, and as I handed it to him, he would walk over to my window so he could see his own reflection and take a long, long time to beautify himself. One cannot talk, can one, when shaving? And it is the same when you are clipping a large mustache.

Over the course of two weeks, Scharff tried all his interrogation techniques on Spicer. He claimed to know as much about Spicer's fighter group as Spicer did, and proposed a competition. He would name a member of the group and then Spicer would have to name a member. Spicer asked for the moustache clipper, strode to the window, and began grooming himself. Scharff named the fighter group's executive officer. Spicer named the group's medical officer, which was of no use to the Germans. Scharff named the group's operations officer; Spicer named its weather forecaster. Scharff named one of the group's squadron commanders. Spicer busied himself with the moustache trimmer for a few moments and then asked, "Oh, excuse me! Is it my turn?" Then he named the group's supply officer, spelling it out as KRANNENSHAKER—"crane shaker." At that point, Scharff recalled, his phone rang, "and I was glad to get a break from this character." Spicer, for his part, was disturbed by how much Scharff seemed to know about Allied air operations in Britain. After two weeks, Scharff gave up on Spicer and released him to Stalag Luft I, a POW camp for Allied aviators in northern Germany, near the town of Barth, on a lagoon of the Baltic Sea.

Stalag Luft I was run by the Luftwaffe. It consisted of two compounds of captured Allied aviators, separated by the German compound. The prisoners' barracks were crudely built, wood-frame structures on small foundation posts. The Germans dug shallow trenches around and under the barracks. Their dogs crept through the trenches at night to listen for the sounds of tunnel digging. At first, the POWs at Stalag Luft I were reasonably well treated. There was little medical care, however, and Spicer worried about his feet, which had not stopped aching since he was adrift in the raft. He feared he might not regain full use of them. Several times a day, he lay on his back and rubbed his legs vigorously to try to restore the circulation. Spicer forced himself to walk the perimeter of the camp every day, although it hurt. He umpired POW softball games, took up knitting, and immersed himself in chess. He and one opponent sometimes played for days without uttering a word.

Like Lieutenant Colonel Schaefer at Oflag 64 in Poland, Spicer was a high-ranking officer in his camp, commanding a company of two hundred other officers. "With his corn cob pipe in his mouth and a big fancy handlebar moustache, he was the picture of authority," wrote fellow pilot and prisoner Mozart Kaufman. He described Spicer as a dynamic leader who "helped the whole compound maintain a feeling of solidarity against the enemy. . . . His philosophy, as I saw it, was to cause as much trouble and play as many tricks as we could get by with in order to harass the Germans."

Spicer wished he could do more than harass the Germans. The better he got to know them, the more he despised them and everything they stood for. It was all he could do to hold his feelings inside. When the chance presented itself, he would speak his mind. His candor would turn him into a pawn in a chess match between Washington and Berlin, binding him to a desperate group of enemy prisoners an ocean away in America.

PART III

Wartime Justice

11

"A Gestapo on the
Free Soil of Kansas"

Ray "Nosey" Green was a nettle in the boots of the army authorities at Camp Concordia, Kansas. No matter how hard they tried to keep a secret, Green, the editor of the daily *Concordia Blade-Empire*, splashed it across the front page. He somehow knew in advance the exact time and date that every new trainload of German prisoners would arrive in Concordia. Nobody could figure out how. Green was an old-school newsman who wore his nickname of "Nosey" like a medal. He had excellent sources and a love of sensational headlines. He knew what to do with a big, juicy story, and on January 11, 1944, his sources at the camp dropped one in his lap.

Camp Concordia had undergone many changes in the three months since the Nazis had forced Capt. Felix Tropschuh to commit suicide there. The camp's lax commanding officer, Colonel Sterling, had been replaced after an embarrassing incident in which his wife was accidentally shot and wounded by another officer during a drunken dispute at the officers' club. (Green and the *Blade* had had a field day with that story, headlining it: "Berserk Captain Shoots Wife of Col. Sterling.") The army had replaced Sterling with a strict disciplinarian, Lt. Col. Lester Vocke, who quickly changed the "country-club" culture at the camp. Vocke kept everyone off balance by constantly riding around the camp on his horse and conducting spot checks to see what the officers, guards, and prisoners were doing. Vocke asked lots of questions. He rooted out more hardcore Nazis and shipped them to the pro-Nazi Camp Alva in Oklahoma. But even he could not dilute their influence at the camp.

Early on the morning of January 11, Green got a tip that a second German prisoner at Camp Concordia had committed suicide. The victim this time was a thirty-nine-year-old private named Franz Kettner. Kettner had fought at Stalingrad on the Russian front and with the Afrika Korps. But the Nazis distrusted him because he was an Austrian and a devout Catholic. He had angered fellow POWs at a branch camp in Peabody, Kansas, by criticizing Hitler. A clandestine "honor court" at Camp Concordia ordered his fellow Germans to shun him, but Kettner did not think that would be the end of it. "I am afraid that the Nazis will kill me for being an anti-Nazi," he wrote to his wife. He concluded the letter, "Long live Austria."

The army had planned to transfer Kettner to a safer camp, but the transfer order got misrouted and delayed. On the night of January 10, Kettner asked to be placed in protective custody. The guards set up a cot for him in the guard house, but he was extremely distraught. Just after midnight, a sentry stopped in and tried to lift his spirits. Four hours later, the guards found Kettner lying in a pool of blood in his cot. He had slashed his wrists. "What went on in his mind is not certainly known," said the army's history of Camp Concordia, "but it is probable that he feared reprisals on his family in Germany." The prisoners' new camp spokesman demanded that Kettner be buried next to Tropschuh, apart from the "honorable" Germans. Vocke refused. He ordered the POWs to dig Kettner's grave. But he could not order them to show Kettner respect, and none of them attended his burial.

Within hours of Kettner's death, Green knew all about it. The *Blade* headlined his front-page story "Fear-Hounded Nazi Captive Slashes Wrists—Feared 'Gestapo.'" Green linked Kettner's death to Tropschuh's and added, "There have been a myriad of rumors and reports to the effect that there is a German Gestapo functioning behind the wires . . . holding 'trials' and passing 'sentences,' and that there is a distinct division among the prisoners along Nazi and anti-Nazi lines." The army was furious. Readers were disturbed. A Concordia man wrote to the *Blade*, "If we can't prevent the functioning of a gestapo on the free soil of Kansas and in our own prison camp, there is no hope for Europe. If the Allies cannot somehow protect and preserve that German minority which is decent and of good repute, then we might as well prepare to kill off the entire Nazi majority."

Bigger regional newspapers picked up the story. "War Captives Live in Terror of Nazi Wrath," *The Wichita Beacon* declared. An editorial in *The Tulsa Tribune* asked, "If we permit [POWs with] fanatic ideologies to kill men while we stand guard within hailing distance, what hopes can we have for postwar Germany after our boys come home?" *The Kansas City Star* described "A Nazi Hold in Prison." Still, the stories in the midwestern newspapers attracted little attention in Washington. The violence in the POW camps remained largely outside the view of the American press and public. That soon would change.

×　×　×

Twenty-three-year-old German POW Werner Dreschler had been a seaman first class on the U-118, an oversized "milch cow" U-boat that delivered supplies to regular U-boats at sea. The U-118 also laid mines, and one of its minefields had sunk three British merchant ships and a Canadian corvette in a convoy near Gibraltar, killing sixty men. On June 12, 1943, the U-118 was on its way to lay more mines when it was spotted by planes from the American escort carrier USS *Bogue,* a miniature aircraft carrier. The planes dropped depth charges that damaged the sub enough to force it to the surface. The pilots machine-gunned the U-boat men when they tried to man the submarine's antiaircraft guns. Another depth charge cracked the U-118 in two. Dreschler suffered wounds in the neck and leg, but he was lucky; only sixteen of the sixty-nine men on the U-boat survived.

After a brief hospitalization, Dreschler was transferred to a secret U.S. interrogation center at Fort Hunt outside of Washington, where all captured U-boat men were taken. Naval intelligence agents found him eager to cooperate. He told them he had been pressured to join the U-boat force and that he resented the Nazis, who had imprisoned his father for five years for belonging to the Social Democrat Party. Dreschler's interrogators found him easy to manipulate—"an individual of immense conceit and vanity, very cooperative if flattered enough." They slathered him with praise and took him out to dinner at Washington restaurants. He told them all he knew about the U-118's design and mine-laying operations, as well as U-boat operations in occupied France. He even identified the U-boat men's favorite brothels in Bordeaux. Dreschler also volunteered to serve as an informant, a "stool pigeon."

At Fort Hunt, stool pigeons were placed among unsuspecting prisoners in bugged rooms, where they posed as loyal comrades while trying to pry loose information their subjects would never disclose to interrogators. A capable stool pigeon was a rare asset. "He must be thoroughly reliable, a quality normally not expected of men who are willing to perform this degrading function," according to a War Department history of the interrogation center. For a while, Dreschler seemed to fit the bill. He mingled with newly captured U-boat men and introduced himself as "Limmer," "Lemhi," or some other false name. He chatted about his time on the U-118 to establish his bona fides. Then he asked the newcomers about the latest U-boat deployments, strategy, and technology, while the Americans listened from another room. Dreschler came on too strong for some of his targets. "I answered his questions in the same way I answered questions when I was interrogated," one submariner said. The captured U-boat men began comparing notes about "Limmer" and spreading word that he was a traitor. Naval intelligence agents quit using Dreschler as a stool pigeon after six months. They turned him over to the army to detain for the rest of the war. The navy stressed repeatedly that Dreschler must be kept in protective custody for his safety. But the army overlooked or disregarded those requests in March 1944 when it consolidated all German navy prisoners in newly built Camp Papago Park in the Arizona desert. The army moved Dreschler out of a secure cell at Fort Leonard Wood in Missouri and put him on a train to Arizona.

Camp Papago Park sat on the eastern edge of Phoenix, within the city limits and close enough to the downtown that prisoners could see the skyline on clear days. The camp was named for the two red-rock Papago Buttes that jutted out of the Sonoran Desert to the south. The camp's eastern edge bordered the Arizona Crosscut Canal, which helped carry water from the muddy Salt River to thousands of acres of cropland. The camp had been sited on a patch of desert so rugged that the army could not build guard towers at all the necessary points along the fences.

Dreschler arrived at Camp Papago Park on March 12, 1944, and was assigned to a company of two hundred U-boat men. They included some of his former boatmates on the U-118 and at least six men from whom Dreschler had tried to wheedle information at Fort Hunt. Within hours of his arrival, everyone in his barracks had heard that a traitor had been delivered into their midst. Dreschler seemed oblivious to the danger he was in. He calmly unpacked his gear, including his pipe and tobacco, and strolled outside to watch a POW soccer match. The first prisoner to engage with him was Otto Stengel, who had been captured when the U-352 was sunk by an American plane off the coast of North Carolina. Stengel had never met Dreschler but had heard others call him a traitor. Stengel struck up a conversation, which grew heated when Dreschler spoke against Hitler. Stengel stalked away after warning Dreschler, "Be careful now what you say, because I won't let you insult our government."

Dreschler also encountered Rolf Wizuy, the tough Nazi "oyster" who had survived the U-615's weeklong firefight with Allied planes in the Caribbean. Wizuy knew Dreschler from Fort Hunt and greeted him by one of the false names he had used there. Dreschler acted puzzled and told Wizuy they had never met. Wizuy was flabbergasted. He reminded Dreschler that he had fetched an icepack for him after an emergency appendix operation at Fort Hunt. Wizuy even recognized Dreschler's old neck wound, which was still visible. Dreschler kept insisting they did not know each other. Wizuy finally cursed him and walked away.

Soon afterward, Wizuy and about a dozen other U-boat men went to the office of a senior German officer, Chief Quartermaster Franz Hox, to ask what should be done about "Limmer." Hox summoned several men who had encountered Dreschler at Fort Hunt. They all agreed he was a traitor. Hox stared up at the ceiling. He told the men, "I can't really advise you what to do. First, I do not know that man, and second, I don't have the right to punish Dreschler." Wizuy and the others decided it was up to them to act. It was night, and the Americans had withdrawn from the German compound. A German noncom suggested Dreschler receive a visit from *Der Heilig Geist,* but the consensus was that he had to die. Another noncom asked for volunteers "who would like to participate in this matter." Wizuy stepped forward, as did four of his fellow enlisted seamen from the U-615, Helmut Fischer, Fritz Franke, Guenther Kuelsen, and Bernhard Reyak, and enlisted seaman Heinrich Ludwig from the U-199. Reyak and Ludwig had been among Dreschler's targets when he was a stool pigeon at Fort Hunt. The six men agreed to hang Dreschler in the company shower room. Wizuy and Franke tried in vain to persuade some of the noncoms and Dreschler's former boatmates on the U-118 to take part. Fischer went to his quarters to fetch a dog leash. Someone brought a clothesline to the shower room. Reyak coiled one end of the line into a noose and tied the other end to a rafter. Ludwig positioned a bench under the noose.

Wizuy sneaked a look into Dreschler's barracks and reported to the others that he was asleep in his bunk. They entered and surrounded him. They shook him awake and demanded he admit betraying them. Dreschler denied it. "Comrades, comrades," he cried, "I'll tell you everything tomorrow." They dragged him out of his bunk. He struggled. They tumbled onto the bunk of another prisoner, who got up and edged away. Dreschler was muscular. He might have outfought any one or two of his assailants, but not all six. They beat him, broke his nose, and pummeled his groin and lower legs. He screamed and they tried to stuff a handkerchief into his mouth. He sank his teeth deep into the middle finger of Wizuy's right hand. Now Wizuy screamed. The men pried open Dreschler's mouth, freed Wizuy's finger, and stuffed the handkerchief in. They carried Dreschler out the door of the barracks. At that moment, an army truck passed the nearest gate and shone a searchlight on the barracks. The men dropped Dreschler. He spat out the handkerchief and stood up. His face was a mass of blood from his broken nose. He taunted his attackers: "Come on over here, boys, if you have the courage." No one came. Dreschler returned to his barracks and got back into his bunk.

Wizuy and the others debated what to do next. Had the *Heilig Geist* visit been enough? Would Dreschler report them to the guards? Wizuy said he had heard that the Americans shipped troublemaking Nazis to extermination camps. He insisted Dreschler must die for betraying the Third Reich. The six men were joined by Otto Stengel, who had argued with Dreschler about Hitler but had not taken part in the attack. Stengel volunteered to help hang Dreschler. He urged the others to hurry before the guards intervened. This time, the men split up and approached Dreschler's bunk from different directions. He was awake, cleaning the blood from his face, when they seized him again. Dreschler shouted at them to let him go. "Comrades, in Washington they made a pig out of me," he cried. He promised again to tell them the full story in the morning. Then, without warning, he sprang out of his bunk and hurled himself at Wizuy, knocking him to the floor.

The others pulled Dreschler off Wizuy. Dreschler screamed for help, but no one in the barracks stirred. They pinned Dreschler's arms and looped Fritz Franke's dog leash around his neck until it cut off his air. They picked Dreschler up and carried him across the yard to the shower room, marching in step. One of Bernhard Reyak's friends blocked his way and warned him not to take part in this. Reyak pushed him aside and hurried to catch up with the others. In the shower room, the men lifted the motionless Dreschler toward the noose. Fritz Franke and Guenther Kuelsen stood on the bench and fitted his head into it. Someone kicked over the bench, leaving Dreschler hanging with his feet just above the floor. Reyak ran into the shower room just in time to hear the bench clatter to the floor and see Dreschler sway. Less than six hours had passed since Dreschler's arrival at Camp Papago Park.

The killers emerged from the shower room to see most of the men in the company waiting outside the door. Dozens of them peeked into the shower room for a look at Dreschler. Wizuy, Stengel, Fischer, Franke, Ludwig, Kuelsen, and Reyak scattered. They insisted they had only done their duty by stopping a traitor from killing more U-boat men. Wizuy wrote that the killing "probably will be considered a bloody deed, but I want to state emphatically that we considered the crime as a military action." Wizuy felt certain the Americans had delivered Dreschler into the Germans' hands because they were finished using him and wanted to dispose of him.

The guards found Dreschler's body after he failed to show up for the 6 a.m. head count the next morning. An autopsy showed he had died by strangulation after a severe beating. The guards lined up every prisoner in the company and examined them for marks of a fight. Wizuy avoided scrutiny of his severely bitten finger by darting forward into a row of prisoners who already had been examined while Franke darted back into his place. The guards did not notice they had examined Franke twice. Any POW in the company could have named the seven killers. But they all claimed not to have recognized any of them in the dark. None of the Germans attended Dreschler's burial service.

12

The *Rollkommando*

Lt. Cmdr. Leon Jaworski looked up from his desk at the Army Judge Advocate General's Office in Dallas to see his superior officer, Col. Julien C. Hyer, standing with an agitated look on his face, holding a photograph of a young man. "His name was Geller," Hyer said, placing the photo on Jaworski's desk. "He was only twenty-one." The man in the photo had dark hair and a thin, sensitive face. Jaworski thought he looked like the Hollywood actor Montgomery Clift. Hyer said the man was Hans Geller, a German prisoner at Camp Chaffee in Arkansas. Geller had just been beaten to death by a Nazi gang, only two weeks after the murder of Werner Dreschler at Camp Papago Park. Geller's offense? Eagerness. "The kid made the mistake of volunteering for some work he could not be compelled to do," Hyer told Jaworski. "The gang wanted to make an example of someone who did more than he absolutely had to." The investigation at Camp Chaffee was being stonewalled by the prisoners, Hyer said. Gen. Richard Donovan of the Eighth Service Command wanted Jaworski to go there and take it over. The general specifically wanted Jaworski to target the ringleader, the man who had organized the fatal beating. The Americans, too, could try to make an example of someone.

Jaworski needed no further motivation. Geller's murder was the fourth in the POW camps, along with two forced suicides at Camp Concordia, in a little over five months. The killings "had escalated to a point where the United States government was gravely concerned," Jaworski wrote. The army was supposed to protect its prisoners of war. "Now it looked like we were losing control." Jaworski was still troubled by his experience prosecuting the murder case at Camp Tonkawa in Oklahoma a few months before. Some of the killers considered themselves honorable men, even after their anger had driven them to kill. They reminded Jaworski of the Ku Klux Klansmen he had encountered as a boy in Waco. Like the Klansmen, the Nazis never seemed to settle their differences man-to-man. They ganged up on their victims when they were at their most helpless.

As he had in the Tonkawa case, Jaworski set out immediately for the scene of the crime. Camp Chaffee was 275 miles northeast of Dallas, in a rugged part of western Arkansas. The camp sat in the valley of the Arkansas River, amid rolling hills surrounded by mountains. To the east stood flat-topped, 2,700-foot Mount Magazine in the Ouachita Mountains, the highest range between the Appalachians and the Rockies. Just ten miles upriver lay the army's Fort Smith, which had been built in the early 1800s to protect settlers from the Cherokee and Choctaw tribes. This part of Arkansas had been outlaw country, the jurisdiction of Judge Isaac Parker, the "hanging judge" who sentenced 160 people to death. By the 1940s, the river valley was thinly populated with farms and settlements and the little town of Barling.

The army bought the land for Camp Chaffee from local farmers, with plans to establish a training base for its armored divisions. But the mass surrender of the Afrika Korps brought three thousand German and Italian POWs instead. A few months before the killing, an army inspector had warned that Chaffee was volatile. No serious effort had been made to weed out the dangerous Nazis. The camp spokesman was an ardent Nazi who had served on General von Arnim's staff before the Afrika Korps surrender in North Africa.*

---

* Von Arnim ended up being held at Camp Clinton in Mississippi with nine other German generals. Army authorities tried to give the generals a favorable impression of the United

Camp Chaffee transferred the camp spokesman and seven more "proven, violent Nazis" to Camp Alva, but they obviously were only a sliver of the problem.

Jaworski presented his ID card at Camp Chaffee's main gate and drove through. In the camp's central yard, he noticed about fifty fit, sun-bronzed POWs marching in formation, "their leader shouting hoarse cadence as desert boots struck up misty puffs of Arkansas dust." Jaworski went straight to the army investigators to see what they had learned about the killing of Hans Geller.

Geller had seemed an unlikely target. A Luftwaffe paratrooper, he had been wounded in action twice. He had lost three brothers to the war. But the Nazis at Camp Chaffee thought he was too helpful to the Americans. He had done extra work in the camp infirmary to earn money to send home to Germany. The Nazis also suspected him of being an informant. In fact, on the day of his death, March 25, Geller had gotten two POWs kicked off a work detail for being disruptive. That night, Geller was cleaning a transistor radio in his barracks when an unfamiliar prisoner walked in and asked if anyone there was from Sundern, a town in Germany's Westphalia region. The stranger said a newly arrived prisoner from Sundern wanted to talk with someone from home. Geller was from Sundern. He set his radio aside and followed the stranger outside. The night was cold, windy, and cloudy. The man led him to the dimly lit edge of the company compound, where a wire fence separated it from an adjoining compound. Prisoners from the two compounds often met at the fence to speak.

There was no newcomer from Sundern. Instead, several men with cloth coverings over their faces converged on Geller with clubs and boards with protruding nails. Geller held his hands over his head to ward off the blows. He shouted that he was not guilty. He tried to run but collided with a prisoner who happened to emerge from the orderly room in a nearby building. Both men fell to the ground. One of Geller's attackers, "a large, robust individual," struck him in the head

---

States, taking them on tours of Williamsburg, Mount Vernon, and a modern American high school. Von Arnim remained an obdurate Nazi.

four times in quick succession with a spiked board. One of the blows buckled Geller's knees. He stumbled into the orderly room as his assailant fled. Geller veered around the room as if drunk, breathing hard and holding his head. "Oh, those swine!" he raged about his attackers. Someone asked who they were. Geller replied that he knew but "wasn't going to tell anything, he was going to take up that matter with each man by himself." He returned to his barracks and lay down in his bunk. He went to sleep but awoke in the night vomiting and crying out. Then he fell silent. He was found the next morning and could not be revived. An autopsy showed he had died of skull fractures and a ruptured artery to the brain.

Geller's fellow prisoners insisted they had no idea who had attacked him. Before Jaworski arrived, one prisoner had toyed with the Camp Chaffee investigators, insisting he could pick out the killers if he got a good look at each prisoner. The investigators had accommodated him, staging a fake "dental checkup" in which every prisoner took a turn in the dentist's chair while the would-be informant looked at them from behind a screen. The process took all day, and some prisoners treated it as a joke. It was. After the last prisoner had risen from the dentist's chair, the would-be informant shrugged and said he had not seen any of the killers.

At first, Jaworski had no better luck questioning the prisoners than Camp Chaffee's investigators had had. Hours of interviews, he wrote, "shed very little light on the identity of the guilty parties." Eventually, however, Jaworski identified several witnesses who seemed to want to talk but were holding back, out of either fear or loyalty. The POW company's senior officer, Sgt. Franz Raba, seemed to fit into the latter category. Jaworski transferred Raba to a nearby hospital, where he could interview him twice a day without any of the other prisoners knowing. Raba seemed to enjoy the visits. He was proud of his service to Germany. He showed Jaworski a photograph he had taken of Rommel in North Africa. Raba hesitated, however, when it came to discussing the killing. He told Jaworski he had not taken part in it and even had tried to prevent it. But he said that as senior leader in the company, he had to accept responsibility for it. Jaworski suggested he instead name the men who truly were responsible. Raba was so con-flicted that when Jaworski offered to inject him with "truth serum," he said yes. The drug was most likely scopolamine, the most common of several drugs sometimes used by U.S. interrogators in World War II to try to lower the inhibitions of suspects and witnesses and loosen their tongues.* The effectiveness of "truth serum" was debatable, and no statement obtained from a person under its influence was admis-sible in American courts. Jaworski thought giving the drug to Raba was "a long shot." But after the injection, Raba became "somewhat unsteady in his sitting position" and soon started speaking more freely. He named the ringleader of the killing: a Luftwaffe veteran and dedicated Nazi named Edgar Menschner, who served as the POW company clerk.

Raba told Jaworski that Menschner had not taken part in the fatal beating. He had established an alibi by arranging to be in another part of Camp Chaffee, teaching a class to some of his fellow prison-ers, while the attack took place. But Menschner had told Raba he had the power to unleash a *Rollkommando,* or beating squad, against any prisoner whose loyalty he questioned. Raba said Menschner "doesn't quite recognize me as company leader. He was always a little bit above me. He felt himself that way." Weeks before, Raba said, Menschner had told him that he was planning to sic a *Rollkommando* on a different prisoner in the company. The intended victim, whose name was Baguette, had volunteered for a job driving trucks, which the Geneva Convention did not require him to do. Raba ordered Men-schner to call off the beating, saying "we could not set up ourselves as judges." Menschner had stalked away snarling, "Okay, then as far as I'm concerned, you can let them all go over to the other side." And

---

* Scopolomine is a plant-based drug originally used in the 1910s to relieve pain for women during childbirth, and later to help traumatized soldiers recover from horrors they had witnessed. During World War II, American interrogators sometimes used it and barbitu-rates such as sodium pentothal and sodium amytal. Using "truth serum" in interrogations is now banned in the United States and in most democracies, but is still common in some parts of the world. Indian authorities used a "truth serum" in 2008 on a suspect in a ter-rorist rampage that killed 170 people in Mumbai.

Menschner had not called off the beating. That night, a stranger walked into Baguette's barracks and announced that someone wanted to talk with Baguette at the wire fence. Fortunately for Baguette, he was away from his quarters. Geller would not be so lucky.

On the morning of the fatal beating of Geller, Raba told Jaworski, two German noncoms were kicked off a work detail for "political activity." Menschner felt certain that Geller was behind it and told Raba, "That bum, Geller, he ought to be killed." Raba agreed Geller might deserve to be beaten at some point, but not killed. Menschner evidently "decided to organize the thing himself," Raba told Jaworski. "And he never said another word about it to me." Raba pointed out that Menschner's job as company clerk gave him access to Geller's personnel file, where he easily could have learned that Geller was from Sundern—the bait the killers used to lure him away from his radio and out to the fence.

After Raba finished his account, the aftereffects of the "truth serum" appeared to kick in, Jaworski said. Raba announced he was going to sleep, "and immediately he fell over and went into a sound sleep."

A second prisoner, Fritz Endlein, told Jaworski that a few weeks before the killing, Menschner had warned him to stop going out to the wire fence to speak with a man in the adjacent compound. That man "is not a National Socialist," Menschner said. Endlein replied that the man was his brother-in-law and that he intended to keep speaking with him. They never talked politics. Menschner said he did not care who the man was or what they talked about. If Endlein ever spoke with him at the fence again, Menschner told Endlein, "I knew what was coming. I knew what means of power they had at their disposal." What power? Jaworski asked. "That one can be beaten," Endlein said. After Geller's death, Menschner sought out Endlein and told him, "You can go to sleep all right. You don't have to be afraid of anything, I give you my word of honor. Nothing is going to happen to you." Then Menschner got to his real point: if the Americans questioned Endlein about Geller's death, he should not "say a lot of things or confuse a lot of things."

Jaworski summoned Menschner for questioning. He found him "a fine specimen, six foot one, blond and blue-eyed." Menschner had been a leader of the Hitler Youth, which he told Jaworski was much like the Boy Scouts of America. Menschner denied any part in Geller's killing. Jaworski tried to rattle him, asking how any intelligent person could swallow Nazi ideology. Menschner's "eyes flashed, face reddened, and he gritted his teeth," but he admitted nothing. He taunted Jaworski: "No one will talk. You have nothing. You can prove nothing."

Jaworski was sure Menschner had gotten help from another prisoner, an orderly at the camp infirmary, who would have been in a position to witness the "extra" work Geller did there. The orderly had been a model prisoner. Before the war, he had been studying for the ministry. But Jaworski sensed something false about him. He ordered a search of the man's belongings, which yielded his diary. It contained no mention of Geller's killing but revealed the writer's true feelings, as well as the extent of Nazi influence at Camp Chaffee. Among the entries:

> We are still German soldiers even in captivity. Those who do not subject themselves to our old principles and order are rejected from our community. This happened to traitors, deserters, and communists. . . .

> Among us were some former Poles and Austrians who had deserted! They were supposed to be [killed] but the Americans rescued them in time. But first we really beat them up until they were bleeding when the Americans got them.

Jaworski hid the diary in a drawer and summoned the orderly for more questioning. Jaworski suggested to him that as a man of God he surely must deplore the violence in the camps. Certainly, the orderly said, but the violence could not be stopped: "After all, it is too late to change my comrades." Without a word, Jaworski placed the diary on a table between them. For several seconds neither man spoke. Then

Jaworski asked the orderly to explain what he had written. Several more seconds passed. The orderly finally said, "You just do not understand." Jaworski reflected that it was the only true sentence the man had spoken. Jaworski never hit suspects, he wrote, but at times like this, "their arrogance made me want to slap them silly." As revealing as the diary was, it did not tie the orderly to the killing. Jaworski reluctantly brought no charges against him. He considered the orderly "a psychopath" and was troubled by the thought of him eventually being released to prey on others in postwar Germany.

Despite his efforts, Jaworski failed to identify any of the members of the *Rollkommando* who had beaten Geller. Hardly anyone had witnessed the beating, and the attackers had been recruited from companies other than Geller's. The planning had been sophisticated. The only man Jaworski managed to charge was Menschner, and the charge was premeditated murder. The evidence was circumstantial, and Jaworski's key witness, Sergeant Raba, was nervous. The day after the "truth serum" injection, Raba told Jaworski he regretted talking to him and stopped accepting cigarettes and other gifts. He calmed down after Jaworski promised to transfer him to a camp far from Camp Chaffee where no other prisoners from Camp Chaffee ever would be sent. That promise was probably empty, given the army's indifferent transfer of the "stool pigeon" Werner Dreschler. Jaworski worried how Raba would hold up on the witness stand. But he felt confident he could win a murder conviction against Menschner before a military tribunal.

×   ×   ×

The day after Hans Geller's body was discovered at Camp Chaffee, seventy-six Allied aviators tunneled their way out of Stalag Luft III, a German POW camp in Sagan, Poland, in what became known as "the Great Escape." The aviators had spent months digging a 336-foot tunnel from a barracks to the woods just outside the camp's perimeter fence. One by one they crept through the tunnel on hands and knees and in makeshift carts pulled along by ropes. The Germans finally spotted them emerging from the tunnel in time to stop dozens more from getting away.

All but three of the seventy-six escapees were soon recaptured. But the escape was the largest of World War II. The subsequent manhunt kept German troops busy for weeks. Hitler was furious. He ordered all seventy-three of the recaptured escapees to be shot. He backed off when his advisers warned that a mass execution might bring reprisals against German prisoners in Allied hands. But Hitler still insisted that "more than half" of the escapees be executed. He left the details to Heinrich Himmler, the chief of the SS, who decided to shoot fifty. Many of the victims were transported in trucks by the SS and Gestapo into the countryside. They assumed they were on their way to new camps. The trucks stopped and the prisoners were told to get out and stretch their legs. When they did, they were shot. The Germans killed forty-seven of the fifty. Three survived by playing dead and made their way back to Allied lines to tell the story. Germany announced that all of the dead had been "shot trying to escape." No Americans took part in the Great Escape, although a few helped with the early planning before they were transferred out of Stalag Luft III. Most of the escapees were British, but they also included aviators from Canada, Norway, Poland, New Zealand, Australia, France, Belgium, Czechoslovakia, Lithuania, Greece, and Argentina. The three who evaded the German manhunt were two Norwegians and a Pole, who managed to reach the Baltic coast and board ships to neutral Sweden.

The execution of the forty-seven escapees sent a chill through Allied prisoners of war in Europe. Hitler's troops had murdered thousands of Soviet prisoners, but he had never before sanctioned a mass killing of prisoners from the Western allies. The German commandant at Oflag 64 in Poland warned "King Kong" Schaefer, James Schmitz, and the other POWs that the Gestapo had threatened to kill anyone who escaped. The senior American officer at Oflag 64 immediately suspended all escape planning and tunnel digging. News of the executions would have struck a deep chord with Col. Henry Spicer and his fellow prisoners at Stalag Luft I in Barth, which like Stalag Luft III was a camp for Allied aviators. Spicer may even have known some of the dead from his days flying his P-51 Mustang from a British air base. Being a prisoner of Nazi Germany suddenly felt more dangerous.

13

"Reeducating" the Nazis

Only ten days after Hans Geller's murder in Arkansas, guards at Camp Aiken in South Carolina discovered the body of a young German private, Horst Guenther, hanging by a crude noose from a light pole. Camp Aiken was a "branch" camp for about 250 POWs, just across the Savannah River from the much larger Camp Gordon in Augusta, Georgia. The Aiken camp was a cluster of canvas tents with wooden floors, surrounded by a security fence. It was conveniently sited amid Aiken County's fourteen thousand acres of peanuts, which the prisoners were put to work harvesting. The Germans were "fine physical specimens," *The Augusta Chronicle* reported, and "there has been no evidence of laziness or attempts to shirk their tasks. They go about their work with a will, sing and whistle and joke with one another. . . . It is little wonder that the farmers in this section of Aiken County are handing bouquets to the war prisoners. Their efforts make the difference between success and failure of the county's peanut crop."

The locals may have been delighted to have extra sets of hands in the fields, but behind the scenes, Camp Gordon and Camp Aiken had a strong Nazi presence. The Nazis at Camp Gordon had plotted unsuccessfully to murder a Catholic priest who served as a chaplain there. They shadowed fellow prisoners. POW Radbert Kohlhaas was summoned to a secret "honor court" after being overheard saying he might not want to go home to Germany after the war. The court had threatened to send word back to Germany to harm his family. Kohlhaas wrote that life inside the camp "was well regulated on the surface, but it could be dangerous underneath." Finally, on April 5, the tension in Camp Aiken's hidden hierarchy erupted into violence.

Horst Guenther had made enemies at both Camp Aiken and Camp Gordon because he seemed too close to the Americans. He played American jazz and popular hits on his transistor radio, and occasionally belted out "Deep in the Heart of Texas." Rumors spread about him. He was said to keep a notebook of misdeeds by fellow prisoners. In his job at the camp mess hall, he supposedly dished up larger portions to the Americans than to his fellow Germans. He was suspected of warning the guards of a planned work strike. Guenther vehemently denied all those allegations. He had quarreled with his accusers, one of whom had torn his shirt in a scuffle. Then on the morning of the fifth, he was found with his head in a noose.

Army authorities assumed at first that Guenther had committed suicide, even though he was hanging with his knees just off the ground. The noose hung loosely, suspended from an electrical pole strung between two tents. Then the guards discovered blood on the electrical pole three and a half feet above Guenther's head, and more blood inside a folded-up tent seventeen feet from the body. The prisoners were questioned, and for a change, several wanted to talk. They said that while Guenther was obnoxious, he had done nothing to deserve being killed. He had posed no threat to his fellow prisoners or to the cause of Nazi Germany. The informants named the killers as German sergeant Erich Gauss and private Rudolf Straub. The Provost Marshal General's Office in Washington dispatched Capt. Henry Irlenborn of the Corps of Military Police to obtain confessions from them. Irlenborn was of German descent and spoke fluent German. On April 17, he interrogated Sergeant Gauss.

Gauss was a thirty-one-year-old professional soldier. He was not the highest-ranking noncom in his POW company but was widely considered its leader—"a comrade and a soldier through and through," as one young prisoner described him. Gauss had fought in Yugoslavia, France, and Russia before being captured in 1943 in Sicily. He still believed Nazi Germany could win the war. On the anniversary of the Third Reich's founding, he had organized a secret celebration for the prisoners and given a passionate speech urging his comrades never to forget their duty to the Fatherland.

Irlenborn told Gauss that the evidence against him was damning and that he might as well admit killing Guenther. Irlenborn suggested Gauss would become a Nazi hero like Leo Schlageter, who was shot by a firing squad for blowing up train tracks in France. Gauss said he would never compare himself to Schlageter. He said only a German court had the authority to judge him. Irlenborn told him, falsely, that he might get his wish and be tried in Germany if he told the truth now. Gauss decided to trust Irlenborn "because I saw before me a fellow countryman who, while he was in the American Army, was not an American." Gauss wrote a statement in which he did not describe the killing but said he alone "had carried out and executed this judgment." Gauss added that deserting the German cause, as Guenther had, was "the greatest crime of all." He said the Americans had no business meddling in an affair of German honor: "For you it is no more than a formal matter, the procurement of the written proof for the death and whereabouts of soldier Guenther. But I see all those millions of dead heroes of the world war and the current war rise before me who have given their lives for the honor of their German people."

Irlenborn read Gauss's statement to Straub, the other German accused by the informants. Straub filled in the details of the murder. Straub was thirty-eight years old and had been a pattern cutter before the war. He had tried to enlist in the Wehrmacht twelve times before being accepted. To him, Gauss was a role model. When Gauss declared that Guenther had to die, Straub immediately offered to help, even though he had never met Guenther. Gauss said they must act on the night of April 5 because Guenther was to be transferred back to Camp Gordon the next day. Gauss would lure Guenther to his tent on the edge of the camp after the evening movie. When the time came to kill him, Gauss would say the German word for dog, *"Hund!"*

Another prisoner who heard Gauss's plan slipped away to warn Guenther but could not find him. After the movie, Gauss led Guenther to his tent. Straub and two other prisoners were inside. Guenther, unsuspecting, sat on Gauss's bunk. The prisoners joked around. Then Gauss abruptly accused Guenther of defecting to the United States. Guenther said he would never fight against Germany; his brother was a German officer. The argument grew heated. Gauss yelled, *"Hund!"* Straub looped a tent rope around Guenther's neck, but Guenther forced his hands inside the rope to keep it from being pulled tight. Straub grabbed Guenther by the collar of his overcoat, pulled him onto the bunk on his back, and wrestled his hands away from the rope. Gauss sprang at Guenther just as someone turned out the lights in the tent.

The killers considered dumping Guenther's body into a freshly dug latrine pit that had filled with rainwater. They decided instead to hang him from a light pole as a warning to others whose loyalty might waver. Later, an army lawyer reviewing Gauss's and Straub's statements that documented the grisly details of the murder had to remind himself to stay focused on the legal issues and block out his personal feelings about the Germans. "It is obvious . . . that they think not as we do, but in a way alien and even abhorrent to us," he wrote. "They are indeed strangers in a strange land." Two weeks after the killing, army prosecutors charged Gauss and Straub with premeditated murder. Three other prisoners who had been in the tent agreed to testify against them. The killing of Guenther, prompted by little more than rumor and conjecture, was surely the most pointless of the five POW camp murders. It also was the easiest to solve.

By the spring of 1944, too many murders were occurring for the East Coast press not to notice. On April 24, the syndicated columnist Dorothy Thompson wrote a column headlined "Nazis Plot and Train in U.S. Prison Camps." Thompson, whom Hitler had expelled from Germany a decade earlier, asserted that German POW camps across the United States were quietly ruled by Nazis through terror and violence. Thompson blamed the army for contributing to the problem by allowing the Germans to maintain their military traditions in the camps. She quoted a letter from a German prisoner assuring his family that faith in Hitler was strong in the American camps. "And if any among us think differently, be sure we will make him faithful."

The *New York Herald Tribune*'s Dorothy Dunbar Bromley got the army's permission to visit a German POW camp in Breckinridge, Kentucky, and found the camp commander surprisingly candid. He told her political violence was common. An American officer at the camp had given an anti-Nazi prisoner a bottle of perfume to spray on anyone who attacked him, to help identify his killers if he did not survive. The famous war correspondent William L. Shirer, who had chronicled the Nazis' rise from Berlin, wrote that violence in the American camps "could be stopped overnight by simply letting the Gestapo-minded prisoners know that this democracy simply will not tolerate this nonsense." Shirer added that the United States was missing "a magnificent propaganda opportunity" by failing to reeducate hundreds of thousands of captive Germans who had been propagandized by the Nazis. An anti-Nazi German publication in New York declared, "Our Nazi prisons can be schools for democracy."

The columnists' concern about violence in the camps soon reached the White House. Dorothy Thompson and Dorothy Bromley shared their findings with their friend First Lady Eleanor Roosevelt. Eleanor was taken aback. In the spring of 1944, she invited Maj. Maxwell McKnight, the army's chief of POW camp operations, to join her for dinner at the White House. After the main course, she told him she had heard reports of violence and terror in the camps. Were they true? McKnight wondered how much to say. "Here's the Commander-in-chief's wife, what do you tell her?" he wrote later. "After all, I was only a Major." McKnight suggested the reports were true but told Eleanor he would need approval from his superiors to go into details. Eleanor said that she understood and that they must speak again. "I'd like to dig into this," she told McKnight. "I think it's very important." The next day, McKnight consulted Assistant Provost Marshal General Blackshear M. Bryan, who apparently authorized him to speak frankly to the First Lady. A few days later, Eleanor invited McKnight to tea on the South Portico of the White House. He described the murders and forced suicides and the ongoing tension in the camps. When he finished, Eleanor told him, "I've got to talk to Franklin. Right in our backyard, to have these Nazis moved in and controlling the whole thought process! What do you think this does to us?"

President Franklin Roosevelt had not devoted a lot of thought to German POWs in America. After telling reporters in 1942 that the prisoners would be put to work on American farms, he had rarely mentioned them in public. Wars were not won by POWs but despite them, and Roosevelt was focused on winning a world war on two fronts. In the spring of 1944, he was planning the D-Day invasion; trying to hold together a fragile alliance with Joseph Stalin and Soviet Russia; and awaiting word on the race to develop the atomic bomb. Roosevelt also was running for reelection, while growing sicker all the time.

Roosevelt had left the management of German POWs to Secretary of War Henry L. Stimson and the War Department, which oversaw the army and the Provost Marshal General's Office. In 1944, Stimson was a fit seventy-six years old, nearing the end of a life of adventure and public service. Born into wealth and educated at Yale and Harvard Law School, Stimson had been a federal prosecutor and a Wall Street lawyer. He had served as President William Howard Taft's secretary of war and as President Herbert Hoover's secretary of state. During World War I, at age fifty, he had enlisted in the U.S. Army and briefly commanded an artillery unit in France. Though a Republican, Stimson had agreed to serve as Roosevelt's secretary of war because he admired the Democratic president's "great insight and keenness of vision" on foreign policy. Stimson liked to say he was the only member of Roosevelt's cabinet who ever dared to disagree with him in a meeting.

Like Roosevelt, Stimson was too busy managing the army and running the war overseas to spend much energy on prisoners on the home front. He had devoted more space in his diary to planning the army-navy football game than to the German POW camps. Stimson was irked by the columnists' assertions that Nazis ran the camps. He acknowledged only that "occasionally, groups of Nazi prisoners have attempted to dominate their fellow prisoners." He declared that the army already was solving the problem by segregating fervid Nazis from anti-Nazis and other prisoners and holding them in separate camps. The army certainly was making progress. But it still had a long way to go. It had unwittingly assigned two Gestapo agents to one of its main anti-Nazi camps at Fort Devens in Massachusetts. After the Gestapo men had collected all the information they wanted about the anti-Nazis at Fort Devens, they had revealed their true sympathies and asked to be transferred to a pro-Nazi camp. (The army had kept them at Fort Devens.) At Camp Hearne in Texas, the army had carelessly allowed Nazis to gain control over the main post office handling all the POWs' mail. For seven months, until the army caught on, the Nazis used the post office as a national center for gathering intelligence. They developed a wide network of Nazi contacts in other camps, passed uncensored mail, and compiled a blacklist of anti-Nazi prisoners in the United States.

Eleanor Roosevelt made good on her vow to speak to the president about the camps. She told Franklin the army needed to tamp down Nazism and promote democracy in them. Franklin and some of his senior advisers doubted the Nazis could be reformed. (Secretary of War Stimson saw little hope for the German government "until the Nazi-educated generation has passed from the stage.") But Roosevelt ordered the army to devise a plan to fix the problems in the camps and "reeducate" the German POWs. Such a plan already had been devised a year earlier but had been shelved as "inadvisable." One problem with it was that "reeducating" the Germans might violate the Geneva Convention's rule against "de-nationalizing" prisoners. Another problem was that if America started "reeducating" the Germans, the Germans might decide to "reeducate" American POWs. But now all those concerns were set aside. The army plucked the plan from oblivion and set out to implement it.

The reeducation plan included sending a trained army officer to each large, "main" camp to help the camp commanders cull out entrenched Nazis. The new officers also would promote democratic values among the prisoners through classes, newsletters, books, and movies. The most receptive prisoners would be sent to secret reeducation schools in Virginia and Rhode Island whose aim was to produce leaders for a democratic postwar Germany. Secretary of War Stimson insisted the reeducation program did not violate the Geneva Convention. But he had enough doubts that he ordered the program kept secret until after Germany surrendered.

As busy as Stimson was, he could not avoid getting involved in the German POW murder cases for long. In late April 1944, the appeal of the five condemned Germans from Camp Tonkawa in Oklahoma landed on his desk as part of the formal review process for courts-martial resulting in death sentences. The secretary of war's office was the Germans' last level of appeal before President Roosevelt. With characteristic diligence, Stimson spent hours reviewing the file of the Camp Tonkawa case with the army's judge advocate general, Myron Cramer. The five murder convictions and death sentences had been approved by General Donovan of the Eighth Service Command and two Army Review Boards. But a dissenting reviewer on one of the army boards had questioned the severity of the charges and death sentences. The Swiss observer at the court-martial, Werner Weingaertner, thought the Germans had committed no worse crime than manslaughter, the reckless but unintentional taking of a life. The Germans' chief defense lawyer, U.S. Army Lt. Col. Petsch, irritated his superiors with an unusually passionate appeal. Petsch wrote that the military tribunal's verdicts conflicted with the evidence and "were surely animated by a war spirit and hysteria prevalent only in the time of war." Petsch warned that hanging his five clients would be "an open invitation for the courts of Germany to 'pay back in kind' American prisoners."

Stimson concluded that the Camp Tonkawa defendants deserved to be executed. In his diary, he wrote that their murder of Johann Kunze was "typical of what the German prisoners are doing in their different camps. They are keeping their discipline and their Nazi hatred." Stimson sent the case on to Roosevelt, making it clear that he favored executing the Germans. Stimson was not worried about how the German government might respond. He referred Roosevelt to a statement by Army Provost Marshal General Archer Lerch that "I have considered the effect, if any, which execution of this sentence might have upon American prisoners of war in German hands."

But neither Lerch nor Stimson had considered it carefully enough. Soon, fifteen American prisoners of war in Germany would be caught up in the POW camp murders in the United States. They already had fallen one by one into German hands. Some, like "King Kong" Schaefer and James Schmitz, had been captured on the battlefield at the point of a gun. Others, like Col. Henry Spicer, had been shot out of the sky. The last of the fifteen Americans had parachuted into Nazi-held Italy in the dark of the moon. Louis Biagioni was a spy.

14

Blind Drop

Louis Biagioni was born on September 12, 1924, in the Tuscany region of Italy. When he was in grade school, his father, Albert, sailed to America in search of better opportunities for his family. He was part of a wave of millions of Italians fleeing poverty and political violence in rural southern Italy and Sicily. Like many of his fellow immigrants, Albert came to the United States alone with the idea of establishing himself and then bringing his family—a process known as "chain migration." After his ship docked in New York, Albert wasted no time. He found a job in Brooklyn as a porter at a radio manufacturing shop. He rented an apartment in an Italian neighborhood on Fourth Avenue and applied for American citizenship. Then he sent word for his family to follow him across the ocean. Nine-year-old Louis sailed into New York Harbor in 1933 with his mother, Aurora, and his brother, Juliano.

The Biagionis lived in a three-story brownstone. Albert and Aurora turned their share of the narrow backyard into a year-round vegetable garden like the ones they had cultivated in Italy. Aurora worked as a dress finisher. A pious Catholic, she carried a rosary at all times and paused frequently during her day to murmur a string of prayers for dead relatives in Tuscany. Her husband, Albert, had more going on than a menial job at the radio shop. He made wine in the basement of the brownstone and often met behind closed doors with strangers in expensive suits. Those men always slipped the boys a little cash. Louis suspected they were gangsters but never asked his father, who might consider the question disrespectful. Albert responded to any perceived show of disrespect from one of his sons with a swift, stinging blow to the head.

Louis finished junior high school in Brooklyn and enrolled at Chelsea Vocational High School to study aircraft mechanics. He attended church with his mother and joined an athletic club. After two years, he quit high school and took a job running a quilting machine in a factory for twenty-three dollars a week. Three months of that work was more than enough for him, and on November 13, 1942, he enlisted in the U.S. Army. Private Louis Biagioni was twenty-one years old, with a handsome face, black hair, and eyes that always seemed to squint. He was slightly built at five foot eight and 130 pounds, but he was wiry and had learned on the streets how to fight. The army decided to train him to be a radioman and sent him to a special five-month school in Sioux Falls, South Dakota. At the start of 1943, he was approached by a recruiter for the army's Office of Strategic Services, or OSS, the forerunner of the CIA. The OSS was looking for Italian-speaking American soldiers to send behind German lines to gather intelligence. Biagioni's recruiter thought he might be "very useful." Aside from growing up in Italy, he was in good physical shape, was "fairly alert," and knew how to use a radio. The recruiter put Biagioni on a train to Washington, D.C. From there, he was sent to an OSS office in Virginia, where, he said, "two men in trench coats told me I was going to parachute into Italy."

The OSS gave Biagioni special weapons training and a .45 caliber pistol. He completed four practice parachute jumps under the supervision of a British unit. In the summer of 1943, after the Afrika Korps surrendered in North Africa, Biagioni was sent to Algiers. A few months later, he was assigned to a three-man team to establish a spy post in northern Italy. His two teammates were officers of the Italian Army who had joined the Allied cause after Italy surrendered on September 3. The three were to parachute at night into enemy territory. They would establish a safe base, set up the radio, and send regular reports to the OSS about German troop movements and the activities of local partisan groups. Biagioni's chief responsibility was the radio. He was trained to operate it with all the critical security codes and also to repair it. His official title was radio operator, but he was in every sense a spy. The OSS did not bother giving him a fake identity, "because he is a secret agent." If caught by the Germans, he could expect no mercy. Two members of another OSS team had been shot by the Gestapo. Biagioni knew the risks. But he loved the idea of fighting for America while helping to liberate the country of his birth. He still had relatives living under the Germans' thumb in Italy. Biagioni seemed to have been born for this mission. A superior officer called him "an extremely brave soldier with abounding patriotism and enthusiasm for his work."

The OSS code-named its teams for types of fruit. Biagioni's team was "Grape." His superiors decided to drop the team north of Milan, in the hills above Bergamo and Lake Como. To reduce the risk of being spotted, the jump would take place on a night with no moon. It would be a "blind drop," with no one to meet them on the ground and no specific knowledge of what awaited them there. Their radio would be dropped at the same time with its own parachute.

The first drop was canceled in midflight because of bad weather. So were the second and third drops. The fourth was halted at the last moment when a German searchlight found the plane and the sky lit up with bursts of antiaircraft fire. The fifth drop was aborted in a white-knuckle emergency that Biagioni described in a report:

> They took off at 20:40 with the same plane that had returned the night before on account of engine trouble. The weather conditions were not very good all along the way, but they had no trouble with the plane until 24:30.
>
> A half hour before reaching the target there seemed to be something wrong with the motor, therefore the pilot decided to turn back. On their way back the motor failed completely and we started to lose altitude. They flew over the sea and dropped everything overboard (including the radio) in order to make the

plane lighter. After dropping all available material, we were called to emergency stations to hook up and be ready to jump at a moment's notice. In the meantime, they were flying toward land over enemy country.

The balance of the trip was uneventful.

The sixth try proved the charm for "Grape." Biagioni and the two Italians jumped from a British Halifax bomber on the moonless night of April 1, 1944. As Biagioni drifted down in the dark, he was mesmerized by shimmering lights below him. It took him a couple of seconds to realize they were high-tension power lines and that he needed to steer the chute away from them. The team landed safely and hunted for the radio. There was no sign of it. The teammates grew worried and then frantic. The radio was their sole, indispensable link to the OSS; they were virtually useless without it. They scoured the rugged hills until the sun rose and they had to hide. The OSS concluded the Germans had intercepted the radio, which meant they nearly had intercepted the "Grape" team.

Biagioni and the two Italian officers discussed what to do next. They decided to contact an OSS operative in the nearby city of Milan and ask him to obtain a new radio for them. The operative was Dr. Enzo Boeri, an Italian biophysics professor, but Biagioni and his teammates knew him only as Dr. Enzo. They hiked across the mountains for three days to the town of Lecco. Biagioni stayed in Lecco while one of the Italian officers, Lt. Emanuele Carioni, kept going to Milan to hunt for Dr. Enzo. After three days, Carioni returned and said he could not find him. The three agreed to relocate at once to Milan, where they could hide among its population of more than 1.5 million and continue searching for Dr. Enzo.

Milan was crawling with German soldiers and Gestapo agents, but it was also a center of the Italian Resistance.* Most of its war-weary

---

* Milan had been the center of Italian dictator Benito Mussolini's rise to power, but after partisans executed him in April 1945, they famously put his body on display in the city's Piazzale Loreto.

citizens were just trying to stay alive until the shooting stopped. Biagioni and his teammates had no trouble blending in. A few days later they found Dr. Enzo. He told them he already knew about their lost radio and had requested a replacement for them. Days passed, then a week. Dr. Enzo had not told them how to reach him. Biagioni grew frustrated and started looking elsewhere for a radio. A friend introduced him to a British major who had lost his radio operator. The major offered to let Biagioni use his radio if he would handle the major's radio communications as well. Biagioni reluctantly decided to accept the offer. But the major did not show up for their next meeting.

Biagioni again ran into Dr. Enzo. He said that in a few nights the OSS would drop two agents and a new radio for "Grape" in the mountains above Lecco. Biagioni and the Italians hiked back up there and camped on a ridge where Dr. Enzo had told them to go. Two nights later, two planes flew over them without lights. Parachutes bloomed. The planes dropped guns, ammunition, and other supplies for the partisans, but no agents and no radio. Biagioni walked back down into Lecco and rented a room in a house owned by three sisters. Carioni went back into Milan to voice his frustration to Dr. Enzo. The other Italian officer on the team gave up and left. Carioni returned from Milan disgusted. He told Biagioni he had joined the OSS to fight for his homeland and could not stand to sit around any longer waiting for a radio. He was going to start his own band of partisans. Biagioni understood Carioni's frustration but saw trouble ahead. The team's mission was to gather intelligence while keeping the partisans at a distance. Dr. Enzo had warned them that some local partisan bands had been infiltrated by the Gestapo.

Carioni was not dissuaded. He started holding meetings in the sisters' house in Lecco. Men stopped in on their way up into the hills to join partisan groups. Too many strangers were passing through the house to suit Biagioni, who still hoped to use it as a secret radio base. One night in late May, Carioni brought home three Russians who supposedly had fought alongside the partisans in a skirmish against SS troops. Biagioni had a bad feeling about the Russians. After they left the house the next day, he asked Carioni to find somewhere else to organize his partisan group. Three days later, Carioni called another meeting at the house. Biagioni got angry. He told Carioni it would be the last meeting there. Carioni agreed. He said he was moving out as soon as the meeting ended. He was relocating to Milan, where he was scheduled to meet one of the Russians the next morning. Carioni left the house around midnight. Biagioni, relieved, went to bed.

He was awakened at 3 a.m. by the chiming of the front doorbell. It chimed the team's signal of three double rings. Before Biagioni could get up to answer it, the three sisters hurried into his room. They said the Germans had surrounded the house. Biagioni was unarmed. He had left his .45 in Milan at the urging of Carioni, who thought they were safer traveling without guns. Biagioni tried to flee out the back door, but as soon as he stepped through the doorway, a German soldier shoved the barrel of a machine pistol into his stomach. Biagioni felt certain the Russians had betrayed him. He was thrown into an isolation cell in San Vittore prison in Milan. The nineteenth-century stone prison had housed the anarchist killer of Italian king Umberto I in 1900. Now it held mostly political prisoners and Jews. Carioni also was at San Vittore, having also been betrayed by the Russians.

A German officer questioned Biagioni about the team's radio but already seemed to know all about it. The officer boasted that the Germans had seized more than one thousand Allied radios in Italy and France. He also showed Biagioni documents he said came from partisan groups he had destroyed. Biagioni told him nothing. He was led back to his cell. Italian police officers at the prison warned him and Carioni that the Germans knew all about their team and that they "must tell the Germans a straight story to save our lives." Biagioni admitted to his next interrogator that he worked for the OSS, but he lied in all his other answers. He said he had no idea where OSS headquarters in Italy was. The interrogator said it was in Naples. Biagioni "told him he knew more than I did."

After twenty-eight days in solitary confinement, Biagioni was moved on June 30 from San Vittore to a German concentration camp at Fossoli near Carpi in northern Italy. There he was sentenced to death for espionage, apparently by a German military court, although

Biagioni provided no details. Carioni had been moved to Fossoli too, along with dozens of other prisoners. Soon after they arrived at Fossoli, the guards called out the names of seventy prisoners who they said were to be transferred to a camp in Germany. Carioni's name was called but not Biagioni's. Carioni and the others on the list were locked in a separate barracks, Biagioni wrote, "and in the morning they were taken to the camp's firing range and machine-gunned into a mass grave."

OSS officials in Washington concluded that DANIEL, their code name for Biagioni, was "in grave peril." They worried he might be made to talk. His immediate superior in Italy assured them that DANIEL could not possibly tell the Germans much about OSS operations in Italy because he did not know much. He had not been told about any of the other teams in the field. "To our knowledge, he has not endangered ourselves or other teams." Even so, Biagioni's bosses wanted him out of German hands. "Naturally, it would be ideal if we could exchange a German political prisoner of the same type as DANIEL on an equal basis," an OSS officer suggested. A different exchange would soon be attempted, under circumstances far from "ideal."

15

"The Dachau Treatment"

Fort Leavenworth was, and is, a storied fortress on a bluff overlooking the Missouri River in northeastern Kansas, 170 miles east of Concordia. Established in 1857 to guard the frontier, it soon became the most important fort in the West. It was a jumping-off point for settlers, explorers, and scouts like James "Wild Bill" Hickok on the Oregon and Santa Fe trails. The latter-day fort was home to the Army Staff College, whose graduates included Generals Douglas MacArthur, Omar Bradley, and Dwight D. Eisenhower. Eisenhower had been the commanding officer there of a young lieutenant named F. Scott Fitzgerald, who was working on the novel that would become *This Side of Paradise*.

This fortified crossroads of American history also contained the U.S. military's only maximum-security prison, the U.S. Disciplinary Barracks, which was surrounded by high stone walls and dominated by a massive, six-story stone rotunda that everyone called "the Castle." Eight wings of cells radiated out from the rotunda. The Castle's inmates had included the gangster George "Machine Gun Kelly" Barnes and the serial killer Carl Panzram, who confessed to twenty-two murders. As the U.S. military expanded for the war, so did Leavenworth's prison population. In mid-1944, the Disciplinary Barracks at Leavenworth was overflowing with three thousand inmates. The army had to open satellite prisons. The Castle was reserved for the most dangerous inmates and those awaiting execution, including the German POW camp killers.

The five Germans from Camp Tonkawa had been transferred to Leavenworth in late February 1944, five weeks after having been secretly sentenced to die by the military tribunal at Camp Gruber, Oklahoma. Their chief defense lawyer, Lieutenant Colonel Petsch, had followed his orders and withheld the verdicts from the condemned men until they reached Leavenworth, their designated place of execution. Petsch was waiting at Leavenworth when they arrived. He immediately told them the bad news, which by then the Germans probably were expecting. Walter Beyer, Berthold Seidel, Hans Demme, Hans Schomer, and Willi Scholz were installed on Leavenworth's death row. It consisted of two rows of cells facing one another, in a basement wing of the Castle. The world of each man was now reduced to a single cell, with concrete walls in the back and bars in the front and sides. The Germans could see and speak with each other through the bars. They could write and receive heavily censored mail. Several times a day they were allowed to walk out into the corridor to stretch their legs. They never went anywhere else.

In June 1944, the five Germans from Camp Tonkawa were joined on death row by Erich Gauss and Rudolf Straub, who had strangled Horst Guenther at Camp Aiken, South Carolina. Gauss and Straub too had been sentenced to die by a secret military tribunal, this one at Fort McPherson, Georgia, on June 17. The defense attorneys, two U.S. Army lawyers, had asked the tribunal to consider that the Germans "are not the same kind of men we have over here, that these people are ruled entirely differently in their emotions and their actions." The prosecutor suggested the defendants were exaggerating their patriotic ardor to justify having murdered a man just because they disliked him. The tribunal had convicted both men of premeditated murder. They were put on a train to Fort Leavenworth and joined the five from Camp Tonkawa on death row. The Germans would soon have more company.

On July 2, Jaworski presented his circumstantial murder case against German sergeant Edgar Menschner, the "ringleader" in the murder of Hans Geller at Camp Chaffee, Arkansas. The secret military tribunal was held at Camp Gruber, Oklahoma, the same site as the Camp Tonkawa court-martial. Five of the nine members of the Camp Tonkawa tribunal, including its president Colonel Desobry, were chosen by General Donovan to sit on the tribunal in the Camp Chaffee case.

Jaworski's star witness, Sgt. Franz Raba, took the stand. He described how Menschner told him he had the authority to unleash a *Rollkommando* on anyone whose loyalty he questioned. Raba described how Menschner had wanted to kill Hans Geller. As Raba testified, Menschner furiously took notes at the defendant's table. Jaworski thought it was a silent warning that Raba's words would be remembered in Germany. Raba held up under the pressure. Another prisoner, Cpl. Hermann Burmeister, testified that Menschner had blamed Geller for getting several loyal Nazis transferred out of Camp Chaffee, including Menschner's best friend. Burmeister said he had heard Menschner tell his friend as he departed, "We shall see. If we can prove anything on him, we shall send you a death notice." Burmeister was one of the men whom Geller had gotten kicked off the work detail on the morning of the killing. He said that he had complained about Geller to Menschner and that Menschner had told him, "Nothing is to be done to him and nothing is to be said to anybody. We shall wait."

The defense lawyers called no witnesses. They argued that prosecutors had failed to prove that Menschner organized the beating or that he intended to kill Hans Geller. They pointed out that investigators had failed to identify a single prisoner who actually had beaten Geller. Jaworski admitted to the tribunal, as he had in the Camp Tonkawa case, that most of the killers were going unpunished, but he urged the members to punish "the man who was the chieftain, the master mind." Jaworski peppered his arguments with Texas slang, calling the fatal beating of Geller a "whipping" and the individual blows "licks." He said Menschner had "set himself up as Lord High

Executioner to determine who should be punished and who should not be."

After three days of testimony and deliberation, the tribunal secretly convicted Menschner of premeditated murder and conspiracy and sentenced him to death. The army put Menschner on a train to Fort Leavenworth, where he joined his comrades from Camp Tonkawa and Camp Aiken. That brought the number of condemned German POWs on Leavenworth's death row to eight.

×　　×　　×

Jaworski was making a name for himself in the Judge Advocate General's Office, just as he had in his private law practice in Houston. A few days after the verdict against Menschner, he received a letter of praise from General Donovan of the Eighth Service Command. The general wrote that he did not usually commend subordinates for doing their jobs but that he considered Jaworski's work on the Camp Chaffee case exceptional. Donovan had followed the case closely. He wrote that the verdicts "are not only beneficial to the maintenance of military discipline but . . . personally gratifying to me." He concluded the letter, "Well done!"

Jaworski's results stood out. The army was not enjoying similar success in its investigation into the killing of the U-boat crewman Werner Dreschler at Camp Papago Park in Arizona. Two weeks of questioning his fellow U-boat men had produced "nothing of the least evidentiary value." Camp Papago Park fell under the command of Maj. Gen. David McCoach of the army's Ninth Service Command at Fort Douglas, Utah. General McCoach thought that allowing Dreschler's killing to go unpunished would be "an admission that murder in the United States may not necessarily be a crime." The general assigned his chief of intelligence, Lt. Col. Gerald Church, to lead a panel of three officers to find the killers.

The panel asked for records of Dreschler's work as a stool pigeon, thinking they might offer clues, but were told no such records existed. The investigators flew in a lie detector expert from Chicago, who examined 125 prisoners in a laborious process that took almost a month. Still no one talked. But the lie detector whittled down the pool of suspects. Twenty of the U-boat men had failed every single pertinent question about the killing. They clearly knew something. They included Otto Stengel, Rolf Wizuy, Helmut Fischer, Fritz Franke, Guenther Kuelsen, Heinrich Ludwig, and Bernhard Reyak. All twenty were confined to isolation cells. But investigators still had no evidence. They needed a confession to break the case. Lieutenant Colonel Church was summoned to Washington "and received certain instructions known only to him," according to an army memorandum. Soon, the twenty suspects "were transferred to a questioning center in California."

The center was Byron Hot Springs, a secluded spa resort northeast of San Francisco that once had attracted Hollywood royalty such as Clark Gable, Charlie Chaplin, Mae West, and baseball star Joe DiMaggio. The resort could not be seen from the road. It offered a park, tennis courts, and natural hot springs for soaking. When the United States entered World War II, the army took over Byron Hot Springs and used it as an interrogation center, mainly for Japanese POWs and Japanese Americans suspected of spying. Captured German generals, including General von Arnim of the Afrika Korps, also had been questioned there. Colonel Church and his investigative panel moved into Byron Hot Springs so they could be called into session to hear testimony on short notice. The U-boat men's chief interrogator introduced himself as Capt. Oscar S. Schmidt of the army air forces, but that was not his real name. "Schmidt" took the interrogation of the U-boat men to a new level. He made them stand for hours in awkward positions, screaming at them, until they faltered. The first to break were two German noncoms. They said they feared they would be held responsible for the killing because of their rank unless they identified the real killers. The noncoms said Otto Stengel had told them a traitor had arrived at Papago Park and might be killed.

"Schmidt" summoned Stengel. He interrogated him over and over, in sessions that lasted a couple minutes to several hours. Stengel said the sessions grew progressively more intense. In an unsworn statement, he described the interrogation on June 1 that finally broke him: "It commenced with a ride of four hours at a speed I have never experienced previously. I was driven in the car for the length of time and inside of that car was a steel bar and it moved back and forth." Blindfolded, Stengel ducked and dodged frantically as he heard heavy objects whiz past his head. The driver finally stopped, and someone asked Stengel if he was ready to confess. He said no and they roared off again.

After several rides, Stengel was dragged into a hot room where several overcoats were layered onto him. He said he was shoved against hot steam pipes that burned his skin. There, Stengel said, "Captain Schmidt" was assisted by a sergeant who gave the false name of Paul Held. An American lieutenant produced a gas mask, "which was put upon my head," Stengel said. Then "Captain Schmidt" asked Stengel if he would rather confess or receive "the Dachau treatment"—an apparent reference to a Nazi concentration camp that used poison gas. Stengel insisted he did not know who the killers were. At that point, Stengel wrote:

> Somebody got an onion and garlic which was smashed and put into the gas mask. The Lieutenant stood next to me and pushed me and stubbed me every time I closed my eyes. . . . [He] closed the inlet holes of the gas mask. At that time, he was looking at his watch to find out how long I could stand without air. The American Captain said, "Now you see how it is if slowly the air gets out. That is the way you have done it with Dreschler." When he has done this with me about eight times . . . I collapsed unconscious. I was not altogether conscious when they got me up and already reached for the gas mask again. "Do you want any more of that stuff?" yelled the Captain. I said no, it is enough for me.

Finally, Stengel admitted to "Captain Schmidt" that he had helped to kill Dreschler. He said Rolf Wizuy had too. He claimed not to know any of the other killers. "Schmidt" summoned Wizuy, who continued his denials. Wizuy described being taken on wild rides in a vehicle that abruptly accelerated, stopped, bounced over ditches, and veered around curves, throwing him around. Then he was forced to stand at attention for hours, first with his arms crossed and then with them clasped behind his back. When he complained he had not eaten for twelve hours, he was told that a "superman" should be able to stand it. "Captain Schmidt let me know that this condition would not change until I would talk."

Wizuy capitulated in the early morning hours of June 2. "I did not have any help to make my rights as a Prisoner of War of value," he wrote. He admitted helping Stengel kill Dreschler. Wizuy also named the five other killers—Fischer, Franke, Ludwig, Kuelsen, and Reyak. "Schmidt" turned his attention to them. Ludwig gave in right away. The other four held out for six more days before their collective resolve failed and they gave written statements describing their roles in Dreschler's killing. Colonel Church's investigative panel concluded there was enough evidence to charge all seven of the U-boat men with premeditated murder. The panel sent a summary of its findings to General McCoach at Fort Douglas, who passed them on to the War Department in Washington.

The suspects and key witnesses were transferred out of Byron Hot Springs and split up in solitary cells at Fort Douglas and in four nearby military hospitals. Church ordered the POWs to be held in absolute secrecy. On June 29, General McCoach appointed the Ninth Service Command's chief prosecutor, Maj. Francis P. Walsh, to consider charges in the case. Walsh had been a member of Church's investigative panel. He knew the U-boat men's confessions were the only real evidence against them. He also knew that "Schmidt's" aggressive interrogation methods might taint the confessions. An army appeals court had just overturned a conviction in an unrelated case because a confession was coerced. The Geneva Convention defined torture as "any act by which severe pain or suffering, whether physical or mental, is intentionally inflicted on a person for such purposes as obtaining from him . . . information or a confession." The wild, blind-folded rides and the heavy coats might meet that standard; the onion-filled gas mask and the shrinking of Stengel's air supply surely did. Major Walsh sent an investigator, 1st Lt. Harry Baldwin of the Judge Advocate General's Office at Fort Douglas, to obtain statements from the Germans that were indisputably voluntary. Baldwin visited each of the seven suspects in his cell and offered him a chance to write a second statement to elaborate on his first statement. Baldwin did not mention that their first statements were probably worthless as evidence. Wizuy, Stengel, and the others leapt at the chance. Surely, they could better explain their actions after a month away from "Schmidt" and Byron Hot Springs. The U-boat men's second statements differed little from their first, except that they were infinitely more useful to prosecutors. The Germans even signed a document swearing they had given the second statements voluntarily, "without any offer of reward, threats, promises or duress of any kind whatsoever."

General McCoach ordered the seven U-boat men to be court-martialed on August 15 at Camp Florence in Arizona, southeast of Camp Papago Park. The general appointed two army officers as defense attorneys and ordered the Swiss to be notified so they could send an observer to the court-martial. General McCoach warned that any evidence presented about "methods and operations employed by the United States Military Establishment" would be secret. The Swiss did not send an observer. Like the previous courts-martial, the Papago Park case was heard in secret before a tribunal of U.S. military officers. The prosecution used the Germans' second statements to make its case. Some of the Germans asked to make unsworn statements in court. The Geneva Convention entitled them to choose their own translator, but the army had given that job to "Schmidt." As a result, Stengel and Wizuy had to rely on the man who had tortured them to translate their descriptions of his actions to the jury. Stengel at one point awkwardly described being abused by "the Captain who is here." Whether or not "Schmidt" accurately translated their testimony, the tribunal heard the Germans describe the blindfolded rides, heavy jackets, and the onion-filled gas mask. The defense called

"Schmidt" from the interpreter's chair to the witness stand. He deflected questions from both the defense and the judge:

DEFENSE ATTORNEY: Did you see [Stengel], during an interrogation by yourself, dressed in an Army overcoat?

SCHMIDT: I cannot answer that question, sir.

JUDGE: You will answer the question.

SCHMIDT: I am not allowed to divulge interrogation methods.

JUDGE: You will answer this question as to whether you saw him or not.

SCHMIDT: I don't remember seeing him with an overcoat on.

DEFENSE: Did you use any forceful means or third-degree methods in any way or in any form?

SCHMIDT: What constitutes third-degree methods?

JUDGE: Answer yes or no.

SCHMIDT: I used ordinary interrogation methods.

DEFENSE: What are the ordinary interrogation methods that you refer to?

SCHMIDT: I am not allowed to divulge those methods.

JUDGE (ADVISING THE DEFENSE): Ask him leading questions about what he did in this case.

DEFENSE: Is it not a fact that you did use a method upon prisoner of war Otto Stengel which involved the use of a gas mask upon prisoner of war Otto Stengel?

SCHMIDT: Yes.

DEFENSE: Did you use a method which involved the use of an overcoat?

SCHMIDT: I think I did see an overcoat.

DEFENSE: In what manner was a gas mask used on prisoner of war Otto Stengel?

SCHMIDT: I do not quite understand, sir.

DEFENSE: How was the use made of the gas mask?

SCHMIDT: It was put on his head and face and used in the ordinary manner.

DEFENSE: Was an onion used in the gas mask?

SCHMIDT: There was.

After that testimony, chief defense attorney Maj. William A. Taylor argued that the Germans' first and second statements were both tainted. He said the U-boat men had given their second, "voluntary" statements only to try to undo the damage from their first statements, which had been obtained through torture. The prosecutor, Major Walsh, called the Germans' claims of torture lies, saying that Otto Stengel "should have been a novelist. He is one of the greatest story tellers I have ever heard." Walsh pointed out that the victim, Werner Dreschler, had been severely beaten before he was choked to death. If anyone in the case had been brutalized, Walsh said, it was not the killers but Dreschler.

After two days, the tribunal voted in written, secret ballots. The members unanimously convicted all seven of the Germans of murder and sentenced them "to be hanged by the neck until dead." Walsh recorded the verdicts in longhand. The Germans were brought back into the courtroom and told they would not learn the results until later. They were returned to their isolation cells at Camp Florence. Walsh sent a summary of the verdicts to General McCoach at Fort Douglas. The author Richard Whittingham wrote that prosecutor Walsh "felt no joy, no satisfaction, in the way it had turned out; deep within him he did not want to see seven young men, enemies or not, go to the gallows." But when Walsh had had the chance to ask the tribunal to spare the men's lives, he had not. The seven death sentences brought the total number of condemned German POWs to fifteen. The army informed the State Department, which notified the Swiss. The Swiss reported the death sentences to Nazi Germany.

×   ×   ×

By the summer of 1944, Germany was mortally wounded and increasingly desperate. It was hemorrhaging men and territory on both fronts of the war. In France, American, British, and Canadian troops were driving inland from the D-Day invasion beaches. U-boats had to abandon their impregnable bunkers on the French coast and retreat to Germany. Italy was in Allied hands. On the Eastern Front, the Soviet Red Army reached the outskirts of Warsaw after sweeping through Belorussia and killing or capturing 350,000 Germans. On July 24, some German army officers tried to assassinate Hitler with a suitcase bomb at his eastern headquarters, the "Wolf's Lair." The explosion left Hitler with minor injuries and more paranoid than ever. He gave his SS more latitude in all German army operations, including POW camps.

The Germans at this point held thirty thousand American prisoners in a network of fifty-seven camps, mostly in Germany and Poland. The deteriorating living conditions in the camps gave the POWs a firsthand look at how desperate the Germans were becoming. The guards kept threatening to shoot escapees. SS men barged into the prisoners' barracks shouting insults, brandishing guns and hand grenades, and scattering the prisoners' belongings. The Germans found creative ways to cut back on the POWs' food. They served horse heads and the nether parts of animals as the daily meat rations, along with rotten potatoes and stale bread. The twice-weekly Red Cross food packages arrived less regularly. The Germans blamed the Allied bombing of the rail lines for the spotty deliveries, but the prisoners suspected the Germans were intercepting the food.

Germany had begun the war trying to treat Western prisoners according to the Geneva Convention but was increasingly failing, concluded MIS-X, the secret military intelligence service helping Americans behind enemy lines. Some problems like widespread short-ages were beyond the Germans' control, MIS-X acknowledged, but the Germans also were committing "numerous willful violations" of the Convention, from withholding prisoners' food to "full-scale atrocities." OSS agent Louis Biagioni witnessed the full range.

On August 2, 1944, after thirty-three days at the Germans' Fossoli concentration camp in Verona, Italy, Biagioni heard his name called by the guards. He and dozens of other prisoners were to be transferred to a different camp. Biagioni wondered if he was about to be executed. Only days before, his "Grape" team comrade Lieutenant Carioni had been called out with a group of prisoners who supposedly were to be transferred but instead were shot. The Germans did not shoot Biagioni. Instead, they loaded him and the others into boxcars, which carried them south across the Austrian border, through the lush hills that lined the Danube River, about one hundred miles upstream from Vienna. On August 9—less than a week before the U-boat men in Arizona were convicted of murdering Werner Dreschler—Biagioni arrived at Mauthausen.

Biagioni had never heard of Mauthausen. It was a forced-labor camp run by the SS. Mauthausen was designed to work prisoners on meager rations to the breaking point, although it increasingly had come to serve simply as a killing ground. It held mostly Jews and political prisoners, including Italian Catholic priests, Russian POWs, Polish intelligentsia, Czechs, Brits, Belgians, Dutchmen, Italians, and Roma. Biagioni could tell which men belonged to which group by the color-coded triangles sewed onto their prison garb. He was one of just a few Americans. He did not know that several of his fellow OSS agents had been executed at Mauthausen in December, along with agents of Britain's Special Operations Executive (SOE). Holding Biagioni among the noncombatants at Mauthausen violated the Geneva Convention. But Mauthausen violated every law of man and God. The camp's main workplace was a large granite quarry. At the bottom, the prisoners were organized into long columns, five men abreast, and made to haul one-hundred-pound chunks of granite up 186 stone steps to the top. Men collapsed on the steps and were beaten, whipped, shot, or even thrown into the pit by SS men in their *Totenkopf* skull-and-crossbones caps. "Every night saw its procession of dead and injured, trundled into camp on wheelbarrows and stretchers, oftentimes there were two or three dozen," an inmate wrote. Sometimes prisoners could stand no more and jumped to their deaths from a cliff near the top of the granite steps. The SS men mockingly called it "the Parachutists' Leap."

Upon his arrival at Mauthausen, Biagioni was shaved from head to foot with a dry razor and put in a barracks where dozens of prisoners slept on bare floors. His mother, Aurora, in Brooklyn received a handwritten letter in Italian through the International Red Cross. "Dear Mom," it said, "I'm in a concentration camp. Please don't worry about me, everything is fine and I'm in good health. Send packages and letters via the Red Cross." The letter no doubt reassured Aurora. But her son had not written it.

Biagioni was spared the Sisyphean labor of hauling stones up the steps. He was given the job of stonecutter, chipping and grinding the chunks of rock into different shapes and sizes for roads, walls, and buildings. He worked a short distance from the camp's crematorium. "I heard human screams continuously from the crematorium," he wrote in his report to the OSS. "Smoke came from the chimney . . . almost every day and night. At night the flames rose up over the chimney, creating a steady glow over that part of the camp. The smell of burning human flesh permeated the air over the camp." The victims included women and children. Many were Jews, but Mauthausen also consumed the lives of Russians, Poles, Hungarians, Yugoslavs, Roma, Spaniards, Brits, and Americans. SS doctors at Mauthausen performed inhuman experiments on prisoners. The total death toll at Mauthausen will never be known but has been estimated at between 122,000 and 320,000.

Every morning at Mauthausen began with the guards calling out the names of a dozen or so prisoners, who were led away never to be seen again. The names seemed to be chosen at random. A guard told Biagioni he was on the list one morning but his name was crossed out by the camp commandant. Biagioni never believed anything the guards told him, but he could not help but wonder why he was still alive in a place designed for suffering and death.

16

Boiling Point

A t Oflag 64 in Poland, where Lt. Col. William "King Kong" Schaefer and Lt. James Schmitz were held, an incident in late August
showed how life had changed even in German camps that were not
death camps. Four American lieutenants—John H. Rathbone, Seymour Bolten, Pat Teel, and George Durgin—were being marched back
to Oflag 64 through the town of Posen, where they had seen a dentist.
The guards ordered them to get off the sidewalk and walk in the street.
They refused. They said the order had no purpose except to degrade
them. The guards threatened to shoot them but did not. When they
got back to Oflag 64, Zimmerman, the despised Nazi security chief,
charged all four with "obstructing the functions of the German
Reich"—an offense punishable by death.

The defendants were allowed to choose a fellow prisoner to defend
them in court. They chose U.S. Army Capt. Clarence Ferguson, who
had practiced law before the war. The court-martial was in Gnesen, a
train ride away from Oflag 64. They were escorted from the camp to
the train by Zimmerman and an unusually large number of guards. At
Gnesen, "we were met at the train by an ominous detachment of
guards dressed in full field uniforms," Ferguson wrote. The guards
marched the Americans down the middle of the street. All traffic had

been rerouted. Townspeople stared from the sidewalks. "No famous criminal in this country or anywhere was more ostentatiously secured as we were on that day," Ferguson wrote. A representative of the Swiss "Protecting Power" introduced himself as Mr. Franz and said he would observe the court-martial. He privately told Ferguson that Allied POWs should cease all attempts to escape because the assassination attempt on Hitler had created an environment where "anything can happen." The situation in Berlin, he told Ferguson, was "very grave. The Germans will kill anyone who tries to get away now. . . . If Hitler wins out, he will order the execution of every escapee. If others win, peace will come soon and you'll not need to escape."

The court convened in an old stone church surrounded by a high stone wall. A German army colonel presided over a tribunal including two other officers. Zimmerman helped present the prosecution's case. The guards from Oflag 64 testified that all four defendants had refused clear, direct orders to get off the sidewalk. The German colonel asked the guards why they had not simply shot the prisoners—a question the guards interpreted as threatening. They said they had not wanted to hit any civilians by accident. Ferguson, the defense attorney, conceded that his clients had disobeyed an order to walk in the street. But he argued that the order was pointless, petty, and "an affront to their dignity as a soldier." Ferguson quoted some famous German jurists about human dignity. To his surprise, the court acquitted the four Americans. The acquittal was a rebuke of Zimmerman, but it only seemed to energize him. On the train back to Oflag 64, Zimmerman warned Rathbone, Bolten, Durgin, and Teel that he would make sure they were tried a second time for walking on the sidewalk. First, however, Zimmerman turned his attention to William Schaefer and Jimmy Schmitz.

Schaefer had clashed with Zimmerman almost from the day he arrived at Oflag 64. He considered Zimmerman "a Party man and, though not in name, the real leader of the camp." When Zimmerman ordered the prisoners to hand over their identification cards, Schaefer called the order unlawful and threatened to report him to the Swiss. The dispute ended up in the hands of Colonel Schneider, the camp commandant, who told Zimmerman to cancel the order. Soon afterward, Zimmerman's assistant told Schaefer he would never leave Germany alive. Schaefer brushed off the threat, but Zimmerman waited for a chance for revenge.

On September 22, 1944, two German sergeants walked into the small office where Schmitz did paperwork. After Schmitz's rough treatment following his capture on the Gari River in Italy, he had settled into a relatively comfortable routine at Oflag 64. His greatest challenge was boredom. Schmitz wrote to his friend and political patron Fred Hart in Streator, Illinois, that "he was engaged in office work at the prison camp, and that his only contact with the outside world was through mail from friends and relatives." Schmitz added, "Life in a prison camp is certainly dull, and I'm sick of it all." The arrival of the German sergeants in Schmitz's office would change that. They carried posters Zimmerman had ordered them to put up on every bulletin board in camp, including the POWs' bulletin board just outside Schmitz's office. That was unusual; the Germans had never posted anything on that bulletin board before. Schmitz got up and asked to see the posters.

They were warnings in large letters that all escapees would be shot. "To all Prisoners of War!" they began. "The escape from prison camps is no longer a sport!" England was engaging in "gangster warfare," and so, to protect Germany from spies and saboteurs:

> It has become necessary to create strictly forbidden zones, called death zones, in which all unauthorized trespassers will be immediately shot on sight.
>
> Escaping prisoners of war, entering such death zones, will certainly lose their lives. They are therefore in constant danger of being mistaken for enemy agents or sabotage groups.
>
> Urgent warning is given against making future escapes!
>
> In plain English, Stay in the camp where you will be safe! Breaking out of it is now a damned dangerous act. . . .

The chances of preserving your life are almost nil!

All police and military guards have been given the most strict orders to shoot on sight all suspected persons.

Escaping from prison camps has ceased to be a sport!

Schmitz considered the poster pure propaganda. He thought it insulted and demeaned the prisoners. He worried about the cumulative effect of the Germans' constant insults on the younger American POWs. As reluctant as Schmitz was to cause trouble, he could not let the posters go unchallenged.

He asked the Germans not to put them up until he spoke with his superiors. The camp's senior American officer was not at his desk, so Schmitz went to his second-in-command—Schaefer. He showed Schaefer one of the posters. Schaefer became irate. He rushed out to the camp's baseball field and halted a game in which his superior, Col. George Millett, was playing. Schaefer explained the situation. Colonel Millett did not want to interrupt the ball game. He told Schaefer to make "a vigorous protest" and then let the Germans put up the posters. Schaefer was always game for a vigorous protest.

Schaefer returned to Schmitz's office, where the German sergeants waited. Schmitz had gone back to doing paperwork at his desk. Schaefer told the Germans the posters were garbage and did not belong on any billboard, much less the POWs' billboard outside Schmitz's office. He told the Germans they would have to use force to put one up there. The Germans said they intended to follow Zimmerman's orders. They started leaving Schmitz's office. At that moment, Schmitz happened to get up from his desk to head out on an errand. Schaefer ordered him to stop in the doorway and block the Germans' exit. Schaefer told Schmitz it was merely a gesture and to move aside if the Germans touched him. Schmitz did not like being a human chess piece, but he followed Schaefer's order. One of the German sergeants smiled at the idea of a confrontation with affable Jimmy Schmitz. He laid a hand lightly on Schmitz's left shoulder and Schmitz all but sprang out of his way. The sergeants put up the posters on the POWs' bulletin board and the rest of the bulletin boards at Oflag 64. Within a week the posters were gone. Schaefer felt satisfied he had made his point. He and Schmitz assumed the matter was over.

Two weeks later, Zimmerman summoned Schaefer and Schmitz to his office. He was conducting a formal investigation of the poster incident. One of the German sergeants gave an accurate account of it, including how Schmitz had quickly stepped aside. Zimmerman demanded that Schaefer and Schmitz write formal statements or "it would go hard with them." Schmitz wrote a statement; Schaefer refused. Zimmerman announced he was charging both of them with "using threats or force to prevent a superior from carrying out his orders," which carried a possible death penalty. Schaefer was angry; Schmitz was stunned. Zimmerman was framing their brief, symbolic gesture as a capital crime. Zimmerman placed Schmitz in solitary confinement. He told Schaefer he was being transferred immediately from Oflag 64 to Colditz Castle, a prison in a Renaissance-era castle near Dresden. Zimmerman claimed that Colditz Castle needed a high-ranking U.S. officer like Schaefer to command other American POWs there. None of Schaefer's fellow prisoners at Oflag 64 believed it. "It was the opinion of the camp that Colonel Schaefer was being moved because he was causing so much trouble, they wanted to get rid of him," one POW recalled.

Zimmerman ordered Schaefer's guards not to feed him during the three-day train journey to Colditz, but they sneaked him food. They even included him in an unauthorized stop in Dresden to visit one of the guards' mothers. They found civilian clothes for Schaefer, and he posed as a German while they stopped at the mother's house. Schaefer even got a slice of homemade cake, which he noticed contained no sugar. But his mood darkened the next day when he got his first glimpse of *Schloss* Colditz, a forbidding-looking stone castle perched on a rock outcropping above the Mulde River. "I became angry," Schaefer wrote. "I told my guards off. I told them this was not a prisoner of war camp but a penitentiary. I told them what I thought of the Germans for treating me in such a manner." The Nazis first had used Colditz Castle to house Jews, communists, anti-Nazis, and criminals.

Now the castle held prominent prisoners, such as Churchill's nephew, as well as prisoners the Germans classified as incorrigible, such as Schaefer. Inside the castle, Schaefer was placed back into solitary confinement. He resumed his mental exercises to fight off "infinity." He was not told what to expect next. At that point, the Germans probably did not know either. The next chapter in Schaefer's story was being written in Washington, D.C.

×   ×   ×

Secretary of War Stimson received the appeal of the two German POWs sentenced to death for the murder at Camp Aiken, South Carolina, in early October. The army and the U.S. Attorney General's Office already had turned down the appeal; Stimson's review was the last step before President Roosevelt got the final say. Stimson did not hesitate to approve the death sentences for Erich Gauss and Rudolf Straub. "I feel very strongly that we should be very severe in these cases," he wrote in his diary October 5. "It is the old snake of Nazism beginning to raise its head in our present camps." The Aiken case reminded Stimson that after five months President Roosevelt still had not acted on his recommendation to confirm the death sentences of the five Germans from Camp Tonkawa. Roosevelt, Stimson wrote, "had gotten some wrinkle in his head of the question of law involved" and had referred the case to an adviser who was busy with other matters. Stimson telephoned one of Roosevelt's top aides at the White House and suggested the president take up the Tonkawa case promptly. Four days later, on October 9, Roosevelt approved the death sentences of the Tonkawa killers, Walter Beyer, Berthold Seidel, Willie Scholz, Hans Demme, and Hans Schomer.

The War Department ordered the commandant of Fort Leavenworth to prepare to hang the five Germans as soon as practicable after January 9, 1945. Article 66 of the Geneva Convention required a three-month grace period between the formal notification of the death sentences to Germany and the executions. The War Department gave the Swiss two full copies of the Tonkawa court records, including transcripts of the court-martial, but told the Swiss not to share those documents with Germany. The only document the War Department wanted sent to Germany was a three-page letter from Assistant Provost Marshal General B. M. Bryan. The letter announced Roosevelt's approval of the death sentences and listed the charges and convictions. It offered no details about the killing or the evidence presented at the court-martial. A State Department representative hand-delivered Bryan's letter to Werner Weingaertner at the Swiss Legation's headquarters on Massachusetts Avenue in Washington. Weingaertner forwarded a copy of the letter to the Germans.

Two weeks later, the German Foreign Ministry sent a message through the Swiss to Secretary of State Edward Stettinius Jr. demanding more information about the Tonkawa case. The Germans complained that they had been told "only the most essential points of the charge" and that the lack of detail "makes it difficult or impossible for German authorities to form an opinion about the case." The Germans wanted to know what testimony had been presented in the court-martial and what kind of defense had been offered. They pointed out that the Geneva Convention required the Americans to "set forth in detail the nature and circumstances of the offense." The Germans said the three-month grace period before the executions should not begin until they had received all the information to which they were entitled. They urged the Americans not to be hasty in taking "the lives of five human beings in their prime"—a strange plea from the murderous Nazi regime.

The Swiss pressed the State Department for a quick response to the Germans. The State Department replied that the matter was "receiving urgent consideration." But all the State Department could do was forward the Germans' message to the War Department, which was solely responsible for the condemned Germans. An undersecretary of state complained in a memo, "It would be appreciated if the Department of State might be informed of the views of the War Department." Secretary of War Stimson was not inclined to hurry to accommodate the State Department, which he considered a collection of "ambassadors and ministers and consular agencies, none of which do anything except write and talk." But Stimson soon would be compelled to respond.

On October 26, the Swiss reported "a further urgent cable" from Germany, reiterating its demand for the Tonkawa court records. The Germans also demanded the court records from the Camp Chaffee and Camp Aiken murder cases, as well as the Camp Papago Park case, in which seven U-boat men had been sentenced to die for killing a traitor. The Germans' new cable included a warning: "Should this not be agreed to by the American authorities, the German Government very soon will have to adopt the procedure of the American authorities with respect to court-martial trials of American prisoners of war." The War Department was playing a dangerous game with Nazi Germany, and the stakes were being increased.

The Papago Park case already had raised red flags from army reviewers at the Ninth Service Command at Fort Douglas, Utah. Col. Archibald King, an expert in the Geneva Convention, thought "Schmidt's" interrogation of the Germans at Byron Hot Springs was "a vicious throwback to medieval cruelty." King further criticized the army for choosing "Schmidt" to translate the Germans' testimony about his harsh treatment of them. King suggested the army investigate the interrogation methods at Byron Hot Springs. Still, King did not think the U-boat men deserved mercy because they had been tortured. He approved of their death sentences.

Other army reviewers at Fort Douglas disagreed, taking a more nuanced view of the killing of "stool pigeon" Werner Dreschler. The two other members of King's review board recommended commuting all seven of the Germans' sentences to life in prison. So did Maj. Gen. William E. Shedd, who had replaced General McCoach at the Ninth Service Command at Fort Douglas. General Shedd's new chief prosecutor, Col. Thomas White, added: "I entertain an almost conscientious objection to the imposition of the death sentence upon a soldier who murders a fellow soldier known to be a traitor. . . . I cannot but wonder if my own natural self-restraint would not be overcome by hatred and contempt for a fellow soldier who betrayed me and my comrades in arms."

General Shedd forwarded the case, along with the various recommendations, to the Army Review Board in Washington. That board often reduced heavy sentences from outlying army commands, but in this case it unanimously approved the murder convictions and death sentences. So did Col. William A. Rounds of the Judge Advocate General's Office. Rounds argued that any sentence less than death would embolden the Nazis in the POW camps in the United States. The appeal in the Papago Park case was sent on to Secretary of War Stimson, who had yet to realize how it and the other POW camp murder cases would endanger American prisoners in Germany.

×   ×   ×

A few weeks after the poster incident at Oflag 64, Col. Henry Spicer put his life at risk at Stalag Luft I with a speech. Spicer, the pipe-smoking P-51 Mustang fighter pilot, had survived being shot down into the English Channel and had resisted the interrogation of Hanns Scharff. At first, life at Stalag Luft I on the Baltic Sea was better. But in September the guards conducted a rough search of the prisoners' barracks, breaking their belongings and scrawling obscene images on their family photos. On another occasion, SS men burst into the barracks and seized all the Americans' uniforms. The Germans' new aggressiveness infuriated Spicer. He also complained to the German camp commandant, Maj. Hans Steinhauer, about the food. Daily rations at Stalag Luft I had dwindled to barley, sauerkraut, and cabbage, with occasional sausages and cottage cheese. Spicer's fellow POW Mozart Kaufman wrote a tongue-in-cheek letter to the etiquette columnist Emily Post:

Dear Miss Post,

I am a POW in Germany. One of the main foods the Germans give us is barley. Often, due to the season of course, we find large worms in the barley. I would like to find the correct way of disposing of said worms. Some say to go ahead and eat them rapidly. If I do this, I always vomit. Others say to place them nonchalantly by the side of the bowl. But then everyone else vomits. Please set me straight.

Emily Post did not respond.

The Red Cross sent the prisoners seeds for beets, carrots, tomatoes, and sweet corn. The POWs planted them but hoped to be long gone from Stalag Luft I by the time they sprouted. Many thought Germany would be beaten by Christmas, although what an Allied victory would mean for Allied POWs was unclear. Some of the guards predicted Hitler would order all the prisoners shot. Spicer thought the guards were trying to provoke the Americans into stepping out of line so that they could be punished. He especially hated the "Ferrets," the English-speaking German guards who circulated through the camp during the day, acting friendly while looking and listening for information. Spicer thought some of his men were getting too comfortable around the Ferrets.

One morning near the end of October, the Germans forced the prisoners to stand outside in a cold rain for more than an hour conducting a routine head count. The Germans kept saying the numbers did not add up. Spicer finally decided the Germans were just harassing his men and ordered them back to their barracks. The Germans threatened but did not stop them. On October 30, some of Spicer's men stole a steel bar from the door of a latrine. The German commandant, Major Steinhauer, told Spicer that if the steel bar was not returned by noon the next day, he would cut off the prisoners' ration of coal, their only source of heat. Winter came early to Stalag Luft I in Barth, with gray skies and cold winds blowing in off the Baltic Sea. Even with coal, the little ceramic stoves in the barracks struggled to beat back the chill. "I spent many days in bed with my clothes on underneath a blanket and with more clothes piled on top," Mozart Kaufman wrote. "The only things sticking out were my head and one hand holding my book."

Spicer normally encouraged acts of defiance like the theft of the steel bar from the latrine door. He detested the Germans for using the cold as a weapon against the prisoners. He would complain to the Swiss. But first he had to get the steel bar back, or the men would suffer. Spicer told Major Steinhauer he would make a personal appeal to the prisoners. After the head count the next morning, Spicer told the 1,400 American officers under his command to stay for an announcement. He stood on the top step of his barracks to make sure everyone heard him. Major Steinhauer and two German noncoms stood at the base of the steps to listen. Spicer began:

Lads, as you can see, this isn't going to be any fireside chat. Someone has taken the steel bar off the south latrine door. The Germans want this bar back. They have tried to find it and I've tried to find it. We have had no success. The Germans have threatened to cut off our coal ration if this bar isn't found by 12 noon. I don't know if this is a threat or not, but we must return this bar to the Germans. Anyone having information, report to my room after this talk. There will be no disciplinary action taken.

Spicer paused. Major Steinhauer and the German noncoms looked satisfied. But Spicer was not finished. He told the men that even though the Germans had started ordering them to salute German officers of lower rank, the Geneva Convention did not require them to do so. "The more he talked, the angrier he got, his handlebar moustache bristling magnificently," recalled ex-POW James R. Ferrin. Then Spicer began speaking from the heart, or possibly, as he wrote afterward, from "a bitter, black hate boiling up." Spicer told the men: "I have noticed that many of you are becoming too buddy-buddy with the Germans. Remember that we are still at war with the Germans. They are still our enemies and are doing everything they can to win this war. Don't let [a German] fool you around this camp because he is a dirty lying sneak and can't be trusted."

Spicer described German atrocities he had heard about from a British paratrooper who had just been captured in Arnhem, Holland. German troops had machine-gunned British prisoners in their beds in a hospital, Spicer told his men, and they had shot a woman with a baby in her arms for flashing a "V for victory" sign to some British prisoners. Spicer's emotions took over. He tried to recall exactly what he said next: "I really couldn't give you the rest of the speech verbatim, but I spent the rest of the time, five or ten minutes, on morale, and I stated that nearly all the things the Germans were doing, they were trying to heckle us and break down our morale and force us into things where they could get the axe on us, committing violations or other acts against the guards etc."

Spicer commended his men for staying strong. Then he delivered his conclusion: "For the benefit of the German officers and NCOs present, this is not an attempt to incite mutiny, riot, revolt, or rebellion, but is surely an expression of my own personal opinion. As far as I am personally concerned, I would be very happy to rot in this hole for the next ten years, if, during the meantime, the German Army is being wiped off the face of the earth."

Spicer had just called for the annihilation of the German army. For a moment, his men stood in silence. Then they cheered. Spicer suddenly realized he had said far more than he had intended. Major Steinhauer and the German noncoms glared up at him from the base of the steps. Spicer told the prisoners, "That is all, men, and remember what I have told you." They returned to their barracks.

Mozart Kaufman "realized that Colonel Spicer had made a momentous speech that should not be lost. As soon as I returned to my room, I gathered my roommates around to help me write down his speech word-for-word." Kaufman wrote it in a notebook and buried it in a coffee tin under the barracks. Within hours the steel bar reappeared on the door of the latrine. But Major Steinhauer was livid. When Spicer reported to the commandant's office for a previously scheduled meeting, Steinhauer told him he was under arrest and would be court-martialed. He ordered the guards to put Spicer in the "cooler," a brick isolation cell six feet wide and eight feet long, with a small window too high to see out of. The next morning, Steinhauer summoned Spicer and told him to sign a typewritten statement. Spicer refused, saying the statement mischaracterized his speech. Steinhauer ordered Spicer taken back to his cell. The senior American officer at Stalag Luft I, Col. J. R. Byerly, complained to Steinhauer, who wrote him a terse note ending with "I most energetically reject your insolent tone." Spicer was not told what offense he was charged with or what would happen next.

17

Bargaining Chips

O n November 6, 1944—the same day Roosevelt won an unprece-
dented fourth term in the White House—the Swiss Legation again
called on the U.S. government to provide Germany with details of the
Camp Aiken murder case. "Since these details have not yet been received," the Swiss continued in stilted diplomat-speak, "the Legation
would greatly appreciate it if the Department of State would lend its
kind assistance in this matter." But as before, State Department officials could not compel the War Department to act; they could only
ask, and then fume over the War Department's reticence.

A few days later, Roosevelt approved the death sentences given to
Erich Gauss and Rudolf Straub for killing Horst Guenther at Camp
Aiken, South Carolina, ending their legal appeals. General Bryan, the
assistant provost marshal, ordered the commandant of Fort Leavenworth to prepare to hang Gauss and Straub as early as February 17,
1945. Bryan notified the Swiss of Roosevelt's decision so that they
could inform the Germans. Bryan offered no more details of the Camp
Aiken case than he had of the Camp Tonkawa case. He cautioned the
Swiss that the War Department considered the case top secret and
that they should not release any details to anyone.

The Provost Marshal General's Office and the War Department

again rebuffed German and Swiss demands for details about the Camp Tonkawa case. On November 8, Bryan sent the Swiss a lawyerly, four-page letter explaining why he refused to provide them. Bryan wrote that the two sides obviously disagreed on what constituted a "detailed" summary. He said the United States already had provided all the information required by the Geneva Convention. He called it a shame that U.S. and German courts did not have the same rules. Bryan wrote that court records in the Camp Chaffee and Camp Papago Park murder cases were "not available," because no one had requested them, and that the army was not required to provide them anyway. Bryan declared that postponing the execution of the Camp Tonkawa killers beyond January 9 would "serve no useful purpose." He added that neither Germany nor Switzerland "has the authority to interpose on behalf of the prisoners." Nevertheless, on December 10, the Swiss asked the State Department to "act with the utmost expediency" to postpone the Tonkawa executions, which were to take place in less than a month.

By mid-December, the army was ready to declare the violence in its POW camps under control. Eight months had passed without a murder or obvious forced suicide. Four of the five murders had been at least partially solved, and fifteen Germans had been sentenced to die. In a "Strictly Confidential" memo to a subordinate, a senior officer in the War Department declared: "The Gestapo is not running our camps. There have been isolated instances of violence among the 305,000 prisoners of war. There are isolated instances of violence in cities of 305,000. The people found guilty in the cases of violence or forced suicide in prisoner of war camps are under sentence of death. Non-cooperative prisoners of war are swiftly removed and placed where they can do no further harm."

That was a rosy view. Spasms of violence still convulsed the camps, and only luck and fast action by the guards prevented more killings. In mid-December, Nazi prisoners at Camp Grant in Illinois tried to kill a newly arrived group of forty-two anti-Nazis by locking them in a barracks and setting the building on fire. And some of the seventy-two POW deaths the army classified as suicides almost certainly were forced suicides or murders that the untrained guards in the camps failed to recognize as such. Some of the "suicides" supposedly hurled themselves in front of trains or trucks; one was said to have given himself a fatal enema with a fire extinguisher. The French author Daniel Costelle estimated that as many as 167 prisoners in the U.S. camps were the victims of clandestine killings. The exact number will never be known.

For his part, Leon Jaworski had hoped that aggressively prosecuting the killers in the five obvious POW camp murders would send a message to the Nazis in all the camps. But the secrecy of the courts-martial limited their broader impact. And the murders were no longer Jaworski's cases; his success with the Camp Tonkawa and Camp Chaffee prosecutions had won him even more high-profile army assignments. The most likely explanation for the reduced violence in the camps was the army's increased emphasis on identifying hardcore Nazis and confining them to pro-Nazi camps such as Camp Alva in northwestern Oklahoma. Camp Alva was located in the Cherokee Outlet, a fifty-seven-mile-wide stretch of land that had been given by treaty to the Cherokee tribe but then opened to settlers for homesteading, grazing, and wheat farming. By late 1944, Camp Alva housed six thousand of the most incorrigible Nazis in the United States. The Nazi officers "were a hard lot and eyed the guards with hatred at all times," a former guard wrote. The camp was a grim and tense place that operated like a prison. Doctors and other visitors were warned never to wear neckties. The only POW work details were cutting the grass inside the fences and unloading supplies at the train station.

Another reason for the reduced violence in the camps was the army's new POW reeducation program, born out of Eleanor Roosevelt's teatime conversation at the White House with Major McKnight. The reeducation program arrived at Camp Concordia, Kansas, in December 1944 in the person of a bright and energetic U.S. Army captain, Karl C. Teufel. Teufel was fluent in German. He posed as a translator to hide his real purpose from the prisoners. He personally interviewed each of Camp Concordia's 3,500 POWs to get a feel for the camp's political climate. He concluded that 545 Germans at Concordia were dedicated

Nazis and another 847 were "lukewarm" Nazis willing to follow their more forceful leaders. The true anti-Nazis numbered only 160. Teufel found that the vast majority of prisoners at the camp had little interest in politics but were "heavily propagandized." An influx of new German prisoners after the D-Day invasion was changing the dynamic at all the camps in the United States. The newcomers, unlike the Afrika Korps men, had experienced a series of defeats. Many expected Germany to lose the war. At Camp Concordia, Teufel wrote, "Fanatical Nazis were doing their best to control a waxing war-weariness and decaying confidence in Herr Hitler." It was still dangerous for prisoners at Concordia to speak openly against Hitler, and Teufel felt he had to work "with subtlety." He developed sources among German officers who opposed the Nazis. They included lawyers, teachers, ministers, and a business executive married to an American heiress. They told Teufel what the Nazis were doing behind the scenes. When 145 Nazis gathered for a "secret" ceremony to honor Hitler, the guards burst in. Dozens of the celebrants were sent to Camp Alva.

Teufel discovered that Concordia's Nazi leaders had filled the camp library with Nazi-themed books. He got rid of 440 books, including Hitler's autobiography *Mein Kampf* and writings by Nazi propaganda chief Joseph Goebbels. Teufel replaced them with books Hitler had banned, including the works of Thomas Mann, Sigmund Freud, Berthold Brecht, and Oscar Wilde. Teufel also discovered that most of the movies in the prisoners' film collection dramatized American crime and corruption. He switched out films such as *Lady Scarface, Seven Miles from Alcatraz,* and *Legion of the Lawless* for more wholesome fare like *Abe Lincoln in Illinois* and *The Adventures of Mark Twain.* Teufel screened packages from the German Red Cross for contraband. In one parcel, he found walnuts stuffed with messages to the prisoners to keep faith in the Nazi cause and keep their mouths shut.* Teufel transformed Camp Concordia's prisoner newspaper

---

* The Germans were not alone in trying to smuggle contraband to POWs in food shipments. MIS-X inserted compasses, maps, and other escape materials into tins of food shipped to Germany. The Germans discovered the tactic and began opening all the tins when they arrived, which significantly reduced the shelf life of the food inside.

from a cautious supporter of Nazism into "a forthright instrument of democratic indoctrination." He replaced Concordia's POW-taught classes with a narrower curriculum including geography, English, and American history. The University of Kansas offered college credit for some of the classes and even sent professors into the camp to lecture. Teufel recommended several prisoners for the army's secret reeducation schools at Fort Kearney on Narragansett Bay in Rhode Island and Fort Eustis in Newport News, Virginia. Those schools were designed to teach the value of democratic institutions in an effort to counter Nazi propaganda.

×   ×   ×

Even though the camps had quieted down by the end of 1944, Nazi Germany still fought ferociously on the battlefields of Europe. The Germans repelled Allied efforts to cross bridges into Germany. They rained V-1 and V-2 terror rockets on London and the Allied supply port of Antwerp, Belgium. Then, on December 16, they launched their last major offensive, which would affect POWs on both sides of the Atlantic. The German Fifth and Sixth Armies, spearheaded by fast-moving tanks and SS divisions, burst through a thin Allied line in the snowy Ardennes Forest in Belgium. The Germans drove a deep bulge into the Allied lines. At what would become known as the Battle of the Bulge, the Americans were caught off guard. Foul weather kept Allied planes on the ground.

On the battle's second day, SS troops captured a convoy of American soldiers in Baugnez near the town of Malmedy. The Germans herded the Americans into a farmer's field and executed them with small arms and machine-gun fire. They killed seventy-two, but a few survived by fleeing or playing dead. American soldiers heard about the executions and began shooting captured SS men, with at least tacit approval from their superiors.

By the first week of January 1945, the Germans had run out of fuel and were forced to retreat from Allied counterattacks. They had lost 80,000 dead, wounded, or missing; the Americans had suffered 75,000 casualties including 8,407 dead; and the British had lost 1,408 dead. The Battle of the Bulge had the savagery of a battle on the Russian Front. With the massacre at Malmedy, the Germans had crossed another line. By the end of 1944, the Germans held more than seventy thousand American prisoners. U.S. authorities wondered how many more of them might be murdered.

× × ×

Behind the scenes, on December 23—at the height of the Battle of the Bulge—an "urgent" cable arrived at the Swiss Legation from the German government. The Germans were furious that the War Department still refused to provide court documents from the Camp Tonkawa case. The executions were only two weeks away. The Germans said hanging the convicted killers before Germany had a chance to review the court record would violate the Geneva Convention. They concluded their message with a new warning to the United States: "Should the sentence be executed regardless, the German Government would reserve the right to draw such conclusions as deemed appropriate in the light of such a violation of the Convention."

U.S. officials softened their stance. Bryan suggested the Swiss review their copies of the court records and share the relevant sections with the Germans. The Swiss refused, saying they could not tell which sections were relevant. They urged Bryan again to release the entire Tonkawa court record to the Germans. On December 20, Stimson agreed to postpone the executions of Camp Tonkawa killers for two weeks, until January 25. Stimson also agreed to allow the Swiss to release the full court record to the Germans. The Germans already were taking matters into their own hands, however. They were going to turn American POWs into bargaining chips.

On Christmas Day, a guard at Colditz Castle handed "King Kong" Schaefer a document saying his actions in the poster incident at Oflag 64 had "hindered the German war effort." Schaefer showed it to the senior American officer at Colditz, Col. Florimond Duke, who visited Schaefer in his solitary cell once a day to bring him food. Duke

was an OSS agent who had been captured trying to foment an upris-
ing against the Nazis in Hungary. He was a colorful character with a
handlebar moustache even more extravagant than Col. Henry Spicer's. Duke seemed to have connections everywhere in Colditz Castle.
Duke showed Schaefer's document to a British prisoner, Lieutenant
Alan "Black" Campbell, who had been a barrister before the war and
was the prisoners' resident expert in German military law. Campbell
took a bleak view of Schaefer's situation. He told Schaefer that the
Germans "could, if they wished, sentence me to death and actually
execute me with impunity." Campbell vowed to lodge a formal protest. Schaefer had no time to dwell on his situation. The next day, the
guards told him to collect his few belongings. He was to travel by
train under "maximum security" to Gnesen, Poland, to face a court-
martial. The guards led him out through Colditz's main gate to the
train station to begin the five-hundred-mile journey.

Two days later, on December 27, Lt. James Schmitz received a similar court-martial summons at his camp, Oflag 64. Schmitz did not
need as much time as Schaefer to reach Gnesen, which was only fifty
miles from Oflag 64. The Germans allowed Schmitz to choose an
American POW as a lawyer to defend both him and Schaefer in court.
Schmitz chose Capt. Clarence Ferguson, who had won the surprising
acquittal for the four Americans who had refused to get off the sidewalk. Oflag 64's senior American officer, Col. Paul Goode, was allowed to attend the court-martial too. Goode tried to notify the Swiss
to send an observer, but there was no time. The Germans denied
Schmitz's request for a second lawyer, which suggested to Ferguson
that "we were in serious trouble." Ferguson feared not only for his
clients' lives but for his own. He had defended several prisoners against
German allegations. In Schmitz and Schaefer's case, he worried he
might be a witness to a war crime. "Tomorrow I might be killed,"
Ferguson wrote, "but until then I needed to concentrate on a defense
for these men. That night I went to bed and prayed that I might go to
sleep quickly to escape the misery and the cold."

Ferguson awoke before dawn to meet Colonel Goode and Schmitz,
who was to be brought from his solitary cell. As Ferguson passed

through the barracks in the darkness, sleepy prisoners stirred and quietly wished him good luck. "They didn't know how welcome such brief encouragement was," Ferguson wrote. He met Goode and Schmitz under guard in the camp administration building. Their greetings were "quiet and reserved." The guards escorted them to Oflag 64's main gate. The weather was bitterly cold. About twenty feet beyond the gate a detail of six guards waited. One of them fumbled at the lock. No one spoke. The guard got the gate open, and the prisoners marched out into the street.

Goode told the Germans the POWs intended to walk on the sidewalk. "It is not permitted," a German sergeant replied. He reached into a pocket of his tunic and produced an order saying that any prisoner refusing to walk in the street would be shot. While Ferguson read the order, "each member of the guard detail lowered the muzzle of his rifle and made ready to fire." They looked deadly serious. "Without further protest," Ferguson wrote, "we moved into the street . . . through ice and snow toward the little railroad station about a mile away."

Zimmerman arrived at the station and took command of the guard. He settled into the train's first-class section, leaving the prisoners and guards to shiver in an unheated car near the rear of the train. The car had no seats and the ride was rough. The train arrived at Gnesen in the afternoon, and the prisoners were marched through the town's business district into a large, official-looking building. Ferguson told the guards he needed to confer with Schaefer before the court-martial. They said they would tell their superiors. As night fell, the guards took the prisoners' shoes to prevent them from trying to escape. "You don't escape into the night in subzero weather barefooted," Ferguson wrote. The Germans put the Americans in an empty room on an upper story of the building. The prisoners slept on the floor in the clothes they wore, wrapped in thin blankets they had brought with them. There was still no sign of Schaefer.

Schaefer was being held in a jail about ten blocks away. On Zimmerman's orders, he had been given no food during the long train trip from Colditz Castle to Gnesen. He was famished and weak. When he arrived at Gnesen, one of his guards took pity and promised to find him some food. Presently a German woman entered his room, set a bowl of chicken noodle soup in front of him, and said, *"Essen sie gern!"*—"Eat well!" Schaefer did. After a few hours, guards led him down a corridor and ordered him to stand in the doorway of a small room. Inside, Zimmerman and another German officer were eating a meal and sharing a bottle of wine. They pretended not to notice Schaefer. Finally, Zimmerman looked up said, "Oh, Colonel, we are sorry we cannot invite you to eat with us. Some other time perhaps. Maybe after the war." Zimmerman laughed. Schaefer wanted to tell him, "No thanks, I just ate," but could not without betraying the people who had fed him. Still, Schaefer could not resist baiting his captors. He faked a yawn and told his guards he needed to lie down in the doorway. They hissed at him to stay upright. At last Zimmerman said, "Take him away."

The guards took Schaefer to a small room with an iron cot. One guard stood outside the door and a second followed Schaefer into the room. The second guard explained apologetically that he had been ordered to sleep in the bed with Schaefer to make sure he did not escape. Schaefer felt sorry for the young German. "I told him I understood. . . . Would he please not talk so much and come to bed so I could sleep? He stripped to his underwear, and we went to bed together." Schaefer still had not seen Schmitz or their defense lawyers. Despite his worries, he was so exhausted that he "slept like a newborn babe."

18

"I Could Not Do Otherwise"

The morning after William Schaefer arrived at Gnesen for his trial over the poster incident, he and his German guards "had quite a visit together," Schaefer wrote. "We talked about everything. They had good minds but limited experience and education." Schaefer asked where Schmitz was, but the Germans did not reveal he was being held several blocks away. Schaefer asked for something to eat. A German captain explained apologetically that he had been ordered not to feed him. A sergeant asked if he could give Schaefer a piece of wurst. The captain turned his back, and the sergeant gave Schaefer the wurst. Schaefer asked again to confer with his lawyers before the court-martial. Zimmerman arrived and told him that was impossible. Schaefer insisted the Geneva Convention gave him that right. Zimmerman said he would ask the presiding judge. He returned with Captain Ferguson and Colonel Goode and told the Americans they could talk if Zimmerman remained in the cell. Colonel Goode exploded. He said the Americans could not discuss their legal strategy in front of Zimmerman, who spoke fluent English. Zimmerman agreed to leave but insisted a German sergeant stay in the room. The sergeant spoke little English. The Americans decided it was the best they could do. Ferguson said he planned to argue in court that Schaefer and

Schmitz had offered only token resistance to the Germans putting up the poster. Ferguson added he did not know how much of a defense he would be allowed to present.

The trial began at five o'clock in the evening on December 28. The judges were German army lieutenant general Erich Schroeck and two colonels. Schaefer noted that the courtroom was full of spectators but did not specify whether they were soldiers or civilians. The spectators did not include a representative of the Swiss "Protecting Power," which had not been notified of the court-martial. The Germans insisted they had not needed to notify the Swiss because the defendants had American lawyers. General Schroeck, the senior member of the three-judge panel, announced that a German lawyer would assist with the defense but was running late. The lawyer appeared just before the trial began, dressed in a black silk suit. He did not approach the Americans and took no part in the proceedings. That left Ferguson and Goode to present the defense, and they felt woefully unprepared. The Germans had refused to let them see the law on which the charges were based. Ferguson had no idea who the prosecution's witnesses would be or what they would say. He felt helpless.

The prosecution's first witnesses were the two sergeants who had encountered Schmitz and Schaefer while putting up the posters. Both men described the incident more or less accurately, although one of them, Manfred Heise, made it sound more serious by claiming he had feared being assaulted by Schaefer. Ferguson tried to discredit that claim in his cross-examination of Heise:

FERGUSON: Did either of the accused ever attempt to use force against either you or [the other German sergeant]?

HEISE: No.

FERGUSON: You posted a number of posters all over camp, did you not?

HEISE: Yes.

FERGUSON: Was there either a threat or a show of force by either of the Accused or as far as that is concerned, by any officer in camp?

HEISE: There were a number of officers standing around the board when these were posted.

FERGUSON: Did any of these officers make threats, use force or in any way disturb you from performing your duty?

HEISE: No.

In many courtrooms, Heise's testimony would have prompted an immediate dismissal of the charges. Even Judge Schroeck seemed confused. The trial was "so raw," Shaefer wrote, that the judge stopped it at one point and told the prosecutor, "This is silly. These charges cannot be the true reason [Schaefer] is here. What is the reason?" The prosecutor replied that Schaefer was a troublemaking and dangerous prisoner. Over Ferguson's objections, the prosecutor called Zimmerman to the witness stand to elaborate. Zimmerman surely relished the moment. He "painted a very black picture" of Schaefer's behavior as a prisoner. He said Schaefer insulted the Germans constantly; led a rebellious group of POWs in the camp; and had been caught with "escape material" in his room. Zimmerman's testimony seemed to satisfy the judge, who allowed the court-martial to resume. The prosecution called no more witnesses.

Schmitz took the stand in his own defense. He testified he thought that the poster's threat to shoot escapees violated the Geneva Convention and that its reference to "gangster warfare" insulted Allied POWs. Schmitz testified that after calling the poster to Schaefer's attention, he had gone back to typing a document. He had paid little attention to the argument between Schaefer and the German sergeants until he got up to run an errand and Schaefer ordered him to block the doorway. Schmitz stressed that he immediately had stepped aside when one of the Germans touched his shoulder.

Schaefer testified he had not expected to get into a confrontation with the sergeants over the poster. He had expected them to take the matter to the commandant, who Schaefer felt would have resolved it with ease. Schaefer said the poster protest was merely a symbolic gesture, to stress the Americans' objections to the poster so that he later could file a formal complaint with the Swiss. Schaefer pointed out that the German sergeants went on to put up the posters all over the camp unimpeded.

In his closing argument, the German prosecutor quoted from the law Ferguson had not been allowed to see. He said the evidence showed Schaefer and Schmitz had impeded German soldiers in the performance of their duties. He said the law allowed for the death penalty because the offense was committed "in the field." Ferguson objected, saying a POW camp was not "in the field." The judge overruled him, saying "in the field" could mean "in time of war." Goode pointed out that Schaefer and Schmitz had used no force whatsoever. Goode said Oflag 64 was an orderly camp. He called the poster incident minor and said Schmitz should not have been prosecuted at all. Shaken by the court's treatment of the law, Ferguson saw little point in making his own closing argument. But he collected himself and made a plea for honor and justice. He told the judges that even though Americans and Germans were enemies, "all of us, like all of you, are people of honor, dignity, integrity; and unless we maintain that status, our lives have been in vain."

In total, the testimony and arguments took about three hours. Schaefer and Schmitz were required to stand for the entire time. The court recessed for twenty-five minutes and returned with guilty verdicts and death sentences for both men. The prosecutor thrust his right hand into the air and declared, *"Heil Hitler! Schuldig und totschlagen!"*—"Guilty and to be executed!" At that moment, Schaefer's hunger and exhaustion caught up with him. He stiffened and stood very erect, his face showing no emotion. Then, Ferguson wrote, Schaefer "reeled ever so slightly as if he had been struck by a tremendous force. He paled noticeably and dark blotches appeared on his face. He could not recover his composure and suddenly his knees began to buckle." Ferguson glanced at the judge for permission to grab Schaefer. He was afraid of being shot if he moved. The judge nodded. Ferguson caught Schaefer and supported him until he could stand on his own again.

Before court adjourned, General Schroeck told the defendants their sentences were not final; they could be appealed both to the German High Command and to Hitler personally. Then, as court was being dismissed, General Schroeck lowered his voice and spoke directly to Schaefer: "Colonel, you are a professional officer with long service. So am I. . . . I have done what I was ordered to do. I could not do otherwise." He told Schaefer to make an appeal only to the German High Command. "Do not make it to Hitler or to the party or to the government. Make it to the Wehrmacht. To the Wehrmacht and no one else, do you understand? Maybe we can delay your execution for quite a while. Colonel, will you make this appeal?" Schaefer replied he would be a fool not to. He was led from the courtroom to be taken back to Colditz Castle. He never saw Schmitz or his lawyers again.

Unlike Schaefer, Schmitz was not a professional officer with long service, and General Schroeck did not offer him any advice. Schmitz and the defense lawyers were led from the courtroom by an entirely new contingent of guards. They were young, sharp-eyed men in crisp uniforms who ignored all the POWs' attempts at conversation. As soon as the group stepped outside the court building into the cold and snow, Ferguson fainted. Schmitz kept him from hitting the ground. Ferguson quickly regained his senses and resumed walking. The guards took the Americans back to the room where they had spent the previous night, and took their shoes again. An armed guard stayed inside their room. Zimmerman perched on a chair just outside the door. Ferguson feared Zimmerman would take the opportunity to kill them, perhaps by claiming they had tried to escape. A desperate thought flickered through Ferguson's mind: Should the Americans jump the guards and try to kill Zimmerman? Ferguson kept a small, razor-sharp pocketknife hidden in his tunic. But no opportunity presented itself. The men slept again on the hard, cold floor in their clothes, wrapped in their thin blankets.

Ferguson kept watch over Schmitz "to help in case he became unduly depressed." Ferguson once had considered Schmitz an unusually docile and compliant prisoner, but the trial had shown otherwise. "During the night I told him I thought he was one of the bravest men I had ever seen," Ferguson wrote. "During all the trial and sentencing, he was a perfect example of calmness and stability. . . . I would always remember him as a person without fear." In the night, Ferguson heard Schmitz "crying and praying ever so quietly," but "when morning came, he showed very little sign of that horrible night."

The train took Schmitz, Ferguson, and Goode back to Oflag 64. There Schmitz was led away from the others to his isolation cell. "It was heartbreaking when he was separated from us," Ferguson wrote. "I knew that [his] days in solitary confinement would be long and dismal." Other than Zimmerman, the Germans at Oflag 64 were "dumbfounded" by the results of the court-martial, Ferguson wrote. The camp commandant, Colonel Schneider, told him the imposition of the death sentences was one of the worst things he had ever heard of. Although the guards had to keep Schmitz in solitary confinement, they gave him special favors when they could get away with it. Ferguson struggled to sleep for days after the verdict. "I was ashamed that I could not separate myself from the unjustness and total depravity of a nation which would use . . . a court of justice to commit premeditated murder," he wrote. Not having heard General Schroeck's advice not to make a direct appeal to Hitler, Ferguson helped Schmitz write a letter to the Fuhrer:

To His Excellency The Fuhrer of The German Reich,
German Headquarters:

I, Lieutenant James R. Schmitz, POW No. 270163, was
adjudged guilty in carrying out certain orders which are
enumerated in the statement of my trial. I desire to make a
plea for clemency on this judgment and to ask His Excellency
to judge the grounds of this plea. On January 22, 1944, I

became a Prisoner-of-War of the German Government and since that time have conducted myself in a manner so as to reflect credit upon the uniform of a soldier. Since my arrival at Oflag 64, I have worked in the Camp Office and have had contact daily with all German Ranks in control of the camp. An investigation of both German Officers and Soldiers will reveal that heretofore there has been no difficulty between them and myself, and that on this particular occasion there was no intention whatever of interference with (the two sergeants) in performance of their duty.

Schmitz summarized his actions in the poster incident, stressing that he had not used violence, had not intended to prevent the Germans from putting up the poster, and had only been following Schaefer's orders. In conclusion, he wrote:

I have not only never received a disciplinary punishment as a Prisoner-of-War, I have never even been investigated for any breach of regulations or crime either as a Prisoner-of-War as an Officer and a Soldier in my own Army nor as a civilian prior to my military service and I have always read, obeyed and followed every German Order ever issued to me while in Germany.

I am a stranger in distress in a foreign country but I cling to the hope that the native country of my forefathers will adhere to its honor in meting out justice and mercy; that this plea for clemency will be heard, and that my life may be spared that I may return to my family and loved ones. I humbly beg His Excellency to remit the death sentence and I hereby place myself at his mercy.

James R. Schmitz
2nd Lt., U.S. Army
POW No. 270163
Oflag 64, Germany.

As Schmitz and Ferguson worked on the appeal to Hitler, Schaefer began his return trip to Colditz Castle. Zimmerman had ordered that Schaefer not be fed on the three-day trip. His guards considered taking him to a restaurant on their way out of town but feared Zimmerman might walk in. The trains were all overcrowded and they had to stand in line all day. Still they could not get seats on the last train of the night. The guards put Schaefer in some kind of furnace room where at least it was warm. They tried to get food for him at an officers' club but were turned away. A woman finally brought him a bowl of soup.

At Colditz Castle, Schaefer was placed in a boxlike cell with thick stone walls, iron bars, and a painted-over window. He feared that another long stay in solitary would addle his mind: "I was now faced with the old problem of maintaining my humanity and the divinity within me." The senior Allied officers at Colditz also tried to encourage him. The British barrister, Lieutenant Campbell, helped him write his appeal to the German High Command. The OSS agent Florimond Duke assured Schaefer that, if necessary, he could be "ghosted," hidden from the Germans in a secret passage inside the castle. Colditz was honeycombed with hidden passages and rooms where the Germans never went. In one large, hidden chamber on an upper floor, some prisoners were building a glider they hoped to fly out of the castle. Duke told Schaefer that whoever flew the glider surely would be recaptured, but the pilot could claim Schaefer had been in the plane with him, which would keep the guards from looking for Schaefer in the castle. Duke had a thousand ideas. Schaefer liked how his mind worked: "If he ever goes to Hell, within three days he will be able to subvert the Devil and get him to run Hell the way Colonel Duke wants it run."

For all its unfairness, the court-martial of Schaefer and Schmitz was a model of jurisprudence compared to the trials of OSS agent Louis Biagioni and P-51 pilot Henry Spicer.

19

"Nasty Smiles"

On the same day William Schaefer and James Schmitz were sentenced to death, December 29, OSS agent Louis Biagioni turned out for the morning roll call at the forced-labor camp at Mauthausen. Life at the camp felt more precarious every day. The guards continued to pull prisoners from the ranks every morning at random and take them off to be executed. One icy morning, the SS guards announced that doctors had come to the camp to treat anyone who needed medical attention. About four hundred prisoners had stepped forward, but instead of receiving treatment, Biagioni wrote, "they were required to take several cold showers and stand naked in the cold open air during the course of the day and night. In the morning when I observed them there were about fifty left." A guard beat the survivors to the ground with a bat, and a second guard crushed their heads with a hammer. Other prisoners were ordered to carry the bodies to the crematorium. Biagioni noticed that the Jews in the camp, who previously had mingled with the other prisoners, were being segregated into some kind of tent village in a gulley north of the barracks. He later realized they were not being relocated but executed and then burned in the crematorium.

After the roll call on December 29, three guards ordered Biagioni to accompany them. One said he was being transferred to a normal POW camp. He did not believe it. He was given a haircut so that the one-and-one-half-inch bare strip down the middle of his head was less obvious. He was given a baggy suit and a fedora so big that it pushed his ears down. An SS officer escorted him to the main gate, where a black car idled. He was told to sit in the backseat between two SS men in civilian clothes. In the front sat the driver and an SS officer. Biagioni had never seen any of them before. They rode through the wintry countryside in silence. Biagioni remarked that the weather was extremely cold, but the Germans did not reply. They did not say where he was going, but after a short time they reached a city, which Biagioni thought must be Linz. Allied bombers had caused great damage to the city. In the railroad yards, train cars "were strewn about like broken toys." To Biagioni, the bomb damage looked like a bad omen.

The black car pulled up outside an office building, and Biagioni was led inside and then into a courtroom. Five or six Wehrmacht officers were seated at what looked like a judge's bench. The only other person in the room was a German in civilian clothes who Biagioni thought was an interpreter or possibly his lawyer. "He didn't say a word and no reason was told why I was there, although it really wasn't needed," Biagioni wrote. The German officers started speaking. Biagioni did not understand German, and no one translated. Soon after the proceedings began, an air-raid siren sounded, and everyone hurried into the basement. "All was quiet and everyone was looking up at the ceiling as if anticipating the falling bombs," Biagioni wrote. "I thought it ironic that I might be killed by American bombs." But after a few minutes, the all-clear sounded and everyone returned to the courtroom.

Biagioni assumed he was being court-martialed, despite the absence of witnesses or arguments. "A few more words were spoken by the officers, then they went out of a door to their right and without hesitation reentered by a door to their left," Biagioni wrote. "One of them said a few last words and the civilian told me in broken English that I was sentenced to death as a spy." Biagioni already had been sentenced to death six months earlier, soon after his capture in Italy. Why had the Germans gone through the process again? After the verdict, he was taken to an adjoining dormitory of SS men and locked in a cell. He had not eaten since the previous night, but no one offered him food.

The next morning, the same SS men in the black car picked up Biagioni from the dormitory. This time, the Germans had a lot to say on the drive, in German. The only words Biagioni understood were "American swine." The SS men became especially vocal when the car passed through bombed-out areas. Biagioni wrote, "I thought for sure that I was being taken on a one-way ride." But he was taken back to Mauthausen, where he was processed like a new prisoner, stripped of his clothes, and ordered to shower. When he was soaking wet, the guards ushered him outside and ordered him to stand at the base of a wall. Biagioni had seen prisoners cruelly executed in this way—forced to stand in the cold while wet until they died of exposure. He wondered if he was being executed. He already was stiff from the cold when another prisoner, apparently on orders from the Germans, helped him inside.

×   ×   ×

On the same day Biagioni was sentenced to death, Col. Henry Spicer, the pipe-smoking P-51 Mustang pilot, was court-martialed for his emotional speech at Stalag Luft I. Spicer had been taken from his isolation cell at Stalag Luft I the previous day and escorted under armed guard by train to Anklam, Germany, a small town on the Polish border about one hundred miles from the camp. Anklam, too, had been devastated by Allied bombs. Spicer was placed in an isolation cell for a few hours before guards led him down a flight of stairs to a room where a German officer sat at a desk. The officer handed Spicer a document in English that laid out the charges against him. He was accused of misusing his authority by telling his men they did not need to salute Germans of equal or lesser rank; of spreading propaganda and defaming the German character; and of inciting his men at Stalag Luft I to riot. Spicer found the last charge absurd. He had not urged his men to do anything other than "rot in this hole for the next ten years." They had not rioted or even demonstrated after his speech; they had quietly returned to their barracks. Spicer asked the officer at the desk if he could keep a copy of the charges against him and was told no.

At around 10:30 a.m., Spicer was introduced to his German defense lawyer, who spoke no English. A translator helped the two men review the charges. "I was convinced in my own mind that this was the first time the defense counsel had reviewed my case," Spicer said. The court-martial commenced before the lawyer had even explained what defense he planned to offer. The panel of judges consisted of a German brigadier general and two colonels. Spicer did not get their names. Once again, the Swiss had not been notified of the court-martial. The prosecution called as witnesses Major Steinhauer and the two German noncoms who had listened to Spicer's speech. Neither Spicer nor his lawyer was allowed to cross-examine them or to call witnesses. After the prosecution's three witnesses finished testifying, the German brigadier general said the panel had heard enough. He asked Spicer in English if he wished to speak. Spicer decided he had nothing to lose.

He began by defending his advice to his men that, despite the Germans' orders, the Geneva Convention did not require them to salute enemy soldiers of lesser rank. He asked Major Steinhauer, who had remained in the courtroom after testifying, whether any POWs at Stalag Luft I had refused to salute since his speech. The judge interrupted and called the question irrelevant. Then Spicer told the judges he only had spoken the truth when he called German soldiers dishonest and untrustworthy. He said his guards routinely stole his belongings. (While he was in court, they stole his cigarettes from his cell at Anklam.) Spicer elaborated: "I gave them examples of lying, cheating & thieving—and summarized that anyone possessing *these* virtues naturally could not be trusted. Further stated that with proper opportunity and a chance to prepare my case I could give them unending examples of same. (Nasty smiles from the judges—the bastards.)"

Spicer told the judges he had learned of recent German atrocities on the battlefield from reliable sources.

Of course, they asked for names—the skunks—which I denied knowing. (Those boys don't have to worry about that.) They asked if I believed the stories. Answer—"Certainly!" So I was informed that the [German] soldier is incapable of such action (Interesting, eh?) and that I of course was merely spreading horror stories of my own manufacture. . . . Next, the boss-judge reeled off a long line of crap about the many atrocities committed by the Americans, and their inhuman treatment of POWs.

Spicer had no idea what the "boss-judge" was talking about. He knew nothing about the German POW murders in the United States or the fifteen Germans on death row at Fort Leavenworth. After the judge finished lecturing, Spicer wrote, his German defense lawyer "got up and delivered a long, impassioned speech of about 60 [seconds] duration—I don't know what he said. The contents were not translated." Then Spicer and everyone except the judges and prosecutor were ushered from the courtroom to allow the panel to consider Spicer's fate.

After only about ten minutes, Spicer wrote, he was brought back into court to hear the prosecutor read from a typewritten document that he had been sentenced to "the supreme penalty of death." Spicer wondered where the document had come from: no typist or court reporter had attended the court-martial, and no one would have had time to prepare the document after the verdict.

The farcical court-martial took less than an hour. Guards took Spicer back to his cell and then to the prosecutor's office. He was allowed to write a short appeal, although the prosecutor suggested it was a waste of time. He told Spicer that the Swiss would be notified of the verdict and that the German High Command would have to approve it before it became final. The prosecutor implied that approval by the High Command was a formality. He told Spicer he was to be executed in three months, on March 30, 1945.

Spicer was returned to his isolation cell at Stalag Luft I. He described his court-martial in a series of short notes he smuggled to a fellow POW who brought him his meals. He was served the camp's meager rations but was denied the Red Cross parcels. Spicer addressed the notes to "Lydia Pinkstuff" to avoid implicating his friend in case the Germans intercepted the notes. Spicer wrote that he did not regret giving the impromptu speech that led to his death sentence. "Why I said these things, I really don't know, but I guess it was just bitter, black hate boiling up. My only regret (now) is that I missed a good chance to really spread it thick—do a thorough job."

Spicer asked "Lydia Pinkstuff" to tell his men he was in good spirits—"I am OK, can eat & sleep." He was allowed to spend an hour a day walking the camp perimeter accompanied by an armed guard who "wasn't very good company." Spicer passed the time by embroidering a picture of an English garden from a Red Cross kit. He carried on imaginary conversations with his mother. He wrote upbeat letters home, omitting any mention of his death sentence. In one note to "Lydia," he mocked the new security measures the Germans had applied to him since his return to Stalag Luft I: "These bastards won't put anybody next door to me—have double guards on all the time—and take away my knife, fork & spoon at night. Tsk! Tsk! Maybe I'm really a nasty desperate character."

Spicer did not want his men to put themselves at risk by lashing out at the Germans on his behalf. He wrote, "DON'T THINK OF DOING ANYTHING DRASTIC! TAKE IT EASY!" He projected confidence and combativeness. One day, some of his men were being marched past his isolation cell and called out to ask if he needed anything. "Send me machine guns!" he shouted back. "Don't give in to them and keep fighting!" Beneath his bravado, however, Spicer worried. He signed one of his notes, "P.P: Prison Pallor." He wrote that he was eager to speak with a representative of the Swiss "Protecting Power." Rumors swirled around the camp that he might be exchanged for a condemned German POW in the United States. Spicer asked "Lydia" to look into whether the Swiss ever brokered such exchanges. "If so, it's my best bet," he wrote. Spicer was wrong about that.

× × ×

The death sentences rendered against Spicer, Biagioni, Schaefer, and Schmitz were only part of a larger German strategy. In the final days of 1944, the Nazis sentenced at least seven other American POWs to death and set the dates of their executions.

On the same day Spicer was condemned to die, December 30, a German military court in Holland pronounced a death sentence against Lt. Franklin Dent Coslett, a U.S. Army Air Forces bombardier turned operative for MIS-X, the covert branch of the U.S. government helping Americans behind enemy lines. Eight months before, Coslett's B-24 Liberator bomber had been hit by flak on its way back from bombing a railway station in Berlin. The flak wrecked one of the plane's four engines, destroyed its oxygen tanks, and punctured its fuel tanks. The bomber straggled out of formation, and soon a second engine failed. Coslett and his fellow crew members bailed out just before the bomber crashed into a farmhouse in Uddel, a Dutch village near the town of Apeldoorn. The ten Americans split up to avoid attracting attention, and Dutch Resistance fighters found them before the Germans did. The Dutch shuttled them between safe houses and helped some of them escape on bicycles into Allied territory in Belgium.

Franklin Coslett probably could have escaped too. But he was inspired by the Dutch Resistance fighters. He wanted to stay in Holland as a "pilot helper" rescuing other downed fliers. He had no training for that work; before becoming a bombardier, he had been a sports radio announcer in Wilkes-Barre, Pennsylvania. But he proved so adept at coordinating escapes that MIS-X recruited him as an agent. Coslett's network of Dutch contacts included duck farmers, business executives, doctors, and socialites. The covert nature of his work, like Louis Biagioni's, left Coslett outside the protections of the Geneva Convention. It also prevented him from writing home. His fiancée, Margaret Smith, kept a daily vigil for him at St. Stephen's Episcopal Church in Wilkes-Barre.

Coslett stayed one step ahead of the Gestapo for seven months. He set up an office in the Dutch village of Zwolle and an escape network that ran through Zwolle, Amsterdam, Arnhem, Deventer,

Harderwijk, Groningen, and Sneek. He was briefly detained by the Germans in November after SS general Hanns Rauter was wounded in a partisan attack. The Germans released Coslett but avenged the attack on General Rauter[*] by executing thirty Dutch partisans as well as the pilot of Coslett's B-24, 1st Lt. Bill Moore, who also was helping the Resistance.

Coslett's luck ran out on Christmas Eve, when German intelligence agents captured him in the snowy woods near the village of Hoenderloo. They took him to their base in Velp, where he was sentenced to death for terrorism and espionage. He was taken to de Kruisberg prison in Doetinchem to await execution. Six days later, on December 30, Coslett was sentenced to death again, this time on a charge of being a *franc-tireur,* a French term for a partisan operating behind enemy lines. Coslett did not understand why the Germans had sentenced him to die twice. He had no way of knowing that German POWs in America were on the verge of being executed for murder or that Nazi Germany was rushing to condemn American POWs like him to offer in trade.

On December 29 and 30, German military courts sentenced six other American POWs to death for minor or questionable offenses.

Three of the condemned were American bomber crewmen: Lt. John Joseph Walsh of Waltham, Massachusetts; Staff Sgt. Edward J. Walsh of Jersey City, New Jersey; and Staff Sgt. Marvin P. Martin of Harrison, Indiana. Their B-24 Liberator bomber, the "Betty Jean," had been hit by flak on a raid on the Perugia Aerodrome in Italy in January 1944. Smoke boiled from the engines as the plane lost altitude. The Americans bailed out just before the bomber smashed into the side of a mountain. The crew evaded the Germans for several days with the help of Italian partisans. One crewman recalled seeing Marvin Martin "in the hands of a Rebel Band aiding the Allies." Martin, Walsh, and Walsh were soon captured. For nearly a year, the Germans

---

[*] General Rauter was the head of the SS in Holland and answered directly to Heinrich Himmler. The partisans who wounded him had not even known he was riding in the truck that they attacked in order to steal food. Rauter was tried for war crimes at Nuremberg, sentenced to death, and executed in 1949.

had classified them as ordinary POWs. Now, suddenly, at the end of December 1944, the Germans reclassified them as *franc-tireurs* and sentenced them to die.

The other three American POWs were condemned for hitting German guards.

Also on December 29, a German military court in Dresden condemned U.S. Army Sgt. Thomas Jefferson Snowden, a twenty-two-year-old blacksmith from Rutland, Ohio, for punching a guard in the jaw. The guard, a noncommissioned officer, had knocked a piece of breakfast bread out of Snowden's mouth after motioning for him to finish eating and get back to work. The guard had responded to Snowden's punch by punching him back. The exchange went no further but Snowden was placed under arrest for assaulting a superior officer. Court documents suggest the incident took place at Stalag IV C at Wistritz in German-occupied Czechoslovakia. At his court-martial on December 29, Snowden was represented by a German lawyer who argued that his offense merited no worse punishment than a prison sentence. The court disagreed, saying Snowden had struck a superior officer "in the field" in front of witnesses.

On December 30, a German military court in Leipzig condemned Staff Sgt. Angelo Nicosia of Bethlehem, Pennsylvania, for striking a guard at Stalag II B in Hammerstein, Germany, in October. The guard had been haranguing a sick POW for slacking on a farmwork detail. The POW had just vomited and complained he was too sick to work. The guard said he should not have come on the work detail. Nicosia, working nearby, heard the exchange and cursed the guard. The guard struck him in the back with his gun butt. Nicosia spun around and punched the guard above the left eye, knocking him down. Nicosia seized his gun and pushed it between the guard's legs to prevent him from shooting. Nicosia handed the gun to the German foreman as soon as he arrived. At Nicosia's court-martial, his German lawyer argued that the guard was partly to blame for the incident and that Nicosia had taken hold of the gun only to avoid being shot. The court was not swayed.

On the same day, the Leipzig court sentenced Private Willard Davis to death on a charge of attacking a guard. Davis had been part of a work detail at a potato factory in November when he came upon a struggle between a guard and a second POW. Davis tried to pull them apart but backed away when other guards arrived. The second POW stopped fighting and raised his hands, but a guard shot him to death anyway. At Davis's court-martial on December 30, he was represented by a German doctor who questioned the guards. Davis did not understand anything they said and was not given a chance to speak. "It looked like they already had had the trial and I was just taken in to hear the end of it," he wrote. "They just ignored me when I tried to talk to them." The trial took less than an hour. The panel of judges comprised two German officers, a sergeant, and two privates. They deliberated only ten minutes before passing sentence. Davis thought the Germans wanted to execute him because he had witnessed a war crime: "I think it was a frame-up to clear the guard from the responsibility of killing the prisoner."

The Geneva Convention allowed capital punishment for assaulting guards in "especially serious" cases, but neither Nicosia's, Snowden's, nor Davis's actions seemed to approach that threshold.

While the covert agents Biagioni and Coslett might have expected to be executed if caught, none of the other Americans—"King Kong" Schaefer, Jimmy Schmitz, Henry Spicer, Edward Walsh, John Walsh, Marvin Martin, Thomas Snowden, Angelo Nicosia, or Willard Davis—had committed offenses worthy of the death penalty. Under ordinary circumstances, they would have received prison sentences or a few weeks in the "cooler." But their circumstances were extraordinary, and were about to become more so.

PART IV

Hostage Diplomacy

20

A Startling Offer

On January 5, 1944, the government of Nazi Germany laid its cards on the table. The German Foreign Office sent, via the Swiss Legation, an "urgent" cable offering to exchange five of the freshly condemned American POWs for the five Germans convicted of killing Johann Kunze at Camp Tonkawa. Before the cable arrived at 10 a.m. Washington time, U.S. authorities had been unaware that the German military courts had handed down a flurry of death sentences.

The following members of the American armed forces have been condemned to death by sentence imposed by the Reich Court Martial and other courts-martial:
Sentenced November 22, 1944, for treason:

Lieutenant James Meloyne Greyfield, born January 31, 1915, in Shawsheen Village, Massachusetts.

Captured as *francs-tireurs;* sentenced December 30, 1944:

Lieutenant Franklin Dent Cosolet [*sic*], Identification number 0/801353/2/42/03

Lieutenant Johann Josef Walsh, born June 12, 1922, in Waltham, Massachusetts.

Sergeant Marvin Palver Martin, born November 24, 1921, in Palmira, Indiana.

Sergeant Edward Adolf Walsh, born March 19, 1922 (presumably in Jersey City. Exact details regarding place of birth will be furnished at a later date).

The condemned prisoners were captured in civilian clothes. Therefore, they are not to be considered prisoners of war, even though they are members of the American armed forces. . . .

The German government has deferred execution of the sentences pending receipt of information from the United States Government as to whether it is prepared to exchange them against prisoners of war Beyer, Seidel, Demme, Schomer and Scholz, of Prisoner of War Camp Tonkawa, who were condemned in the United States. Should the United States Government agree to this proposal, the exchange could be carried out in the course of the forthcoming exchange of seriously wounded.

The "forthcoming exchange" referred to the next scheduled of six total exchanges of sick or injured prisoners arranged between the Western Allies and Germany during World War II. The exchanged prisoners sailed across the Atlantic aboard the Swiss-operated ocean liner MS *Gripsholm* and were exchanged in neutral ports such as Goteborg, Sweden. The next exchange, scheduled for January 16, involved three hundred American and British POWs and four hundred German POWs. Over the course of the war, more than 2,200 Allied and 4,800 German POWs would be repatriated in this way. Exchanges of prisoners on humanitarian grounds were as old as warfare. But none of the German prisoners in Germany's exchange offer on January 5 were sick, injured, or noncombatants. They had been convicted of murder in Oklahoma.

Soldiers of the German Afrika Korps surrender to the Allies in Tunisia, North Africa, in May 1943. More than 120,000 of them would end up in POW camps in America.

POW Camp Concordia in remote north-central Kansas was typical of the more than 150 "main" camps scattered across the United States during World War II. Each camp was surrounded by barbed-wire fences with strategically sited guard towers.

German POWs harvest corn in a farmer's field near Hampshire, Illinois, in 1944. The Germans worked in farms and factories all over the United States.

German POWs dig into a big meal at a POW camp in the southeastern United States. Food in the camps was plentiful and usually prepared by German cooks and bakers.

German POWs playing soccer before a crowd of fellow prisoners at a camp in the southeastern United States. All camps of any size had athletic fields for soccer and other sports.

A large collection of contraband— including objects that could serve as weapons—seized from German prisoners in a surprise shakedown/ inspection of a POW camp. Many of the objects had been smuggled into the camp from work details.

Lt. Col. Leon Jaworski, an army prosecutor who led the investigation and prosecution of two of the POW camp murder cases, in 1944.

Injured German U-boat crewman Werner Dreschler, *left,* is helped ashore at the Norfolk Naval Base in Virginia by a fellow member of the U-118 crew after the U-boat was sunk by Allied planes in June 1943. Dreschler ended up betraying the Nazi cause and was murdered by his fellow captives at Camp Papago Park in Arizona in 1944.

REYAK

WIZUY

FISCHER

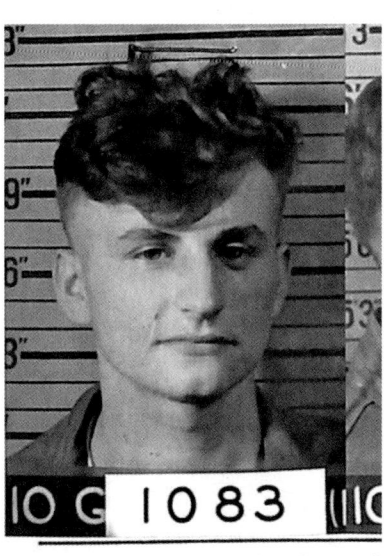

FRANKE

Four of the German POWs who were convicted of murdering U-boat crewman Werner Dreschler and subsequently were hanged at Fort Leavenworth, Kansas. *Clockwise from top left,* Bernhard Reyak, Rolf Wizuy, Fritz Franke, and Helmut Fischer.

U.S. Army Lt. Col. William "King Kong" Schaefer as a POW at Oflag 64 in Poland in 1944.

U.S. Army Lt. James Schmitz in 1943 before his capture in Italy.

U.S. Army Air Forces Col. Henry Spicer in the cockpit of his P-51 Mustang fighter in 1944 before he was shot down over the French coast and captured.

OSS agent Cpl. Louis Biagioni at his enlistment office in 1942.

The German poster at Oflag 64 that led to death sentences for Lt. Col. William Schaefer and Lt. James Schmitz.

To all Prisoners of War!

The escape from prison camps is no longer a sport!

Germany has always kept to the Hague Convention and only punished recaptured prisoners of war with minor disciplinary punishment.

Germany will still maintain these principles of international law.

But England has besides fighting at the front in an honest manner instituted an illegal warfare in non combat zones in the form of gangster commandos, terror bandits and sabotage troops even up to the frontiers of Germany.

They say in a captured secret and confidential English military pamphlet,

THE HANDBOOK
OF MODERN IRREGULAR
WARFARE:

". . . the days when we could practise the rules of sportsmanship are over. For the time being, every soldier must be a potential gangster and must be prepared to adopt their methods whenever necessary."

"The sphere of operations should always include the enemy's own country, any occupied territory, and in certain circumstances, such neutral countries as he is using as a source of supply."

England has with these instructions opened up a non military form of gangster war!

Germany is determined to safeguard her homeland, and especially her war industry and provisional centres for the fighting fronts. Therefore it has become necessary to create strictly forbidden zones, called death zones, in which all unauthorised trespassers will be immediately shot on sight.

Escaping prisoners of war, entering such death zones, will certainly lose their lives. They are therefore in constant danger of being mistaken for enemy agents or sabotage groups.

Urgent warning is given against making future escapes!

In plain English: Stay in the camp where you will be safe! Breaking out of it is now a damned dangerous act.

The chances of preserving your life are almost nil!

All police and military guards have been given the most strict orders to shoot on sight all suspected persons.

Escaping from prison camps has ceased to be a sport!

U.S. secretary of war Henry Stimson in 1944. He would play a key role in the German POW murder cases.

Colditz Castle in Germany, where Lt. Col. William Schaefer was held before and after his court-martial for the poster incident.

The U.S. Disciplinary Barracks at Fort Leavenworth, Kansas, where the fifteen condemned Germans were held on death row and fourteen ultimately were hanged. The "Castle" is the rotunda that dominates the prison grounds.

A scene of utter devastation in the bombed-out heart of Berlin in early 1945, as negotiations for an exchange of condemned POWs were under way.

MAUTHAUSEN C.C. (MAY 8, 1945)

OSS agent Louis Biagioni, *center,* after U.S. troops liberated the Mauthausen concentration camp in Austria in 1945.

The graves of the executed Germans at the secluded prisoner cemetery at Fort Leavenworth, Kansas.

President Franklin D. Roosevelt, *right,* and his vice president, Harry S. Truman, who would succeed Roosevelt after the latter's death in April 1945. The decisions of whether to execute the condemned Germans would fall to Truman.

The water tower of POW Camp Tonkawa in Oklahoma is practically all that remains of the camp today.

Secretary of War Henry Stimson was livid at the German offer. "In the opinion of the War Department," he wrote, "the German authorities have trumped up charges against these five Americans in order to compel the release of the German murderers or the deferment of their executions." The bellicose German message seemed out of sync with Germany's increasingly bleak prospects in the war. Stimson asked the State Department to warn the Germans that they were violating the Geneva Convention and should vacate the Americans' verdicts and death sentences and retry them fairly.

U.S. authorities also were puzzled by the Germans' list of condemned American POWs. They quickly identified the three B-24 crewmen, although Edward Walsh's middle name was not "Adolf" but John, and Marvin Martin's middle name was not "Palver" but "Palmer." But the Germans' misspelling of Coslett's name as "Cosolet" created confusion. The serial number the Germans had listed for him—his U.S. military identification number—belonged to a different aviator who was still flying. And there was no record of a "Lieutenant James Meloyne Greyfield" anywhere in the U.S. armed forces. Was Greyfield a civilian? The State Department asked the Swiss to find out who Greyfield and "Cosolet" were.

On the same day the Germans offered the exchange, they sent word through the Swiss that a reviewing judge had "canceled" the previous acquittals of the four Oflag 64 lieutenants who had refused to get off the sidewalk and walk in the street. The four men—John Rathbone, Seymour Bolten, George Durgin, and Pat Teel—were to be retried for that offense, as the spiteful Captain Zimmerman had promised. Their new trial was scheduled for January 25 in Posen, the site of the first trial. Given the context of the message, the four men seemed likely to be sentenced to death rather than acquitted a second time.

On January 8, Secretary of War Stimson received a visit from an ex-POW, U.S. Army Col. Thomas D. Drake. Drake had been a senior American officer at Oflag 64 in Poland until September 1944, when he was repatriated to the United States in one of the exchanges of sick and injured prisoners. Drake described the treatment of American

POWs at Oflag 64 as "very poor." He told Stimson the Germans responded better to threats and "rough talk" than to reason. Drake said he once had obtained the release of two American POWs, "whom the Germans had intended to execute and had already put into a Polish prison camp," by threatening to report the name of the German camp commandant to the Allies for prosecution after the war. It's unclear which two Oflag 64 POWs Drake was talking about. He had not saved Schaefer, Schmitz, or the four officers who had refused to get off the sidewalk. He may have thought he had saved them. Drake had been repatriated before Schaefer and Schmitz were sentenced to death and before the Germans announced plans to retry the other four after their original acquittals. In any case, Stimson took to heart Drake's advice about using threats and "rough talk" against the Germans.

ON JANUARY 12, a new cable from the Germans offered details about the five American POWs on the list. They said "Cosolet," the MIS-X agent in Holland, had been convicted of illegal possession of arms by a court of the Second Parachutist Detection Corps. He had been "captured in civilian clothes behind German lines in a pillbox. Arms, ammunition and maps were near him." The three B-24 bomber crewmen, John Walsh, Edward Walsh, and Marvin Martin, had been "captured in civilian clothes . . . carrying Italian language leaflets in which the Italian population was invited to offer resistance to the German troops and to help the enemy." The Germans said Greyfield, whose middle name they now spelled "Melvyn" rather than "Meloyne," had taken a job at a German news service in order to gather sensitive information and then "communicated to American organizations state secrets which had become known to him."

The same day, a series of telegrams from the American ambassador in Berlin, Jerome Klahr Huddle, provided a great deal of information, which he apparently had learned from Swiss diplomats, that appeared to raise the stakes even further.

Huddle's first telegram revealed to U.S. authorities for the first time that Sgt. Thomas Jefferson Snowden had been sentenced to die for striking a German guard. Huddle wrote that the Swiss already had protested Snowden's case on two grounds: the Germans had moved up the court-martial on the calendar from its original date without notice, which had prevented the Swiss from sending an observer; and other Allied POWs who had committed similar offenses had received much less severe sentences. The Swiss had argued that Snowden's death sentence was excessive and should be "canceled."

A second telegram from Huddle reported Sgt. Angelo Nicosia's death sentence for punching and disarming the guard who had harassed the sick POW. Huddle wrote that, as in Snowden's case, the Swiss had not been told of a change in the trial date. The Swiss said they had heard that a German lawyer was appointed to defend Nicosia but did not know if he had done so. The Swiss had protested Nicosia's death sentence as too severe and had called on the Germans to void it.

Ambassador Huddle's third telegram reported Schaefer's and Schmitz's death sentences. It briefly summarized the poster incident at Oflag 64. It said the men's court-martial, like Snowden's and Nicosia's, had been moved up on the court calendar without notice. Once again, the Swiss had protested Schaefer's and Schmitz's sentences as too severe and had asked the Germans to cancel them.

Huddle's fourth and final telegram disclosed Pvt. Willard Davis's death sentence. Huddle said the Germans claimed that Davis, "together with another prisoner, assaulted a superior." Davis's court-martial also had been rescheduled without notice to the Swiss. Huddle had no further information about Davis's case. He stressed that none of the Americans' sentences were final until Hitler approved them. The Germans had not yet mentioned the death sentences of P-51 Mustang pilot Col. Henry Spicer or OSS agent Louis Biagioni. But at least ten Americans now faced the prospect of being executed, most of them for relatively minor offenses. The four lieutenants who had refused to get off the sidewalk seemed likely to join them.

Secretary of State Stettinius, who had been appointed to his post only weeks earlier to replace the ailing Cordell Hull, vented his anger over the Germans' actions in a ten-page telegram to the U.S.

ambassador in Switzerland. Stettinius wrote that the United States had followed the Geneva Convention in convicting the German POWs of murder. The Germans, by contrast, had illegally reclassified the three B-24 crewmen from POWs to *franc-tireurs* and condemned them to die for the sole purpose of offering them in exchange. The fact that Coslett, Walsh, Walsh, and Martin had been captured in civilian clothes was not enough to declare them partisans, he wrote. None of the German guards who had been struck by the POWs had been injured. Stettinius pointed out that four German POWs in the United States had been tried for striking American guards: three had received short prison terms; the fourth had been given a life sentence because he also had incited a riot. Stettinius wrote that the death sentences of Schaefer, Schmitz, Davis, Nicosia, and Snowden "are plainly indefensible in their severity." He added that the Germans had provided "only scanty and inadequate information" about the Americans' trials and death sentences—the same complaint the German authorities had made for months about the murder cases in the United States.

The Germans' prisoner exchange offer roiled emotions in the Pentagon, which had just opened at its current site as a supposedly temporary headquarters for a wartime U.S. military.* The Joint Chiefs of Staff proposed warning Nazi Germany that for every American POW it executed, the United States would "dispose of" one thousand German POWs after the war, either "by turning them over to the Russians for forced labor or otherwise." Stimson did not immediately reject the idea but finally concluded it would only bring reprisal from an enemy who lacked "normal humane considerations." Stimson also felt the idea too closely resembled the Nazis' practice of taking revenge for the killings of German soldiers in Nazi-occupied nations by staging mass executions of innocent local citizens. Stimson decided to wait for the Germans' next move. They had not yet offered to exchange

---

* The U.S. government's original plans called for the Pentagon to be converted after the war into a hospital, an office complex, or warehouses. Secretary of War Stimson reflected the newness of the Pentagon in 1945 by referring to it as "the Pentagon building." The land on which the building stood, and stands, had been part of Confederate general Robert E. Lee's estate, which was confiscated by the federal government after the Civil War.

Schaefer, Schmitz, Snowden, Nicosia, or Davis for any of the other ten Germans on Leavenworth's death row. But U.S. authorities fully expected them to. The speeding-up of the Americans' trials, the severe sentences, and the timing of the notice to U.S. authorities made it hard to conclude otherwise. The army prepared a document listing all ten of the condemned American POWs, drawing a line between the five the Germans already had offered to exchange and the five the army expected them to offer later. The name of the mysterious Greyfield had a question mark after it. Greyfield apparently was not an American service member or civilian. Was he a spy with a false name? Had the Germans made him up? The State Department urged the Swiss to keep trying to find a serial number or some other ID for Greyfield.

Five days after the flurry of telegrams, Edwin Plitt, the chief of the State Department's Special War Problems Division, wrote to Assistant Secretary of State James Dunn that he had helped the War Department prepare a "strong protest" of the death sentences of the ten American POWs. Plitt wrote that the Americans obviously "have been sentenced in reprisal for the sentencing of the German prisoners of war in this country." He pointed out that the German exchange proposal still had not been answered directly. He suggested the War Department set aside any outrage over the unfairness of the proposal and consider accepting it to save the lives of the American prisoners. Otherwise, Plitt wrote, "should the American public become aware of the German proposal and our failure to accept it, widespread repercussions may result."

The War Department's silence on the German exchange proposal also troubled Henry P. Leverich of the State Department's Division of European Affairs. In a memo to Assistant Secretary of State Dunn, Leverich wrote that no formal protest was going to stop the Germans from executing the ten American prisoners, "against whom they have quite obviously trumped-up charges." He suggested Dunn contact high-ranking officials in the War Department and try to persuade them to accept the German offer. The Swiss minister in Washington also tried to intervene. He approached the poet and playwright Archibald MacLeish, who had accepted a wartime appointment as an assistant secretary of state. The Swiss minister suggested to MacLeish that German prisoners who killed traitors "might perhaps be considered as less culpable than those who commit crimes of violence for reasons having nothing to do with the sense of loyalty or discipline." MacLeish forwarded the minister's remarks to his superiors at the State Department, adding that he had refrained from either agreeing or disagreeing with the minister.

While the exchange offer dangled, army authorities set out to execute the five Camp Tonkawa killers as their superiors at the War Department had ordered. On January 17, Col. A. M. Tollefson, director of the army's POW Operations Division, announced the rejection of Germany's latest request to postpone the Tonkawa executions past January 25. Tollefson wrote that the War Department saw no reason to discuss an exchange of the five Germans for "five American soldiers alleged to have been sentenced to death." But only three days later, Secretary of War Stimson agreed to postpone the Tonkawa executions until March 31. Stimson still did not address the exchange proposal. He wrote that giving the Germans three additional months to review the Tonkawa court records "will effectively deprive the German Government of any plausible pretext for protest or reprisal when the sentences are executed." That was wishful thinking, as the Germans immediately proved.

On January 26, German lawyers savaged the Camp Tonkawa murder case in a lengthy message transmitted through the Swiss. The Germans wrote that the trial transcripts made it clear that the victim, Johann Kunze, was a traitor. They blamed his death on army authorities because "after having used him for their purposes they left him to remain among honor-loving German prisoners of war, although [they] undoubtedly had been aware that he would be in danger there." The Germans wrote that testimony at the court-martial made it clear that none of the five men who had been sentenced to die had delivered the fatal blows or even had seriously injured Kunze. The German lawyers concluded that the death sentences were unjustifiably severe and clearly were "intended, under the pretext of the court proceedings, to terrorize German prisoners of war."

Secretary of War Stimson responded with a two-page letter dismissing all the German lawyers' contentions. Stimson wrote that the army bore no blame for Kunze's death because it had no obligation "to ascertain the political beliefs of prisoners of war in its custody or to segregate them on that basis. Furthermore, it is obvious that a conspiracy among prisoners of war to murder one of their fellow prisoners cannot be justified on the ground that they consider him to be a 'traitor.'" Stimson wrote that the five Germans at Tonkawa "had received the same justice in the case as would have been meted out to American offenders for a like crime," and that how a German court might view the case was "wholly irrelevant." Judge Advocate General Cramer agreed with Stimson's arguments but did not think they would sway the Germans. Cramer thought that taking a strong position, as Stimson was doing, might only make things worse. He suggested stalling by simply acknowledging the German complaints and saying they were being considered.

The same week, a State Department official in Marseilles, France, sent an urgent telegram to Washington recounting his conversations with American POWs who had passed through Marseilles in the latest exchange of sick and injured prisoners. The POWs had provided a few details about Schaefer's and Schmitz's trial. They also had informed U.S. authorities for the first time that Col. Henry Spicer had been sentenced to death for giving a speech to his fellow prisoners "that he would be willing to stay in this hole for ten years if it would result in the death of the German army."

Two weeks later, the Germans sent a telegram through the Swiss to the State Department offering to postpone the executions of the condemned Americans while negotiations for an exchange were pending. The Germans wrote that they also were willing to postpone the execution of OSS agent Louis Biagioni—adding Biagioni to the exchange discussion for the first time.

The Germans' scathing review of the Camp Tonkawa murder case left American authorities wary of how they would react to the court records from the other three murder cases. The Camp Aiken records already had been released to the Germans. But President Roosevelt had not yet confirmed the death sentences in the Camp Chaffee and Papago Park cases, and so those records had not been sent to Berlin. The Camp Chaffee case, in which Jaworski had used circumstantial evidence to convict the "ringleader" of the killing, was sure to be criticized by the Germans. But the real problem was the Camp Papago Park case.

The seven death sentences of the Papago Park U-boat men were the most in any of the murder cases. A careful reading by the Germans of the trial transcripts would show that the army had dropped a well-known traitor into a barracks full of U-boat men, allowed them to kill him, and then tortured some of them into confessing. The testimony about the onion-filled gas mask was potentially explosive. Assistant Provost Marshal General Bryan warned Judge Advocate General Cramer that the Papago Park record contained "obnoxious material" that should not be shared with the Germans. Bryan suggested that when the time came, the army should withhold the court records of the Camp Papago Park and Camp Chaffee cases and provide the Germans only with "a substantial summary" of the cases, without the "obnoxious material."

The testimony about torture in the Papago Park case also caught Secretary of War Stimson's attention when he reviewed the case. Stimson did not think "Schmidt's" harsh interrogation of the U-boat men was grounds for sparing their lives. But Stimson refused to approve the verdicts and sentences until he received a report on the interrogation methods at Byron Hot Springs. He ordered the report on his desk in four days. Army files contain a list of questions, possibly asked by Stimson:

1. What authority was there for the use of third degree interrogation methods, and who gave them?
2. What was the necessity for third degree interrogation methods?
3. Who participated in these third degree methods from within the [Ninth] Service Command?
4. Who participated from without the Service Command?

5. What offices or agencies did they represent?
6. Who is Captain Oscar Schmidt? Full identification is required.
7. Who is Sergeant Held? Give his full identity.
8. Give full report of the facts in connection with this incident.

Stimson's demand for a quick report set off a scramble by senior army officers in Utah and Washington. Most of them were blindsided by the torture allegations. Army files contain the transcript of a telephone call in which Provost Marshal General Archer Lerch in Washington and the chief of staff of the Ninth Service Command in Utah agreed they knew nothing about what went on at Byron Hot Springs. The two men wondered how much Colonel Church knew and how they might avoid the fallout. They agreed Church should be summoned from a conference in Texas and put on a train to Washington so that he could speak to Stimson in person.

Church apparently never spoke directly to Stimson. Instead, he spoke with Brig. Gen. John Weckerling, the deputy assistant chief of staff of army intelligence, or G-2. Stimson also received a memorandum from Weckerling's boss, Maj. Gen. Clayton Russell, the assistant chief of staff of G-2, dismissing all of the U-boat men's torture claims as either false or exaggerated. Russell wrote that the vehicle in which the Germans were taken for rides at Byron Hot Springs "is not and has never been equipped [with] a moving steel bar of any sort." The U-boat men were not burned by hot steam pipes because the heat was turned off at the resort at the time. Russell wrote that the gas mask had been used "without authorization" because the commander of Byron Hot Springs was away at the time. The commander would not have allowed it, "since methods of this sort are distinctly forbidden." Russell added that "Schmidt"—whose real name he did not disclose—had felt justified in using the gas mask and other strong interrogation methods because the U-boat men "were extremely arrogant and considered themselves heroes because of the part they had played in this murder."

Stimson wrote in his diary that "Weckerling has made a thorough investigation and after hearing it I decided that no failure of justice had been occasioned." The secretary of war approved the U-boat men's murder convictions and death sentences and forwarded the case to President Roosevelt. In a letter to Roosevelt, Stimson wrote that he had investigated the torture complaints and decided they were "either unfounded or are grossly exaggerated. Whatever improper treatment there may have been had no effect on their later confessions which were voluntarily made." Even so, Stimson added, "I have taken steps to see that no further instances of this kind will occur." War Department files contain a draft warning from Stimson to POW camp commanders to avoid extreme, "third-degree" interrogation methods. Those methods not only violate the Geneva Convention, Stimson wrote, but might later come to light and bring "retaliation upon American prisoners held by the enemies."

Stimson was rethinking the War Department's failure to acknowledge the Germans' exchange offer. His worries extended beyond the condemned American POWs to the more than eighty-five thousand Americans being held by the Germans. Fifteen thousand American soldiers had been captured in January alone in the Alsace region of France. The growing number of American prisoners in German camps created "a very ticklish and trying situation," Stimson wrote in his diary. "We are now afraid that there will be mass murders as the Russian troops and our troops converge on the present camps in Germany where our prisoners are being held."

21

Pandemonium

U.S. authorities were just beginning to weigh the Germans' offer to exchange condemned POWs when the Russians roared into the picture. By mid-January, the Soviet Red Army was battering the outnumbered and outgunned Germans all along the Eastern Front. The Russians were exacting revenge for three and a half years of German brutality in Soviet lands. The Germans had killed more than ten million Soviet prisoners and civilians, including at least three million who were worked to exhaustion and then executed at places like Mauthausen—"discarded by the Reich for disposal as if they were worn-out nags sent to the abattoir," in the words of British historian Catherine Merridale. Now it was the Russians' turn. A Russian soldier wrote to his father, "You said that we should do the same things in Germany as the Germans did to us. The court has begun already; they are going to remember this march by our army over German territory for a long, long time." In advance of the Soviet onslaught, tens of thousands of terrified Germans in Poland and East Prussia fled west with whatever they could carry. At Oflag 64 in Schubin, Poland, Lt. James Schmitz and his fellow POWs heard the clatter of the refugees' horse-drawn wagons on the cobbled roads just outside the camp.

On January 20, Oflag 64's German commandant announced that

the camp was to be evacuated immediately. The Russians were just thirty-six hours from the gates. The prisoners were to be moved 345 miles west and north to a new camp in the German city of Brandenburg. The Geneva Convention required that POWs be kept a safe distance from battle zones, but Schmitz and his comrades doubted they were being moved for their safety. They suspected the Germans wanted to keep them as potential hostages. Schmitz knew that to be true in his case. He was assigned two personal guards to make sure he did not escape during the move to Brandenburg.

An air of panic permeated Oflag 64 the night before the evacuation. The Germans kept the lights burning in the barracks all night so the guards and prisoners could collect what they wanted to carry. In the camp hospital, a German doctor moved from bed to bed deciding which prisoners were too hurt or sick to survive the rigors of the journey. Dozens of newly arrived prisoners from the Battle of the Bulge were still recovering from wounds; scores of others suffered from stomach ailments and upper respiratory tract infections from the camp's inadequate food and heating. The German doctor allowed eighty-six POWs to remain in the hospital to await the Russians. Since no Germans dared to stay with them, they essentially were being set free.

Schmitz was among the 1,471 prisoners deemed healthy enough to evacuate the camp. The Germans announced they would march the POWs fifteen miles to Exim—the Germans' new name for the Polish village of Kcynia—to board a train that would carry them to the camp in Brandenburg. Even marching fifteen miles was a daunting prospect for the malnourished prisoners. A severe winter gripped northern Europe. The temperature at the camp hovered just below freezing. Several inches of snow and slush covered the streets. Icicles hung from the trees and telephone lines, and a fine mist off the Baltic Sea coated everything with a sheen. Schmitz and his fellow prisoners prepared as best they could. They fashioned mittens out of old shirts and sewed blankets together to create sleeping bags. Some prisoners built sleds out of bookshelves and bed boards and piled their gear on top. One POW hid the camp's secret shortwave radio in his set of bagpipes so the men could keep listening to the BBC news. The prisoners packed most of their remaining Red Cross food, uncertain when they would be fed next. Few could sleep, so they smashed up their wooden bunks and stuffed the pieces into their stoves, filling the barracks with a warmth they had not felt in weeks.

Early the next morning, January 21, almost all of the able-bodied POWs assembled at the camp's parade ground. A few hid in a half-finished tunnel to wait for the Germans to leave. The prisoners formed ragged ranks on purpose to make it difficult for the guards to count them. For the first time the men heard the rumble of Soviet artillery in the distance. Colonel Schneider, the camp commandant, threw open Oflag 64's main gate and told the prisoners, "Gentlemen, I have orders to march you from here back into Germany. I want your cooperation, but whether I get it or not, I will take you out of here." He climbed into a surrey drawn by a mule and headed out the gate. The prisoners formed ranks five-across and followed, with guards on either side. Some of the guards were old men. One was so feeble that the prisoners helped him carry his pack. The prisoners trudged alongside one of the German refugee caravans, a long line of overloaded carts pulled by horses and oxen. A woman on a wagon cursed the Americans but they did not respond. They had too much else to worry about. At the village of Exim/Kcynia, no train waited for them. The Germans said they were going to have to walk the remaining 325 miles to Brandenburg. But that plan sounded ad-libbed and tenuous. Ferguson caught a glimpse of Schmitz in one of the columns and felt relief that his former client had gotten at least this far without being executed.

The POWs spent the second night of the march shivering in an abandoned barn. Some of the guards grew dispirited. Schmitz's two personal guards vanished. Dozens of prisoners slipped away. An American officer led a group of them back toward Oflag 64 to wait for the advancing Russians. But they were intercepted by the hated Zimmerman, now in command of a small SS force. Zimmerman marched them toward Berlin instead. Schmitz had stayed with the main body of marchers. For almost two years, he had never tried to escape, thinking his best chance to get home alive to Ottawa, Illinois, was to follow the rules and wait. But the poster incident had showed him the rules no longer applied. He decided his best chance was to escape. At the end of the next day's march, he darted out of formation and buried himself in a large stack of straw. The next morning, the march went on without him. For a few hours, Schmitz was free. But an SS unit trailed behind the march to sweep up stragglers and escapees. The SS men stopped at the straw stack. They "fired a few shots into it and threatened to throw grenades in it, so I climbed out," Schmitz wrote. To his surprise, he had not been alone in the stack. Several other Americans climbed out with hands raised.[*] The SS men loaded them into a truck and drove them ahead to rejoin the main body of marchers. Schmitz resolved to try to escape again.

The Germans turned the marchers west, away from Brandenburg and in the general direction of Berlin. Exactly where they were going was unclear to the prisoners and probably to their captors. Day after day, Schmitz and the other marchers labored along icy, snowy roads. The sleds that some men had built to haul their gear fell apart. The prisoners spent the nights in whatever barns, stables, or abandoned houses they happened upon as darkness fell. Every night they camped wet and exhausted. The Germans rarely allowed them to build fires. There was little water for drinking and none for bathing. The daily food ration consisted of a bowl of turnip soup, some potatoes, a cup of coffee or tea, and a half slice of bread. The prisoners bartered food from families along the roads. They walked for forty-five days, averaging fourteen miles a day, before they were loaded into boxcars. By then, hundreds of prisoners had escaped from the march. Only 490 of the original 1,471 prisoners remained. Schmitz was among them.

---

[*] Straw stacks were a favorite hiding place for escaped prisoners. Another American escapee hid deep enough in a stack that he could stay concealed even when the Germans probed it with pitchforks. The Germans did not shoot into the stack.

×　　×　　×

The evacuation of Oflag 64 was reported to U.S. authorities in Washington by the Swiss and other sources. On February 14, the Swiss relayed a message from the German High Command that two hundred of the American prisoners who had been marched out of the camp "had been abandoned enroute and are now in Soviet hands." As encouraging as it was to learn that those Americans were free from the Germans, U.S. authorities worried how the Russians would treat them. The Red Army had liberated nearly thirty thousand Americans from German POW camps, but Stalin refused to allow Allied planes to land in Poland or other Soviet-controlled territory to pick them up. Stalin insisted they all be transported to the Ukrainian port of Odessa and sent home by sea. Collecting and transporting Allied POWs was a low priority for the Red Army in the middle of a great battle, and many newly "liberated" Americans suffered more than they had in German hands. Some were detained by Soviet troops in abandoned buildings with little food or water and had to scour the ravaged countryside for firewood in order to stay warm.

As the Soviets advanced, sometimes by as much as fifty miles a day, the Red Army took what it wanted from German civilians, sometimes by deadly force. "The Russians dearly love to murder German civilians," one American POW wrote. "It is a relatively common practice to rape, then murder." Some POWs who had been freed by the Russians reported they were friendly until they got drunk, at which point they often grew boastful and chided the Americans for not fighting harder and advancing faster. One American POW recommended that Russian and Allied troops never be quartered in the same town with time on their hands. A postwar poll found that 56 percent of the American prisoners freed by the Red Army thought they had received at least adequate treatment, given the harsh weather and battlefield conditions. Life was hard for the Russian soldiers too.

Army intelligence agents tried to track the evacuations of Allied POWs from camps all along the fast-changing battlefront. Tens of thousands of prisoners were being marched like the Oflag 64 POWs for long distances in frigid weather to camps deep in Germany and Austria. In some cases, the Germans started moving prisoners without knowing where to take them. The U.S. ambassador to Switzerland, Leland Harrison, sent telegrams to the State Department summarizing the latest reports on prisoner movement. One read:

One. *Stalag IIA*: POWs moving west

Two. *Stalag XXB*: Moving towards Neu Brandenburg

Three. *Stalag IIC*: 4,000 Poles overrun by Russians; remainder moving west.

Four. *Oflag 64*: 266 officers moved by train have reached Stalag IIIA; 200 officers left on roadside. Remainder moving west.

Five. *Stalag IIIB*: POWs arrived *Stalag IIIA*. After few days stay were to be marched to new camp 18 kilometers west of Luckenwalde.

Six. *Stalag Luft III*: About one half Americans now *Stalag VIIA*. Remaining half moved to [Nuremberg]. Of British POWs who reached *Stalag IIIA*, about one half remaining IIIA, balance moving on towards *Marlag* and *Milag Nord*. All Norwegian POWs arrive *Stalag IIIA*, also 950 Polish officers from Hungary.

Seven. *Stalag 344*: POWs held for moment at Konnigratz until decision as to what destination made.

Eight. *Stalag VIIA*: Now has 100,000 POWs.

The State Department complained to the Swiss that the chaotic movement of POWs was "extremely at variance" with the Geneva Convention, not only on the marches but in the overcrowded receiving camps. The State Department cited one instance in which 682 Allied prisoners, including wounded men, were crammed into a room only eighty feet long and seventy feet wide for ten days with no toilet facilities, scant food, and one cup of water per man per day. When the prisoners begged for more food, a German officer told them, "I would rather shoot you than feed you."

Stimson was growing furious at the Swiss, who he felt were half-heartedly protesting the mistreatment of American POWs. Stimson complained that even when Swiss inspectors found grossly inadequate food, heat, and medical attention in German camps, they "lacked aggressiveness and persistence in pressing those issues." The Swiss replied they could only do so much. At many camps, the Germans were not intentionally withholding food and other necessities from the prisoners; they simply no longer had them to provide. The German people were starving and shivering too, the Swiss said, "and it is, of course, very difficult for us to demand from the German authorities things for the prisoners of war which the people themselves do not have."

Word of the forced marches also reached U.S. senator Thomas Connally of Texas, who had helped Jaworski become an army prosecutor. Connally wrote a letter to Stimson urging him to warn Allied pilots not to bomb marching columns of prisoners by mistake. Connally also suggested that General Eisenhower issue a warning that any German officer responsible for mistreating "our boys . . . will be hung or shot as any criminal." Connally wrote that threats were "the only language the Germans understand": "They think our Government consists of a lot of 'softies' and really make fun of the generous treatment accorded their men in American prison camps. Some of the American prisoners of war in Germany have been and will no doubt continue to be tried on trumped-up charges of minor natures and will likely be punished or executed unless our Government takes a firm stand and threatens them with retaliation." Connally hardly needed to add, "The whole thing makes my blood boil."

Not all the American POWs were on the move in February. The Red Army was still too far from Stalag Luft I in Barth to rescue the P-51 Mustang pilot Col. Henry Spicer, and American troops were still too far from Mauthausen in Austria to free OSS agent Louis Biagioni. Biagioni had been moved from his stone-cutting job near the crematorium to a job in the camp garage. He was surprised to learn from a Czech doctor at Mauthausen "that the execution of my sentence was postponed for a possible exchange of a German POW." The doctor, Stransky Milos, secretly burned all of the camp's documents relating to Biagioni, hoping the Germans would lose track of who he was. Milos also burned the documents of another American prisoner at Mauthausen, U.S. Navy Lt. Jack Taylor.

Colditz Castle also remained far enough from the battlefront that the Germans saw no need to evacuate its prisoners, including "King Kong" Schaefer. Months of solitary confinement were taking a toll on Schaefer, wrote Swiss inspector Rudolf Denzler, who visited Schaefer in his isolation cell. "His nerves were not up to it. He lost his hair and teeth." On February 2, another Swiss inspector found Schaefer "in a fair physical condition" but suffering from "the enormous anxiety of uncertainty." The inspector told Schaefer his death sentence was the result of the Germans "trying to get even for their POWs being sentenced to death in the United States." The inspector had heard rumors of a plan to exchange condemned POWs, but he "took the whole thing with a grain of salt" and suggested Schaefer do the same.

Though Colditz Castle was still beyond the reach of Allied troops, nowhere in Germany was beyond the reach of Allied bombers. On the night of February 13, Schaefer witnessed the devastating firebombing of Dresden, only thirty miles from Colditz. Dresden, on the Elbe River, was Germany's seventh-largest city and the capital of the German state of Saxony. Dresden was so lovely that some called it "Florence on the Elbe." The city had been spared from serious bombing, and its residents joked that Winston Churchill had an aunt living there. Now, near the war's end, Dresden was overflowing with three hundred thousand refugees from the battle zones farther east. The Allies decided to bomb it because Stalin asked them to disrupt German troop movements in the area.

The drone of the first wave of bombers filled the night just after 10 p.m. on the thirteenth. Over the next few hours, eight hundred British bombers dropped 1,700 tons of explosives and incendiary bombs on the city. Flames whipped by high winds created a firestorm that uprooted trees and incinerated parts of Dresden. Historian Donald Miller described the scene on the ground: "People's shoes melted into the hot asphalt of the street, and the fire moved so swiftly that many were reduced to atoms before they had time to remove their shoes. The fire melted iron and steel, turned stone into powder and caused trees to explode from the heat of their own resin. People running from the fire could feel its heat through their backs, burning their lungs." U.S. Army Pvt. Kurt Vonnegut Jr. was a POW in Dresden and survived because he was held in an underground meat locker. "Dresden was one big flame," Vonnegut wrote in his antiwar novel *Slaughterhouse Five*. "The one flame ate everything organic, everything that could burn."

Schaefer had been moved from his tiny solitary cell into a larger one with a window where, "except that I was awaiting execution, life was much more comfortable." He watched the bombers strike Dresden: "*Schloss* Colditz was bathed in the reflected light of the explosions and fires at Dresden. By standing at the lefthand wall of my cell as I faced the window and looking diagonally out of the window, I was able to see Dresden. In the light given off by the explosions and the fires I was able to see many buildings fall."

Schaefer thought he saw a British bomber shot down, but Dresden was virtually defenseless. Its antiaircraft guns had been moved east. No guards came to Schaefer's cell that night, but he could tell that the Germans in the castle were badly shaken. Many of them lived in Dresden or had family there. "From the noise of people running back and forth and from the tremendous shouting outside my cell, I deduced that there was tumult in *Schloss* Colditz," Schaefer wrote. "Many Germans may have thought they were seeing Pandemonium, the Capital of Hell, at nearby Dresden."* After daybreak, American bombers dropped another 1,200 bombs. The unsentimental British air chief marshal Arthur "Bomber" Harris was asked to assess the

---

* The well-read Schaefer was quoting the seventeenth-century English poet John Milton, who in his epic poem *Paradise Lost* envisioned Pandemonium as the Capital of Hell, created by the fallen angels, ruled by Satan, and swarming with demons.

damage to Dresden. He replied, "Dresden? There is no such place as Dresden."

Late on the morning after the bombing, the guards came to fetch Schaefer for his daily walk along the castle's parapets. It was the only exercise he was allowed. Schaefer was puzzled to see small strips of tinfoil everywhere. The guards explained that the British had dropped clusters of tinfoil before the bombing to confuse the German radar, which could not distinguish the falling tinfoil from aircraft. That reminded Schaefer of a lesson at West Point: every technological advance in wartime leads to a responding advance by the enemy. "Whatever man can invent, man can circumvent." Germany, however, was running out of chances for circumventing.

The firebombing of Dresden upended life at Colditz Castle. "German morale thereafter simply did not exist," Schaefer wrote. His comparison of Dresden to Pandemonium was not far from the truth. The firebombing killed an estimated twenty-five thousand people. Schaefer and the other Allied prisoners viewed Dresden's destruction as a sign they soon would be free. They might have felt differently had they known of Nazi propaganda minister Joseph Goebbels's reaction. Goebbels suggested to Hitler that for every German civilian killed in Dresden, one Allied POW should be executed. Hitler was talked out of it by other advisers, who argued that such a glaring violation of the Geneva Convention would come back to haunt Germany.

A few days after the Dresden bombing, three German officers marched down the corridor to Schaefer's cell just before dawn. They bowed and the officer in the center told Schaefer to collect his belongings. Then they marched away. Schaefer feared he was about to be executed. "I made a bundle of my possessions," he wrote. "It was tiny. I wrote notes telling who I was, the date, and that I was being taken out for execution. I hid them in the cracks in the stone walls with the hope that someday they would be found by someone who would make a proper report." The Germans did not return. Instead, after a period of time, OSS agent Florimond Duke appeared at the door of Schaefer's cell, looking "a bit excited," Schaefer wrote. Duke opened the cell door with a key, looked in at Schaefer and yelled, "Come on, Colonel, get out of here before the old bastard changes his mind." Schaefer turned to pick up his bundle of belongings, but Duke yelled, "Come on! Fast! Never mind anything else. Just let's get out of here." On the way down the corridor, Duke explained that the German commandant—"the old bastard"—had very reluctantly agreed to let Schaefer move out of his solitary cell because that side of the castle was exposed to American artillery. Colditz Castle still looked like a formidable fortress and would be a natural target for any attacking force. Duke added pointedly that Schaefer must leave all future dealings with the commandant to others. Schaefer was just glad to be out of the cell. "Try to fathom the military mind," he told Duke. "They sentence me to death. Now they move me out of death row because I might be killed."

The German commandant of Colditz Castle feared the SS more than he feared the Americans. An SS unit with a band of Hitler Youth in tow had decided to make a stand in the town of Colditz, which lay practically in the castle's shadow. The SS barricaded the main streets and posted snipers in houses on the edge of town. The Hitler Youth began digging trenches just outside the castle walls. "Boys and girls of all ages could be seen at work with spades and pickaxes alongside their elders in uniform," a prisoner wrote. The commandant worried the SS would take over the castle and kill everyone inside, including him. The SS already had come and taken away the so-called *Prominente*, twenty-one prominent prisoners including Polish and French generals, British aristocrats, and British military officers, including a pilot who was a nephew of King George VI. The lone American among the *Prominente* was a B-17 bomber pilot, John Winant Jr., whose father, John G. Winant Sr., was the U.S. ambassador to Britain and a former governor of New Hampshire. The younger Winant had conversed with Schaefer through a pipe that ran through both men's isolation cells at Colditz, Schaefer wrote. "I set my head on the iron pipe with my jawbone and ear along its length and started talking loudly," and Winant did the same. Just before the SS came for the *Prominente,* Schaefer wrote, Winant told him through the pipe, "Colonel, they are taking me away somewhere. They are taking me away.

They came and told me so." Schaefer had promised to report it to Allied authorities if he could.

Just hours after Schaefer was freed from solitary confinement, the German commandant struck a deal with the prisoners to try to ensure their mutual survival. The German guards and Allied POWs would no longer be captor and captive, but partners. They would run the castle jointly. When the Americans inevitably arrived, the prisoners would try to ensure that their former captors were treated well. Until then, the Germans would maintain the facade that they still ran Colditz Castle, to try to prevent the SS from attacking it.

×   ×   ×

By mid-February, as the men in Colditz Castle held their breath, the War Department in Washington had left the Germans' POW exchange proposal unanswered for more than a month. Meanwhile, details of Schaefer's and Schmitz's court-martial reached American authorities from an officer in the latest group of sick and injured prisoners to be brought home by the *Gripsholm*. Lt. Col. Nathaniel R. Hoskott of the Eighty-Second Airborne Division had been held at Oflag 64 with Schaefer and Schmitz and knew all about the poster incident, the courts-martial, and Schaefer's transfer to Colditz Castle. He said Schaefer's and Schmitz's prosecutions were part of an ominous pattern: "It was the story around camp that the Germans were trying to get some American officers under the death sentence to use for trading purposes as to some Germans that we have under the death sentence." Some German guards told Hoskott that if no trade could be arranged, the Americans probably would be executed just before Germany surrendered.

The War and State Departments also received further details about the death sentences of Sergeant Snowden, Sergeant Nicosia, and Private Davis. The Swiss forwarded a three-page memo from Snowden's German defense attorney, a Dr. Lommatzsch from Dresden, who described himself as a "Lawyer, Notary and Tax Advisor." Lommatzsch recounted the court-martial and his futile efforts to spare Snowden from the death penalty. He had not disputed that Snowden had struck the guard. But he had questioned the seriousness of the offense, and whether Snowden had understood the guard's earlier gestures to finish eating. The court nonetheless had sentenced Snowden to die. Lommatzsch attached a memo describing a similar case in which a British POW had received only two and a half years in prison for striking a guard. Lommatzsch also attached a bill for his services. The new information about Nicosia and Davis similarly explained what they had been accused of doing, and the defense efforts on their behalf. The memo seemed to contain exactly the level of detail the Germans had demanded initially about the POW camp murder cases in the United States. The State Department formally appealed the verdicts, but it had grown clear that legal appeals were pointless. The cases against the Americans were not going to be thrown out on legal grounds. They were not really cases at all. They were a last-ditch attempt to save the lives of the fifteen Germans at Fort Leavenworth.

The condemned Germans had not given up. They knew enough about the war to know that Germany was losing, and enough about the law to know they were almost out of time. But they lodged a series of complaints about Leavenworth with visiting Swiss inspectors, who forwarded the complaints to U.S. authorities. One of the convicted Camp Tonkawa killers, Sgt. Berthold Seidel, claimed that doctors at the prison were refusing to treat him for severe cramps. The doctors insisted they could find nothing wrong with him. Seidel's codefendant at Tonkawa, Sgt. Walter Beyer, reported his mail was not being delivered promptly. The army promised to expedite it. Edgar Menschner, the convicted "ringleader" in the murder of Hans Geller at Camp Chaffee, Arkansas, demanded court documents in his case. He was told he would receive them after President Roosevelt reviewed his verdict and death sentence.

On February 8, the killers from Camp Aiken, South Carolina, Sgt. Erich Gauss and Pvt. Rudolf Straub, wrote a letter to President Roosevelt asking for executive clemency. The letter was nothing like James Schmitz's letter to Hitler. Gauss and Straub declared they were not Nazi leaders or Gestapo agents but only soldiers who had taken their oath of duty to heart. Gauss wrote that the killing of Horst Guenther "was not murder but was a manifestation of our defense of the honor of our fatherland." Gauss further insisted that only German courts had jurisdiction over German POWs. Gauss and Straub ended their letter by asking Roosevelt to "help us forget our frightful experiences and return us to the peaceful ways of private citizens." Roosevelt did not reply, but the letter prompted Provost Marshal General Lerch to order notices posted in all POW camps to remind prisoners that they were subject to the laws of the United States.

The army also received complaints from the seven U-boat men from Papago Park, Arizona, who were still being held in isolation cells in nearby Camp Florence, Arizona. The Germans objected that they "were not permitted to talk with each other, to sing or to whistle." Soon afterward, the army put them on a train to Kansas City and then in a windowless bus to Fort Leavenworth. Their arrival united all fifteen of the condemned Germans in the basement wing of the "Castle." There they could just as readily be hanged or put on an eastbound train for a journey home.

22

Hostage Diplomacy

The plight of William Schaefer and James Schmitz was gaining attention in the U.S. Congress. On March 2, U.S. senator C. Wayland Brooks from the two men's home state of Illinois wrote to Secretary of State Stettinius. Brooks, an army veteran who had been wounded in World War I, held a seat on the Senate's powerful Appropriations Committee. Somehow he had learned that Schaefer and Schmitz had been condemned to die for "impeding the progress of the Reich." Brooks did not know any of the details. But he also had heard the Swiss were trying to broker an exchange of Schaefer and Schmitz for two condemned German POWs. Senator Brooks asked the secretary of state to "see that I am informed the minute any information is received from Switzerland concerning this case." Acting Secretary of State Joseph C. Grew wrote back to Brooks that U.S. authorities were appealing the sentences and felt confident neither man would be executed "in the near future." Grew promised to "bring all the pressure we can upon the German Government not to proceed with the executions." He did not mention the German exchange proposal. He did not want that dilemma to become public. He told the senator that the War Department considered the cases of Schaefer and Schmitz "highly confidential" and asked him not to disclose anything about them to anyone until the War Department "is willing to have the information published."

The same day, the Swiss floated the possibility of exchanging "King Kong" Schaefer and Jimmy Schmitz for a high-ranking SS officer, Lt. Col. Max Wünsche, who had been captured in Normandy and was being held by the British in Scotland. The Swiss said a German Foreign Office representative in Bern had told them informally that "highest German officials" were "very interested" in such a trade.

In Congress that day, Army Provost Marshal General Lerch gave a speech to a House committee about the German POW camps in the United States. He said dealing with the Nazi element in the camps "has not been easy. . . . It required painstaking intelligence work, screening and more screening to separate the good from the bad." But no murders had occurred in the camps since April 1944, Lerch said, and the killers in the earlier murders had been brought to justice, though "the sentences have not been officially announced." Lerch did not mention that the sentences had put the lives of American POWs in danger.

While Lerch was addressing Congress, a new message from the Germans arrived via the Swiss at the State Department. It was a new exchange offer for Schaefer and Schmitz. The Germans would trade them for Erich Gauss and Rudolf Straub, the two German POWs convicted of strangling Horst Guenther at Camp Aiken, South Carolina. This looked like an official offer, unlike the earlier inquiry involving the SS officer in Scotland. In making the offer, the Germans were suggesting an equivalency between two cold-blooded killers and two Americans who had briefly interrupted the posting of a placard on a bulletin board. The tactic of bringing excessive charges against foreign citizens to force their governments to release prisoners dates back centuries and is still in use today. The twenty-first-century term for it is *hostage diplomacy*.

In the same message, the Germans repeated their January offer to exchange five of the other Americans who had been sentenced to death at the end of December—the B-24 crewmen Edward Walsh,

John Walsh, and Marvin Martin; the Holland MIS-X operative Franklin Coslett; and the mysterious James Greyfield—for the five Germans convicted in the Camp Tonkawa killing. The Germans also provided more information about Greyfield. He was "an agent for an American news service" who had "secured employment in a political news office under a false name while outside Germany." He claimed to have graduated from West Point in 1938 and to have been promoted to captain in 1943. Greyfield had given the names of both his parents, as well as a home address in tiny Shawsheen Village, Massachusetts. But the War Department found no trace of his parents or of any such address in Shawsheen Village. Greyfield remained a cypher. The Swiss ended their message by saying they believed that "any proposal from the United States for the exchange suggested in this telegram would be entertained favorably by the German authorities." Why the Germans were supposedly so eager was impossible to guess. They seemed determined to bring their condemned prisoners home alive.

Later that day, the State Department asked the Swiss to expedite their inquiries into the status of Col. Henry Spicer and Capt. Wilbur McKee. McKee was a U.S. Army doctor who had accused a Gestapo agent of stealing canned food intended for sick and wounded prisoners. He was to have been court-martialed in the Polish city of Neustettin for "insulting a German officer in the performance of his duties," a potential death penalty charge. But the Russians had captured Neustettin before the scheduled trial, and U.S. authorities did not know where McKee was. In fact, the Germans had transferred McKee to Stalag Luft I in Barth, where Spicer was awaiting execution.

Two days later, on March 9, the U.S. government notified the Swiss that America had accepted the German offer to exchange condemned POWs. In fact, the United States was willing to expand the exchange to include all fifteen of the Germans on death row at Fort Leavenworth. The telegram did not indicate who had written it, but a notation at the bottom said the offer had been cleared all the way up through the War Department to Stimson, and Stimson may have notified the White House. The telegram said that although the

United States insisted the American prisoners' death sentences were unlawful,

> the Government of the United States . . . is nevertheless prepared to give consideration to exchanging for the American prisoners in German custody who are named below, a like number from among the German prisoners who are named below, as follows:

American Personnel

Biagioni, Louis	Schaefer, William H.
Coslett, Franklin Dent	Schmitz, James
Davis, Willard H.	Snowden, Thomas Jefferson
Greyfield, James Meloyne	
Martin, Marvin P.	Walsh, Edmund Joseph
Nicosia, Angelo J.	Walsh, John Joseph

German Personnel

Walter Beyer	Helmut Fischer
Berthold Seidel	Fritz Franke
Hans Demme	Guenther Kuelsen
Hans Schomer	Heinrich Ludwig
Willi Scholz	
Erich Gauss	Bernhard Reyak
Rudolf Straub	Otto Stengel
Edgar Menschner	Rolf Wizuy

The list included four men—Biagioni, Davis, Nicosia, and Snowden—whom the Germans had not yet offered to exchange. Greyfield was to be part of the trade, even though American authorities were not even sure he existed. The total of eleven Americans was still four short of the total of fifteen Germans. The United States offered the Germans two ways to balance the totals: choose eleven out of the fifteen condemned Germans to save; or add to the list four Americans who either had been sentenced to die or faced charges that could bring death sentences. Specifically, the telegram listed four additional American POWs who were rumored to have been sentenced to death—Col. Henry Spicer, Capt. Wilbur McKee, and two army lieutenants, John Rathbone and George L. Durgin. Rathbone and Durgin had been among the four POWs at Oflag 64 who had been acquitted after refusing to get off the sidewalk. U.S. authorities had received unconfirmed reports that the men had been retried for that offense and sentenced to death. In fact, Rathbone and Durgin had been evacuated from Oflag 64 along with Schmitz before they could be retried. They might have been retried in absentia, although the Germans had not reported it. The Germans still had not reported bringing any charges against Spicer.

In the same telegram on March 9, the United States offered to accept Spicer, McKee, Rathbone, and Durgin, "or any other members of the United States armed forces in German custody" facing death sentences, to raise the total number of Americans in the exchange to fifteen. The United States suggested a group exchange in Switzerland under the auspices of the Swiss government. It said both sides should agree not to execute any of the thirty men until April 5, in order to ensure there would be enough time to complete the negotiations. An internal note at the bottom of the telegram said the fifteen-for-fifteen exchange had been cleared with Stimson and with army colonel Maurice Bernays, who was gathering information for future war crimes trials.

The Provost Marshal General's Office took immediate steps to prevent mistakes that might wreck the exchange. It notified the commandant of Fort Leavenworth not to execute any of the five German POWs from Camp Tonkawa until at least April 5. It halted the process of requesting Roosevelt's final confirmation of the death sentences of the seven U-boat men from Camp Papago Park and the Camp Chaffee "ringleader" Edgar Menschner. It notified the Judge Advocate General's Office to report any pending charges against German POWs in the United States that might possibly result in death sentences, and not to pursue any more such cases without prior approval from the

War Department. The army also decided that before the exchange could take place, Roosevelt would have to rescind his approval of the seven death sentences from the Camp Tonkawa and Camp Aiken murders.

The rapid disintegration of Nazi Germany was disrupting the negotiations. The American offer of a fifteen-for-fifteen exchange did not reach the Germans immediately. Instead, on March 12, the Germans offered to exchange "the American journalist Biagioni" for the two Camp Aiken killers, Erich Gauss and Rudolf Straub. The Germans obviously considered Biagioni an especially valuable bargaining chip. If the United States did not want a two-for-one exchange, the Germans said, they were willing to trade both Schaefer and Schmitz for Gauss and Straub. The Germans added they could not provide court documents for some of the American POWs' cases because those courts had been "moved"—which in this case meant that the cities containing the courts had been evacuated. The Germans promised to send the documents "as soon as this is technically possible."

Meanwhile, Ambassador Harrison in Switzerland sent a series of ominous telegrams to the State Department. The first said the Swiss ambassador in Berlin was hearing "uncontrollable rumors" that the Nazis planned to "liquidate Allied POWs rather than let them fall into Allied hands." In a second telegram, Harrison paraphrased a report from "a well-known German diplomat who declares he was never a [Nazi] party member": "When bad reports which can no longer be withheld are given to Hitler he becomes [a] raging xenophobe and yells violent threats against all foreigners in his power whether workers, POWs or prominent individuals. . . . Well-informed Germans believe that should Hitler and high Nazi chiefs once determine [to] execute threats, foreigners would lose lives."

Harrison wrote that a Stockholm newspaper had reported that Heinrich Himmler, the head of the SS and architect of the Holocaust, was preparing a plan to murder all POWs, foreign workers, and concentration camp inmates once the Third Reich was "definitely defeated." Harrison wrote that such reports were impossible to confirm.

They might be gossip or "pure invention." Or they might be a German tactic to scare America and Britain into negotiating a peace favorable to Germany. Even as the Allies considered the war won, they increasingly feared for the safety of prisoners in Germany.

Days after the German prisoner exchange offer, on March 7, Allied tanks and infantry rumbled into Germany across the Rhine River on the Ludendorff Bridge at Remagen, which the Germans had tried but failed to blow up. The U.S. First Army began driving into Germany's industrial heartland from the west. The Russians bludgeoned their way toward Berlin from the east. Stalin tricked his American allies into believing he viewed Berlin as just another city that happened to be in the Soviets' path. In fact, Stalin considered Berlin a prize. He pitted his top generals against one another in a race to see which of them could reach it first, regardless of Red Army casualties. Thousands of German refugees streamed into Berlin, hoping for refuge but finding only severe shortages of food, water, and shelter. Berlin's population had swollen to more than three million, including 120,000 infants, but Hitler had made no plans to provide for them. He was in his underground bunker, raging at his advisers and ordering his hollowed-out armies to launch impossible counterattacks.

While most Americans cheered the approaching victory in Europe, the families of thousands of American POWs feared their loved ones would be murdered or simply allowed to die of neglect as the Third Reich collapsed. Relatives of POWs wrote personal letters to Roosevelt. Lucy M. Camps of New York pleaded with the president to find a way to bring her son Felix home from captivity:

> For three years now we have hoped and prayed and waited patiently with all the other American families for a quick victory to bring our loved ones back. At this time, however, I feel I cannot wait much longer. Grandmother is 84 years old, has had diabetes for 25 years, and is now steadily losing her sight. She weeps daily for "her lost son" and asks only that she see him one more time before she is totally blind.

A Brooklyn man wrote to Roosevelt: "Press reports state that Jewish prisoners of war in Germany are being segregated for some fiendish purpose. As the father of one of them I strongly urge you to tell the Mad Dog of Germany that you will take the lives of ten Nazi [POWs] for every one of our boys they may harm."

On March 14, Secretary of War Stimson and Secretary of State Stettinius jointly issued a warning that any German leaders overseeing an area in which Allied prisoners were abused "will be relentlessly pursued and brought to punishment." They added that it made no difference whether the abuses were committed by German soldiers, Nazi party activists, or civilian reserve units. The secretaries wrote that American, British, and Canadian armies had liberated twenty-seven POW camps but that seventy thousand American prisoners were still suffering in overcrowded camps behind German lines. The American Red Cross and other aid organizations rushed food and other supplies to the German border, but the collapse of the German transportation system made it difficult to get them to the prisoners. Stimson and Stettinius blamed the situation on "Germany's fanatical determination to continue in a hopeless war, with a resultant disintegration under disastrous military defeat."

No American POWs were in greater danger than those who had been sentenced to death. By March 25, two weeks had passed without a German response to the Americans' offer of a fifteen-for-fifteen exchange. The silence worried American authorities. Had the Germans rejected the offer? Had they even received it? Secretary of State Stettinius pressed the Swiss to make sure the latest American prisoner exchange proposal had gotten through:

Make every effort to see that the message is delivered to responsible German authorities before April 3 and to report when the message was delivered and to what German authority it was delivered. If it can be delivered to more than one German agency . . . the Department would appreciate if this was done. . . .

The Government of the United States would not wish to have the pending proposals fail of proper consideration by the two Governments involved.

The State Department added that the United States had extended its deadline for a German response from April 5 to May 1. Stettinius pledged to postpone any executions of the German POWs until then and asked the Germans to reciprocate. The negotiations were fraying. The American prisoners' best hope might be the advancing Allied armies.

× × ×

Lt. James Schmitz's new camp in Hammelburg, east of Frankfurt, fit Stimson and Stettinius's description of a wretched, overcrowded camp. The quarters were shabby and the rations meager. The camp's air-raid sirens wailed constantly, and the 1,500 POWs lived in fear of being bombed by their own planes. The prisoners included dozens of Serbs who had been held by the Germans since 1941. The Serbs gave Schmitz some of their clothes, which he donned to disguise himself as one of them. The Germans in fact had lost track of Schmitz toward the end of the long journey to Hammelburg, but they believed he was still in the camp. Guards kept asking other prisoners to point him out, but so far, no one had. When a Swiss inspector visited Hammelburg on March 25, Schmitz asked him discreetly to check on the status of his appeals of his death sentence to Hitler and the German High Command. Schmitz also asked the Swiss to send a welfare message to his mother, Kathryn, in Ottawa, Illinois, telling her he was "in excellent health and spirits." Schmitz added, "Request this welfare message not mention death sentence."

Two days after the Swiss visit, on March 27, Schmitz noticed a commotion in the camp. He was shocked to see American tanks just outside the main gate. The tanks were part of a task force sent by Gen. George S. Patton to liberate the Hammelburg camp, and specifically to liberate

Patton's son-in-law, U.S. Army Lt. Col. John K. Waters, who was being held there. A few days earlier, Patton had written to his wife, Bea, "We are headed right to John's place [of captivity] and may get there before he is moved. Hope to send an expedition . . . to get John." Hammelburg was nearly sixty miles behind the German lines. Patton originally had wanted to send a large force but decided a smaller one could race to Hammelburg, liberate the camp, and get back inside the Allied lines before the surprised Germans could react. The officers assigned to lead the "Hammelburg Raid" were not so sure. They did not know that Patton's son-in-law was in the camp and could not understand why they were being sent on such a risky mission. But they followed orders and set out for Hammelburg at the head of a column of three hundred men, sixteen tanks, twenty-seven half-tracks, three assault guns, and seven jeeps. Patton wrote to Bea that he was "nervous as a cat" about the raid. He had good reason.

The task force came under heavy fire as it approached Hammelburg. Nevertheless, the German commandant decided to surrender the camp and sent Lieutenant Colonel Waters out through the main gate clutching an American flag and a white bedsheet. A young SS man, acting on his own, raised his pistol and shot Waters just below the hip. With the truce shattered, American tanks crashed through the camp's perimeter fence. The prisoners cheered and crowded around their would-be rescuers. But reality quickly set in. Patton had not realized the camp held 1,500 prisoners; the task force could carry out fewer than 200. The task force commander, twenty-four-year-old Capt. Abraham Baum, "could have cried" when he saw how many prisoners he would have to leave behind. As dusk fell, Baum's men loaded up all the prisoners they could carry. Patton's son-in-law, Waters, was too badly injured to go. The task force did not rescue Schmitz either, possibly because he was hiding among the Serbs. Baum climbed up on a tank and told the prisoners who were being left at Hammelburg that they had two choices: wait in the camp for the Germans to return, or take your chances and flee into the countryside.

Schmitz chose to flee. He and two other Americans set out through the main gate and plunged into a forest. They had no food, no compass, and only a vague idea of where the Allied lines might be. The first night, they were chased with dogs by the Volkssturm, the local home guards. The next day Schmitz happened upon a U.S. Army reconnaissance team. "I thought my worries were over," he wrote, "but my freedom didn't last long." The Germans ambushed the recon team, and Schmitz suffered a minor head wound in the ensuing firefight. He was captured again and taken back to Hammelburg. He would have fared no better if he had been "rescued" by Patton's task force. The task force was wiped out by stronger German units before it could return to Allied lines. Twenty-five of its three hundred men were killed and thirty-two were injured, including its leader, Captain Baum, who threw his dog tags into the woods to prevent the Germans from discovering he was Jewish. All but a few of the other task force members were captured. Most of the POWs who had ridden out of Hammelburg with the task force gave up before the firefight was over and trudged back to the camp. They got back there before Schmitz did.

Afterward, Patton, under scrutiny, falsely claimed he had not known his daughter's husband was being held in the camp. He insisted his only mistake had been sending too small of a force. General Eisenhower called the Hammelburg raid "Patton's latest crackpot actions." But at this stage of World War II, the hard-charging Patton was too valuable to hold accountable for it.

Back at Hammelburg, Schmitz resumed his pose as a Serb. A Serbian doctor who knew his real identity tried to protect him by destroying all his records, including those of his death sentence, just as a Czech doctor had done for Louis Biagioni at Mauthausen. The Serbian doctor also admitted Schmitz to the camp infirmary, where the Germans seemed less likely to find him. His best hope now was to lie low as the war staggered to its end.

23

"Unfavorably Terminated"

B y the first week of April, the Germans still had not responded to the U.S. proposal to exchange the fifteen Germans at Fort Leavenworth for fifteen Americans. Nazi Germany was collapsing. Russian artillery had reduced the city of Königsberg in East Prussia to rubble. A Soviet assault on Berlin seemed imminent. American troops fought their way to the Elbe River to join with Soviet troops and cut Germany in two. Berlin lost contact with many of the POW camps around the country.

A Swiss POW camp inspector in Germany, Gabriel Naville, reported he could no longer effectively perform his job. He visited as many camps as he could and found all of them overcrowded and lacking in basic necessities for the prisoners. But complaining to the Germans at any level was pointless because they had no resources with which to solve the problems. Naville could not even report to his own superiors in a timely way, because the German telephone network had failed and overworked telegraph operators refused to transmit long messages. Naville understood U.S. authorities' fears for the condemned Americans and promised to do all he could to obtain information about them. But his message was not reassuring.

On April 6, the Forty-Seventh Tank Battalion of Patton's Third

Army liberated James Schmitz from the Hammelburg POW camp, this time for good. The return of the tanks came too late for most of the American officers in the camp, who by then had been marched from Hammelburg to a camp near Nuremberg.* Their departure had left only about sixty prisoners at Hammelburg, including injured men and groups of Poles, Yugoslavs, and Serbs. Schmitz was still hiding among the Serbs. He revealed his true identity to Patton's troops. After eighteen months of captivity and a death sentence, Schmitz was free. He wrote a letter to his mother, Kathryn:

> I have waited a long time to write what I can joyously reveal in this letter—now I find it hard to express my deep feeling of gratitude to the doughboys of the American army who have liberated me from the Germans.
>
> As of 2 p.m. April 6 I was liberated from German hands and I crossed the German border today. Eating good American food once again, and getting a few days' rest here, makes me feel great. I am very happy and have much to talk to you about and tell you as soon as I can see you.
>
> Love, Jimmy

Schmitz still did not tell his mother that the Germans had condemned him to die; he would save that detail for when he got home, if then. His hometown newspaper the *Ottawa Republican-Times* reported that Kathryn Schmitz had received her son's letter while doing volunteer work at the La Salle County Courthouse and "was almost hysterical with joy when she learned of his release." The same day, one of Kathryn's neighbors in Ottawa received a letter from *her* son, a doctor at a U.S. Army hospital in Germany where Schmitz was taken. The doctor wrote:

---

* Those officers reached Nuremberg to find its POW camp had no room. Then they were marched to a camp in Moosburg, Germany, which had no room either. Their guards kept marching them day and night until an American armored force overtook them.

When I walked into my ward tonight, who should I see but
Jimmy Schmitz, sitting there bright as day. He has finished his
nightmare as a prisoner of war and is [at the hospital] for a
few days.

He is well and we are feeding him and I don't think I have
ever seen a happier boy. Had a long talk with him and he
would just sit there and say, "Doc, it seems just like make-
believe. I can't believe it even yet." He ate a peanut butter
sandwich and said it seemed just like cake to him. He feels that
he is a very lucky boy.

On the same day Schmitz was freed, two of the American POWs
who had been sentenced to death for striking guards, Sgt. Thomas
Jefferson Snowden and Pvt. Willard Davis, were liberated after a long,
forced march from overcrowded Stalag II B camp in Hammerstein,
Germany. The German Foreign Office announced that the retreating
German forces would leave all POWs in the camps behind if they
agreed not to take up arms and rejoin the fight. Secretary of State Stettinius favored the German proposal but was not sure the French
would. He told the U.S. ambassador in Paris to make it clear that the
United States was going to accept no matter what France said.

As Allied troops drove deeper into Germany, the exchange negotiations fell into confusion. On April 10, the Germans sent a telegram to
the Swiss denying they had executed any of the condemned American
POWs. Two days later, the Germans sent an urgent cable accepting
the Americans' month-old offer of a fifteen-for-fifteen exchange of
condemned prisoners. The State Department responded immediately.
It reiterated that Germany still had named only eleven American
POWs who had been sentenced to death. It said two of those eleven
already had been liberated. It did not specify whether it meant
Schmitz, Snowden, Davis, or others. The State Department again
asked the Germans whether more than eleven American POWs had
been condemned to die, and if so, who. U.S. authorities still had received no word from the Germans about Col. Henry Spicer, Capt.
Wilbur McKee, Lt. George Durgin, or Lt. John Rathbone.

Despite the confusion, the State Department tried to move the exchange forward. It proposed that as soon as the two sides agreed on which prisoners to exchange, the U.S. government would transport the fifteen German POWs "as expeditiously as possible to a convenient point on the Swiss-French frontier." The fifteen condemned Americans would be assembled at a different location, on the border of Switzerland and Germany. Then the Swiss would coordinate a simultaneous exchange.

The prospects of completing such an exchange seemed increasingly dim. The State Department may even have been stalling, trying to keep the condemned Americans alive until Allied armies could reach them. The wonder was that the Germans were still negotiating at all. With the Third Reich disintegrating and Berlin under siege, someone in the German High Command was still trying to save the lives of fifteen German POWs five thousand miles away in Kansas.

On April 12, President Roosevelt collapsed and died of a cerebral hemorrhage at the age of sixty-three at his favorite retreat in Warm Springs, Georgia. Goebbels gave Hitler the news in a phone call to his bunker. "My Fuhrer, I congratulate you!" Goebbels exulted. "Roosevelt is dead. It is written in the stars that this will be the turning point for us." But the fifty-six-year-old Hitler would outlive Roosevelt by only eighteen days. Roosevelt's vice president, Harry S. Truman, was sworn in to face a thousand difficult decisions, among them the fates of the Germans at Leavenworth.

Two days after Roosevelt's death, Canadian troops liberated de Kruisberg prison in Holland and freed Lt. Franklin Coslett, the bombardier-turned MIS-X operative who had been sentenced to death twice for helping the Dutch Resistance. Coslett had spent 110 straight days in solitary confinement. He sent a cablegram telling his fiancée, Margaret Smith, and his parents in Wilkes-Barre, Pennsylvania, that he was free. Like Schmitz, Coslett did not mention that he had been sentenced to death. Rather than go home immediately to Wilkes-Barre, Coslett stayed in Holland and resumed helping Allied aviators who had been shot down behind German lines.

At Colditz Castle, "King Kong" Schaefer, his fellow prisoners, and their new German "partners" braced for attacks from both sides. The U.S. First Army was close enough that the men in the castle could hear its guns. Below them, the SS Unit and the Hitler Youth were dug into their positions in the town of Colditz. "Artillery has been plainly heard since 1:30," a British prisoner wrote on April 14. "The camp was in a furor of excitement and every inch of window space was crowded with leaning, crushing bodies." That night, he wrote, "we have a red hot rumor of a large tank concentration four miles west of Colditz."

The battle for Colditz began on the morning of April 15. Six American tanks appeared on a hillside above the town and exchanged fire with Germans in machine-gun nests. German 88mm artillery hurled shells at the tanks from the edge of a forest near the castle. An American artillery round slammed into the castle's main guard house—near Schaefer's old isolation cell. A second American shell crashed into the third-floor cell of a British airman. The airman was outside in the castle's interior courtyard, where the prisoners arranged blankets and mattress covers to spell out "POW" in large letters. They hoped the message would protect them from being mistakenly attacked by the American P-47 Thunderbolt fighters that roared over the castle on their way to strike German positions in the town.

The U.S. Army troops bearing down on Colditz Castle had endured hard fighting in recent weeks and lost dozens of men killed and wounded. Near Colditz, they had liberated a Nazi forced-labor camp where emaciated bodies lay next to an incinerator. They had been told there was also a POW camp in the area, but they did not guess it was in the old castle on the bluff. American infantry attacked the town of Colditz and fought house-to-house with the SS men and the Hitler Youth. The Americans retreated just across the river as night fell, but gave every indication they would renew the attack. Overnight, the Germans withdrew. Now the prisoners in the castle feared only friendly fire. The next morning, April 16, they raised American and British flags.

When the first U.S. soldiers of the Third Battalion, 273rd Infantry, Sixty-Ninth Infantry Division reached the castle's main gate, American and British officers strode out to meet them, holding American and British flags. The infantrymen were cautious at first, wary of a trap. Then they realized they had found the POW camp. The first few GIs to pass through the main gate were greeted like conquering heroes. Schaefer joined the celebration. After one year, eight months, and sixteen days as a captive, he was free. One officer described Schaefer as "shaking uncontrollably, tears streaming down his face."

Later, Schaefer was told that some newly arrived American officers wanted to see him. He ascended to a large room in one of the castle's upper floors where about twenty American officers stood at attention around a long, polished hardwood table. "Each of them had a full bottle in front of him," Schaefer wrote. "To my left at the fireplace was a woman. She was the first I had seen at close range for a long time. She seemed very beautiful to me." She was Lee Carson, a fearless war correspondent for International News Service. She wrote the first accounts of the liberation of Colditz Castle and its 1,365 prisoners. One of the American officers at the table had been Schaefer's adjutant in Panama before the war. He persuaded Schaefer to drink a Grand Marnier. "In my weakened condition with my weight about one hundred pounds I took too much," Schaefer wrote, "but it was good." He was given "a full meal of American rations." As he finished it, a photographer from the Army Signal Corps took his photo. On his way back to his cell, Schaefer passed a line of German guards, who were now prisoners. Some of them greeted him, he wrote. "I think they were genuinely glad I had not been executed."

Schaefer was flown to a hospital in England and then taken by train to London, where he was lodged at a fine hotel and given spending money. A man dressed as an American lieutenant colonel approached him and told Schaefer he was on leave and had nowhere to sleep. He asked to share Schaefer's room. Schaefer agreed to leave it unlocked. When he returned to the room, his money and watch were gone. A police officer who took his report "told me I was a sap and that there was little hope of getting back either my money or my watch." Schaefer knew the officer was right on both counts. The hotel management took pity on Schaefer and gave him his room and meals for free.

Word of Schaefer's liberation took days to reach Washington. In the meantime, on April 20, the U.S. Embassy in London sent a telegram to the State Department with an unconfirmed report that Schaefer had disappeared from a waiting room at a train station between Colditz and another camp. The sender of the telegram was the U.S. ambassador to London, John Winant Sr., whose son, John Jr., was the member of the *Prominente* who had spoken with Schaefer through the pipe. The twenty-one *Prominente* had been taken from Colditz to Tittmoning Castle, a thirteenth-century redoubt in the Bavarian Alpine region where the Nazis were falsely believed to be planning a last stand. In his final days, Hitler ordered an SS officer to travel to Tittmoning Castle and kill all the *Prominente*. The officer wrote of Hitler: "His hand was shaking, his leg was shaking and his head was shaking; and all that he kept saying was, 'Shoot them all! Shoot them all!'" But the execution order, like most of the orders coming from Berlin in those last days, was never carried out. Nazi Germany was collapsing too fast.

On April 27, an alarming dispatch from the German High Command reached the State Department. It had been sent by the Germans nearly a month before. Why it had taken so long to arrive was a mystery. The communiqué listed sixteen additional American POWs—not including any of the fifteen already on the list—who had been charged with death penalty offenses ranging from espionage to "plundering" to assaulting guards. The German dispatch suggested that the defendants already had been tried but that "the results are not available." The Germans assured U.S. authorities that none of the sixteen men on the new list would be executed while negotiations for an exchange were pending. But the Germans' assurance was now a month old. Were negotiations still pending? Were all the Americans on this list still alive? The late-arriving German message raised the unsettling question of what other messages from Berlin might have been delayed or lost in the growing chaos.

The next day, the Swiss told the State Department they were not sure if the prior offer by the United States of a fifteen-for-fifteen exchange on the Swiss border had ever reached the German negotiators.

German diplomats in Switzerland could no longer contact "responsible authorities" in Berlin because of an "interruption" in the German communications system. Two days later, the German diplomats acknowledged they no longer knew the whereabouts of the American prisoners listed for the exchange. The Swiss speculated that some of the Americans had been taken deeper into southern Germany. They promised to try to find them but suggested it would be very difficult "under the circumstances."

U.S. authorities did not know enough about what was happening in Germany to assess what the breakdown of negotiations foretold for the condemned Americans. It was possible they were out of danger. But it also was possible that their captors would give up waiting for orders and just execute them. American and Swiss diplomats debated whether to try to resend the latest exchange offer. Ambassador Harrison decided against it. At this uncertain point, he wrote, pursuing it might only jeopardize the lives of the American POWs by drawing attention to the fact that negotiations had been "unfavorably terminated." Harrison suggested U.S. authorities avoid saying or doing anything and hope the Germans still felt bound by their promise to delay the executions.

Later that night of April 30, Hitler shot himself to death in his underground bunker. About 130 miles north in Barth, the Germans abandoned Stalag Luft I, where Col. Henry Spicer and Capt. Wilbur McKee were held. The Red Army was closing in. The Germans tried to force the three hundred remaining POWs in the camp to evacuate with them, but the prisoners refused, and the Germans left without harming them. Spicer was still in his isolation cell across the camp from the barracks. A friend and fellow prisoner, Luther Richmond, found the key to the cell, flung open the door, and told Spicer he was free. Spicer had been asleep. He rolled over, looked at his watch, and said, "I'll tell you what, Richie, this is my six-month anniversary in here. Just leave the door unlocked and I'll see you in the morning." Spicer went back to sleep. When Spicer emerged from his cell the next morning, the men gathered around him. He told them, "Seeing and hearing you made solitary confinement worth it."

The Americans, now in charge of Stalag Luft I, moved into the guards' quarters, which were larger and had real mattresses instead of sacks of straw. They sent scouts into the surrounding countryside to make contact with the approaching Russians. The scouts brought back a small Red Army unit, and the senior American officers greeted the Russians at the main gate. Spicer wrote that a Russian "Cossack" galloped through the gate on horseback and declared he was liberating the prisoners. The Americans told him the Germans already had freed them. He ignored them and boasted that he was freeing prisoners all over Germany. He ordered some of the camp's fences torn down, and they were. For the next few days, the Americans and Russians celebrated. The Russians slaughtered cattle and set up barbecues throughout the camp. Spicer and his fellow aviator Mozart Kaufman got drunk with the Russians. "I don't remember where the liquor came from," Kaufman wrote, "but we had a ball. It was hard to believe that a bunch of Americans who spoke no Russian and a group of Russians who spoke no English could have such a great time." One Russian signed Kaufman's ledger, "To the comrades in arms in a joint struggle against fascists." Spicer wrote that the Russians "all loved the Americans. They would see one, yell, '*Americanski,*' grab him and kiss him." Spicer called the cheap Russian vodka "not bad. There comes a time when anything tastes good."

The "Cossack" also liberated a forced-labor camp near Stalag Luft I. Most of the captives had been marched west toward an unknown fate. Only three hundred emaciated survivors remained, most of them European Jews. Kaufman wrote that the survivors wandered "zombie-like" through the streets of Barth, bowing to passing Allied soldiers "in humble subservience," seemingly unable to comprehend that they were free. Kaufman wrote that the Russians ransacked the town, and when an American ex-POW complained his shoes were worn out, a Russian soldier shot a German civilian to death and gifted his shoes to the shocked American.

As the days passed, Spicer and Kaufman grew impatient with their new Russian comrades, who treated them with respect but seemed in no hurry to help them get out of there. Kaufman wrote that the Russians "continued to drink toasts to the destruction of Germany and to the great friendship among the Russians, the Americans and the British, but their toasts and bravado did not ring true. They seemed to say one thing and do another." Finally, after two weeks, Stalin agreed to allow American B-17 bombers to land at an airfield near Barth to pick up the liberated prisoners. As the ex-POWs were boarding, Kaufman wrote, "some of the guys kissed the planes and said, 'This is American. This is home.'" The prisoners were flown to a large Allied transit camp near Le Havre, France. News of Spicer's deliverance from a death sentence made headlines across the United States. War correspondents in France asked him about his fateful speech—the "prisoner pep talk" that had enraged his captors and earned him a death sentence. "I guess some of the things I said made the Germans sore," Spicer told one reporter. "But all I really did was to explain to the men that things would be pretty bad and I wanted them to keep up their fine morale." Spicer was asked how he had managed to smoke his pipe for more than a year as a prisoner with no reliable source of tobacco. He said, "You don't know what all will burn in a pipe."

×　　×　　×

The same day Spicer was freed, Red Army troops liberated Stalag Luft III in Sagan, Poland—the site of the 1943 "Great Escape"—and freed the condemned B-24 crewmen John Walsh, Edward Walsh, and Marvin Martin.

Four days later, on May 5, an eight-man patrol from Patton's Third Army happened onto Mauthausen and freed OSS agent Louis Biagioni and his fellow prisoners. The SS had fled Mauthausen and left it in the hands of German police. An American soldier handed Biagioni a pistol and invited him to shoot the SS men's dogs, which had been left in a kennel and were unmanageable without their masters. Biagioni shot them all. Some of the liberated prisoners uprooted fence posts and used them to club to death their former "kapos"— fellow prisoners who had helped the Germans subjugate them. American officers soon established order and stopped the killing. Biagioni appeared on a newsreel grinning broadly and saying, "God bless America." But his time at Mauthausen was not over. The OSS put him to work taking photos to document the Germans' crimes at the camp, which were worse than he had realized. His photographs included the piles of emaciated bodies in shallow trenches near the crematorium. After completing his work at Mauthausen, Biagioni accompanied Patton's troops into the Po Valley and the northern Apennines before Germany surrendered on May 8.

×   ×   ×

Schaefer happened to arrive in New York City on a plane late on the day of the German surrender. He found the streets of Manhattan littered with ticker tape. That night, more than 250,000 revelers filled Times Square, including thousands of men and women in uniform. Schaefer was too broke and exhausted to join the party. At POW camps all across the United States, the army announced the surrender to German prisoners over the loudspeakers: "The organized resistance of the German armed forces has ceased. The National Socialist Movement of Germany no longer exists. The Allied occupying authorities exercise all power in Germany. Members of the German armed forces are released from any obligation entered into with a government which no longer exists."

Many of the prisoners expressed relief. Some of the hardcore Nazis refused to believe Germany had surrendered. The army compelled all POWs to watch grisly newsreel footage of the newly liberated German death camps. Many German prisoners insisted they had known nothing of such horrors, or refused to believe they had occurred—despite the fact that many incidents of violence against Jews had taken place in Germany before the war.

The army announced it would stop shipping German POWs to America. The last group of three thousand sailed into New York on May 13. A *New York Times* reporter described them as "bedraggled and grimy." They included a thirteen-year-old boy and a grizzled sixty-five-year-old veteran of the First World War. The prisoners seemed to harbor few illusions. Unlike earlier arriving POWs, they had not expected Manhattan to be wrecked by German bombs. "We knew our air force was too cracked up to do anything like bomb New York," one prisoner said. Another German asked his captors if they could help him stay in the United States. He would be among thousands of German prisoners to make that plea.

The 371,000 German POWs in the United States were told they would have to stay in the camps for the foreseeable future and keep working. They would not be sent home immediately because the United States was shifting most of its resources to the ongoing war against Japan. But the Army Provost Marshal General's Office was determined to act quickly on one piece of unfinished business with the German POWs: hanging the fifteen condemned killers at Fort Leavenworth.

24

The Elevator Shaft

Secretary of War Stimson could hardly wait to fire the Swiss as the Protecting Power for German and American POWs. On the day Germany surrendered, Stimson wrote to Secretary of State Stettinius complaining that the Swiss had failed to protect American POWs in Europe and had criticized the German POWs' death sentences in the United States as too severe. Stimson did not want to press the Swiss to change. He suggested to Stettinius that America just dismiss Switzerland as Protecting Power with Germany, since the German government no longer existed. A day later, the United States discharged Switzerland as its Protecting Power in Europe but retained the Swiss as Protecting Power in the Pacific. Stimson asked Stettinius to help him keep a close eye on the Swiss efforts with the Japanese.

Provost Marshal General Lerch wanted to get on with hanging the fifteen Germans at Fort Leavenworth as soon as possible. The end of the war had not changed his perspective on the murders in the camps. But before he started executing the Germans, he wanted to make sure that all fifteen of the condemned American POWs were safely back in Allied hands. That was no small task in the chaos following Germany's surrender. In a memo on June 12, Lerch wrote that ten of the fifteen Americans on the exchange list had been confirmed as safe so far. Four others—Angelo Nicosia, Thomas Snowden, Wilbur McKee, and George Durgin—were still unaccounted for, as was the man the Germans called Lt. James Greyfield. Despite the confusion, Lerch concluded, there was no reason to think any of those men were still being held hostage by the Germans, and therefore no reason to delay the executions of the Germans any longer. Lerch recommended that the five Germans from Camp Tonkawa and the two from Camp Aiken, whose death sentences had been approved by Roosevelt, be executed as soon as July 15. He recommended that the final appeals of the other eight Germans, which had been halted during the exchange negotiations, be sent immediately to President Truman.

Maj. Stephen Farrand, who had been the War Department's chief liaison with the Swiss, had laid out the U.S. government's options for executing the Germans in a memo on May 16 to senior War Department leaders. Farrand wrote that America had the legal right under the Geneva Convention to hang the Germans. But did the United States have any moral obligation to commute the Germans' death sentences? Farrand noted that Germany had kept its side of the bargain by not executing any of the Americans, until its defeat ended the negotiations. "The moral aspect of the matter," Farrand wrote, "is one of policy for higher authority." Lerch was the higher authority, and he was unmoved.

On June 26, Col. Harrison A. Gerhardt, an aide in the War Department, notified his superiors that three of the five Americans on the list who had been unaccounted for—Nicosia, McKee, and Durgin—had been confirmed safe, liberated by Allied armies. Snowden officially remained missing, but the army merely appeared to have lost track of him. He had been liberated in April from a camp at Hammerstein, Germany. As for James Greyfield, Colonel Gerhardt wrote, the army had conducted a "persistent search in all U.S. records, enlisting the cooperation of the FBI and various local authorities. Search was also made of British records. No such officer has ever been identified."

Eleven days later, on July 3, Judge Advocate General Myron Cramer asked President Truman to conduct a final review of the Papago Park death sentences. Cramer forwarded the Army Review Board's report on the Papago Park case to the White House. In a memo to Truman's chief of staff, Cramer noted that army reviewers had recommended commuting all seven of the U-boat men's death sentences to life imprisonment. But Cramer and Stimson recommended Truman uphold the death sentences and allow the Germans to be hanged. Truman approved the death sentences of the U-boat men that same day.

But the Camp Chaffee murder case, in which Jaworski had prosecuted the "ringleader" of the fatal beating, gave Cramer pause. The Army Review Board had split on the case. Two of its three members agreed Sgt. Edgar Menschner had organized the gang of men who had killed fellow POW Hans Geller. But the board's third member had written a strong dissent, citing the circumstantial nature of the evidence. Cramer concluded that Menschner had organized the gang but that the evidence he intended to kill Geller was "tenuous and conjectural." The crime of organizing a gang to commit violence carried a maximum penalty of life in prison. Cramer recommended Truman commute Menschner's death sentence to twenty years at hard labor. On July 6, the president did so. Menschner received the news from an army lieutenant who appeared at the door of his basement cell on death row with two guards. The lieutenant told Menschner to gather his belongings to move to a more permanent cell upstairs in Leavenworth's "Castle." According to the author Richard Whittingham, the guards allowed Menschner to shake hands with each of his fourteen comrades on his way out. Whittingham's source appears to have been the late U.S. Army captain George Towle, a Catholic priest and chaplain at Fort Leavenworth who spent hours with the condemned Germans. Truman's decision to commute Menschner's sentence reduced the number of Germans on death row to fourteen.

Truman had to reissue his approval of the Papago Park and Camp Chaffee death sentences two weeks later when the army discovered that the documents it originally had provided to him had contained dated language about forwarding copies to the Swiss. Truman signed new documents with the old language deleted. The army told the commandant of Fort Leavenworth's Disciplinary Barracks, Col. William S. Eley, to execute the Germans as soon as he was ready.

Fort Leavenworth had no gallows; it had been conducting executions at the nearby Kansas State Penitentiary. So army engineers at Leavenworth quickly built a temporary gallows in an elevator shaft in an unused three-story salvage warehouse about 250 yards from the Castle. The elevator was secured on the third story of the shaft to keep it out of the way. The gallows occupied the second story, the ground level, and the basement. On the second story, a four-by-ten-inch wooden crossbeam was laid to secure a rope seven eighths of an inch in diameter. The rope dangled to a point head high above the ground level and ended in a noose. On the ground level, the army installed a wooden floor with a black border and a black circle painted in the center to mark the trapdoor on which the condemned men were to stand. They would be hanged one at a time. Once the noose was tightened and the trap sprung, each man would drop seven feet into the basement of the elevator shaft, with his feet suspended several feet above the basement floor. There was enough rope on the second level that after each hanging, the section with the noose could be cut off and a new length of rope could be lowered and fashioned into a noose.

The Germans were to be hanged in three groups, on three different days. The five convicted in the Camp Tonkawa killing would go first, followed by the two in the Camp Aiken killing and then finally the seven U-boat men from Camp Papago Park. The army gave Colonel Eley detailed instructions about how to conduct the hangings. The guard detail for each execution would consist of one technical sergeant, two sergeants, two corporals, and eight privates, all under the command of an officer designated by the fort's supervisor of prisoners. Twenty-four hours before the execution, the men to be hanged would have their hands cuffed behind their backs and would be taken from their cells into the adjoining corridor, where Colonel Eley would read their formal execution orders to them in English. A lieutenant at his side would translate the orders into German. While the condemned men stood in the corridor, guards would enter their cells and remove "all articles which could be readily used by a man to injure himself, such as neckties, belts and razors." The men would then be returned to their cells and freed from the handcuffs. Two guards would be posted outside their cells to keep them under constant observation. They would be fed at the normal times but "allowed only a spoon for eating purposes." They were asked to provide names and addresses of loved ones who could receive their personal effects. Willi Scholz, one of the condemned Germans from Camp Tonkawa, could think of no one.

The Germans would be allowed to die in their uniforms, which would be checked by the supervisor of prisoners "for cleanliness and neatness." When each man's time came, he would be taken from his cell with his arms bound behind his back. Flanked by guards and escorted by a clergyman of his choice, he would be led out of the Castle and placed in a vehicle for the short ride to the warehouse and the elevator shaft. The two sergeants in the guard detail would lead him to the painted black circle on the temporary floor. The army provided a map to show exactly where in the death chamber each person should stand. Eley would address the condemned man by name and ask if he wished to make a last statement. After giving him time to speak, Eley would tell him, "May God have mercy on your soul." The sergeant of the guard would place a black hood over the prisoner's head and adjust the noose around his neck while other soldiers bound his ankles. Then Eley would give a hand signal to push a brake-like handle that sprang the trapdoor. The surgeon of the prison hospital would check the hanged man and record the time of death. Immediately after the execution, Eley was to report all pertinent information to the Provost Marshal General's Office, including any last words by the condemned and any "unusual circumstances" of the hangings.

Despite the secrecy and careful preparations, the army feared the executions might cause other prisoners at Leavenworth to riot. As a precaution, all officers in the Prisoners' Department were ordered to remain on duty from an hour before each hanging until they were dismissed. A reserve force of twenty armed guards would wait just outside the fort's main gate until Eley dismissed them. The army initially wanted no publicity but reversed course at the last minute and invited reporters from *The Kansas City Star, The Leavenworth Times,* and a local TV station to witness the executions. The army may have concluded that there would be no public outcry in the United States about the hangings. New depths of Nazi depravity came to light every week in reports from liberated death camps such as Auschwitz, Buchenwald, and Bergen-Belsen. On July 5, *The New York Times* reported the discovery of a "murder factory" in Bavaria where "hundreds of men, women and children—all Germans—allegedly mentally defective or physically deformed, were killed by intramuscular injections or slow starvation." The story, from the Reuters news agency, said inmates at the facility had been used as "guinea pigs" in experiments aimed at purifying the Aryan race. Eighteen American soldiers who had accompanied doctors into the "murder factory" were reported to be "so outraged by what they saw that they volunteered to serve as an execution squad for those culpable." The same day, the *Times* reported that 239,533 American military personnel had been killed so far in World War II. (The final tally would be 407,316, plus 9,521 merchant mariners.)

On Sunday night, July 8, Colonel Eley marched down the corridor in Leavenworth's death row, flanked by guards, Father Towle, and a Protestant chaplain. The echoes of their footsteps preceded them down the long corridor. Eley called the five Camp Tonkawa killers from their cells, and the guards went in to conduct the searches. Eley and the translator read the execution orders. Eley told the Germans he would return for them just after midnight on July 10, in about twenty-eight hours. Richard Whittingham wrote that Eley allowed the chaplains to remain behind to help the Germans "salvage whatever peace of mind they could in the awful gloom of that block of cells."

A few hours after Eley's visit to Leavenworth's death row, and while the Camp Tonkawa Germans awaited their fate, a guard in a tower at a POW branch camp in Salina, Utah, threaded a cartridge belt into his .30-caliber machine gun and methodically emptied it into the tents where 250 Germans lay sleeping after a day's work in Salina's beet fields. The guard killed nine prisoners and wounded twenty others as the Germans ran screaming from the tents. Confronted by a superior, the guard asked for more ammunition. In fifteen seconds, he had killed more POWs than had all the Germans on death row. It was the single worst act of violence against German prisoners in America during the war.[*]

On July 9 in Leavenworth's death row, the five Germans convicted of murdering Johann Kunze at Camp Tonkawa ate a last meal of stew, steamed rice, creamed asparagus, coffee cake, bread with butter, and coffee. A few minutes before midnight, Colonel Eley returned as promised and led them one by one to the elevator shaft. They were taken in order of rank. First went Sgt. Walter Beyer, the thirty-two-year-old career soldier who had called the mass meeting to expose Kunze as a traitor. Like most of his comrades, Beyer wore his Afrika Korps uniform, with black pants, a khaki jacket with four "accordion-like" pockets, and a long-billed cloth cap, according to a detailed account of the execution by William H. Radford, a staff writer for *The Kansas City Star*.

The death chamber in the warehouse was brightly lit inside, but the windows were draped with heavy army blankets so that no light was visible from the exterior. In the elevator shaft, Radford wrote, "Beyer had stood stolidly four feet in front of [Colonel Eley]" as the latter read his death sentence. Beyer "appeared none too robust and his cheeks were drawn. A black stubble, matching his hair, indicated he had not shaved for at least twelve hours. His eyes were those of a trapped beast. They moved nervously from right to left. But he never moved his head or turned his chin from its jutting position." Asked if he had a statement to make, Beyer "blurted out something in German that the interpreter said was, 'I have no statement to make. I can't see why this should be done to me.' Then he mumbled something that the interpreter did not understand." Eley, following the army's script, told Beyer, "May God have mercy on your soul." One of the American sergeants pulled the hood over Beyer's head, and someone gave "a brittle command of 'Right face! Forward march!'" Beyer pivoted on

---

[*] The Utah massacre was not the only case of POWs being attacked. In 1944, someone fired a shotgun into a camp near West Helena, Arkansas. Two shots were fired into tents at Camp Ashby in Virginia Beach, Virginia. No one was hit in either of those incidents.

his right heel and marched the last thirty feet to the gallows, in step with the four U.S. soldiers flanking him on each side. "His bearing was military to the last," Radford wrote. The noose was fitted around Beyer's neck and the trap was sprung on Eley's command. It was seven minutes past midnight on July 10. Beyer was pronounced dead sixteen minutes later.

After Beyer's body was removed and a new noose was coiled at the end of the rope, Eley and the guards returned to death row for Sgt. Berthold Seidel. Seidel had punched Johann Kunze in the face several times at the start of the fatal beating. Seidel declined to make a final statement. As he was led to the gallows, Radford wrote, the Protestant chaplain, a Major Sagan, followed close behind him, chanting, "Lord, have mercy upon us, Christ, have mercy upon us, Lord, have mercy upon us." The chaplain stood in front of Seidel as the noose was being fitted around his neck and said the Lord's Prayer over and over until the trap was sprung.

Following Seidel was Hans Demme, the 108-pound sergeant who had tackled Kunze in the kitchen and sent dishes flying. Demme tried to appear brave, but he began breathing hard as his death sentence was read. He started to make a last statement, Radford wrote, but he got only as far as "A wrong is being done." Then "his voice broke, and he groped for words that did not come, and the black hood was fastened over his head."

Demme was followed by Hans Schomer, who had confessed to throwing two cups at Kunze during the melee in the mess hall. Schomer made no final statement. He was the only Catholic of the five, and Towle, the Catholic chaplain, recited the Prayer of the Dying and gave Schomer absolution. Towle crossed himself as the trap was sprung and Schomer dropped from sight into the basement of the elevator shaft. Towle then "hurried down to the basement, where Schomer's body was swinging in the noose." The chaplain cut open the black hood, splashed Holy Water on the dead man's face, and administered last rites.

The last of the five, Willi Scholz, "was extremely nervous and wavered in his last steps to the gallows," Radford reported. "However, he met death as had the others, without further word." He dropped to his death at 2:11 a.m.—a little over two hours after Eley had first appeared on death row. An army surgeon reported it took an average of sixteen minutes for the men's hearts to stop after they plunged through the trapdoor. The *Star* noted with a hint of triumph, "There were no defiant, 'Heil Hitlers' as they marched to their doom."

The Kansas City Star ran its story on the executions at the top of its front page, but newspapers farther from Leavenworth paid less attention. There was too much else happening. Fierce fighting continued in the Pacific, and conflict was growing with the Soviets over the control of postwar Europe. *The New York Times* reported the executions on page 12 with a story from the United Press newswire under the headline "Five Nazis Hanged by Army in Kansas." The story quoted the army as calling the hanged men "fanatical Nazis."

Since no one in Germany could possibly claim the bodies at that point, the army buried them, without military honors, in the Military Prison Cemetery, a half-acre graveyard sitting on a ridge about a mile northwest of the main part of the fort. The prison cemetery held only 240 graves, and no one had been buried there since 1929. It was reserved for prisoners who had died in confinement and thus, under U.S. military regulations, were not eligible to be buried among the honored dead.

Two nights after the Tonkawa executions, at 9:30 p.m. on July 12, U.S. Army Lt. Col. Nathan Cockrell visited death row to inform the two Camp Aiken killers, Erich Gauss and Rudolf Straub, that they would be executed in a little over twenty-seven hours—just after midnight on July 14. *The Kansas City Star* reported that Gauss, the thirty-two-year-old sergeant who had lured Horst Guenther to his tent and helped strangle him, bore the news stoically. Straub, a thirty-nine-year-old private who had looped a tent rope around Guenther's neck, "had to be assisted to a chair when he heard the execution order read." As with the Tonkawa killers, Straub and Gauss were taken one at a time under heavy guard to the elevator shaft. Straub went first. He blinked several times from the bright lights in the death chamber but "walked forward briskly with head erect, face expressionless," wearing his olive-drab Afrika Korps field jacket, tan trousers, boots, and a cloth cap with a Nazi insignia. His last words were "I stand here not guilty. What I did was done as a German soldier under orders. If I had not done so, I would have been punished when I returned to Germany." The trap was sprung at seven minutes past midnight; he was declared dead fifteen minutes later. Gauss followed him. He wore a uniform but no cap. Asked whether he had a final statement, he said he had a question. He was told he was not permitted to ask questions. He said, "I can say no more than that a great injustice is being done. I committed no murder. There is nothing else I can say." The army buried Gauss and Straub in the prison cemetery next to the five Tonkawa killers.

×　　×　　×

The executions of Gauss and Straub left only the seven U-boat men on Leavenworth's death row. They waited. Weeks passed. "Do you think they've forgotten us?" Otto Stengel half-jokingly asked Chaplain Towle, according to Richard Whittingham. But "they" were only temporarily distracted. While the world stood still for the condemned Germans, it was changing dramatically outside Leavenworth's stone walls. President Truman signed the seven Papago Park death warrants on July 28 from the Berlin suburb of Potsdam, where he was meeting with Stalin and Churchill to discuss who should control postwar Europe and especially Germany. Truman hoped to gain leverage over Stalin by revealing to him that America had successfully tested an atomic bomb on July 16. Unbeknownst to Truman, Stalin's spies already had told him America had the bomb. The Soviets were racing to build their own. One of Stalin's reasons for wanting to reach Berlin first was to seize a cache of enriched uranium the Nazis were hiding there.

With the Japanese defending every island to the death, Truman concluded that dropping the atomic bomb would save countless American lives by ending the war quickly. The first bomb hit Hiroshima on August 6, killing at least eighty thousand people. Three days later, the United States dropped a second bomb on Nagasaki, killing some thirty-five thousand people. (The hills around Nagasaki shielded thousands of Japanese from direct exposure to the blast, limiting the death toll.) Six days later, on August 14, Japan surrendered.

Nine days after the Japanese surrender, on the stifling hot Kansas night of August 23, Colonel Eley appeared on Fort Leavenworth's death row and told the seven U-boat men they would be executed soon after midnight on the following day, August 25. Helmut Fischer went first. He made no final statement but "moistened his lips and spoke in silent prayer," *The Kansas City Star* reported. The next two submariners, Fritz Franke and Guenther Kuelsen, faced their deaths silently and stoically. Kuelsen "was chewing gum and he easily joked with the others as he went from cell to cell saying goodbye," wrote Gene W. Dennis, a TV reporter and witness. "The last two men slapped [Kuelsen] gently on the back—and as he left the room, he turned his head back and smiled faintly. It was an apparent gesture that he was going to die like a man. He did!" Dennis took comfort in the grim process by imagining that the Germans had killed Americans before being captured. Dennis wondered how Nazi leaders such as Hermann Goering "will do beneath the black hood."

Heinrich Ludwig used his last words to thank the two chaplains for supporting him during the final weeks of his life. Bernhard Reyak laughed and shook hands with his two remaining cellmates, who soon would follow. Otto Stengel affected a jaunty manner at first. "Walking through the bright moonlight to the gallows, he glanced around the open prison yard and remarked—'nice flowers,'" Dennis wrote. But when Stengel stepped into the black circle, he grew serious. A Catholic, he used his last statement to thank Chaplain Towle for giving him a final Holy Communion. Stengel also thanked Colonel Eley, who he said "was very correct in handling us and we received excellent treatment while here." Eley had let Stengel walk to the gallows with a photo in his breast pocket of his wife and two children, including a three-year-old son he had never met.

Rolf Wizuy went last. He asked Eley if a fellow prisoner at Leavenworth—most likely Menschner, whose death sentence had been commuted—could be allowed to see his grave in order to be able to describe it to Wizuy's mother back in Germany. Eley did not reply because questions were forbidden. Wizuy said, in English, "I am glad that I had Father Towle beside me for my last few hours. Father Towle, I thank you." Richard Whittingham wrote that Wizuy thanked Towle again as he was falling through the trapdoor. None of the U-boat men used their last words to profess innocence. *The Kansas City Star* reported that they went to their deaths "without murmur of hatred for their executioners."

The Fort Leavenworth News, the army base newspaper, printed a short story on the hangings that focused on logistics. "The trap was sprung on the first man at 12:10 a.m. and the last man went to his death at 2:48 a.m." It had taken only two hours and forty-eight minutes to hang the seven men, and the *News* estimated that the apparatus in the elevator shaft had "saved more than an hour in the procedure." *The New York Times* ran a story on the hangings on page 15. The front page was dominated by stories about the tense start of the U.S. occupation of Japan. American warships were preparing to enter Tokyo Bay for the formal surrender ceremony, while in front of the Japanese Imperial Palace, Japanese citizens were said to be committing hara-kiri in disgrace. The executions in Kansas attracted little attention from the American public. Secretary of War Stimson was traveling in the Adirondacks of upstate New York at the time, enjoying a hard-earned vacation with his wife, Mabel. He resigned from his post, and government service, two weeks later, at the age of seventy-eight. He would live only five more years.

The hanging of the seven U-boat men was not the last mass execution in U.S. history or even U.S. military history. In 1955, the army hanged three Black U.S. soldiers for fatally beating and robbing a cab driver in Missouri. But the execution of the German prisoners marked a unique moment in American history just before the fever of World War II broke. Soon afterward, two of the five POW camp murder cases would be reopened. How they were pursued showed how the national mood had changed.

25

"Everything Comes Out
Under the Sun"

Leon Jaworski's vigorous prosecution of the POW murder cases and other cases in the United States had won him a choice assignment in Europe. He was to investigate Nazi war crimes, as part of a vast effort by the Allies to hold Nazi leaders legally accountable. The army had flown Jaworski to Paris in December 1944 carrying 132 pounds of documents alleging crimes by German soldiers and civilians. "Unfortunately," Jaworski later wrote, "there was a lot of material to work with," including "case histories that turned your stomach and made you want to weep." In early May, Jaworski had flown to London to view footage from newly liberated death camps. It was all he could do to sit through it. After Germany's surrender on May 8, he witnessed the start of the tumultuous celebration in London and then flew into Paris in time to stroll along the Champs-Élysées during the French celebration. But the joy of V-E Day offered Jaworski only a brief respite from the grim business he had gone to Europe to conduct.

In mid-July 1945—soon after five Camp Tonkawa killers were executed at Leavenworth—Jaworski prosecuted the first war crime case of World War II. The case was from the small German town of Rüsselsheim, which had long been under U.S. control, and where investigators could operate freely. The defendants were eleven civilians from

Rüsselsheim who had beaten six captured American bomber crewmen to death a year earlier. The Americans were being marched through Rüsselsheim by guards on their way to a POW camp. They had to travel through the town on foot because British bombers had struck Rüsselsheim the night before and damaged its rail line. As the Americans entered the town, people emerged from their homes jeering and cursing. A mob of fifteen to twenty men and women, egged on by an ardent Nazi and two housewives, attacked the airmen with fists, clubs, and stones. The Americans shouted that they had not been the ones who had bombed Rüsselsheim. They tried to fend off the blows; when one of them collapsed, others carried him. After seven blocks they all lay bleeding and motionless in the street. They were "tossed into a cart, trundled off to a nearby graveyard, and unceremoniously dumped into a common grave," Jaworski told the court.

The court was a U.S. military tribunal of six army officers led by a brigadier general. But this trial, unlike those of the German POWs, was open to the public, and the courtroom in the nearby city of Darmstadt was packed every day with German spectators. The choice of a large venue was purposeful. "We looked to the educational effect of these trials," Jaworski told a reporter in Germany. "I think the effect will be permanent and beneficial." One day, the members of the tribunal walked the seven blocks in Rüsselsheim where the victims had been attacked. The tribunal convicted ten of the eleven defendants of murder and acquitted the eleventh. Seven of the ten were sentenced to die, including the main Nazi agitator and the two housewives. The women's sentences were commuted later to forty years. Two other defendants were sentenced to twenty-five years in prison and one to fifteen years. Jaworski was amazed that most of the killers claimed to be devout Christians. He could not square it with his own worldview.

After the trial ended, two former POWs came forward with a startling epilogue to the Rüsselsheim story. They had been part of the air crew that was attacked in the street. They had been piled into the cart while still alive and taken to the cemetery. One of them had been unconscious and the other, covered with his own blood, had played dead. While the Germans were preparing to dump them all into a mass grave, an air-raid siren had sounded. The gravediggers fled for cover. The two Americans struggled out from among their dead friends and hid in the cemetery's chapel while the burial was completed. No one noticed their absence. They soon were captured by a German patrol and taken to a POW camp. Even after they were liberated, they told no one about their ordeal until news reports about the trial prompted them to write Jaworski. They told him they had kept the secret for so long "because they did not want relatives of their buddies to know what kind of death they met."

The Rüsselsheim beating victims were not the only aviators lynched in Germany. One historian has estimated that roughly one thousand American fliers were assaulted or murdered after being shot down over Nazi-occupied territory, though the exact number will never be known. Many airmen were officially listed as "missing." Nazi leaders Goebbels and Martin Bormann encouraged *Lynchjustiz*—"lynch justice"—against the "terror flyers" as fitting punishment for the destruction wreaked by the bombers. Allied bombs killed roughly half a million German civilians during the last two years of the war.

Jaworski's next war crime case was in some ways even more chilling. The German defendants had run a sanatorium in Hadamar, a picturesque village near the city of Limburg in western Germany. The Nazis used the sanitorium for murdering Polish and Russian slave laborers who had grown too sick or weak to work. The staff pretended to ease their pain with hypodermic injections of morphine, which killed them. Their bodies were buried in a large common grave. "Children whose parents were slave laborers were put to death alongside their mothers and fathers," Jaworski wrote. By early 1945, the Nazis were sending healthy men and women to Hadamar to be murdered. Jaworski had evidence of about four hundred murders at Hadamar but felt certain the real number was much higher. He convicted seven staff members at the sanatorium of murder. The chief administrator and two male nurses were sentenced to death; the head physician, an elderly man in ill health, received life imprisonment; the keeper of the Hadamar's records was sentenced to thirty-five years; a gravedigger to thirty years; and a female nurse to twenty-five years. All insisted they had had no choice; if they had not murdered their patients, the Nazis would have murdered both them and the patients.

Jaworski's successful prosecutions of the Rüsselsheim and Hadamar cases prompted the army to offer him a place in the upcoming Nuremberg trials of the surviving leaders of Nazi Germany, including Luftwaffe chief Hermann Goering, deputy Nazi Party leader Rudolf Hess, and Nazi Party ideologist Alfred Rosenberg. Himmler had committed suicide by biting on a cyanide capsule while in British custody. The Nuremberg trials were the biggest stage possible for an ambitious army lawyer. But Jaworski had had enough of the Nazis. By the end of 1945, he had been in Europe for almost a year, immersed in horrific work. He missed his wife and children. He missed Texas. He asked to be sent home. Jaworski agreed to stay long enough to finish investigating war crimes at the infamous concentration camp at Dachau, Germany, where prisoners were used as the subjects of barbaric experiments. Jaworski, ultimately, professed relief at having skipped the Nuremberg trials. He thought they dragged on too long to be effective because so many nations were involved. He also was uncomfortable with the vagueness of some of the war crimes charges.

Jaworski arrived back in Houston on December 3, 1945. He was welcomed back to his old law firm of Fulbright, Crocker, Freeman, and Bates, which soon added his name to its name. Jaworski eventually would ascend to an even bigger stage than Nuremburg. But he never got over his experiences with the Nazis. He would spend the rest of his life contemplating, and writing about, the nature of the evil he had confronted in postwar Europe and in the POW camps in the American Midwest.

Those camps were starting to empty out by the time Jaworski's plane touched down in Houston. The U.S. government was moving by fits and starts to send the more than 370,000 Germans back to Europe. The repatriation posed not only logistical problems but economic, strategic, and even moral ones. Many POWs had lived in America for the better part of three years and had lost touch with their loved ones back home. They knew Germany was short of food, fuel, homes, and jobs. Its military was being disarmed and largely disbanded. Germany itself was divided into four zones of Allied occupation—one each for the United States, Britain, France, and the Soviet Union. Even Berlin was divided, with the American section a virtual island in the Russian zone. A *Pravda* correspondent reported that Berliners were "confused in conscience and in soul. . . . They understand a new existence is beginning. They want to know what kind of existence." Thousands of German POWs wanted to stay in the United States. "No one wanted to leave," recalled a prisoner in Camp Mexia in Texas. "If I could have . . . I would have stayed—and even tried to do so." But American authorities decided to send all the Germans home. They would be allowed to return and resettle in America only by going through the lengthy process of obtaining visas, securing American sponsors, paying their way across the Atlantic, and applying for U.S. citizenship.

But for the army, deciding and actually getting the Germans home were two different matters. Article 75 of the Geneva Convention called for repatriation of POWs "with the least possible delay after the conclusion of peace." But the absence of a functioning German government and the immense destruction in Europe complicated the process. Some Americans wanted the Germans shipped home at once. Labor unions argued that the ex-prisoners were clinging to jobs that were needed by returning GIs. Veterans' groups called the Germans' continuing presence on American soil an insult to soldiers who had fought and died in Europe. U.S. senator Burnet Maybank (D-South Carolina) declared, "The prisoners of war in this country should be returned to their native lands so that our boys who made possible the great victory in Europe, the gallant soldiers, will not find them here." Senator Maybank quickly reversed his position when farmers and business owners in his home state informed him they still needed POW labor. Assistant Provost Marshal B. M. Bryan declared that the army would find a middle ground: "We'll get them out of here just the minute any labor becomes surplus. . . . If there's a civilian for the job, he gets it."

U.S. authorities also struggled with the question of which Germans to send home first. The army announced that the first to go would be "useless" POWs, including unrepentant Nazis and officers and noncoms who were not required to work. That plan brought howls of protest. "Genuine Nazis are being rewarded for their convictions with a speedy reunion with their families, whereas German prisoners who cooperate by relieving the labor shortage are kept from their homes for an indeterminate period of time," a man wrote to *The New York Times*. An editorial in *The Washington Post* questioned the wisdom of injecting tens of thousands of rabid Nazis into an "anarchic and chaotic" postwar Germany. The U.S. government agreed to start instead with prisoners who were skilled in mining and manufacturing, and thus could help restart Germany's economy. The army also would send home graduates of its secret reeducation schools, who could help run the new West German government. An instructor in the reeducation program, Dr. William G. Moulton, said his students understood they would struggle at first in their ruined homeland: "We would get them there, turn them loose, and they would face misery. But at least they'd be in Germany."

More than half of the German POWs in the United States did not go straight home to Germany, however. The U.S. government secretly agreed to hand over more than 170,000 of its German prisoners to Britain, France, and other Allied nations. The prisoners would be forced to work to help repair the destruction the Nazi war machine had caused. Most of them would spend more than a year, and some as long as three years, laboring on farms, in coal mines, or in hazardous jobs such as clearing mines and disarming unexploded ordnance. The Geneva Convention allowed once-warring nations to work out the details of repatriating prisoners, but the writers of the treaty certainly had not envisioned those arrangements. France detained thousands of German POWs until 1947, when other Allied nations intervened to get them released. By that point, some Germans in France had cut short their prison sentences by joining the French Foreign Legion and fighting in the jungles of Vietnam—where they eventually would be replaced by a new generation of American soldiers.

Some German POWs in the United States did not realize they were not going straight home to Germany until their transport ships docked at Liverpool or Le Havre rather than at German ports. POW Helmut Horner found a message scrawled above his bunk on his ship saying, "Everything is only lies!" Prisoners who had developed a high regard for America felt betrayed. Many German POWs already had been caught by surprise when the army cut food rations in the camps after Germany's surrender. The army insisted the cutbacks only reflected food shortages in the United States, but they followed a new wave of public criticism about the "coddling" of German prisoners in the Fritz Ritz.

The Soviet occupation of eastern Europe posed another dilemma for repatriating the POWs. German prisoners from nations occupied by Stalin's Red Army, including Poland, the Baltic states of Estonia, Latvia, and Lithuania, and the eastern part of Germany, feared being shot or enslaved in the Soviet Gulag if they returned. At Fort Dix, New Jersey, more than 150 prisoners, many of them anticommunist Russians who had fought for Germany, barricaded themselves in their barracks the night before they were to board a ship to a Soviet port. When guards fired tear gas into the barracks, the prisoners rushed out at them brandishing homemade weapons. Some prisoners called to the guards to shoot them. The guards fired low and wounded seven prisoners, quelling the riot. Inside the barracks, three prisoners hanged themselves before the guards could stop them. The other rioters eventually were shipped back to the Soviet Union and uncertain fates. At Camp Shanks, New York, two Czech POWs committed suicide rather than board a ship for eastern Europe. Three others broke free of their guards on the docks and fled. They were quickly recaptured and sent "home." Secretary of War Stimson and General Eisenhower, among others, thought delivering Soviet-born German POWs into Stalin's hands was unconscionable. "To force those people to go back to a life of terror and persecution is something that would violate every moral standard by which America lives," Eisenhower declared at the time. But he was not yet in a powerful enough position to prevent it. Truman considered granting the Soviet-bloc POWs political asylum but decided that doing so would further exacerbate tensions in Europe.

The mood was gloomy even on repatriation ships bound for West Germany. American merchant seaman Norman Palmer said the Germans with whom he spoke felt hopeless. "They were going back to nothing—no home, no family, no work, no food, no money, no pension from the Army," Palmer recalled. "They did not know how they were going to live." Many of those men spent weeks at sea and then in cold, muddy processing camps in Britain and France. They traveled the final leg home the same way they had traveled to fight in the war: in boxcars. One prisoner wrote that as his train of boxcars neared the German border, he noticed "a tenseness in the men. I could see it in their eyes. They crowded to the doors for that first glimpse. Then they saw. They saw and they'll remember for all time. Ruin, desolation and destruction were framed in that open door." Another prisoner recalled, "From the windows in the houses, women and children waved at us. Many women cried. The way we looked was cause enough for that, considering that we had not washed or shaved for six days. Plus, hollow-eyed because of hunger." People along the tracks "threw food and tobacco for us to catch," he wrote. "But to the shame of the German prisoners, I have to admit that those things were rarely shared as good companions would do. Whoever stood at the window . . . took those things and kept them for himself." Twelve years under the Nazis had hardened many Germans, wrote ex-POW Franz Haber. "It was hard to discuss politics intelligently without a fight breaking out. . . . Everyone bargains over the simplest things." The German historian Harald Jähner entitled his book on life in postwar Germany *Wolfzeit*— "the time of wolves."

But as Jähner made clear, hundreds of thousands of Germans overcame hardships and rebuilt their lives in their wrecked country. Karl Gassman, who spent most of the war as a POW at Camp Concordia in Kansas, returned home to find his house destroyed by bombs, his father still a prisoner of the Russians, and his brother still a prisoner of the French. But his mother was still alive, and so was Gassman's spirit. He went to school and became an architect.

×   ×   ×

In the U.S. Army's rush to send the Germans home, it had all but forgotten the POW murder cases. The army had made efforts to help the widows of two of the Germans who had been hanged at Fort Leavenworth, U-boat man Otto Stengel and Camp Aiken killer Erich Gauss. The widows had written to U.S. authorities seeking documents to help prove in German courts that their husbands had been executed unjustly. Stengel's widow was trying to get help from a German welfare agency for her children. Gauss's widow was trying to obtain his pension. The army sent the widows several documents but not the court records they were seeking, which remained classified.

Despite the fifteen convictions and fourteen executions, no one could argue that all the POW camp killers had been brought to justice. Two of the five murders remained largely unsolved. No one had ever been charged in the killing of Hugo Krauss at Camp Hearne, Texas. And although Jaworski had convicted Edgar Menschner as the "ringleader" in the fatal beating of Hans Geller at Camp Chaffee in Arkansas, investigators had never identified the men who had beaten Geller. Those two cold cases were about to be reopened.

In December 1945, a German POW awaiting repatriation at a camp in Texas confessed out of the blue to killing Hugo Krauss at Camp Hearne. Guenther Meisel, a soft-spoken corporal, had never even been a suspect. He was a trustee, so well regarded that as part of his job repairing trucks, the army had let him drive between bases in Texas unsupervised. On one of those trips, he told a fellow prisoner, he noticed a young woman on the side of the road with her car's hood open. Meisel stopped and fixed the problem. He and the woman exchanged addresses and then letters. Meisel admitted he was a German prisoner, not a long-haul trucker as he first had told her. She continued to write. She told him she was a Christian and hoped he was too. She offered to send him a Bible. Meisel grew increasingly attached to her. He confessed to her that he had helped kill a man. She said he must confess to the authorities. He fought it for several days but finally contacted an American officer at Camp Fannin, a branch camp in Texas. The officer asked Meisel if he realized "what I was saying and doing to myself." Meisel said he did.

Meisel told the investigator that every POW in Company 3 at Camp Hearne disliked the victim, Hugo Krauss, for constantly praising America over Germany. Krauss kept saying he wanted to defect. His parents lived in New York City. His mother had sent him a transistor radio, and Krauss told his fellow prisoners the Allied war news was more accurate than the German war dispatches, which the prisoners heard on a hidden shortwave radio. When the guards found the shortwave radio, the prisoners blamed Krauss. On the day of the killing, Meisel told investigators, the POW company's ranking officer, Sergeant Anton Boehmer, announced that Krauss should be beaten. Another prisoner quoted Boehmer as saying he would not mind if Krauss was killed. Meisel said Boehmer's statement was "a spark." A prisoner named Helmut Meyer circulated through the barracks talking up the beating. A German corporal, Erich Von Der Heydt, recruited several rugged volunteers from another company. Meisel decided to help beat Krauss. "Everybody was for the beating," he said, "but many of them were too clever to join in. They encouraged us by talking for it." Meisel offered an insider's account, starting with a meeting of the gang by candlelight:

> At the meeting we figured out what everybody was going to do. We had some guards standing outside to watch the tower guards. During the attack Boehmer was to remain in bed to prevent suspicion of him. Six or eight of us were to beat Krauss. Everybody at the meeting had brought sticks of wood with them. I had a piece of pipe about nine inches long and about ½ to ¾ inch in diameter. I sharpened a piece of wood and drove it into the pipe so I could handle it. Several of the sticks brought by the others were 2-inch by 4-inch sticks about three feet long with one end whittled down so they could hold them. Spikes about 4½ inches long had been driven through the sticks and the points of the spikes stuck out about 2½ inches from the boards. . . . Someone was to turn off the light switch in Barracks 1. Everyone was instructed to bury their sticks at any place they could, immediately after the beating was finished. Nobody said how much Krauss should be beaten.

Meisel said he had brought the metal pipe specifically to destroy Krauss's radio—"I hated that radio and wanted to beat it." He knew only one of the others who took part in the beating, Cpl. Heinrich Braun. Braun showed up at the candlelight meeting without a club, and when someone asked why he had not brought one, he had said his fists were strong enough. Braun berated one of the lookouts for not having enough guts to take part in the beating.

Krauss somehow knew he was going to be attacked, but he apparently thought he could protect himself. "Let them come, I am not afraid," he told another prisoner on December 17, 1943, before going to sleep. A little before midnight, Cpl. Werner Hossann peered into Krauss's barracks and reported to the gang that he was asleep. Hossann stood by the light switch to make sure no one turned it on. Meisel, Braun, and several others surrounded Krauss in his bunk and began beating him. Krauss screamed loudly enough for everyone in the barracks to hear. "We were supposed to hit him in certain places, but we got nervous and hit him anywhere we could," Meisel told investigators. The beating lasted only a minute. Meisel smashed the hated radio. Krauss managed to get up from his cot, screaming, and his attackers scattered. He walked on his own to the latrine, where Meisel saw him. "He was bleeding all over. He said nothing, except he continued to cry and yell. He had been yelling since the beating started. He kept crying until he was taken to the hospital." Sergeant Boehmer got out of bed to escort Krauss to the hospital.

Meisel said he was surprised six days later to learn Krauss was dead. "I had not intended to kill Krauss or help the others kill him," he said. "I just wanted to beat him. I had tried not to hit him on the head because I did not want him to die." Meisel did not mention the girl on the roadside or his religious conversion in his statement. Asked why he had come forward and confessed to a murder, he replied, "To get it off my chest, everything. . . . Because my mother always told me everything comes out under the sun." He was asked, "Did you talk with anyone about religion prior to the time that you signed this statement?" "Yes, I did," Meisel said. "For three months."

On the basis of Meisel's confession, he and Braun, Boehmer, Von

Der Heydt, Meyer, and Cpl. Werner Jaschko were charged with murder. Jaschko had served as a lookout. The army took credit for breaking the case, claiming disingenuously that the charges had grown out of "a searching investigation over a two-year period" rather than a killer's unexpected act of conscience. On January 30, 1946, after a five-day court-martial, a U.S. military tribunal at Camp Swift, Texas, convicted all seven Germans of murder. Krauss's killing was as brutal as any of the others. But the war was over. The POWs were going home. Rather than sentence the Germans to hang, the tribunal sentenced each of the seven to life imprisonment at Fort Leavenworth.

×　　×　　×

The Camp Hearne killers were unlucky they were still in America when Meisel confessed. The army was clearing out the camps at a fast pace. It shipped 38,000 German prisoners to Europe in January 1946, 73,000 in February, 68,000 in March, 56,000 in April, 47,000 in May, and 37,000 in June. By July, the only German POWs left in the United States were those who either were too sick to travel, were in transit, or were finishing their studies in the army's reeducation program. Just 26 German POWs out of more than 371,000 were unaccounted for. The army assumed they had escaped from their camps and made it back to Europe or died trying. But the escapees were hiding in plain sight in the United States. They would reveal themselves years and even decades later.

The last large batch of German POWs left American soil at 3 p.m. on July 22, 1946. They departed from Camp Shanks on the Brooklyn waterfront aboard the harbor boat *General Yates,* which carried them to a larger vessel for the voyage across the Atlantic. They included many young men, including an eighteen-year-old who had been captured the previous April while he was still seventeen. He considered himself lucky to have been captured. He had spent his time in America working on a farm on Long Island and later as an interpreter. The last prisoner to board the boat, a twenty-two-year-old electrician from Heidelberg, patiently walked back and forth across the gangplank several times to allow all the news photographers to capture the moment. The United States was the first Allied nation to get rid of all its POWs. "Considering the numbers," a War Department spokesman said, "we feel we got them out in a hurry." As the *General Yates* edged away from the pier, Camp Shanks's commanding officer, Col. Harry W. Maas, summed up America's experience in imprisoning German POWs: "Thank God that is over!"

But the POW murder cases were still not over. In September 1946, two months after the last group of prisoners left Camp Shanks, the Army Adjutant General's Office reopened the Camp Chaffee case. The reason is not clear from the court files. It may have been a response to President Truman's decision to commute the death sentence of "ringleader" Edgar Menschner to twenty years in prison. Aside from Menschner, no one had ever been charged with the murder of Hans Geller. The army ordered Gen. Courtney Hicks Hodges, commander of the First Army at Fort Jay, New York, to try to identify the men who had fatally beaten Geller and hold them accountable.

Despite the fact that two and a half years had passed since Geller's murder, army investigators quickly found witnesses who identified nine ex-POWs as having been involved in the killing. The suspects were scattered across two continents. Three were finishing classes at schools in the army's reeducation program—which cast doubt about the program's screening process. Two others were about to be sent home on a ship to Germany. The army ordered all five to be held in the United States until further notice. Four other suspects already had been sent home to Germany. The army started the paperwork to bring three of them back to America to face charges; the fourth man had disappeared.

The investigation seemed to be gathering momentum. The army took steps to detain more than a dozen potential witnesses who also had been about to be sent home to Germany. But in February 1947, army prosecutors at Fort Jay concluded they could not prove murder charges against any of the suspects. Chief of Staff Maj. Gen. W. B. Kean explained: "The evidence against the accused and suspects . . . is unsatisfactory, being conflicting, fragmentary, secondary and inconclusive. The successful prosecution of all accused depends in a great part, if not wholly, upon their willingness to waive their immunity against self-incrimination. In any event, the trial of any number of these individuals promises to be a lengthy affair, difficult in nature, expensive in time and money and doubtful as to ultimate conviction." General Kean added that since the end of the war, the United States had adopted a policy of commuting the sentences of ex-POWs who had committed crimes against other prisoners and sending them home. Convicting men of the three-year-old Camp Chaffee murder was "useless and impractical" if they were just going to be sent home to Germany, Kean wrote. He recommended dropping the case. Two years before, the army had hanged some of the German POWs on less evidence than the new Camp Chaffee investigation had uncovered. But the end of the war had changed everything. The army decided not to pursue the men who had murdered Hans Geller. Now the POW murder cases were over.

26

Closing the Ledger

The German POW camps that once spanned the United States are mostly forgotten today, swallowed up by the rural landscapes where they operated so briefly. The U.S. government quickly dismantled the camps after the prisoners departed. It auctioned off the land, the buildings, and their every salable component, from lumber to pipes to gravel to barbed wire. Wood from Camp Concordia in Kansas helped frame the Concordia Lutheran Church, and a boiler from the camp heated the church for a half century. Much of the farmland where the camps sprawled was too laden with cement foundations to support crops again. Buyers found other uses. The land on which Camp Huntsville in Texas stood is now owned by Sam Houston State University, which for years used the barracks for married student housing. The desert site of Camp Papago Park in Arizona is covered mostly by a housing development in what is now the city of Scottsdale. A patio built by German POWs for a one-room stone schoolhouse at Camp Chaffee in Arkansas is still used by the Stonehouse restaurant, which occupies the old school building. A few vestiges of the camps survive because they are just too big and costly to dismantle. The massive, sixty-foot-tall concrete base of Camp Tonkawa's old water tower, now overgrown with ivy, looms over an industrial park dominated by the roar of a battery recycling plant.

Most of the old camp locations are either unmarked or marked with blink-and-you-miss-them roadside historical signs. Scattered hole-in-the-wall museums preserve camp documents and artifacts. A half dozen camps around the United States have been partially restored or preserved by nonprofit groups and turned into tourist attractions. Camp Concordia in Kansas holds an annual Victory Day celebration in a restored barracks decorated with POWs' landscape paintings of Cloud County's rolling hills. The museum documents how Camp Concordia went from being one of the nation's most troubled POW camps to a model camp as its army inspectors saw it. One of Concordia's old guard towers still stands at the museum's main entrance. In Algona, Iowa, an elaborate, sixty-five-piece Nativity scene built by German prisoners in 1945 still attracts thousands of visitors every Christmas season. An ex-POW who built some of the creche figures out of wire, wood, and plaster wrote to an Algona grade school class, "I am very glad that the nativity scene still helps to heal the wounds of war." The little Camp Algona POW Museum in Algona offers artifacts and information about the old camp. A restored barracks at the Camp Hearne Historical Site contains artifacts and exhibits, although most of the old camp has been swallowed up by juniper, scrub pine, and Johnson grass. Visitors can ride a golf cart into the woods to see the spot where Hugo Krauss was murdered, under a sign that marks "The Scene of the Crime."

Krauss's body and those of the other victims of the POW murders and forced suicides were disinterred from their original graves and reburied in military cemeteries. Krauss and Hans Geller lie in Fort Sam Houston National Cemetery in San Antonio; Horst Guenther in the Fort Gordon Post Cemetery in Georgia; Johann Kunze in the Fort Reno Post Cemetery in Oklahoma; Werner Dreschler at Fort Bliss National Cemetery in El Paso; and Felix Tropschuh and Franz Kettner at the Fort Riley Post Cemetery in Kansas.

The fourteen men who were executed for the murders are buried in the back row of an isolated prisoners' graveyard at the U.S. Disciplinary

Barracks at Fort Leavenworth. Even for a graveyard it's a lonely place, hemmed inside a chain-link fence on a wooded ridge a half mile from the National Cemetery where American military veterans are buried. The prisoners' cemetery is immaculately maintained. Edgar Beyer, whose father, Walter, was executed for the Camp Tonkawa killing, visited his father's grave at least twice in the 1990s. He told reporters he had no memory of his father, who last saw his family at Christmas 1942. "I was four years old when my mother found out he died," Edgar said. "I remember her crying. I'll never forget her cry." She did not tell him his father had been executed for murder until he was a teenager. In 1992, *The Kansas City Star* reported that flowers kept mysteriously appearing on the convicted killers' graves. Today no one visits the graves except occasional tourist groups.

The convicted killers who avoided being hanged in 1945 ended up spending little time behind bars. Edgar Menschner, the "ringleader" of the Camp Chaffee killing whose sentence was commuted at the last moment from death to twenty years, was sent home to his wife and children by President Truman in 1948. Truman also paroled Guenther Meisel, whose religious conversion broke open the Camp Hearne murder case, after Meisel had spent only three years at Fort Leavenworth. Meisel's codefendants were sent home too. Meisel apparently did not stay in touch with the American girl who had persuaded him to confess.

×　　×　　×

The most durable legacy of the German POW camps in the United States is the thousands of former German prisoners who resettled in the United States after the war. The U.S. government did not keep track of how many ex-POWs immigrated to America, but some historians have estimated the number at five thousand. Many of those men kept in contact with farmers and other American supporters after they were repatriated. Their early letters from Germany described their privations. "Not even for infants can one receive necessary food," one former prisoner wrote to a Midwest farm family. He yearned "for the better time I had in America. I wish I were still there. Better to be a prisoner forever in America than to endure this continual hunger." He asked the farmer to send him seeds so he could try to grow sorghum.

Gerd Kruse, a former Afrika Korps artilleryman, vowed to return to America as soon as he was repatriated. "When I set foot on German soil and I saw what happened, I just as soon turned around," he said. He had made a good impression on a farmer in remote Deshler, Nebraska, and when a group of farmers decided to send care packages to deserving prisoners, that farmer chose Kruse. The farmer's daughter, Ella Kuhlman, handled the mailing and started exchanging letters with Kruse, and then long letters. She eventually traveled to Germany, married Kruse, and brought him back to help run the family farm. The couple lived a quiet life working and rearing a family. Kruse died in 2005. His and Ella's two sons now farm parts of the property. There were other love stories. A Black U.S. Army nurse married a former POW who had worked with her in the hospital at Camp Florence in Arizona.

Other German ex-POWs returned to the United States and became doctors, lawyers, business executives, and artists. "We came here with two suitcases, and today we have a manufacturing company and a retail store," said Frieda Goedecke, whose husband, Heinrich, was a prisoner. "And you can do it here in America. I think that is the only place where you can do it." Even the master Luftwaffe interrogator, Hanns Scharff, who had matched wits with Col. Henry Spicer, resettled in the United States in 1950. He prospered as an artist in Los Angeles, specializing in mosaic work. He created mosaics for the Los Angeles Civic Center, Disney World, Epcot Center, and the floor of the California State Capitol in Sacramento. Scharff tracked down some of the American pilots he had interrogated, and reminisced with them. He apparently never reminisced with Spicer.

The prospect of a brighter future in the United States also beckoned to German escapees who remained at large after the war. Sixteen remained unaccounted for in the army's final tally. They had never left the United States. They melted into American society, establishing fake identities and staying out of trouble. They started businesses, bought homes, got married. One by one, over the course of the next forty years, they came forward or gave themselves away, were arrested by the FBI, and were deported. The last six to remain at large included Reinhold Pabel, who slipped away from a branch camp in Illinois and hid in Chicago, claiming to be a Dutchman. When FBI agents arrested him in 1953, he was running a bookstore in the city's North Side. Another ex-POW, Luftwaffe paratrooper Harry Girth, became a wealthy decorator. He was caught after his photo appeared in a *Collier's* magazine article. The last ex-POW to remain at large, Georg Gaertner, had escaped from Camp Deming in New Mexico to avoid being repatriated into Soviet territory. He caught a freight train across the desert to California, where he worked as a lumberjack, ski instructor, and tennis pro. Using the name "Dennis Whiles," he played tennis with Swedish icon Bjorn Borg and socialized with Hollywood stars including Robert Stack and Lloyd Bridges. In September 1985, Gaertner read about himself in a book by the historian Arnold Krammer, telephoned the author, and revealed his true identity. He faced no charges but was sent back to Germany. He wrote a book entitled *Hitler's Last Soldier in America*.

×   ×   ×

Gaertner, by coming forward, effectively closed the ledger on the POW camps in the United States. The army had interned 371,683 German, 49,784 Italian, and 5,080 Japanese prisoners without a single act of sabotage or violent crime against an American citizen. The POWs helped thousands of American farms and businesses stay afloat during hard times. By shipping the German POWs to America, the army enabled thousands of GIs in Europe to fight rather than stand guard duty. America's good treatment of German prisoners saved the lives of countless American soldiers in Europe. Roughly 99 percent of American POWs in Europe came home alive despite their privations in German captivity. And on the battlefields, tens of thousands of German soldiers surrendered rather than fight to the death as Hitler ordered. More than 80 percent of the Germans who surrendered in the few months after D-Day told army interrogators they knew they would be treated well by the United States.

The impact of the army's reeducation program, jump-started by Eleanor Roosevelt, is harder to assess. The U.S. government tracked only a small number of the graduates of the program's secret reeducation schools after they returned to Germany. In the 1970s, the author Judith M. Gansberg set out to gauge the results of the program by interviewing POW participants, instructors, and administrators. She concluded that the program was "blundering, heavy-handed" but that the reeducation schools had produced graduates who helped build a democratic government in West Germany. Gansberg wrote that those graduates "may have tipped the scales; they may merely have added a few more voices to an inevitable movement. But they were there; they helped."

America's experiment with housing four armies' worth of German POWs succeeded despite a series of errors that could have led to disaster, wrote the historian Harold Deutsch, a former high-ranking OSS officer. "We made mistake after mistake: the Nazis weren't segregated until after the damage had been done; the best men were wasted in the wrong areas; and so on. In retrospect, it was only common sense and our basic humanity which saved us." America treated its prisoners better than any other major power did in World War II. In a speech to Congress, Provost Marshal General Lerch said the United States had set an example for the world by resisting the pressures and emotions of a bitter war and hewing to the Geneva Convention.

Lerch did not mention that when the murders in the POW camps became a threat, the army had resorted to torture to stop them and then had been forced to hide its actions from the Nazis. The United States got away with it because it defeated Germany on the battlefield. If Germany had held out a few months longer, the United States probably would have freed all fifteen of the POW camp killers at Fort Leavenworth to save an equal number of Americans. Nor did Lerch mention in his speech that America had handed over thousands of POWs from Soviet-bloc nations to the murderous Stalin.

Since World War II, America has not attempted to detain large numbers of enemy prisoners on its soil. Most captured soldiers from North Korea, China, North Vietnam, Iraq, and the "War on Terror" were held in camps outside the United States. The Cold War communists carried on the fight inside the camps even more savagely than the Nazis did, holding kangaroo courts, murdering fellow prisoners, rioting, taking hostages, and assaulting guards. The Vietcong rejected the Geneva Convention, which had been updated in 1949, and refused to allow the International Red Cross to inspect its harsh camps, where future U.S. senator John McCain and others suffered. America's allies the South Vietnamese executed Vietcong prisoners, and the Vietcong responded by executing several captured Americans.

The stateless terrorists of the twenty-first century have rioted and murdered in their camps too. After the September 11, 2001, terrorist attacks, President George W. Bush declared that terrorism suspects were not prisoners of war protected by the Geneva Convention but would be treated "humanely, and to the extent appropriate and consistent with military necessity, in a manner consistent with Geneva." In practice, Bush turned over the interrogations of some terrorism suspects to the CIA, which subjected them to waterboarding and other "third-degree" methods harsher than those "Schmidt" used on the U-boat men at Byron Hot Springs. The CIA also transferred captives through a process called extraordinary rendition to nations that employed more ruthless interrogation methods than were allowed in the United States. Bush defended aggressive interrogations on the grounds they foiled bombing plots and helped track down terrorist ringleaders such as Al Qaeda's 9/11 mastermind Khalid Sheikh Mohammed. But the use of torture against him and other terrorists created legal issues that have helped snarl the court proceedings against them for two decades, and may ultimately spare them from being executed.

America's treatment of enemy prisoners in the twenty-first century has been governed mainly by "expediency—whatever is required to extract critical information, immobilize enemy fighters, or break the nationalist spirit or religious devotion of opponents," wrote Krammer, the historian. "Whether necessary or not in the face of a new type of warfare, this change signals a sad turn to earlier and more barbaric times." The pendulum of American politics and public opinion has swung back and forth. In 2019, a decorated U.S. Navy SEAL, Special Operations Chief Edward Gallagher, was court-martialed after some of his fellow SEALS reported he had murdered Iraqi civilians. Other SEALS testified on Gallagher's behalf, and a military jury convicted him of only one minor offense. He was pardoned by then-president Donald J. Trump, who called Gallagher one of "our great fighters." But the following year, a U.S. military jury at Guantanamo Bay, Cuba, gave an Al Qaeda terrorist a relatively light sentence of twenty-six years in prison because he had been tortured by the CIA. The jury foreman, a U.S. Navy captain, said the jurors were repulsed by the terrorist's actions but also by the torture, which he called "a stain on the moral fiber of America."

Hostage diplomacy, as employed by the Germans in 1945, is a common practice today. Iran has engaged in it repeatedly since a conservative theocracy took over the country in 1979, detaining foreign journalists, businessmen, and aid workers to exchange for assassins, other prisoners, and money. In 2021, China imprisoned two Canadians on dubious spying charges to force Canada to release an executive of the Chinese firm Huawei Technologies, whom Canada was holding for the United States on fraud charges. U.S. authorities accused China of using trumped-up charges to force the release of a suspect facing legitimate charges—"hostage diplomacy." Chinese government media retorted that the real "hostage diplomacy" was the jailing of the Huawei executive in the first place. At least none of the prisoners in that case faced the death penalty.

In February 2022, the American women's basketball star Brittney Griner was arrested in Moscow for trying to board a plane with two vape cartridges of hashish oil in her luggage. A few days later, Russia invaded Ukraine. By the time Griner was formally sentenced to nine years in prison in October, Russian troops were committing atrocities in Ukraine and Russia-U.S. relations were growing colder every day. The United States finally took the best deal it could get, saving Griner by freeing a notorious Russian arms dealer, Viktor Bout, whose nickname was "the Merchant of Death."

On August 1, 2023, the United States and Russia took part in the largest "hostage diplomacy" exchange since the Cold War, in which a total of twenty-four prisoners were released from captivity in seven countries. The Americans freed from Russia included Evan Gershkovich, a reporter for *The Wall Street Journal* who had been arrested in March 23 and accused of spying; Paul Whelan, a security contractor who had been imprisoned on spying charges since 2018; and Alsu Kurmasheva, a Russian-American editor for Radio Free Europe/Radio Liberty who had been held since 2023 on charges of "spreading false information about the Russian military" after Russia's invasion of Ukraine. The freed Russians included Vadim Krasikov, who had been serving a life sentence in Germany for assassinating a Chechen former rebel fighter in a public park in Berlin in 2019; and Roman Seleznev, a cybercriminal who had been serving a fourteen-year prison sentence in the United States for stealing millions of dollars through online identity theft and bank fraud. Then-president Joe Biden—who had worked out the last details of the exchange just before announcing he would not seek reelection—declared he had been unwilling to let innocent Americans "rot in jail" even if freeing them came at the cost of releasing Russian criminals. Congressional Republicans praised the exchange while warning that "without serious action to deter further hostage taking by Russia, Iran and other states hostile to the United States, the costs of hostage diplomacy will continue to rise." They did not specify exactly what actions could be taken, however. On the day the exchange was announced, the State Department said seventy other Americans were being detained by other nations on questionable charges.

× × ×

The German POW murders left a mark on the Americans who became entangled in them. Leon Jaworski wrote three books in which he reflected on his experiences prosecuting Nazis and their followers. He wrote that the German people had failed a moral test by allowing the Nazis to take over their country at a time "when all Germans of ordinary intelligence knew that Hitler's course was evil and wrong," and subsequently "were willing to accept the fruits of an evil goal instead of repudiating it." Jaworski warned that Germany would not be the last nation to face such a test and that America was not immune. "It must never be forgotten," he wrote, "that the metamorphoses that took place in the German people can occur elsewhere as well."

Back home in Texas, Jaworski gained prominence in political circles as a centrist Democrat. He served on the Warren Commission investigating the assassination of President John F. Kennedy in 1963. He became a close confidant of U.S. senator and then president Lyndon Baines Johnson but voted twice for Republican president Richard M. Nixon. In 1973, Nixon, trying to cover up his role in the coverup of the Watergate break-in, fired the special prosecutor in the case, Archibald Cox, and asked Jaworski to replace him. If Nixon expected Jaworski to go easy on him, he badly miscalculated. Jaworski fended off Nixon loyalists who tried to derail the investigation. In the process, he lost friends and received death threats. He pressed all the way to the U.S. Supreme Court to force the White House to release audiotapes that finally forced Nixon to resign on August 8, 1974. Jaworski was criticized for not prosecuting Nixon or challenging President Gerald Ford's pardon of the ex-president. Even so, Jaworski emerged from Watergate as a national hero, or at least a role model—a man of conscience who pursued the truth no matter where it led.

Jaworski went on to serve as special prosecutor in the "Korea-gate" scandal, in which members of Congress were accused of taking cash from the South Korean government. The diplomatic immunity of key figures in the case frustrated Jaworski, but his investigation sent one congressman to prison and caused three others to be reprimanded. Jaworski retired to his Texas ranch, where he died in 1982 at the age of seventy-seven while chopping wood.

Twenty-five years after Jaworski's death, a secret emerged from one of his high-profile wartime cases. In late 1944, the army had sent him to Fort Lawton in Seattle to prosecute Black GIs for "rioting" in a night of violence that left an Italian POW dead. Jaworski knew it was a career-building case. "Honey, this is a really big job I am on," he wrote to his wife, Jeannette, in Dallas. "It's being watched closely in Washington." Jaworski ended up prosecuting forty-three Black soldiers, three for murder and the others for rioting, in one of the largest courts-martial of World War II. He won twenty-eight convictions, praise from his superiors, and a choice new assignment in Europe.

In 2005, sixty years after the Fort Lawton case and a quarter century after Jaworski's death, journalist-turned-author Jack Hamann discovered that Jaworski had withheld a critical piece of evidence from the Black soldiers' defense attorneys: a scathing report by an army general that the initial investigation was bungled so badly that most of the evidence was lost. The general had gone so far as to recommend that the camp commander be relieved of duty. Jaworski surely would have recognized that the general's report would help the defense and that he was required by law and duty to disclose it. Why he did not is an answer he took to his grave. After Hamann's book *On American Soil* was published in 2005, the U.S. Army Board for Correction of Military Records ordered all the Black soldiers' convictions at Fort Lawton voided because of Jaworski's "egregious error." The army's action was one of a series of steps it has taken in the past twenty years to correct its record on racial justice dating back to the Civil War.

Jaworski never wrote about how his murder prosecutions of German POWs in the United States led to retaliation against American POWs in Germany. It seems likely he learned about the exchange negotiations, although at the time he was busy with the war crimes cases. The fifteen Americans who were listed by the government in the exchange negotiations apparently were told only fragments of the story. The army never publicly announced what happened. The fifteen never held a reunion. William Schaefer and James Schmitz apparently were the only two in the group who ever met. Both Schaefer and Schmitz provided sworn statements against Zimmerman, the Nazi security chief at Oflag 64, for war crimes. Schmitz delivered a signed statement in person to the War Department in Washington. But Allied authorities never found Zimmerman. Captain Ferguson, who had defended Schaefer and Schmitz at their court-martial, heard Zimmerman was dead.

Lt. Franklin Coslett, the bombardier who became a Dutch Resistance operative, stayed in Holland after the war's end to run an MIS-X office that provided financial compensation to Dutch Resistance fighters and their families. Coslett understood their risks and sacrifices after his own seven months on the run. He helped them obtain everything from bicycle wheels to visas to money for hard times. One member of his wartime network "may have been killed," Coslett reported. "His wife probably is in need of assistance." After finally going home to Wilkes-Barre in 1946, Coslett became a television anchorman, hosting the six o'clock news at WBRE-TV for twenty-seven years. He ended each broadcast with a salute and the words "That's it, that's the news." He retired in 1980 and died in 1992.

When Col. Henry Spicer came home, he and his wife, Louise, were feted with luncheons, dinners, and cocktail parties from Hollywood to San Antonio. Spicer never mentioned his death sentence to his children, but he did not normally talk to them about his work. He told the Rotary Club in McAllen, Texas, that he and four other American prisoners "were picked mostly at random" to exchange for five German POWs who had been "properly" convicted of murder. Spicer wasted no time in getting back into the cockpit. In 1952, he flew P-80 fighter jets to Europe to intervene if the Soviets attacked the cargo planes hauling supplies in the Berlin Airlift. His fellow officers considered Spicer an outstanding leader, but his fatherly "Are you all right, laddie?" days were over. He was all business now. "I'd rather have slapped a coiled rattlesnake in the face than disagree with him," recalled a former subordinate. After several years in Europe, Spicer was given command of the Seventeenth Air Force at Wheelus Air Force Base in Tripoli, Libya. He led a search in 1959 that discovered the long-lost American B-17 bomber "Lady Be Good," which had gone missing in 1943. The plane's wreckage had first been spotted from the air by geologists flying over the remote Libyan Desert. (A subsequent mission recovered the remains of eight of the nine crew members.) In his free time, Spicer enjoyed big-game hunting. He shot lions in Africa, wild boar in Turkey, deer in Germany, pheasant in Italy, and reindeer in Norway. But he preferred his meals meatless. Spicer's other interests included history and architecture. He occasionally warbled Texas cowboy laments while strumming a guitar.

Spicer rose through the air force to the rank of major general. He was given command of NORAD's air defense system for the U.S. West Coast and Canada, including radar monitoring and fighter intercepts of unidentified aircraft. Spicer retired from the air force in 1964 in Arizona. He was stricken by bone cancer and moved to Texas for treatment. He died at the hospital at Lackland Air Force Base on December 4, 1968, and is buried at Fort Sam Houston National Cemetery in San Antonio—the same cemetery in which German POW murder victims Hans Geller and Hugo Krauss are buried. Thirty years after Spicer's death, one of his former flying students wrote a profile of him for *Air Force Magazine,* entitled "A Speech Worth Dying For" and quoting the speech at Stalag Luft I that had led to his death sentence.

Louis Biagioni was badly shaken by his experiences at Mauthausen. A doctor who examined him upon his return to the United States found he suffered from "high nervous tension from imprisonment." Another interviewer noted his "moderately severe fatigue and nervous tension." The army considered transferring him out of the OSS and giving him a desk job. But his OSS superiors stuck up for him, and he responded well to a sixty-day furlough. After the OSS was disbanded following World War II, Biagioni continued doing covert work for the U.S. Air Force's Strategic Air Command, according to his son Albert. Biagioni worked mostly in Europe, South America, and the Middle East, but told his family next to nothing about what he did there, Albert said. The only stories Biagioni ever shared were vignettes that shed little light on his missions. In 1961, he told Albert, he helped to brief President John F. Kennedy on the planned Bay of Pigs invasion of Cuba, using a pointer to show the president where the invaders would land. Afterward, Biagioni ducked back into the empty meeting room, hoping to take Kennedy's cup as a souvenir, but someone had already cleared the table.

Biagioni bought his parents the three-story brownstone in Brooklyn they had been renting. He married and fathered four children. He was a disciplinarian like his father. His son Albert recalled seeing him swat his brother in the head for speaking disrespectfully. The blow was so swift and sharp that his brother's eyeglasses seemed to hang in the air for a moment where his brother had been. Biagioni retired from government service after twenty-two years after his superiors asked him to go to Vietnam and serve as an adviser, Albert said. Biagioni settled on Long Island and spent his days fishing for flounder and striped bass. He fashioned his own lures and boasted that he had never needed to buy fish. In 1986, Biagioni provided a sworn affidavit against a former guard at Mauthausen who had been living under a false name in Michigan. The FBI found the ex-guard hiding in a secret compartment under the stairs in his home. He was deported to Germany. In his final years, Biagioni moved to Chesapeake, Virginia, to be closer to his children, who helped care for him. He met friends almost every morning at a local coffee shop. Occasionally a newcomer to the group would express doubt about the Holocaust. Biagioni would firmly set him straight. "It just drove him crazy that people could think like that," Albert said.

Biagioni's OSS superiors apparently told him the entire story of the attempted fifteen-for-fifteen exchange of condemned prisoners. Before his death in 2003, he researched the German POW camp murders in the United States and concluded that he would have been exchanged for one of the condemned U-boat men. As much as Biagioni had suffered in German hands, he did not think the seven Germans at Camp Papago Park had deserved to die for killing a traitor.

Lt. James Schmitz's homecoming to Ottawa, Illinois, made headlines around the Midwest. "It would be good to return to the United States any time," he told the *Chicago Tribune*. "But it is especially wonderful when I think that just a few weeks ago I was in military confinement and momentarily expecting to be executed." Schmitz wanted to plunge right back into politics. He thought his war story would appeal to voters. He gave talks to civic groups and shared stages with visiting politicians, including Senator Brooks, who in April 1945 had queried the State Department about Schmitz's and Schaefer's death sentences. A reporter who covered one of Schmitz's talks wrote that he "touches on mistreatment quite considerably." Schmitz also told audiences that all Germans shared the blame for Hitler's rise, which may not have sat well with some of his German American listeners. Schmitz decided to run for sheriff of Lasalle County and hired his brother as campaign manager. Midway through the campaign he abruptly withdrew without explaining why. His family suspected he was forced out of the race by a political adversary, possibly because of his homosexuality.

Soon after dropping out of the race, Schmitz moved out of small-town Ottawa to Chicago. He owned an ice cream shop in Oak Park, but it burned down. He shared a house with a chef at the Playboy Mansion. Every couple of months he would roar up to his brothers' house in Ottawa at the wheel of a white Cadillac Coupe DeVille or some other gleaming sports car. He always wore a fine suit and often smoked a cigar. He was a larger-than-life figure, gregarious, street-wise, full of fun—the polar opposite of his brothers. He never told his family he was gay, and they never asked. They deduced it from a series of small discoveries, like a leather bomber jacket, far too big for Jimmy, hanging in a closet of a family cabin. Eventually the family just talked about his sexuality as if everyone had known about it for years. His nephews and niece gravitated toward him. "He had the look and the stature of a great man," his nephew John said. "I think he could never achieve that greatness because he was gay. But he gave a lot to people. My ability to handle people came from him. He's always close to me." Schmitz died in 1979 at the age of sixty-five.

After William Schaefer recuperated from his imprisonment at Colditz Castle, the army sent him to Japan to take part in the U.S. occupation. He served on the staff of Gen. Douglas MacArthur in Tokyo. He rejoined the army after the war, and after a refresher course at the infantry school at Fort Benning, Georgia, he returned to active duty. He retired in 1954 as a full colonel and the director of training at Fort Meade, Maryland. Schaefer moved to Columbus, Georgia, where he married and wrote self-published books on leadership, global monetary policy, and his days as a POW. In 1961, the local newspaper printed a feature on Schaefer's success at growing vegetables in Columbus in the winter. Schaefer said he knew he could grow peas, lettuce, and romaine out of season in Georgia because he had grown them at Oflag 64 in Poland. In 1971, Schaefer joined a group of ex-POWs on a tour of the site of Oflag 64. He apparently also revisited Colditz Castle. Schaefer died in 1979 at the Veterans Administration hospital in Tuskegee, Alabama. He is buried at Linwood Cemetery in Columbus.

In his book about life as a POW, *People Too,* Schaefer comes across as a more contemplative and philosophical leader than the "King Kong" his fellow prisoners described. He suffered enormous physical and emotional duress in World War II. He hobbled ashore with an injured leg to lead his battalion in the invasion of Sicily. He was wounded twice by shrapnel, knocked unconscious by a grenade, knocked out again by an artillery shell, captured, strafed, bombed, starved, interrogated, bled with leeches, and isolated in solitary confinement for weeks at a time. He was charged unjustly with a capital offense, convicted in a mockery of a trial, sentenced to death, and locked away in Colditz Castle.

In *People Too,* Schaefer described how helpless he had felt as he stood unsteadily in the German military court and was condemned to die for a dispute over a poster. He could still hear the prosecutor shouting out the verdict: "*Heil Hitler!* Convicted and to be executed!" Everyone in the courtroom, including the German officers deciding the case, knew the proceedings were a sham. Even so, Schaefer wrote, "I ask the reader not to be too hard on this court. I have seen outright injustice in some American courts and you may have seen it also. Injustice stinks just as badly in one place as in another."

Notes on Sources

I have used the following abbreviations and descriptions for frequently mentioned sources:

The National Archives and Records Administration (NARA) Record Group 389, or RG 389, at the Archives II branch in College Park, Maryland, contains the files of the Army Provost Marshal General's Office, which include most of the material about the creation, operation, and inspection of the German POW camps in the United States. NARA RG 59 at College Park contains records of the secretary of state, including communications among the War Department, the State Department, the Swiss Legation, and the German Foreign Office regarding the murder cases against the German POWs and the subsequent negotiations for a prisoner exchange. RG 107 contains records of the secretary of war. RG 153 contains alphabetized records of American POWs in German hands who were believed to be victims of or witnesses to war crimes, including brief summaries of some of the court cases the Germans brought against them. RG 319 contains intelligence reports about the interrogations of German prisoners. RG 226 contains Louis Biagioni's declassified OSS personnel file.

The NARA branch in St. Louis contains the case files of the five German POW murder cases. I reviewed the case files of the murder prosecutions at Camp Chaffee, Camp Hearne, and Camp Aiken in St. Louis. In these notes, those sources will be described coming from NARA St. Louis. The Chaffee case file is designated M-CMR (first defendant Menschner, Court-Martial

Record); the Hearne case is designated B-CMR (Boehmer); and the Aiken case is G-CMR (Gauss).

For logistical reasons, I reviewed the case files of the other two POW murders—at Camp Tonkawa and Camp Papago Park—at the library of the University of California-Davis. Copies of those case files are at UC-Davis because of the persistence of the late Kenneth Knox, a former guard at Fort Leavenworth who became fascinated with the POW murder cases and compiled copies of the case files from the National Archives. The Kenneth Knox Collection at UC-Davis also contains a collection of documents related to the Germans' executions.

At the Hoover Institution Library and Archives at Stanford University in Palo Alto, California, I found a fascinating collection of documents, articles, and news clippings in the Stephen M. Farrand Collection. Major Farrand of the Army Provost Marshal General's Office was the main point of contact between the army and the Swiss "Protecting Power" during World War II and brought a unique perspective to the story of the German POW camp murders.

The Texas Collection at Baylor University in Waco, Texas, contains the personal papers of Leon Jaworski (who earned his undergraduate and law degrees at Baylor), including photos, letters, and documents relating to the prosecutions he conducted both in the United States and in Germany after the war.

Secretary of War Henry Stimson's wartime diary is kept at the Library of Yale University in New Haven, Connecticut. I was able to access the diary online through the assistance of archivist Shawn Kent.

Author's Note

My information about POW Camp Ashby in my home city of Virginia Beach came primarily from local historian Julie Spivey, who shared with me her collection of government documents from the National Archives, old newspaper clippings, and a written account by former POW John Merz of his experiences at Camp Ashby during World War II.

PROLOGUE
A Chair and a Clothesline

My description of farm life in Cloud County, Kansas, comes from my conversations with Lowell May, an army veteran who grew up in the area and has been instrumental in preserving POW Camp Concordia. My information about Camp Concordia, Kansas, comes from my visit to Concordia in 2022 and several other sources, including a wealth of documents May provided to me, including numerous oral histories and "The History of Camp Concordia from Site Survey to Inactivation," a 115-page history of the camp written by its army reeducation officer, U.S. Army Capt. Karl Teufel, in October 1945. May had obtained his copy of the history from NARA RG 389, Box 1612. May has written two books on the topic of POWs in Kansas: *Camp Concordia: German POWs in the Midwest* (Sunflower University Press, 1995) and *Prisoners of War in Kansas, 1943–46* (KS Publishing, 2007), the latter of which he cowrote with Mark P. Schock.

May told me that to POWs the most unnerving thing about remote north-central Kansas was the vast distances between towns and even farms. The description of the wind always blowing at Concordia comes from an oral history by former guard Joe Pickering. Many German POWs described their fears for their families in their recollections of their time in the camps. Army records in RG 389 list POW suicides in the camps before Felix Tropschuh's death at Concordia.

Details of the soccer-ball shooting come from Teufel's "History of Camp Concordia" and from *The Concordia Press*, October 21, 1943. Ex-guards Donald Kerr and Carl Stangel described in their oral histories the high tension in the camp after the soccer-ball shooting; Harriet Fahlstrom described in her oral history the racket emanating from the camp after the shooting.

The army's initial belief that Felix Tropschuh had committed suicide is described in Teufel's "History of Camp Concordia" and *The Concordia Press,* October 21, 1943.

My information about the army's subsequent discovery that Tropschuh had been forced to kill himself comes from Teufel's "History of Camp Concordia"; from newspaper articles in the *Concordia Blade-Empire* on January 11, 13, and 14, 1943, the *Concordia Daily Kansan* story "Fear Caused German Prisoner's Suicide" on January 13, 1944, the *New York Times* article "Prison Camps Rid of Nazi Terrorism" on January 16, 1945, and the *Clyde (Kansas) Republican* on October 1, 1943; and from an oral history by former Concordia POW Axel Bauer. For background I also consulted a 2005 graduate paper by Mark P. Schock, Lowell May's coauthor, at Wichita State University, "Bloodied Kansas: Nazi Retribution in a Kansas POW Camp."

The report of a half-dozen Concordia POWs requesting transfers after Tropschuh's death comes from the Camp Concordia prisoner transfer reports in RG 389.

CHAPTER 1
From *Afrika* and the Sea

Ernie Pyle's column about his interviews with German POWs at Tunis appeared in American newspapers on May 20, 1942. I found the version with the "screwy ideas" headline ("Nazi Prisoners Bare Superior-Race Complex and Other Screwy Ideas") in a clipping from the *Washington (D.C.) Daily News* in the Farrand Collection. I found background material on Pyle in David Chrisinger's biography of him, *The Soldier's Truth: Ernie Pyle and the Story of World War II* (Penguin Press, 2023).

My information about the rise and fall of the Afrika Korps comes from several sources, including Rick Atkinson's book *An Army at Dawn: The War in North Africa, 1942–1943* (Henry Holt, 2002) and Gershom Gorenberg's book *War of Shadows: Codebreakers, Spies, and the Secret Struggle to Drive the Nazis from the Middle East* (Public Affairs, 2021). Gorenberg's book reveals the critical role that stolen Allied secrets played in German field marshal Erwin Rommel's strategies.

The banner headline "Axis Giving Up in Tunisia Trap" appeared in *The Washington Daily News* on May 11, 1943, and I found the clipping in the Farrand Collection. The British captain's expression of relief comes from Atkinson's *Army at Dawn*, page 525.

I found the Harvard historian Dr. Sidney Fay's analysis of the Afrika Korps soldiers' mentality on page 161 of Arnold Krammer's *Nazi Prisoners of War in America* (Scarborough House, 1979). Krammer's book was the first and remains the most authoritative general account of the German POWs' experiences in the United States. It's essential reading for anyone interested in the topic.

My information about Col. Gen. Hans Jürgen von Arnim and his arrogant surrender comes from Atkinson's *Army at Dawn*, pages 528–29, and from Derek R. Mallett's *Hitler's Generals in America: Nazi POWs and Allied Military Intelligence* (University Press of Kentucky, 2013), pages 18–22. Mallett tells the unusual story of how U.S. authorities eventually courted captured German generals in the hope they could persuade the German people to side with the West in the incipient Cold War. They had little success with von Arnim, who led an ardent pro-Nazi faction at the generals' camp, Camp Clinton in Mississippi, where he was sent after his interrogation in Britain. I also drew information from several news clippings from the Farrand Collection, including an account of von Arnim's surrender in *The Washington Post* on May 14, 1943, and Associated Press stories on May 13 and 16, 1943.

My information about Japanese submarine attacks on the American mainland after the Pearl Harbor attack comes from William Breuer's *The Air-Raid Warden Was a Spy, and Other Tales from Home-Front America in World War II* (Castle Books, 2003). The fascinating story of the Japanese fire balloon attacks on the United States is well told in detail in Ross Coen's book *Fu-Go: The Curious History of Japan's Balloon Bomb Attack on America* (University of Nebraska Press, 2014). The U.S. government feared the Japanese might send saboteurs riding on balloons across the ocean but ultimately concluded that a balloon capable of carrying a person and supplies for such a long distance would have to be huge. The balloons carrying the incendiary bombs were twelve feet in diameter.

There are lots of accounts of the Germans' failed sabotage missions in 1942. I draw my brief sketch of the incident and the prosecutions from Michael A. Dobbs's book *Saboteurs: The Nazi Raid on America* (Vintage Books, 2005) and from a June 28, 2016, article in *Smithsonian Magazine,* "The Inside Story of How a Nazi Plot to Sabotage the U.S. War Effort Was Foiled," by David A. Taylor.

The landing of the would-be saboteurs in 1944 was not the last time Germany sent agents to U.S. shores. On the night of November 29, 1944, a U-boat landed two German spies on the Maine coast near Bar Harbor with $60,000 in small U.S. bills (over $1 million in 2024 dollars) and a bagful of diamonds to sell in an emergency. Their assignment was to assess the impact of Nazi propaganda and gather information about American defense industries. They got ashore without being spotted and made it by train to New York City. But their mission fell apart in much the same way as the saboteurs' mission in 1942. One of the two spies to land in Maine, American-born William Colepaugh, gave up on the plan and contacted the FBI, which arrested him and his comrade Erich Gimpel. A U.S. military tribunal convicted both men of espionage and sentenced them to death. Their sentences would be commuted.

An excellent source of information about the role of American industry in World War II is Richard Overy's *Why the Allies Won* (W. W. Norton, 1995).

I found Edgar Mowrer's column on the Geneva Convention in the Farrand Collection. The date of the column was not shown on the clipping.

The quote from *Collier's* magazine comes from the August 1944 issue, as quoted on page 30 of Judith M. Gansberg's book about the POW reeducation program, *Stalag: U.S.A.: The Remarkable Story of German POWs in America* (Thomas Y. Crowell, 1977).

The views of the House Military Affairs Committee on treating enemy prisoners well to protect American prisoners are from page 539 of an article by Provost Marshal General Archer Lerch, "The Army Reports on Prisoners of War," in *The American Mercury* magazine, May 1945. The article is part of the Farrand Collection.

George G. Lewis and John Mewha describe America's initial reluctance to accept any more than "an emergency batch" of fifty thousand German prisoners in World War II, as well as an explanation of why the United States had little choice but to accept a far larger number, on page 83 of their book *History of Prisoner of War Utilization by the United States Army, 1776–1945* (Department of the Army, 1955).

Krammer's colorful comment about "the specter of thousands of escaped Nazi prisoners sabotaging and raping" appears on page 114 of his *Nazi Prisoners of War in America*.

Ernie Pyle's comparison of the large haul of Afrika Korps prisoners to a desirable "white elephant" appears in his "Nazi Prisoners" column.

POW Heino Erichsen's observation that the Nazis still felt powerful even while on ships being taken to America is on page 110 of Michael R. Waters's *Lone Star Stalag: German Prisoners of War at Camp Hearne* (Texas A&M University Press, 2004). I found a reference to Churchill sailing to America with German POWs in a story by the Associated Press dated June 7, 1943. Jim Greer of Omaha, Nebraska, told me about his encounters with German POWs on his merchant ship in a telephone interview in 2021. Lt. Yvonne Humphreys's ill feeling about some of the German POWs on her ship is reported on pages 16–17 of Krammer's *Nazi Prisoners of War in America*.

I found the quote about the German U-boat crewman worrying about being torpedoed on page 27 of Antonio Thompson's book *Men in German Uniform: POWs in America During World War II* (University of Tennessee Press, 2010). POW Rüdiger von Wechmar described his experience crossing the Atlantic in the 2010 History Channel documentary *Nazi POWs in America*. The footnoted information about the sinking of the M/V *Montevideo Maru* comes from a CNN article by Heather Law, "World War II Shipwreck of SS Montevideo Maru, Which Sank with Over 1,000 POWs, Found in South China Sea," April 21, 2023.

I found the saga of the U-615 on pages 29–35 of Richard Whittingham's *Martial Justice: The Last Mass Execution in the United States* (Naval Institute Press, 1997). The interrogation report on Rolf Wizuy as a stubborn Nazi comes from RG 319, "Interrogation of Rolf Wizuy."

I found the quote about the incoming POWs (from Beverly Smith's article,

"The Afrika Korps Comes to America," in the August 1943 issue of *American Magazine*) in Krammer's *Nazi Prisoners of War in America*, page 44.

The account of the German POWs squeezing through a porthole and jumping into the water near Manhattan's West Side docks comes from an Associated Press story on June 16, 1943, that appeared in the *Washington (D.C.) Evening Star* under the headline "Eight Nazis Attempt to Flee Prison Ship." I found the *Star* clipping in the Farrand Collection.

POW Reinhold Pabel's comments about the Pullman coaches are on page 146 of his autobiography, *Enemies Are Human* (John C. Winston, 1955).

My information about some POWs leaping from trains and one being shot on a train station platform comes from NARA RG 389, Statistics on German POWs. The story of Dietrich Kroll mapping out his return route from Nebraska to the sea comes from page 26 of Melissa Amateis Marsh's book *Nebraska POW Camps: A History of World War II Prisoners in the Heartland* (History Press, 2014), which is full of interesting details. The German's comment about turning America into a colony comes from the transcript of the Camp Tonkawa murder trial, which I reviewed in the Knox Collection at UC-Davis. The murder victim, Johann Kunze, had told the Americans that a German sergeant made the comment on the train ride into the rural heart of the United States.

The prisoner's comment about the natural beauty of Houma, Louisiana, comes from a collection of POW comments in the Farrand Collection. The U-boat man's comment comparing the Arizona desert to the sea comes from page 66 of John Hammond Moore's book *The Faustball Tunnel: German POWs in America and Their Great Escape* (Naval Institute Press, 1978). Moore's book is a lively and well-researched account of the mass escape from Camp Papago Park in December 1944.

The POW's comment about the full factory parking lots in America and the absence of blackouts comes from Karl Gassman's oral history at Camp Concordia, Kansas.

CHAPTER 2
"I Just Didn't Lose"

My description of Leon Jaworski's background comes from three of his books, *After Fifty Years* (Gulf, 1961), *Crossroads,* with Dick Schneider (David C. Cook, 1981), and *Confession and Avoidance,* with Ricky Herskowitz (Anchor Press / Doubleday, 1979). I also found some nice details in three in-depth magazine profiles of Jaworski: "The Conscience of Leon Jaworski," by Brock Bower, in *Esquire* magazine, February 1975; "Have Conscience, Will Travel," by Henry Hurt III, in *Texas Monthly*, November 1977; and "Colonel of Truth: How My Grandfather, Leon Jaworski, Saved America," by Jaworski's grandson, Robert Draper, in *Texas Monthly*, November 2003. Jaworski's personal papers in the Texas Collection at Baylor University also provided many insights into his life.

Jaworski described his early life in pages 18–23 of *Crossroads,* including his explanation of why his father immigrated to America and his lyrical quote about the night wind in the cedars. He described his early encounters with anti-German and anti-immigrant bigotry on pages 27–28. He described his impatience with long novels on page 3 of *Confession and Avoidance.*

"Liberty cabbage" was not the last case of the political renaming of food in the United States. A more recent example took place in 2003, when conservative Republicans pressed for renaming French fries "freedom fries" and French toast "freedom toast" in a symbolic rebuke to France for opposing the planned U.S. invasion of Iraq.

Jaworski's personal papers contain a photo of his mother's grave with the cross inscribed in German. He recounted his prewar legal career in all three books. His personal papers are full of documents and court records about his most interesting cases, including his attempt to save a young Black sharecropper from the electric chair. He described his mixed feelings about the death penalty on page 18 of *Confession and Avoidance.* Jaworski explained his reliance on prayer in his decision to move to Houston on page 68 of *Crossroads,* and the new direction his career took at that point on pages 48–72 of *Confession and Avoidance.* His description of the drive and determination that made him successful comes from "Have Conscience Will Travel," his interview with *Texas Monthly.*

Jaworski's personal papers contain letters and documents showing his vigorous efforts to join the army as a prosecutor or a trial judge advocate. His description of his motivations and his "planetary adventure" quote come from *Confession and Avoidance,* pages 74–75.

My figures about the explosion of criminal cases in the wartime army come from Jack Hamann's investigative book *On American Soil: How Justice Became a Casualty of World War II* (Algonquin Books, 2005). It was Hamann who uncovered the fact that Jaworski had withheld critical evidence from the defense in the Fort Lawton, Washington, case.

Jaworski wrote about his view of Nazism as evil in *After Fifty Years,* his first book and his only book devoted entirely to his World War II experiences.

CHAPTER 3
Incoming

My information about the first German POWs arriving at Camp Concordia comes from Lowell May and a collection of oral histories he provided to me, including one by Chester Erickson with a quote that the prisoners looked bedraggled and smelled bad. The reference to the parents' fear for their teen-aged girls—a fear of the American guards, not the German POWs—comes from the oral histories.

The description of the townspeople of Mexia, Texas, turning out to see the POWs arrive comes from page 44 of Arnold Krammer's *Nazi Prisoners of War in America* (Scarborough House, 1979). The "greatest thing since popcorn" quote comes from page 13 of Michael R. Waters's *Lone Star Stalag: German Prisoners of War at Camp Hearne* (Texas A&M University Press, 2004). Beverly Smith's take on the puzzled German POWs arriving in small-town Crossville, Tennessee, comes from her article "The *Afrika Korps* Comes to America," in the August 1943 issue of *American Magazine.*

My information about America's history of dealing with prisoners of war comes from Lt. Col. George G. Lewis and Capt. John Mewha's *History of Prisoner of War Utilization by the United States Army, 1776–1945* (Department of the Army, 1955) and Robert C. Doyle's *The Enemy in Our Hands: America's Treatment of Prisoners of War from the Revolution to the War on Terror* (University Press of Kentucky, 2010). Both books offer thoughtful analysis of America's approach to POWs from the American Revolution onward. George Washington's exchange with General Gage appears on pages 1–2 of Lewis and Mewha's *History of Prisoner of War Utilization*; President Lincoln's ultimatum to the South in the Civil War and General Sherman's use of Confederate prisoners to clear mines appear on page 37; General Pershing's preference to keep World War I German prisoners in France is explained on page 53.

I got my figures on the numbers of German POW camps in the United States and the states in which they operated from an army summary of the camp program in RG 389. The number of branch camps is imprecise because the summary missed some that I found in the course of my research. Some of the camps existed only briefly, or seasonally when crops had to be harvested, which may explain why those camps did not make the list. The description of a typical main camp comes from the army's summary in RG 389 as well as from documents at Camp Concordia, Kansas, and Camp

Hearne, Texas. My detailed description of Camp Concordia comes from official army documents provided to me by Lowell May.

My information about the exodus of workers from Kansas farms comes from page 11 of Lowell A. May and Mark P. Schock's book *Prisoners of War in Kansas, 1943–1946* (KS Publishing, 2007). The letter from one of Congressman Hope's constituents comes from page 243 of David Hinshaw's book *The Home Front* (G. P. Putnam's Sons, 1943).

Rachel Forsberg recalled her fears about German POWs in her oral history at Camp Concordia. The citizen protest of the army's plan to open a POW branch camp in Butler County, Kansas, is described on page 103 of May and Schock's *German Prisoners of War in Kansas*. The Ottawa, Kansas, woman's letter to the editor comes from page 154 of that book.

Most of the quotes about prisoners eating better in the camps than at home come from a collection of prisoner comments in the Farrand Collection. The "we got fat" quote comes from Waters's *Lone Star Stalag*, page 24. The prisoner's quote about using flour to line soccer pitches comes from Lewis H. Carlson's *We Were Each Other's Prisoners: An Oral History of World War II American and German Prisoners of War* (Basic Books, 1997), page 151. The POW's letter reassuring his mother about the food comes from the Farrand Collection, as does the comment about "turkeys big like eagles."

Most of the Nazis' laments about the camps come from the Farrand Collection. The quote about Texas heat inspiring the devil to fight his own grandmother comes from Waters's *Lone Star Stalag*, page 17. The resolute quote ending the chapter comes from the Farrand Collection.

CHAPTER 4
The Fritz Ritz

My information about Jaworski's rise through the ranks of army prosecutors, his prosecution of the GI for cutting off his fingers, and his assignment to prosecute the Camp Tonkawa killers comes mainly from his personal papers at Baylor and from his book *Confession and Avoidance,* with Mickey Herskowitz (Anchor Press / Doubleday, 1979), 78–80. Jaworski's comment about the importance of prosecuting such cases comes from page 81.

Archer Lerch's comment about the Germans working better for a beer reward comes from his article "The Army Reports on Prisoners of War," in the *American Mercury* magazine, May 1945, page 542. He quoted Confederate general Thomas "Stonewall" Jackson on page 540 of that article.

The army's September 17, 1943, memo opening the way to siting new POW camps according to the need for labor comes from RG 389. So does a copy of the German High Command's order to enlisted German prisoners to work, in a message from the Swiss Legation dated February 8, 1944, in RG 389.

The diverse kinds of labor performed by the German POWs are described in numerous books and articles. An Associated Press article in *The Kansas City Star* on May 15, 1945, described the POWs filling sandbags along the Mississippi in the Ste. Genevieve levee district in Missouri. The statistic about the seed cotton in Mississippi comes from Lt. Col. George G. Lewis and Capt. John Mewha's *History of Prisoner of War Utilization by the United States Army, 1776–1945* (Department of the Army, 1955), page 127.

I found Bill Strauss's comment that he could not help but befriend the Germans in Lowell A. May and Mark P. Schock's *Prisoners of War in Kansas, 1943–1946* (KS Publishing, 2007), page 62. Melissa Amateis Marsh's *Nebraska POW Camps: A History of World War II Prisoners in the Heartland* (History Press, 2014) contains a vignette of a farm wife insisting on feeding the Germans on page 133.

The farmer's account of the POW clowning with his son comes from Marsh's *Nebraska POW Camps*, page 79. Ernest Blecha's story about the POW asking to hold his baby comes from page 38 of May and Schock's *Prisoners of War in Kansas*.

Guenther Oswald's quote about his change of heart comes from a collection of POW writings at Camp Trinidad in Colorado that I found in the Farrand Collection.

I include only a few stories about German POWs encountering the South's Jim Crow laws. Unfortunately, there are many more. Robert Trimmingham's letter to *Yank* magazine comes from the Library of America's collection *Reporting World War II: Part Two, American Journalism, 1944–1946* (Literary Classics of the United States, 1995), page 470. I found the account of Lena Horne's experience at Camp Robinson on pages 163–64 of James Gavin's biography of Horne, *Stormy Weather* (Atria Books, 2009).

On page 129 of Judith M. Gansberg's *Stalag: U.S.A.: The Remarkable Story of German POWs in America* (Thomas Y. Crowell, 1977), she quotes an instructor at the army's reeducation school for Germans who described how POWs had frequently asked him how America could boast about its form of democracy while its Black citizens were subjected to virulent racism. The instructor, T. V. Smith, a southerner, told Gansberg he tried to focus on the advances Black U.S. citizens had made since the days of slavery, but "there was never any pretense on my part that 'democracy' is not fascism to our Negroes in certain sections [of America] and at certain times."

The vignette about a news reporter witnessing a performance of *Faust* at Camp Trinidad in Colorado comes from Arnold Krammer's *Nazi Prisoners of War in America* (Scarborough House, 1979), page 52.

The account of a German POW reuniting with an American brother he had not seen in twenty-five years was among the stories I heard in 2023 on a visit to the Camp Hearne Historic Site, which is located between Houston and Waco, Texas. Robert D. Billinger Jr. mentions the rice planters' seafood feast for POWs in his richly detailed book *Hitler's Soldiers in the Sunshine State: German POWs in Florida* (University Press of Florida, 2009).

The "Put them in Death Valley" quote comes from page 45 of Krammer's *Nazi Prisoners of War in America*. I found several references to the term "the Fritz Ritz" in my research. I first saw it in Krammer's book.

Provost Marshal General Lerch tallied the escapes and recaptures of German POWs in his article "The Army Reports on Prisoners of War," pages 545–46. His figures correspond with an army report on escapes in RG 389.

The account of the lone German escapee comes from Gansberg's *Stalag: U.S.A.*, page 34. The account of the Luftwaffe pilot's near escape comes from Krammer's *Nazi Prisoners of War in America*, page 127, and my info about the Detroit escape attempt comes from page 127. My information about the three Nisei Japanese sisters comes from an article by Eric L. Muller, "Prosecution of the Shitara Sisters," in the *Densho Encyclopedia*, last updated June 12, 2020, encyclopedia.densho.org/Prosecution_of_the_Shitara _Sisters/. The SS man's "vacation trip" comes from Billinger's *Hitler's Soldiers in the Sunshine State*, page 116. Franz Bacher's escape for the sake of his art is recounted in Allen V. Koop's book *Stark Decency: German Prisoners of War in a New England Village* (University Press of New England, 1988), pages 54–56. Koop wrote that the guard who bumped into Bacher in Penn Station had known him in Austria before the war, knew he was an anti-Nazi who posed no threat, and may have allowed him to enjoy a few more days of freedom in New York City before turning him in.

My brief summary of the mass escape from Camp Papago Park in Arizona is based on my reading of John Hammond Moore's *The Faustball Tunnel: German POWs in America and Their Great Escape* (Naval Institute Press, 1978).

CHAPTER 5
Little Germanies

Amery's observations on arriving at Camp Hood come from page 103 of French author Daniel Costelle's book *Prisonniers Nazis en Amerique* (Acropole, 2012). His comment that he felt "had come home" comes from page 162 of Arnold Krammer's *Nazi Prisoners of War in America* (Scarborough House, 1979). Camp Hood's parent installation, Fort Hood, had been named for the daring Confederate cavalry officer Capt. John Bell Hood. The fort was renamed Fort Cavazos in 2023 for Gen. Richard Edward Cavazos, the first Hispanic American four-star general and a decorated veteran of the Korean and Vietnam Wars.

Josef Krumbachner's quote about the Nazis at Camp Como, Mississippi, terrorizing other prisoners comes from Lewis H. Carlson's *We Were Each Other's Prisoners: An Oral History of World War II American and German Prisoners of War* (Basic Books, 1997), page 151. My information about prisoners at Camp Mexia, Texas, being forced to listen to readings of *Mein Kampf* comes from Richard Walker's article "The Swastika and the Lone Star: Nazi Activity in Texas POW Camps," *Military History of the Southwest* 19, no. 1 (Spring 1989): 48. The account by the new prisoner of his lecture about "the spirit of Rommel" and his quote about being ruled by the Nazis "in the land of the free" comes from Walker's article. Luca Müller's comment that he enjoyed more political freedom in the Wehrmacht than in his POW camp comes from Lewis Carlson's *We Were Each Other's Prisoners*, page 167.

The description by informant "Karl P." about the Nazis' threats to sic the Gestapo or SS on the families of POWs back in Germany comes from Judith M. Gansberg's *Stalag: U.S.A.: The Remarkable Story of German POWs in America* (Thomas Y. Crowell, 1977), page 51. The vignette about the POW discovering that the Nazis had made good on one such threat comes from Walker, "The Swastika and the Lone Star."

Major McKnight's quote about never considering segregating the different kinds of German POWs comes from Gansberg's *Stalag: U.S.A.*, page 60.

The army inspector's dim view of the quality of American POW camp guards comes from army circular 161, "Camp Establishment—Short Historical Sketch, Background, and Problems Encountered," a summary of a presentation at a regional conference of POW camp authorities at an unspecified date in 1944, which I found in the Farrand Collection. The same circular contains a copy of a speech, apparently from the same conference, in which Assistant Provost Marshal B.M. Bryan quoted a line from Hitler in *Mein Kampf* to the effect that big lies always leave their mark, regardless of how outrageous and readily disproven they are. Army circulars in the Farrand Collection also advised guards how to counter the Nazis' favorite "fantasies" and lies, including that Jews were the source of most problems in Germany and America; and reminded guards to consider what horrors friendly-acting German POWs may have committed before they were captured. A commentary by James Powers about POW camps being dumping grounds for poor U.S. officers also is part of the Farrand Collection.

Major McKnight's striking quote about "kooks and crazy people" comes from pages 42–43 of Gansberg's *Stalag: U.S.A.* Gansberg interviewed McKnight after the war, when he evidently felt free to speak candidly.

The vignette about the churchgoing Germans singing the Horst Wessel Song comes from Krammer's *Nazi Prisoners of War in America*, page 150. Former German POW Horst Kuhnke compared the American guards at Camp Concordia to the incompetent German guards in the TV series *Hogan's Heroes* in his oral history at Camp Concordia.

Sergeant Staff's favorable comments about Nazi discipline come from Krammer's *Nazi Prisoners of War in America*, pages 149–50.

The army camp commander's dismissal of anti-Nazis as "Hitler's scum" comes from Krammer's *Nazi Prisoners of War in America*, pages 149–50. The letter from the anti-Nazi prisoner's plea to the army commander of Camp Campbell in Kentucky comes from page 165. POW Heino Erichsen's observation that the army's love of efficiency led to a "disastrous strengthening" of the Nazis in the camps comes from Michael R. Waters's *Lone Star Stalag: German Prisoners of War at Camp Hearne* (Texas A&M University Press, 2004), page 111.

Several POWs described the Nazi threat to send word home to punish families in the transcripts of the murder trials in the Knox Collection at UC-Davis and the National Archives office in St. Louis. The transcripts also contain several descriptions by German POWs of *der Heilig Geist*. One of the better descriptions comes from the testimony of POW Josef Heidutzek in the Camp Tonkawa murder case. In the transcripts, several prisoners said the Nazis operated such courts in the tradition of secret *Fehme* tribunals in medieval Germany.

I found Fritz Haus's "knife's edge" comment on page 117 of Waters's *Lone Star Stalag*. James Powers's evocation of a Nazi-controlled camp as a "little Germany" comes from his article in the *Atlantic Monthly*, "What to Do About the German Prisoner," in November 1944.

The army's breakdown of the percentages of various types of German POWs comes from the army circular "What About the German Prisoner?" That circular also contains a keen if belated analysis of the Nazis' methods of taking over the camps.

I found the army's estimate of the total number of violent incidents among Germans at the camps in a report in RG 389. Krammer's estimate of the number of Nazi assaults on fellow prisoners comes from page 170 of his *Nazi Prisoners of War in America.*

The incident at Camp Ellis is described in Krammer's *Nazi Prisoners of War in America,* page 170. A report of the Camp Huntsville riot is among Jaworski's personal papers at Baylor. Guard Tex Geyser's colorful quote comes from Waters's *Lone Star Stalag,* page 111.

My account of Camp Concordia's early years comes from Capt. Karl Teufel's "History of Camp Concordia from Site Survey to Inactivation," October 1945 (NARA RG 389, Box 1612, courtesy of Lowell May). The vignette about the anti-Semitic janitor at Concordia comes from the oral histories at Camp Concordia. The information about the transfer of the Gestapo agent from Camp Concordia comes from the Concordia POW transfer reports in NARA RG 389.

The account of the soccer-ball shooting of a POW comes partly from *The Concordia Press,* October 21, 1943. Carl "Casey" Stangel described the incident in his oral history at Camp Concordia. Harriet Fahlstrom's quote comes from her oral history at Concordia.

The army provided a detailed account of its investigation into Tropschuh's death to *The New York Times,* for its story "Prison Camps Rid of Nazi Terrorism" on January 16, 1945. The comments by ex-POWs Karl Gassman and Willi Lelle are in their oral histories at Camp Concordia, as is Purdy's remark about getting rid of the Nazis. I found numerous transfer requests from anti-Nazis in the army's files in RG 389.

CHAPTER 6
"No Place for a Priest"

I reconstructed the mass meeting and murder of Johann Kunze at Camp Tonkawa mainly from the defendants' statements and from the court-martial testimony in the case files at the Kenneth Knox Collection at UC-Davis. Most of my information about the defendants also comes from those files. Copies of the unsigned note about Hamburg and Kunze's letter to his wife are in the files.

I stumbled upon a great description of the British firebombing of Hamburg on pages 203–7 of John Vaillant's book *Fire Weather: A True Story from a Hotter World* (Alfred A. Knopf, 2023).

My information about Leon Jaworski's rise from routine cases to major cases comes from his personal papers at Baylor University and his books *After Fifteen Years* (Gulf, 1961), *Crossroads,* with Dick Schneider (David C. Cook, 1981), and *Confession and Avoidance,* with Mickey Herskowitz (Anchor Press / Doubleday, 1979).

Jaworski expressed his reasons for favoring prosecution of the German POWs on page 81 of *Confession and Avoidance.* My background information about Camp Tonkawa comes from the Oklahoma Historical Society.

My account of Captain Maffitt's preliminary investigation comes from the case files at NARA St. Louis and from court reporter Wilma Parnell's book *The Killing of Corporal Kunze,* with Robert Taber (Lyle Stuart, 1981), pages 27–76. Parnell described Maffitt's outburst on page 68. She was among those startled by the outburst. She described her immediate, favorable impression of Jaworski on page 77. Parnell's book offered a valuable civilian's take on the Camp Tonkawa case. She got to know Jaworski during the proceedings and he graciously agreed to read a draft of her book.

Jaworski described his investigation at Camp Tonkawa in his three books on the topic. I also relied on the case files at NARA St. Louis.

Parnell described her new impression of the Afrika Korps on pages 53–54 of *The Killing of Corporal Kunze.*

The statements of Willi Scholz, Hans Demme, and Hans Schomer come from the trial record of the Tonkawa case in the Knox Collection at UC-Davis.

Jaworski's comments about catching at least some of the killers come from his closing arguments in the Tonkawa court-martial, which are included in his personal papers at Baylor and also in the court transcript.

My description of the violence at Camp Huntsville comes from court documents in Jaworski's personal papers—he prosecuted two of the POWs involved—and from Jeffrey L. Littlejohn and Charles H. Ford's book *The Enemy Within Never Did Without: German and Japanese Prisoners of War at Camp Huntsville, 1942–1945* (Texas Review Press, 2015), page 53.

Wilma Parnell described the awkward junction of the investigation and a holiday dance at Camp Tonkawa in *The Killing of Corporal Kunze,* pages 81–84.

I found Colonel Morrissette's criticism of the Tonkawa murder charges, as well as Jaworski's reaffirming exchange of letters with a JAG prosecutor in Washington, in Jaworski's personal papers at Baylor.

My information about the history of U.S. military tribunals comes from Lt. Col. George G. Lewis and Capt. John Mewha's *History of Prisoner of War Utilization by the United States Army, 1776–1945* (Department of the Army, 1955) and from Beverly Gage's book *G-Man: J. Edgar Hoover and the Making of the American Century* (Viking, 2022), page 274. Jaworski's description of courts-martial versus civilian trials comes from pages 26–27 of his book *After Fifteen Years* and from page 80 of *Confession and Avoidance*.

CHAPTER 7
Secret Verdicts

My background information about Hugo Krauss comes from documents at the POW Camp Hearne Historic Site, from testimony in the court-martial of his suspected killers, and from a story about him in *The New York Times* on January 16, 1945, "Ex-Yorkville Man Slain as Prisoner."

My statement about the American public not knowing the full scope of the German POW camps or much about what went on in them is based on interviews with dozens of people who lived near the camps around the country. Army files in NARA RG 389 illustrate the U.S. government's extreme sensitivity about "bad press" regarding the camps and the army's efforts to limit coverage of them and control the narrative. Army authorities grumbled and raged in internal memos about the relatively few "negative" stories about the camps in newspapers and magazines.

The makeup of the Camp Tonkawa military tribunal and the defense team comes from court documents from the case in the Knox Collection at UC-Davis.

I reconstructed the Tonkawa court-martial from the case file in the Knox Collection at UC-Davis and documents in Jaworski's personal papers at Baylor, which include a transcript of his closing arguments in the case.

Jeffery L. Littlejohn and Charles H. Ford helpfully include a copy of the 1929 Geneva Convention relating to POWs in an appendix to their book *The Enemy Within Never Did Without: German and Japanese Prisoners of War at Camp Huntsville, 1942–1945* (Texas Review Press, 2015).

Jaworski described his worries about the fallout from the Tonkawa murder case on page 81 of *Confession and Avoidance,* with Mickey Herkowitz (Anchor Press / Doubleday, 1979). His and others' statements praising the fairness of the court-martial come from the court record in the Knox Collection at UC-Davis. Defense Attorney Petsch's prescient prediction of how the

German would react to the death sentences of the German POWs also comes from the court record.

CHAPTER 8
King Kong in a Cage

I found background on Schaefer's early years in census records via www
.ancestry.com, and in his obituary in *The Columbus (Ga.) Ledger,* September
17, 1979, under the headline "War Prisoner Dies at 79." Claudia Dant, curator of the Wabash County (Ill.) Museum, described for me what Schaefer's
birthplace of Kitchen's Bridge was like at the start of the twentieth century
when he was born.

My physical description of Schaefer in 1942–44 comes from Clarence Ferguson's book *Kriegsgefangener (Prisoner of War)* (Texian Press, 1983), page
224. Ferguson served as Schaefer's and Schmitz's chief defense lawyer in the
court-martial resulting from the poster incident. Several sources recalled
Lt. Col. William Schaefer's nickname of "King Kong," including Flint Whitlock in his book *The Rock of Anzio: From Sicily to Dachau, a History of the
U.S. 45th Infantry Division* (Hachette, 2005). Whitlock writes that Schaefer
called his men his "knot heads" and quotes some of Schaefer's fellow officers
praising his military knowledge, including Lt. Bill Whitman, who theorized
that Schaefer would have retired as a major general had he not been captured.

The story of Schaefer's angry takeover of his battalion's training program comes from "Col. William H. Schaefer, U. S. Army, Ret.," a reminiscence about Schaefer by one of his men, Dr. Peter Carl Graffagnino, that was
printed in "The Doctor's Lounge," a column in the *Bulletin of the Muscogee
County (Ga.) Medical Society* 10, no. 12 (December 1963): 9. The article was
published on the occasion of a talk Schaefer gave to the society about a book
he wrote and self-published about the international monetary system. Schaefer, who was something of a Renaissance man, self-published books about a
wide range of topics, including one about his time as a POW, which I reference below.

Much of my account of Schaefer's capture, transport, and incarceration
comes from his book *People Too* (Pageant Press, 1971). Schaefer's long-out-
of-print book was extremely hard to find. I finally obtained a copy through
the Oflag 64 veterans' group. Elodie Caldwell, the administrator of the
group's website, www.oflag64.us/, put me in touch with Dave Stewart of
Texas, who literally was about to put his only copy of the book in a box and

mail it to a POW museum in Poland. Dave paused long enough to scan the entire book for me before sending it off. Needless to say, I'm very grateful to Elodie and Dave for going out of their way to enable me to tell Schaefer's story in detail.

Schaefer described his part in the invasion of Sicily and his capture in detail on pages 11–31 of *People Too*. My account of the actor/soldier singing an aria from *Rigoletto* to calm a frightened Sicilian family comes from a United Press story I found in the *Green Bay Press-Gazette*, August 10, 1943, under the headline "U.S. Sailor Sings Rigoletto to Calm Frightened Sicilians."

Schaefer described his dangerous passage in captivity through Italy on pages 32–54 of *People Too*, and his hard times at the Luckenwalde interrogation center on pages 62–76. Schaefer also described his experiences in a postwar report to MIS-X, which I found among Schaefer's entries in NARA RG 153, the files of the Judge Advocate General's Office. Those files include investigations by the U.S. War Crimes Office into possible German war crimes. I found the MIS-X analysis of Luckenwalde in RG 389.

CHAPTER 9
Wrong Side of the River

Clarence Ferguson described Lt. James Schmitz in 1944–45 and the differences between Schmitz and Schaefer on page 224 of *Kriegsgefangener (Prisoner of War)* (Texian Press, 1983). My physical description of Schmitz after the war comes from his army separation report on September 2, 1945, which I found in RG 389.

Much of my background information about Schmitz comes from three of his cousins, Rita Schmitz of Texas, James Schmitz of Illinois, and John Schmitz of Chicago. All of them loved Schmitz and said he had had an outsized impact on their lives. Each of the three wanted me to know he was gay because they thought his sexual orientation had made his life more difficult and his achievements more impressive. It was John Schmitz who described La Salle County politics in the 1940s and called my attention to *Capone's Cornfields*. I also received helpful information about Schmitz's background from members of veterans' groups in Illinois, including the resourceful Jay Less, as well as Dave Mumper and John Duback. More details of Schmitz's background come from news stories written about speeches he gave after leaving the army and attempting to reenter local politics. I found most of the news stories via www.newspapers.com, which like www.ancestry.com is a tremendous resource for researchers.

The account of Schmitz dining with a fellow Ottawa, Illinois, native in Italy comes from a letter reported in *The Times* of Streator, Illinois, "Two Ottawans Meet in Italy," on January 10, 1944.

Ernie Pyle's description of the fighting in the mountains of Italy comes from the chapter "Mountain Fighting" in a new edition of his book *Brave Men* (Penguin Books, 2023). The same chapter contains perhaps Pyle's most famous column—his depiction of soldiers' grief over the death of a beloved officer.

My background information about the battle of Monte Cassino comes from the second volume of Rick Atkinson's trilogy about World War II, *The Day of Battle* (Henry Holt, 2007), pages 339–48, and from Peter Caddick-Adams's book *Monte Cassino: Ten Armies in Hell* (Oxford University Press, 2012), pages 16–32. The role of the cold, rainy weather in frustrating the Allies comes from Caddick-Adams, page 31.

Schmitz told the story of his personal experience in the battle on the Gari River in a series of speeches he gave in Illinois after the war. The speeches were covered in detail by *The Times* of Streator on April 26, 1945—"Ottowan Faced Execution by Nazis, Flees: Lieut. James Schmitz, Well Known Here, Tells of Escape, Liberation"—and on June 1, 1945—"Lt. J. Schmitz Relates Experiences as Prisoner of Nazis." The *Chicago Tribune* also recounted Schmitz's ordeal in a story headlined "Ex-Ottawa G.O.P. Chief Tells of Fleeing Nazis," on April 26, 1945. I found the story of the Germans' propaganda use of the note from the other captured officer on page 87 of Ferguson's *Kriegsgefangener*.

Schmitz briefly described his dangerous journey from capture to Oflag 64, and his disbelief of the Russians who described death camps, in the speeches covered by *The Times* on April 26 and June 1, 1945. Ferguson described the rural Polish countryside on pages 94–95 of *Kriegsgefangener*.

Ferguson described Schmitz's German ancestry and his loyalty to the United States on page 224 of *Kriegsgefangener*.

My description of Oflag 64 comes from the Oflag 64 "alumni" group and from pages 96–99 of Ferguson's *Kriegsgefangener*. Ferguson described the German camp commandant, Colonel Schneider, on page 97, and the spiteful Nazi security officer Captain Zimmerman on page 223. Zimmerman is also described on pages 36, 50, and 54 of Stephen Dando-Collins's book *The Big Break: The Greatest American WWII POW Escape Story Never Told* (St. Martin's Press, 2017) and on page 276 of Jerry Sage's book *Sage: The Man They Called "Dagger" of the OSS* (Dell, 1985).

Schmitz recounted the story of writing the "I give up" note for a German soldier in his speech covered by *The Times* of Streator, Illinois, on June 1, 1945.

A record of Jaworski's prosecution of a Texas GI for sodomy is contained in his personal papers. My information about the Nazis beating some fellow Germans for homosexuality comes from Michael R. Waters's *Lone Star Stalag* (Texas A&M University Press, 2004), page 76. Schmitz's nephew James Schmitz made the comment about his uncle living "in a prison inside a prison" at Oflag 64 in a telephone conversation with me in 2022.

Schmitz's account of starting an Illinois Club at Oflag 64 comes from *The Times* of Streator, Illinois's account of his speech on June 1, 1945.

Schaefer's comment about Oflag 64 being a great improvement over his other POW camps comes from William H. Schaefer's *People Too* (Pageant Press, 1971), page 77. The extraordinary vignette of Schaefer rapidly clacking his false teeth in order to taunt the Germans comes from Sage's book *Sage,* page 277. Schaefer's comment that some of the Germans "hated my guts" comes from *People Too.*

CHAPTER 10
The Bastards Get Lucky

My information about Col. Henry Spicer's background comes from a variety of sources, including his sons Randy Spicer of California and Tony Spicer (for whom he named his P-51 Mustang, "Tony Boy") of North Carolina. Randy sent me a copy of an obscure book about Spicer, *There Was an Eagle Here: The Story of Maj. Gen. Henry R. Spicer and Memories of the 357th Fighter Group in World War II* (Steeley, 2012), that was self-published by Bruce W. Spicer, who may have been a distant relative of Henry Spicer. *Eagle* is packed with recollections of Henry Spicer by his now-deceased fellow aviators, as well as copies of their official mission reports from 1944. Col. Henry Spicer's son Tony, who became a pilot, helped me interpret the reports and gave me valuable background about flying. Randy and Tony Spicer read drafts of this chapter, as did Kevin Knight of Virginia Beach, who retired from flying navy F-14s and now flies jetliners. I also consulted a detailed article about Henry Spicer by one of his former flying students, C. V. Glines, in the October 1995 issue of *Air Force Magazine,* entitled "A Speech Worth Dying For." I found numerous newspaper articles on www.newspapers.com that followed Spicer's career from Colorado to California to Texas, where he was based before being sent overseas.

My information about Spicer's polo skills and the "Horseless Wonders" comes from the *Hollywood (Calif.) News Citizen* story "Hollywood Leader of Flying Group Reported Missing," on April 17, 1944.

The vignette about Spicer's unusual grading practices in flight school comes from Glines, "A Speech Worth Dying For," page 72.

The story about Spicer and his pipe being a fixture at Moore Field in Texas comes from a society column in *The Monitor* (McAllen, Tex.), January 21, 1943.

The sobering statistic about U.S. bomber losses in October 1943 comes from page 817 in the Chronology in the Library of America's compilation *Reporting World War II: Part One, American Journalism, 1938–1944* (Literary Classics of the United States, 1995).

A great deal of information is available online about the P-51 Mustang's role in the war. I got my background information on the plane from several sources, including the website of the Aviation History Online Museum at www.aviation-history.com/north-american/p51.html, which covered all the points relevant to my story.

I found the names of other planes in Spicer's squadron scattered throughout Bruce Spicer's *There Was an Eagle Here,* along with a good summary of the dangers of flying P-51s in the air war over Europe.

My information about Henry Spicer's fast start in flying missions and shooting down German fighters comes from Spicer's and his fellow pilots' mission reports in Bruce Spicer's *There Was an Eagle Here* and Glines, "A Speech Worth Dying For," page 73. Henry Spicer's report on shooting down two enemy fighters on February 24, 1944, is among the mission reports.

My information about Chuck Yeager's white-knuckle experiences as Spicer's wingman comes from page 28 of Yeager's autobiography, cowritten with Leo Janos, *Yeager: An Autobiography* (Bantam Books, 1985). Yeager's own survival story after he was shot down on the same day as Spicer is worth reading.

Spicer's fellow pilot's description of Spicer's being shot down comes from a letter from Lt. Col. Gilbert O'Brien to Bruce Spicer, which the latter includes on page 32 of *There Was an Eagle Here.* Wingman Lt. John Pugh's report on the downing of Henry Spicer's plane comes from Spicer's individual entries in NARA RG 153.

My statistics about the losses of aviators in the English Channel and North Sea come from an online article, "Down in the Drink," by Merle Olmsted, historian, 357th Fighter Group, which I found on the website of P-51 "ace" Emil "Bud" Anderson, at toflyandfight.com/down-in-the-drink

-air-sea-rescue-in-the-english-channel/. The article cites British search-and-rescue historian Sid Harvey's estimate that about two thousand U.S. and four thousand British airmen were rescued from the waters around Britain over the course of World War II. The higher British number reflected the fact that Britain fought the war longer. In fact, downed American aviators stood a much better chance of being rescued from the sea because they flew in daylight while the British mostly flew at night. Harvey estimated that 66 percent of American airmen were rescued, compared to only 40 percent of their British counterparts.

The information that Spicer's wife first learned he was missing from volunteers on shortwave listening stations on the East Coast comes from *The Monitor* story "Spicer Reported War Prisoner in Europe," May 9, 1944.

Mozart Kaufman's take on master Luftwaffe interrogator Hanns Joachim Scharff comes from pages 109–12 of his book *Fighter Pilot: Aleutians to Normandy to Stalag Luft I* (M. and A. Kaufman, 1993).

Scharff's entertaining account of his attempts to draw information from Spicer comes from Raymond F. Tolliver's biography of Scharff, *The Interrogator: The Story of Hanns Joachim Scharff, Master Interrogator of the Luftwaffe* (Schiffer Military History, 1997), pages 168–72.

Kaufman expressed his high opinion of Spicer in *Fighter Pilot*, pages 137 and 147.

CHAPTER 11
"A Gestapo on the Free Soil of Kansas"

My information about the *Concordia Blade-Empire*'s tough editor "Nosey" Green comes from a reading of his articles on microfilm in the Cloud County Historical Society Museum as well as an oral history in Lowell A. May's book *Camp Concordia: German POWs in the Midwest* (Sunflower University Press, 1995). I worked with a few editors like Green during my long career as a journalist before I began writing books.

The account of the officers' club shooting that led to Colonel Sterling's being replaced as commanding officer at Camp Concordia comes from the pages of the *Blade-Empire* and U.S. Army Capt. Karl Teufel's "The History of Camp Concordia from Site Survey to Inactivation," October 1945 (NARA RG 389, Box 1612), courtesy of Lowell May. The "History" also described the disciplinarian style of Sterling's replacement, Lieutenant Colonel Vocke, and Vocke's refusal of the German camp spokesman's demand that Kettner be buried apart from the "honorable" Germans.

My information about POW Franz Kettner's forced suicide comes from Teufel's "History of Camp Concordia"; from *The New York Times* story "Prison Camps Rid of Nazi Terrorism" on January 16, 1945; and from *The Concordia Blade-Empire* stories on January 11 and 13, 1944. The misrouted transfer request that might have saved Kettner is contained in Camp Concordia's POW transfer file in RG 389. That file contains other requests by anti-Nazis to be transferred to camps where they would be safe from the Nazis at Camp Concordia.

"Nosey" Green's story under the headline "Fear-Hounded Nazi Captive Slashes Wrists" appeared on the front page of the January 11, 1944, edition of the *Blade-Empire*. One of my former editors called such stories "Hey, Martha!" stories, in the belief they would prompt readers to exclaim to their wives, "Hey, Martha! Read this!" The letters to the editor, including the one expressing concern about "a Gestapo on the Free Soil of Kansas," come from the *Blade-Empire* after Green's story appeared. I found *The Tulsa Tribune*'s and *The Kansas City Star*'s stories through www.newspapers.com.

My background on the U-118 comes from the U-boat website www.uboatnet.com—an excellent source of information about the U-boat war—and from naval intelligence reports on the interrogation of Werner Dreschler in RG 319. My background information about Dreschler comes from the intelligence report about his interrogation. My description of the secret Fort Hunt Interrogation Center and its use of stool pigeons comes from a narrative history of the interrogation center in Dreschler's file in RG 319. The U.S. Navy interrogators' analysis of Dreschler as conceited and therefore easy to manipulate is part of Dreschler's interrogation file.

The navy's attempts to keep Dreschler in protective custody and the army's failure to do so are laid out in a series of memos in the file "Transfers of Prisoners of War" in RG 165.

I visited the site of the former Camp Papago Park in 2019. Page 26 of John Hammond Moore's book *The Faustball Tunnel: German POWs in America and Their Great Escape* (Naval Institute Press, 1978) contains a good description of what the camp looked like in 1944.

My account of Dreschler's arrival at Papago Park and his death less than six hours later comes from reports on the army investigation and the transcript of the subsequent court-martial of the seven defendants, which I found in the Knox Collection at UC-Davis. NARA St. Louis also has copies of those documents.

CHAPTER 12
The *Rollkommando*

Leon Jaworski described his superior officer dramatically giving him the assignment of finding the "ringleader" in Geller's killing in *Crossroads,* with Dick Schneider (David C. Cook, 1981), page 85. Jaworski wrote more in his books about the Camp Chaffee case than about the earlier POW murder case at Camp Tonkawa, most likely because the Camp Chaffee case proved a bigger challenge for him.

Jaworski recalled his concern that the army was losing control of the POW camps on page 83 of *Crossroads.*

My background information about Camp Chaffee and the history of that rugged corner of Arkansas comes from Camp Chaffee historian Rod Williamson, whom I interviewed by phone in January 2024.

My account of Hans Geller's background and his murder at Camp Chaffee comes from the case file of the murder case at NARA St. Louis, where I spent several days reviewing the Camp Chaffee, Camp Hearne, and Camp Aiken murder cases in 2023.

My account of the flailing initial investigation into Geller's death and the POW's "dental checkup" shenanigans comes from Jaworski's *Confession and Avoidance,* with Mickey Herskowitz (Anchor Press / Doubleday, 1979), page 83.

Jaworski recounted his initial frustrations in investigating the murder and the taunting by Menschner on page 84 of *Confession and Avoidance.*

Jaworski described his use of "truth serum" to loosen the tongue of his eventual star witness, German sergeant Franz Raba, on pages 43–46 of *After Fifty Years* (Gulf, 1961). He noted in the book that no evidence he obtained from Raba while the latter was drugged would have been admissible in court unless Raba repeated the information afterward, which Raba did. Nowhere in the record of the trial was the use of the "truth serum" mentioned. In the book, Jaworski identified Raba as "Abar" and also misspelled the names of other witnesses and suspects. It's unclear whether he was trying to protect them or simply did not get their names right.

I found background information about the use of scopolamine and other forms of "truth serum" in several sources, including an online article published in 2008 by the McGill Office for Science and Society, Joe Schwarcz's "The Truth About Truth Serum," at www.mcgill.ca/oss/article/technology-history-general-science/truth-about-truth-serum, and Kelsie Cassell's "Plants Go to War: A Botanical History of World War II," *Yale Journal of*

Biological Medicine 93, no. 2 (2020): 375–79, containing an interview with American botanist and author Dr. Judith Sumner, at www.ncbi.nlm.nih.gov /pmc/articles/PMC7309670/.

Jaworski described his impressions of the suspected "ringleader" Edgar Menschner on pages 83–84 of *Confession and Avoidance* and on pages 37–39 of *After Fifty Years*. He described his method of getting under Menschner's skin by criticizing Nazism on pages 38–39, and his suspicion that Menschner had used his position as company clerk to determine Heller's hometown in Germany on page 36.

Jaworski explained his theory that a second POW had helped arrange the killing on pages 39–42 of *After Fifty Years*. I have not identified the second POW because he was never charged. Jaworski included entries from the man's diary on pages 86–89 of *Confession and Avoidance*. He described his frustration at being unable to charge the man and thus prevent him from being set free in postwar Germany on pages 48–49. (Jaworski would have been even more frustrated if he had known that Menschner also would end up being sent home to Germany within a few years.)

Jaworski described his efforts to prevent his star witness Sergeant Raba from getting cold feet on pages 46–48 of *After Fifty Years*.

I based my account of "The Great Escape" on Paul Brickhill's *The Great Escape* (Cassell, 2000). Clarence Ferguson described the broader chilling effect that the murder of the Allied escapees had on other Allied POWs in Germany, and specifically at Oflag 64, in his book *Kriegsgefangener (Prisoner of War)* (Texian Press, 1983).

CHAPTER 13
"Reeducating" the Nazis

I found the favorable article about the German POWs at Camp Aiken, South Carolina, as well as background on the sizable peanut crop in Aiken, in the story "German Prisoners Harvest Peanut Crop in Aiken Area" in the September 12, 1943, issue of *The Augusta Chronicle,* which I accessed via www .newspapers.com.

Robert Kohlhaas's recounting of the Nazis' pressure on him comes from an article by Kathy Roe Coker, "World War II Prisoners of War in Georgia: German Memories of Camp Gordon, 1943–45," in *Georgia Historical Quarterly* 76, no. 4 (Winter 1992): 849.

My description of the Horst Guenther's background, the suspicions that grew around him, his murder at Camp Aiken, and the subsequent investigation comes from the case files and particularly the transcript of the court-martial of POWs Erich Gauss and Rudolf Straub, G-GCM, at NARA St. Louis.

The army lawyer's reminder to himself to focus on the facts of the Camp Aiken murder case and ignore his personal feelings about the killers comes from the Army Review Board's lengthy analysis of the case, which I found in the case file at NARA St. Louis. Jaworski's personal papers at Baylor also contain a copy of the document.

Dorothy Thompson's syndicated column on the German POW camps in the United States appeared on April 24, 1944, under various headlines, including "How We Treat Nazi Prisoners of War," in a clipping from an unidentified source that I found in the Farrand Collection. There, I also found Dorothy Dunbar Bromley's two-part story on the camps from *The New York Herald Tribune* on April 12 and 13, 1944. Her first article was headlined "War Prisoners Include Nazis and Anti-Nazis," and her second, "Prison Camps Lack Staff Who Speak German." William Shirer repeatedly expressed his views in print, including in a column in *The Washington Post,* headlined "Shirer Flays U.S. Military on Propaganda for Nazi POWs," on August 20, 1944, and in the January 1945 issue of *Reader's Digest* magazine.

My account of Maj. Maxwell McKnight's encounters with Eleanor Roosevelt comes from Judith M. Gansberg's *Stalag: U.S.A.: The Remarkable Story of German POWs in America* (Thomas Y. Crowell, 1977), pages 61–63. McKnight's description of his meetings with Eleanor provides another example of his candor in postwar interviews with Gansberg.

My brief sketch of Henry Stimson's very full life comes from several sources, including Stimson's autobiography (coauthored with McGeorge Bundy), *On Active Service in Peace and War* (Harper and Brothers, 1947); Godfrey Hodgson's biography of Stimson, *The Colonel: The Life and Wars of Henry Stimson, 1870–1950* (Alfred A. Knopf, 1990); Edward Aldrich's book *The Partnership: George Marshall, Henry Stimson, and the Extraordinary Collaboration That Won World War II* (Stackpole Books, 2022); and Stimson's biography and diary at the Yale University Library in New Haven, Connecticut.

Stimson downplayed the violence in the camps in a somewhat defensive letter to Dr. Warren A. Seavey of Harvard Law School, who had criticized the army's failure to control the camps, in a letter on May 11, 1944. I found a copy of Stimson's letter in RG 389.

My information about the army's blunder in allowing four Gestapo agents to infiltrate the anti-Nazi POW camp at Fort Devens, Massachusetts, comes from Arnold Krammer's *Nazi Prisoners of War in America* (Scarborough House, 1979), page 175. My description of the covert Nazi takeover of the main POW post office at Camp Hearne comes from an army report on the topic on January 9, 1945, provided to me by Cathy Lazarus at the Camp Hearne Historic Site in Hearne, Texas, which I visited in 2023. Michael Waters also provides a good description of the post office takeover on pages 95–109 of *Lone Star Stalag: German Prisoners of War at Camp Hearne* (Texas A&M University Press, 2004). Waters points out that the army asked for trouble by choosing to locate the main post office at Camp Hearne, which by late 1944 had been designated specifically as a camp for "uncooperative" prisoners, and where the murder of Hugo Krauss the year before remained unsolved.

Judith Gansberg traces the unusual journey of the German POW reeducation plan from conception to rejection to implementation on pages 59–63 of *Stalag: U.S.A.*

Stimson described his thorough review of the Camp Tonkawa murder case in his diary. My summary of what he found in the case file comes from my own review of the file in the Knox Collection at UC-Davis. Petsch's warning that the Germans would respond to their POWs being sentenced to death by sentencing American POWs to death is also in the file, as is Stimson's assurance to Roosevelt that all possible repercussions of the death sentences had been carefully considered.

CHAPTER 14
Blind Drop

I got my information about OSS agent Louis Biagioni's background from his son Albert Biagioni, whom I was surprised to discover lived not far from my home in Virginia Beach, Virginia. (Louis Biagioni also had lived near me for several years before his death in 2003.) Albert allowed me to interview him at length and provided me with a trove of documents and photos, including his father's reports to the OSS and the War Crimes Commission about his capture and subsequent ordeal. I also examined Louis Biagioni's declassified OSS personnel file in RG 226 and shared its contents with Albert.

The wave of Italian immigration to America in the late 1800s and early 1900s is well documented by numerous sources. I found all the background I needed for my purposes in the article "The Great Arrival," accessed August 4, 2024, on the Library of Congress website, at www.loc.gov/classroom -materials/immigration/italian/the-great-arrival/.

For background about Biagioni's mission and OSS operations in Nazi-occupied Italy, I consulted a book by his OSS boss Max Corvo, *Max Corvo: OSS Italy, 1942–1945* (Enigma Books, 1990). The book contains four mentions of Biagioni and his ill-fated "Grape" team. I found Biagioni's report on a failed "blind" parachute drop on pages 63–64 of Corvo's book, and also in Biagioni's OSS personnel file.

Biagioni described his frustrating attempts to secure a radio and his search for "Dr. Enzo" in his reports and writings to his son Albert. I found background information about conditions in Milan during 1944 and 1945 in Corvo, *Max Corvo,* and in several online sources, including "Milan: The Capital of the Resistance," accessed August 4, 2024, www.liberationroute.com /themed-routes/31/milan-the-capital-of-the-resistance. I found background about Dr. Enzo Boeri and his vital contributions to the Italian Resistance in Milan in Corvo's book *Corvo* and in an article by Peter Tompkins, "The OSS and Italian Partisans in World War II," accessed August 4, 2024, on the website of the OSS's successor, the CIA, at www.cia.gov/resources/csi/static/oss -italian-partisans-ww2.pdf.

Biagioni's account of his frustrations with his teammate Lieutenant Carioni, his apparent betrayal by the Russians, and his capture by the Nazis comes from his reports in his OSS file in RG 226.

My information that OSS brass in Washington worried that Biagioni/ DANIEL might talk, and their interest in trading a German prisoner for him, are reflected in memos contained in his personnel file in RG 226.

CHAPTER 15
"The Dachau Treatment"

My brief sketch of the colorful history of Fort Leavenworth, Kansas, and the U.S. Disciplinary Barracks (USDB) comes from my visit to the fort and the Fort Leavenworth Museum in 2023; an article in *The Atlantic* magazine by Robert D. Kaplan, "Fort Leavenworth and the Eclipse of Nationhood," in the September 1996 issue; and Peter J. Grande's book *Images of America: United States Disciplinary Barracks* (Arcadia, 2009). Grande also took time to talk with me by phone in June 2024 about the USDB and the executions of the Germans. The vignette about a young Dwight D. Eisenhower commanding a young F. Scott Fitzgerald at Fort Leavenworth comes from an article by

Garrison Keillor, "Scott Fitzgerald Slept Here, Briefly," in *The New York Times* on September 22, 1996.

The description of death row in the Fort Leavenworth "Castle" in 1944–45 comes from Richard Whittingham's book *Martial Justice: The Last Mass Execution in the United States* (Naval Institute Press, 1971), pages 239–41. Whittingham's book is extensively researched but lacks citations of where he got his information. It's clear that he interviewed the USDB's late Catholic chaplain George Towle, who spoke at length with the condemned Germans on death row. But it's not clear how he reconstructed some of the statements he attributed to the Germans, and I have been cautious about using any of those statements in my book.

The information about the military tribunal's verdict in the Camp Aiken murder case, and the defense lawyer's plea that the German defendants were not like normal people, comes from the transcript of the court-martial, G-GCM, at NARA St. Louis.

My description of the court-martial of Gauss and Straub for the Camp Aiken killing comes from the trial transcript in G-GCM at NARA St. Louis. The general's letter of praise to Jaworski is contained in the latter's personal papers at Baylor.

The information about the revival of the investigation of the murder of U-boat man Werner Dreschler at Camp Papago Park in Arizona comes from the court files of the case in the Knox Collection at UC-Davis.

My information about the use of the former resort at Byron Hot Springs as an interrogation center comes from the already-cited history of the Fort Hunt Interrogation Center in RG 319. The information about the Holly-wood celebrities who used to frequent the place comes from an October 31, 2019, article by Aria Bendix, "An Abandoned Hotel in California Was Once a Popular Destination for Hollywood Celebrities. Now Some Think It's Haunted," in Business Insider at www.businessinsider.com/byron-hotel-california-abandoned-haunted-photos-2019-10#the-hotel-was-popular-among-celebrities-in-the-1920s-2.

The account of "Captain Schmidt's" third-degree interrogation methods comes from the written statements and testimony of U-boat men Otto Stengel and Rolf Wizuy in the case files of the court-martial, which I accessed in the Knox Collection at UC-Davis. My account of the court-martial, including the questioning of "Schmidt" by the defense attorneys and judge, comes from the transcript of the court-martial in the Knox Collection.

My updates on the war come primarily from an excellent chronology of World War II in Library of America, ed., *Reporting World War II: Part One,*

American Journalism, 1938–1944 (Literary Classics of the United States, 1995), beginning on page 795.

I found the MIS-X report on the treatment of American POWs in German hands in RG 389.

Louis Biagioni's account of his narrow escape from a massacre of fellow prisoners and his transfer to the Mauthausen forced-labor camp comes from documents shared with me by his son Albert and from documents in his OSS file in RG 226. Albert Biagioni had a copy of the mysterious, upbeat letter that was sent to his father's parents in New York after his transfer to Mauthausen. For background on Mauthausen, I consulted Evelyn Le Chene's book *Mauthausen: The History of a Death Camp* (Corgi Books, 1973).

CHAPTER 16
Boiling Point

My account of the prosecution of the four Americans for refusing to get off the sidewalk and walk in the street comes from RG 153, in Clarence Ferguson's postwar report on the case to the Judge Advocate General's War Crimes Office.

The information about William Schaefer's and James Schmitz's poster incident comes from a large collection of official documents in RG 153, including reports by Schaefer, Schmitz, Ferguson, and others about the incident; from Schaefer's *People Too* (Pageant Press, 1971), pages 80–83; from the previously cited accounts in *The Times* of Streator, Illinois, of Schmitz's postwar speeches; and from Clarence Ferguson's *Kriegsgefangener (Prisoner of War)* (Texian Press, 1983), pages 225–26. RG 153 contains a copy of the German poster.

Schaefer described his journey to the prison at Colditz Castle and his detour to Dresden in *People Too*, pages 84–88. My background information about Colditz Castle comes from Schaefer's book; Ben Macintyre's fine book *Prisoners of the Castle: An Epic Story of Survival and Escape from Colditz, the Nazis' Fortress Prison* (Crown, 2022); and P. R. Reid's book *The Colditz Story* (Coronet Books, 1962).

Stimson's comments about the Camp Aiken murder case come from an October 5, 1944, entry in his diary at the Yale University Library. Roosevelt's approval of the death sentences of Gauss and Straub comes from the Camp Aiken case file at G-GCM at NARA St. Louis.

As mentioned in my notes for chapter 7, editors Jeffery L. Littlejohn and

Charles H. Ford include a copy of the 1929 Geneva Convention's rules on the treatment of POWs in an appendix to their book *The Enemy Within Never Did Without: German and Japanese Prisoners of War at Camp Huntsville, 1942–1945* (Texas Review Press, 2015), starting on page 113.

The German Foreign Ministry's demand to the U.S. State Department for more information about the Camp Tonkawa murder case comes from an extensive collection of telegrams and memos in NARA RG 107, General Records of the Department of State, Central Decimal Files, 1940–1945. The documents in boxes 204, 205, 336, 3336A, 3337, 3348, 3349, and 3350 track on a daily basis the months of communications and POW exchange negotiations between U.S. and German authorities through the Swiss Legation, as well as communications between the State and War Departments. I am grateful to Meredith Lentz Adams, a professor emeritus at Missouri State University, whose notes for her book *Murder and Martial Justice: Spying and Retribution in World War II America* (Kent State University Press, 2011), about the Papago Park case, gave me a head start on finding these documents in the vastness of the National Archives. Dr. Adams also gave me helpful information in a telephone conversation in 2022.

My information about the bumpy review process of the Papago Park murder case comes from the case files in the Knox Collection at UC-Davis. King expressed his concerns about the torturing of Otto Stengel and Rolf Wizuy in his review for the Army's Ninth Service Command, which is included in the Knox Collection. General Shedd's recommendation that the seven U-boat men's sentences be commuted to life imprisonment and his citing of Col. Thomas White's views on killing traitors are contained in the case file in the Knox Collection.

Mozart Kaufman described the increasingly harsh treatment of POWs like him and Col. Henry Spicer at Stalag Luft I on pages 163–66 of *Fighter Pilot: Aleutians to Normandy to Stalag Luft I* (M. and A. Kaufman, 1993). His letter to Emily Post appears on page 166.

Spicer described the events leading up to his fateful speech in a report to the War Crimes Office of the Judge Advocate General's Office on August 4, 1945, which I found among Spicer's entries in RG 153. Other witnesses, including Maj. J. J. Fischer, also filed reports confirming Spicer's story and adding details.

My account of Spicer's speech comes from Spicer's testimony for the War Crimes Office and also from Kaufman's *Fighter Pilot,* pages 137–40. Kaufman was so impressed by the speech that he immediately hurried into his barracks and reconstructed it with the help of some other POWs, wrote it down, and hid it. In places where Kaufman's account of the speech differed from Spicer's, I went with Spicer's, not only because he made the speech but because his account of it was sworn testimony.

Byerly's protest and the German camp commandant's curt response are in Byerly's testimony to the War Crimes Office in RG 153.

CHAPTER 17
Bargaining Chips

The Swiss request that the United States provide more information about the Camp Aiken case comes from the previously cited State Department files in RG 59.

Roosevelt's approval of the Camp Aiken death sentences is part of the court record of the case in G-GCM at NARA St. Louis, as are General Bryan's instruction to the commander of Fort Leavenworth to prepare to hang Gauss and Straub; Bryan's notification to the Swiss about the president's action and the warning to keep the case secret; and Bryan's lawyerly response to the Germans.

The army gave a detailed account of the killings and the prosecutions to *The New York Times*, whose article on January 16, 1945, "Prison Camps Rid of Nazi Terrorism," indicated the problems in the camps had been solved. I found the War Department officer's confident memo, dated December 13, 1944, in RG 389.

The report about the attempted arson and murder of anti-Nazis at Camp Grant in Illinois comes from Arnold Krammer's *Nazi Prisoners of War in America* (Scarborough House, 1979), page 173.

I found Lerch's March 2, 1945, speech to Congress in the Farrand Collection.

My information about pro-Nazi Camp Alva comes primarily from a visit I made to Alva, Oklahoma, in 2022. Little remains of the old camp, but the Cherokee Strip Museum in Alva, which focuses mainly on the region's Native American history, contains two rooms full of documents and artifacts from the old POW camp. Particularly interesting were a history of Camp Alva written in 1992 by Dick Warner of Tulsa, Oklahoma, including notable incidents at the camp (such as the imposition of the no-neckties rule), and an account by an army medical officer, Capt. Miles Kelly, of a year he spent serving at the camp. Newspaper clippings show that some of the "super-Nazis" who were sent to Alva returned to visit there after the war. One of them told a reporter, "They called us Nazis, but we were patriots just like the Americans."

Statistically, Camp Alva was not an unusually violent camp. Political arguments were few among the ardent Nazis, although two "suicides" took place and several prisoners sought protection from their even more fervid comrades. One prisoner at Camp Alva was fatally shot by a guard while trying to escape; forty-two others died of illness, suicide, injuries, and lingering battle wounds. The Nazis at Camp Alva found pleasure in outsmarting their American captors. One prisoner made the guards think he had escaped for two years, hiding in a tunnel during head counts and inspections but otherwise living like a normal prisoner, eating meals and playing soccer with his comrades. After the war, a thorough search of a German barracks at Camp Alva revealed a trapdoor leading to an underground chamber, dominated by a three-and-a-half-foot, beautifully carved wooden statue of an eagle with a swastika in its talons. The Nazis had somehow produced the statue—which is on display in the Cherokee Strip Museum—and used it as a centerpiece for meetings and ceremonies. Camp Alva surely kept other secrets.

Capt. Karl Teufel described his work at Camp Concordia on behalf of the POW reeducation program in chap. 4 of "The History of Camp Concordia from Site Survey to Inactivation," October 1945 (NARA RG 389, Box 1612, courtesy of Lowell May). Teufel's account is the story of an energetic officer doing all he could to eliminate the Nazi influence from what had been a troubled camp.

I got my background on the Battle of the Bulge and the SS massacre of American POWs primarily from Anthony Beevor's book *Ardennes 1944: The Battle of the Bulge* (Viking, 2015). Beevor describes the Malmedy massacre on pages 144–47. On page 222, Beevor writes that U.S. Army Lt. Gen. Omar Bradley tacitly approved the execution of captured SS men. Beevor specifically recounts a story of an officer telling Bradley about questioning captured men from the Twelfth SS Panzer Division and Bradley raising his eyebrows and asking, "Prisoners from the Twelfth SS?" The officer replied, "We needed a few samples. That's all we've taken, sir." Bradley is said to have smiled and said, "Well, that's good." Beevor wrote that the Battle of the Bulge "brought the terrifying brutality of the Eastern Front to the West." The American casualty figures come from the National World War II Museum in New Orleans.

I have a personal connection to the Battle of the Bulge because my father, Raymond H. Geroux, to whom I've dedicated this book, fought in it. Like many World War II veterans, he almost never talked about his war experiences. But he told me he nearly froze to death in a foxhole outside Bastogne, losing consciousness before a buddy noticed his condition and got help. While I was combing through the POW murder trial transcripts at NARA St. Louis, which also is the repository of the National Personnel Records Center, I requested Dad's service records and saw that he had been treated for frostbite at a hospital in Brussels, Belgium. The bulk of his records, like the records of many military personnel from that time, were destroyed in a fire at NARA St. Louis in 1973.

The documents tracking the continuing back-and-forth between the German and U.S. authorities about access to court records from the Camp Tonkawa murder case come from the already-cited records of the secretary of state in RG 59. Petsch's praise of the court-martial proceedings comes from the transcript of the court-martial in the Knox Collection at UC-Davis.

William Schaefer described his attempts to fathom the meaning of a document charging him with a capital offense for the poster incident in *People Too* (Pageant Press, 1971), page 89. Ben Macintyre provides a colorful description of Col. Florimond Duke and his background in *Prisoners of the Castle: An Epic Story of Survival and Escape from Colditz, the Nazis' Fortress Prison* (Crown, 2022), pages 217–22. But Schaefer may have had the best line about Duke, declaring on page 88 of *People Too* that Duke was so shrewd that he could have talked the devil into running hell as Duke wanted it run. Duke revealed his background and personality in his own book about his war experiences, written with Charles M. Swaart, *Name, Rank, and Serial Number* (Meredith Press, 1969).

Schmitz spoke about being summoned to a court-martial for the poster incident in the postwar speeches that were covered by *The Times* of Streator, Illinois. But the best and most complete account of the ominous journey from Oflag 64 to the site of the court-martial in Gnesen, Poland, comes from Clarence Ferguson, his POW defense attorney, in *Kriegsgefangener (Prisoner of War)* (Texian Press, 1983), pages 222–26.

Schaefer described his even more ominous trip to Gnesen for the court-martial in *People Too*, pages 91–93.

CHAPTER 18
"I Could Not Do Otherwise"

Schaefer's account of his talks with his guards and his first meeting with his lawyers comes from *People Too* (Pageant Press, 1971), page 94.

Schaefer described the trial in his already-cited testimony to the War Crimes Office in RG 153 (the source of the exchange between the defense and one of the poster-hanging German sergeants).

Clarence Ferguson described the trial in his testimony to the War Crimes Office in RG 153. He also described it and his swirling fears and emotions in *Kriegsgefangener (Prisoner of War)* (Texian Press, 1983), pages 226–36. In his book, Ferguson wrote that the German officer who testified about Schaefer's track record as a troublemaking POW was not Zimmerman but a German captain who based his testimony on reports that Ferguson was prohibited from seeing. But in Ferguson's sworn statement to the War Crimes Office in 1945, he said the testimony came from Zimmerman. And Schaefer said the same in his sworn statement to the War Crimes Office. I have relied on the sworn statements for my account of the court-martial. Plus, it's hard to believe that Schaefer would have confused Zimmerman with anyone else.

Schaefer recounted the trial in more personal terms, as well as the German general's private advice to him about appealing the case, on pages 96–97 of *People Too*.

Ferguson described catching Schaefer as he appeared to faint in *Kriegsgefangener*, pages 235–36, where he also described Schmitz's outward calm upon being sentenced to die. Ferguson described his own fainting and the immediate aftermath of the court-martial, including his newfound admiration for Schmitz, on pages 236–39. Ferguson described the reaction of the German commandant and guards at Oflag 64 to the death sentences in his testimony to the War Crimes Office in RG 153 and on page 238 of *Kriegsgenfangener*.

I found Schmitz's letter to Hitler among the documents in his entry in the war crimes investigations in RG 153. The *Chicago Tribune* quoted Schmitz on its previously cited story on April 26, 1945, as saying he found the act of writing to the Fuhrer "repulsive."

Schaefer described his return journey to Colditz Castle and his return to his struggle with "eternity" on pages 98–108 of *People Too*.

Ben Macintyre tells about the POWs' extraordinary effort to build a glider in a secret chamber of the castle on pages 242–45 of *Prisoners of the Castle: An Epic Story of Survival and Escape from Colditz, the Nazis' Fortress Prison* (Crown, 2022).

CHAPTER 19

"Nasty Smiles"

Louis Biagioni described the horrors he witnessed at Mauthausen, including the cruel invitation to sick prisoners to step forward, in his postwar report to the OSS, which is contained in his personnel file in RG 226. His son Albert also has a copy. Biagioni's account included his being forced to stand outside in the cold while soaking wet—a common form of execution at Mauthausen. The material Biagioni shared with his son Albert included a photograph of a statue at Mauthausen honoring Russian lieutenant general Dmitri Karbyschev, who was executed by being sprayed with cold water and forced to stand against a wall in freezing weather.

Col. Henry Spicer described his journey to Anklam in his testimony to the War Crimes Office in RG 153 and in a series of notes he smuggled to a fellow POW from his solitary confinement cell at Stalag Luft I after the trial. Spicer's son Randy referred me to the notes, which can be found on a website devoted to Spicer's career and his days at Stalag Luft I, "World War II—Prisoners of War—Stalag Luft I: Col. Henry Russell Spicer," at www.merkki.com/spicerruss.htm. To me, nothing reveals Spicer's raw anger and defiance so clearly as those notes to fellow POW Loren McCollom—a.k.a. "Lydia Pinkstuff"—scrawled in an isolation cell after his death sentence. The Germans never provided U.S. authorities with any documents about Spicer's court-martial. His accounts of it are the only detailed ones I found.

I learned about Spicer's embroidered picture of an English garden and the family's donation of it to the Eighth Air Force Museum from Spicer's sons. A photo of it is on the website www.merkki.com/spicerruss.htm.

My information about Franklin D. Coslett, the army air forces bombardier who went to work for the Dutch underground after he was shot down, comes from several sources, including his statements to the War Crimes Office in RG 153. Those files include an MIS-X escape and evasion report about him.

The downing of Coslett's B-24 bomber and the subsequent execution of his pilot, Lt. Bill Moore, are described on the website Air Crew Remembered, "Archive Report: US Forces, 1941–1945," at aircrewremembered.com/moore-bill.html. Many details of Coslett's covert work in Holland come from "History of the Holland Office of 6801 MIS-X Detachment," June 10, 1946, on the website Netherlands Escape Lines, at wwiinetherlandsescapelines.files.wordpress.com/2014/10/history-holland-office-6801-mis-x.pdf.

Coslett's fiancée Margaret Smith's vigil for him is described in a retrospective story in the *Wilkes-Barre (PA) Times-Leader,* "Nation and a Community Recall Fellowship That Outlasted a War Against Evil," on May 7, 1994.

For background information on Coslett, I referred to Census Bureau records and other sources on www.ancestry.com and also to stories in the *Times-Leader*—"End of an Era: Veteran Broadcaster Franklin D. Coslett Dies at 76"—on February 14, 1992; and the Wilkes-Barre *Citizens' Voice*—Franklin D. Coslett, WBRE Newsman for 28 Years, Dies"—on February 14, 1992. Coslett appears to have kept his harrowing war experiences largely to himself. He was best known in his community as a longtime news anchorman for WBRE-TV in Wilkes-Barre. I was unable to find any surviving family members or close friends of Coslett to elaborate on his war story.

I found information about the B-24 crewmen Joseph Walsh, Edward Walsh, and Marvin Martin, including official reports on the downing of the "Betty Jean" in occupied Italy, on the website of the 449th Bomb Group (W.W. II) under "Phillips Crew," accessed August 4, 2024, at 449th.com /phillips-crew/. I found a few documents in the three men's files in RG 153. I found some background on the men in Census Bureau reports and other documents on www.ancestry.com.

I found memos from the U.S. War and State Departments pointing out that the three fliers had been listed as regular POWs before being suddenly reclassified as *francs-tireurs* in the State Department's files in January and February 1945 in RG 59.

My information about Sgt. Thomas Jefferson Snowden and his death sentence for punching a German guard comes from www.ancestry.com, from the War Crimes Office files in RG 153, and from the State Department files of January-March 1945 in RG 59. Those entries include letters from his German defense lawyer describing the lawyer's efforts to save him from the death penalty.

I got my information about Sgt. Angelo Nicosia from www.ancestry.com, from documents in the State Department files of January and February 1945 in RG 153, and from the War Crimes Office files in RG 59.

I obtained my information about Pvt. Willard Davis and his death sentence for hitting a guard from www.ancestry.com, from the State Department files of January and February 1945 in RG 153, and from the War Crimes Office files in RG 59. The latter files include a report by Davis about witnessing the murder of a fellow POW. Davis told an investigator from the Judge Advocate General's Office that he suspected the Germans wanted to execute him because he was a witness to that killing.

CHAPTER 20
A Startling Offer

The "urgent" January 5, 1944, telegram from the German Foreign Office that first proposed a prisoner exchange for the five German POWs convicted of murder at Camp Tonkawa comes from the already-cited State Department files in RG 59. For this chapter and the next two, those files provide an almost-daily account of the proposed prisoner exchange. Stimson's account of his conversation with ex-POW Col. Thomas Drake comes from his diary entry on January 8, 1945.

My information about the series of exchanges of sick and wounded prisoners and civilian internees aboard the MS *Gripsholm* comes from a variety of sources. Two good places to start are an article by Jan Jarboe Russell on December 21, 2016, "Trade Off: Exchanging German-Americans for POWs in WWII," on HistoryNet, at www.historynet.com/trade-off-exchanging -german-americans-for-pows-in-wwii/, and Brigette C. Kamsler's "The Gripsholm Exchange and Repatriation Voyages," *The Burke Library Blog* (Columbia University), September 17, 2012, at blogs.cul.columbia.edu /burke/2012/09/17/the-gripsholm-exchange-and-repatriation-voyages-2/.
The possibility of using the *Gripsholm* for the condemned POW exchange was discussed in several entries in the State Department files in RG 59 in January-March 1945. The voyage in which the Germans originally proposed exchanging the German POWs was described in *The New York Times* story "Prisoner Exchange in Switzerland Due," on January 17, 1945.

Stimson's angry comment about the "trumped-up charges" is part of the correspondence in January in the State Department files in RG 59. So are the accounts of U.S. authorities about their puzzlement over the identities of James Greyfield and Franklin "Cosolet."

I found no trace of Greyfield in www.ancestry.com or other sources and enlisted the help of Marilyn Helmers of the Andover Center for History & Culture in Andover, Mass. She took the search for Greyfield as a challenge. She could find no trace of him or his parents ever having lived in Shawsheen Village, Massachusetts. Helmers added that the street address quoted by the Germans as being that of the Greyfield family did not exist, although the street did. I cannot say that Greyfield was not who he claimed to be, but I could find no trace of him.

The report that the Germans intended to retry the four American POWs at Oflag 64 for refusing to get off the sidewalk comes from the State Department files in January in RG 59, as do the Germans' additional details on

January 12 about the five American POWs they first offered for exchange. Ambassador Huddle's series of telegrams come from the same series of memos and telegrams in RG 59. So does Secretary of State Stettinius's lengthy telegram to the U.S. ambassador to Switzerland.

The Joint Chiefs' modest proposal is part of the files in January 1945 in RG 59. I got my information about the newly opened Pentagon and the original plan to make it a temporary headquarters for the War Department from an article by Katie Lang on December 19, 2019, "Pentagon History: 7 Big Things to Know," on the U.S. Defense Department website, at www.defense.gov/News/Feature-Stories/Story/article/1867440/pentagon-history-7-big-things-to-know/.

The communications between the State Department and War Department over the Germans' exchange proposal also come from RG 59, including Edwin Plitt's warning that the American public might be angry if the War Department did not try to save the American POWs by completing the exchange, and Henry Leverich's suggestion that the War Department be approached about the subject. Archibald MacLeish's memo about his conversation with the Swiss also comes from the skein of communications in RG 59.

The German lawyers' harsh critique of the Camp Tonkawa murder case and Secretary of War Stimson's dismissal of their arguments come from the January communications in RG 59. So does Judge Advocate General Myron Cramer's warning not to release the case files of the Papago Park murder case with its "obnoxious material" to the Germans.

I found the list of questions about "Captain Schmidt's" interrogation methods at Byron Hot Springs among army files in the Knox Collection at UC-Davis, where I also found documents describing the scramble by army authorities to respond to Stimson's questions. A transcript of the awkward phone conversation between the chief of staff of the army's Ninth Service Command and Provost Marshal General Lerch about who had known about the "third-degree" interrogation methods is in the Knox Collection, as is the letter from the assistant chief of army intelligence, G-2, refuting some of the German POWs' claims of torture and blaming "Schmidt," whom Lerch said had been unsupervised and overzealous. Stimson's description of how he investigated the torture allegations comes from his diary entry on February 10, 1945. Stimson's letter to Roosevelt saying he had taken steps to see that no further such methods were used comes from the Knox Collection at UC-Davis.

Stimson's diary entry about the "ticklish and trying situation" comes from his diary at Yale University Library.

CHAPTER 21
Pandemonium

For background on the Soviet advance, I consulted two excellent books on Russia's World War II experience, Catherine Merridale's *Ivan's War: Life and Death in the Red Army, 1939–1945* (Picador, 2006), and Richard Overy's *Russia's War* (Penguin Books, 1999). Merridale's book includes a helpful chronology of the war on the Eastern Front. My figures about the Germans' killing of Russian prisoners come from Merridale, *Ivan's War,* page 298. The letters from the Red Army soldiers thirsting for revenge come from Merridale, *Ivan's War,* page 302. Merridale and Overy are among the historians who took advantage of a relatively brief period of openness by Russian authorities in the 1990s to examine Russian records and shed considerable light on Russia's experiences in World War II.

Clarence Ferguson wrote about hearing the clattering of the German refugee wagons outside Oflag 64 in *Kriegsgefangener (Prisoner of War)* (Texian Press, 1983), page 239. He described the Germans' plans to evacuate the POW camp and the prisoners' preparations on pages 239–42. Ferguson described the long march on pages 243–55. He mentioned his sighting of Schmitz on page 246. I also draw information on the march from the Oflag 64 website and from Stephen Dando-Collins's *The Big Break: The Greatest American WWII POW Escape Story Never Told* (St. Martin's Press, 2017), which focuses mainly on the march. Dando-Collins characterizes the march as a large, slow-motion, and remarkably successful escape attempt.

Schmitz described his experiences on the march, including his hiding in the straw stack, in his postwar speeches covered by *The Times* of Streator, Illinois, April 26 and June 1, 1945, and in an interview with the *Chicago Tribune* published April 26, 1945. My information about the Allies' attempts to track the forced migrations of POWs as German camps were overrun comes from the State Department communications in RG 59. Stimson's complaints about the Swiss, and the Swiss explanation of the difficulties the Germans faced in caring for POWs, come from there as well. I also found Senator Connally's letter to Stimson in RG 59.

Biagioni's description of the Czech doctor's attempts to save him comes from the documents shared with me by his son Albert. Albert has a copy of a letter the doctor wrote to Biagioni after the war.

The Swiss inspector's report on Schaefer's welfare at Colditz Castle comes from the War Crimes Office's documents on Schaefer in RG 153.

For background on the Allied bombing of Dresden, I consulted Sinclair

McKay's book *The Fire and the Darkness: The Bombing of Dresden, 1945* (St. Martin's Press, 2020) and Michael A. Dobbs's book, *Six Months in 1945: From World War to Cold War* (Alfred A. Knopf, 2012). I found the historian Donald Miller's dramatic description of the bombing on the website of the National World War II Museum in New Orleans.

U.S. Army Pvt. 1st Cl. Kurt Vonnegut Jr. survived the firebombing of Dresden as an American POW after being captured by the Germans during the Battle of the Bulge. He described the devastation in Dresden in his novel *Slaughterhouse-Five* (Dial Press, 2005), pages 226–27. Vonnegut wrote of the bombing's aftermath: "Dresden was like the moon now, nothing but minerals."

William Schaefer described his view of the bombing of Dresden on pages 110–12 of *People Too* (Pageant Press, 1971). The cold-blooded quote from Arthur "Bomber" Harris comes from Dobbs's *Six Months in 1945*, page 96–97.

Schaefer's description of how the bombing changed life at Colditz Castle comes from *People Too*, pages 112–13. My description of the Allied POWs' partnership with their German captors for self-preservation comes from *People Too* and from pages 262–64 of Ben Macintyre's *Prisoners of the Castle: An Epic Story of Survival and Escape from Colditz, the Nazis' Fortress Prison* (Crown, 2022).

Lt. Col Hoskott's description of Schaefer's and Schmitz's incident with the poster comes from the War Crimes Office's examination of the case in RG 153.

The German lawyer Lommatzsch's account of the court-martial of Pvt. Willard Davis and Sgt. Thomas Snowden comes from the State Department files in RG 59.

I found the various complaints by the condemned German POWs at Fort Leavenworth in the Knox Collection at UC-Davis. Erich Gauss's letter to Roosevelt comes from the files of the Camp Aiken murder case at G-CCM at NARA St. Louis. So does Provost Marshal General Lerch's order that the camps post notices that American laws applied to German POWs. The complaints by the Papago Park U-boat men that preceded their transfer to Fort Leavenworth come from the Knox Collection.

CHAPTER 22
Hostage Diplomacy

Senator Brooks's letter and the War Department's response come from the State Department files for March 1945 in RG 59, as does the message from the Swiss floating the idea of an exchange for SS colonel Wunsche.

I found a copy of Lerch's speech to a congressional committee in the Farrand Collection.

The Germans' repeating of their exchange offer, and their release of further details about Franklin Coslett, Joseph Walsh, Edward Walsh, Marvin Martin, and James Greyfield, come from the March 1945 communications in the State Department files in RG 59.

My information about Capt. Wilbur McKee comes from the War Crimes Office's interview with him in RG 153.

The steps taken by the Provost Marshal General's Office to prevent inadvertent actions that could sabotage the exchange come from army documents in RG 59. There are also copies in the Knox Collection at UC-Davis.

The Germans' offer to include Louis Biagioni in the exchange comes from the State Department communications in March 1945 in RG 59.

Ambassador Harrison's ominous warnings to the State Department and his description of the stories in the Stockholm newspapers come from the March entries in the State Department's communications in RG 59.

My information about Stalin's tricking his allies into thinking Berlin was not important to the Soviets comes from Anthony Beevor's *The Fall of Berlin 1945* (Penguin Books, 2003), pages 138–39.

The pleading letters from the families of American POWs to President Roosevelt come from the State Department communications in RG 59. So does the joint statement by Stimson and Stettinius, as well as Stettinius's plea that the POW exchange not be allowed to collapse because of a communication failure.

Schmitz described his efforts to hide his identity from his German captors by blending in with Serbian prisoners in his speeches covered by *The Times* of Streator, Illinois, on April 26 and June 1, 1945, and in his interview with the *Chicago Tribune* published April 26, 1945. Schmitz's letter asking the Swiss to send a reassuring letter to his mother but omitting the fact that he faced a death sentence comes from his entries in the documents of the War Crimes Office, RG 153.

For background on Gen. George S. Patton's disastrous Hammelburg raid, I referred to Rick Atkinson's book *The Guns at Last Light: The War in Western*

Europe, 1944–1945 (Henry Holt, 2013), pages 570–75, and Richard Whitaker's article in the September-October 1996 issue of *ARMOR* magazine, "Task Force Baum and the Hammelburg Raid," which offers a more detailed account of the raid. Patton's telltale letter to his wife acknowledging that he hoped to launch the raid on Hammelburg to free his son-in-law comes from page 570 of Atkinson's *The Guns at Last Light*, and Patton's later note to his wife from page 572. My account of Captain Baum being stunned by the large number of prisoners at Hammelburg comes from Whitaker, "Task Force Baum," page 30. Whitaker also describes Baum's decision to hurl his dog tags into the woods so that the Germans who were about to capture him would not know he was Jewish. The muted response of Patton's superiors to his abuse of authority comes from Atkinson's *The Guns at Last Light*, page 575–76. Patton's disastrous raid was no reflection on his son-in-law, Lt. Col. Waters, who had known nothing about the plan to rescue him. Waters, who was well regarded by his fellow POWs, eventually retired from the army as a four-star general.

Schmitz's account of his short-lived escape after the task force raid comes from his testimony to the War Crimes Office in RG 153 and his speeches quoted in *The Times* of Streator, Illinois, April 26 and June 1, 1945.

CHAPTER 23
"Unfavorably Terminated"

The report by the Swiss inspector on deteriorating conditions in Germany and particularly in its POW camps comes from the State Department's communications in April 1945 in RG 59.

Schmitz's letter to his mother after the true liberation of Hammelburg camp was printed in *The Times* of Streator, Illinois, on April 16, 1945. His mother's reaction, and the letter from an American doctor who saw him in an Allied hospital after his release, come from an undated clipping from the *Ottawa (Ill.) Republican-Times*—which once had employed Schmitz as sports editor. The clip was provided to me by his nephew James Schmitz of Illinois.

The reports of Sergeant Snowden and Private Davis being liberated from the POW camp in Hammerstein, Germany, come from the State Department communications in April 1945 in RG 59. So does the Germans' agreement to leave POWs in the camps as the camps were abandoned, as well as Secretary of State Stettinius's notification to the French.

The German telegram agreeing to a fifteen-for-fifteen POW exchange comes from the April entries in RG 59. So do the State Department's quick response and its proposal to make the exchange at two points along the Swiss border.

I found Joseph Goebbels's upbeat message to Hitler about the death of President Roosevelt in Anthony Beevor's *The Fall of Berlin 1945* (Penguin Books, 2003), page 204.

My information about Franklin Coslett's liberation from a Dutch prison comes from Coslett's interview with the War Crimes Office in RG 153 and from "History of the Holland Office of 6801 MIS-X Detachment," June 10, 1946, on the website Netherlands Escape Lines, at wwiinetherlands escapelines.files.wordpress.com/2014/10/history-holland-office-6801-mis-x .pdf.

I got my information about the arrival of the American pilot John Winant Jr. at Colditz Castle and his subsequent removal from the castle with the other *Prominente* by the SS from Ben Macintyre's *Prisoners of the Castle: An Epic Story of Survival and Escape from Colditz, the Nazis' Fortress Prison* (Crown, 2022), pages 260–68, and from Florimond Duke's *Name, Rank, and Serial Number* (Meredith Press, 1969), pages 129–34. William Schaefer described his communication with Winant through a pipe in *People Too* (Pageant Press, 1971), page 109.

My information about Hitler's frenzied order to "shoot them all" comes from David Stafford's book *Endgame, 1945: The Missing Final Chapter of World War II* (Little, Brown, 2007), page 216.

Florimond Duke described arranging for Schaefer to be moved to a cell that would be safe from Allied artillery, as well as Schaefer's remark to him about the absurdity of being moved out of death row for his safety, on page 135 of *Name, Rank, and Serial Number*. Schaefer described Duke's insistence that he exit his cell fast on page 113 of *People Too*. The Swiss inspector's comment that solitary confinement had taken a toll on Schaefer comes from Macintyre's *Prisoners of the Castle*, page 254.

My account of the battle for Colditz Castle between the U.S. First Army and a contingent of SS men and Hitler Youth comes from Macintyre's *Prisoners of the Castle*, pages 275–82; Duke's *Name, Rank, and Serial Number*, pages 138–43; and Schaefer's *People Too*, pages 112–15.

The POW's description of Schaefer "shaking uncontrollably" and crying upon being set free comes from Macintyre's *Prisoners of the Castle*, page 284. Schaefer described his activities after being set free, including his sighting of the female war correspondent Lee Carson and his drinking of a Grand Marnier, on pages 116–19 of *People Too*.

Schaefer described being flown to London and then being fleeced out of his money on pages 119–21 of *People Too*.

Ambassador Winant's outdated report on Schaefer's whereabouts comes from the State Department communications in April 1945 in RG 59. Macintyre explained the fate of Winant's son and the rest of the *Prominente* on pages 287–89 of *Prisoners of the Castle*.

The disturbing, late-arriving message from the German High Command about sixteen other American POWs potentially facing death sentences comes from the State Department communications in April 1945 in RG 59. The Swiss messages that the POW exchange was falling apart because of a breakdown of the German communication system also come from RG 59, as does Ambassador Harriman's suggestion that continuing to pursue the exchange might only endanger the condemned American POWs.

The description of the Germans abandoning Stalag Luft I, where Col. Henry Spicer was held in a solitary cell to await execution, comes from Mozart Kaufman's *Fighter Pilot: Aleutians to Normandy to Stalag Luft I* (M. and A. Kaufman, 1993), pages 172–73. I found the vignette about Spicer deciding to spend a last night in the cell anyway in the transcript of a speech by fellow POW George Lesko at a 2001 reunion of former Stalag Luft I prisoners in Barth, Germany, in "World War II—Prisoners of War—Stalag Luft I: Col. Henry Russell Spicer," at www.merkki.com/spicerruss.htm. Lesko also described Spicer's fellow POWs' hearty welcome of him back into the world of free men, and Spicer's compliment to them.

Spicer described the Russian "Cossack" riding into the camp in a speech to the McAllen, Texas, Rotary Club, reported in *The (McAllen, Tex) Monitor* newspaper story "Spicer One of Five Sentenced to Death in Revenge for U.S. Executions of Murderers," on June 14, 1945. Spicer's account, as reflected in the headline, suggests he knew only part of the story of the attempted POW exchange. In the same speech, Spicer described the Russians' initially warm greetings for the Americans and his enjoyment of their vodka.

Kaufman described partying with the Russians and slowly becoming disenchanted with them on pages 175–76 of *Fighter Pilot*. His quote about the Russians saying one thing and doing another appears on page 183. Kaufman described the Russians' discovery of a brutal concentration camp near Stalag Luft I on pages 178–81. He described the survivors of the camp wandering like "zombies" through the streets of Barth on page 180. Kaufman recounted another ex-POW's story of a German woman in Barth offering herself to him to avoid being raped by the Russians.

Kaufman described the American POWs gratefully flying out of Poland on B-17s on page 184 of *Fighter Pilot*. I found a video of the Stalag Luft I survivors departing from Poland, "Evacuation of POW's from Stalag Luft 1—# 1," at www.youtube.com/watch?v=HpVnOsX21oE.

Spicer explained his reasons for making the speech that made the Germans "sore" to a war correspondent in an Associated Press story datelined Paris, May 16, 1945. He told the Rotarians in McAllen, Texas, in his previously cited account in the *Monitor* on June 14, 1945, "You don't know what all will burn in a pipe."

Spicer was far from the only notable "alumnus" of Stalag Luft I in Barth. Others included two British aviators who later took part in "the Great Escape" from Stalag Luft III (one of them was shot after being recaptured); British airman Donald Pleasance, who went on to become an actor and played a British POW in the movie *The Great Escape* before his star-making role as the psychiatrist in the horror movie classic *Halloween;* and Bernard L. Barker, an American bombardier who later became a CIA operative and then one of the Watergate burglars—whose capture ultimately led to Leon Jaworski's appointment as a special prosecutor and President Richard M. Nixon's resignation.

I found the newsreel footage of Louis Biagioni, newly freed from Mauthausen, declaring "God bless America" on the website of the United States Holocaust Memorial Museum, at collections.ushmm.org/search/catalog/irn1000313. Biagioni told his son Albert about being assigned after his liberation to document the horror of Mauthausen. He gave Albert some of the grisly photos he took at Mauthausen.

I found a copy of the Western Union telegram announcing Louis Biagioni's liberation in his OSS file. The telegram informed his father Albert in Brooklyn that Louis had been "RETURNED TO ALLIED CONTROL."

Schaefer recalled arriving in New York City on May 8, 1945, the day of the city's joyous V-E Day celebration, but being too broke and exhausted to take part, on pages 119–21 of *People Too. The New York Times* described the celebration in its story "Millions Rejoice in City Celebration," on page 1 of the May 9 edition.

I found the text of the message about the German surrender that was posted in all POW camps in the United States in a United Press story dated May 8 in the Farrand Collection. I found the order to force all German POWs in U.S. camps to watch gruesome newsreel footage of the Nazi death camps in RG 389. Daniel Jonah Goldhagen describes prewar violence against Jews in Germany in his book *Hitler's Willing Executioners: Ordinary Germans and the Holocaust* (Vintage Books, 1997).

The account of the last group of German POWs arriving in the United States comes from the *New York Times* story "3,000 Germans, Last Batch to Come Here, are Ragged but Well Fed—None, of Course, Was Ever Linked with Nazis," on May 14, 1945.

CHAPTER 24
The Elevator Shaft

Stimson voiced his enthusiasm for quickly firing the Swiss as "Protecting Power" on POW matters with Germany in a memo I found among the State Department communications in May 1945 in RG 59.

Provost Marshal General Lerch's order restarting the execution process for the fifteen condemned German POWs comes from the June communications in the State Department files in RG 59.

I found Captain Farrand's May 16 memo laying out the legal and potentially moral issues of going ahead with the executions in the Farrand Collection and also in RG 59.

Memos from Colonel Gerhardt and other army officials updating the search for the fifteen condemned Americans in Germany were among the June entries in RG 59.

Judge Advocate General Myron Cramer's request to Truman to start his review of the seven Papago Park U-boat men's death sentences, and Truman's response, come from the Papago Park murder case file in the Knox Collection.

I found the Army Review Board's detailed ruling on the Camp Chaffee, Arkansas, murder case in the case file of M-GCM at NARA St. Louis. Truman's brief order commuting Menschner's death sentence to life imprisonment is also in that case file.

My description of the army delivering the good news to Menschner at Fort Leavenworth's death row comes from Richard Whittingham's *Martial Justice: The Last Mass Execution in the United States* (Naval Institute Press, 1997), page 260.

My description of the gallows at Fort Leavenworth and its operation comes from army documents in the Camp Tonkawa murder case file in the Knox Collection. The army's detailed instructions to Colonel Eley, the commander of the U.S. Disciplinary Barracks, also come from the Knox Collection.

The New York Times reported the story of the "Murder Factory Found in Bavaria," as well as updated figures on U.S. war casualties, on July 5, 1945.

America was not the only Allied nation forced to cope with Nazi violence in its German POW camps. The British executed a total of ten German prisoners for political murders at camps in Yorkshire and in Comrie, Scotland, and Canadian authorities executed five Germans for two political killings in a camp in Medicine Hat in Calgary, Alberta. The murders in England, Scotland, and Canada were similar in most respects to those in the U.S. camps.

The account of Colonel Eley coming to death row to give notice to the five convicted killers from Camp Tonkawa of their impending execution comes from Whittingham's *Martial Justice*, page 262.

I found accounts of the American guard massacring German POWs in Salina, Utah, in the story "8 Die as GI Machineguns POW Camp," in *The Washington Post* on July 9, 1945, and a retrospective story in *The Salt Lake Tribune*, "Living History: 'Midnight Massacre' in Utah Was Worst Mass Murder at a POW Camp in U.S. History," on November 7, 2016. According to those accounts, the guard, twenty-eight-year-old private Clarence V. Bertucci of New Orleans, had served overseas for eight months but never saw combat, spending most of his time in Britain. He had not previously expressed anger toward POWs, but he twice had been disciplined by the army, including a sentence of three months' hard labor for refusing to go on guard duty. One of his brothers told a reporter that Clarence had been ill "for some time" and had been in and out of army hospitals. His poor service record apparently had prompted the army to relegate him to guarding POWs. Bertucci ultimately was declared insane and sent to an asylum in New York. How long he remained there is unclear. He was buried in New Orleans in 1969.

I found the footnoted references to the shooting incidents at camps in Virginia and Arkansas in the camp inspection reports in RG 389. Julie Spivey also told me about the incident at Camp Ashby in Virginia Beach.

The account of the executions of the five Camp Tonkawa killers comes from a story in *The Kansas City Star*, "Hang Five Nazis," by staff writer William H. Radford, on July 10, 1945. Radford was one of the witnesses to the execution and produced a highly detailed account. *The New York Times* gave the story far less attention that day, burying it on page 12 beneath the headline, "Five Nazis Hanged by Army in Kansas." I found the army's brief press release about the executions of the "fanatical Nazis" in the Knox Collection.

My information about the executions of the two Camp Aiken killers also comes from *The Kansas City Star,* on July 14, 1945. This time, staff writer Alex D. Weimer witnessed the executions and wrote an equally detailed account, headlined "Hang Two More Nazis."

Convicted Papago Park killer Otto Stengel's joking question to Chaplain Towle about whether U.S. authorities had forgotten about the seven U-boat men comes from Whittingham's *Martial Justice,* page 263.

While the Papago Park U-boat men waited and wondered in Leavenworth's death row, the army used the gallows at the nearby Kansas State Penitentiary on August 22 to execute a U.S. Army private for fatally shooting a buddy who had failed to pick him up when he was hitchhiking. The condemned man, Edward J. Reichl of Chicago, used his last words to profess his affection for the Windy City: "Goodbye, Chicago, I love every street and alley in Chicago." The German POWs apparently were told nothing of Reichel's hanging.

I found President Truman's order confirming the Papago Park death sentences in the case file in the Knox Collection. According to the Office of the Historian of the U.S. State Department, Truman was in Potsdam for his meeting with Churchill and Stalin on the day he signed the order. Anthony Beevor's *The Fall of Berlin 1945* (Penguin Books, 2003) describes Truman hoping to use news of the successful testing of the atomic bomb as leverage against Stalin, and notes that Stalin already knew about the bomb from his spies and was racing to build a Soviet bomb, on pages 138–39.

William Radford of *The Kansas City Star* covered the executions of the seven Papago Park U-boat men as thoroughly as he had covered the Camp Tonkawa executions, in his story on August 25, 1945, "Hang Seven Nazis." TV reporter Gene Dennis, who also witnessed the executions, described them to Kenneth Knox in a letter in the Knox Collection. The *Fort Leavenworth News* story on the executions, with its odd focus on logistics, "Seven More Die on Gallows at Post Prison," appeared on August 26, 1945. I found the *New York Times* story on the executions, "7 German Captives Hanged in Kansas," deep inside the paper while stories about the occupation of Japan dominated page 1.

CHAPTER 25
"Everything Comes Out Under the Sun"

Jaworski described his new assignment in Europe, his journey to Paris lugging 132 pounds of documents, and his viewing of the gruesome footage from the Nazi concentration camps on pages 99–101 of *Confession and Avoidance,* with Mickey Herskowitz (Anchor Press / Doubleday, 1979) and pages 93–96 of *Crossroads,* with Dick Schneider (David C. Cook, 1981). He described the V-E celebrations in London and Paris on page 101 of *Confession and Avoidance.*

I found court documents from the Rüsselsheim murder case among Jaworski's personal papers at Baylor. His interview with a war correspondent about the value of the war crimes trial is among his personal papers. He described the Rüsselsheim case in detail in *After Fifty Years* (Gulf, 1961), pages 65–101, and more briefly in *Confession and Avoidance*, pages 102–6, and *Crossroads*, pages 96–100. He described the stunning letter he received after the trial from the survivors of the massacre on page 106 of *Confession and Avoidance.*

I found background information about the Germans murdering other captured American aviators in an article by K. T. Hall, "*Luftgangster* over Germany: The Lynching of American Airmen in the Shadow of the Air War," *Historical Social Research* 43, no. 2 (2018): 277–312, at nbn-resolving .org/urn:nbn:de:0168-ssoar-57690-3.

Jaworski's personal papers at Baylor contain records and photos of his prosecution of the Hadamar sanitorium defendants. He described the Hadamar case in detail on pages 104–23 of *After Fifty Years* and more briefly in *Confession and Avoidance*, pages 107–15, and *Crossroads*, pages 106–18.

Jaworski described his desire to forgo the Nuremburg trial and return home to his family in Texas on pages 125–26 of *After Fifty Years*. I found background on the Nuremburg proceedings in the book *The Nuremburg Trial,* by Ann Tusa and John Tusa (Skyhorse, 2010).

The Camp Mexia POW's quote about wanting to stay in the United States after the war comes from Arnold Krammer's *Nazi Prisoners of War in America* (Scarborough House, 1979), page 224. The vignette about Senator Maybank's about-face on the immediate repatriation of German POWs comes from pages 232 and 234.

General Bryan's promise that the army would find a middle ground in reclaiming jobs in the United States from the POWs comes from a document in the Farrand Collection.

The letter to the editor about "genuine Nazis" being allowed to return home first comes from *The New York Times*, May 31, 1945. The *Washington Post* editorial questioning the early return of hardcore Nazis to Germany appeared on April 24, 1945.

Moulton's comment about the POWs at least being able to go home to

Germany comes from Judith M. Gansberg's *Stalag: U.S.A.: The Remarkable Story of German POWs in America* (Thomas Y. Crowell, 1977), page 159.

Krammer offers an excellent overview of the issues and the process of repatriating German POWs on pages 230–34 of *Nazi Prisoners of War in America*. My information about the French keeping thousands of German POWs at hard labor for years after the war and about some German POWs in postwar France choosing to join the French Foreign Legion and fight in Vietnam comes from Robert C. Doyle's *The Enemy in Our Hands: America's Treatment of Prisoners of War from the Revolution to the War on Terror* (University Press of Kentucky, 2010), page 193.

Helmut Horner's discovery of the message on his transport ship that he might not be going straight home to Germany comes from Antonio Thompson's *Men in German Uniform: POWs in America During World War II* (University of Tennessee Press, 2010), page 131.

My account of the Fort Dix riot comes from a retrospective story about the incident in *The Philadelphia Inquirer,* "POWs, Suicide Plan at Ft. Dix," on September 4, 2018. My account of the short-lived escapes at Camp Shanks, New York, comes from the *New York Times* story "3 POWs Caught, Escape at Shanks," on July 1, 1946. Norman Palmer, a former U.S. merchant mariner, told me about his shipboard conversations with disheartened ex-POWs in a phone conversation.

The ex-POW's description of the final leg of his journey home to Germany in a boxcar comes from Krammer's *Nazi Prisoners of War in America*, page 250.

The title of the English-language edition of Harald Jähner's book, which I consulted for background about life in postwar Germany, is *Aftermath: Life in the Fallout of the Third Reich, 1945–1955* (Vintage Books, 2021).

Karl Gassman told his success story in his oral history at Camp Concordia, Kansas.

I found background on the immigration of former German POWs to the United States, along with numerous personal stories, in Barbara Schmitter Heisler's book *From German Prisoner of War to American Citizen: A Social History with 35 Interviews* (McFarland, 2013).

The U.S. government's efforts to aid the widows of Otto Stengel and Eric Gauss are reflected in documents in the Papago Park murder case file in the Knox Collection and the court files of the Camp Aiken murder case, G-CGM, at NARA St. Louis.

Texas historian and author Michael Waters, a professor at Texas A&M University at College Station, Texas, uncovered the fascinating story behind

Guenther Meisel's change of heart and confession to the murder of Hugo Krauss at Camp Hearne, Texas, through his contacts with ex-POW Fritz Haus, in whom Meisel confided. Waters details Haus's account of his dealings with Meisel on pages 127–29 of *Lone Star Stalag: German Prisoners of War at Camp Hearne* (Texas A&M University Press, 2004). Waters graciously took time to discuss the Meisel story with me by phone in 2024. The case file of the investigation and court-martial, M-GCM, in NARA St. Louis makes only vague mention of why Meisel chose to come forward and confess.

My account of the court-martial of Meisel and his codefendants, and the subsequent commutation of their sentences by President Truman, comes from the Camp Hearne trial transcripts in the case file, M-GCM, at NARA St. Louis.

The information about the last American POWs from the camps being shipped out from Camp Shanks, New York, comes from the *New York Times* story "Camp Shanks Ends War Missions as Last German PW's Start Home" on July 23, 1946.

I found the story of the army's aborted 1946 attempt to identify and prosecute the men who had beaten Hans Geller to death at Camp Chaffee in the case file at M-GCM at NARA St. Louis. Major General Kean's memo recommending the army drop the case is contained in that file.

CHAPTER 26
Closing the Ledger

I visited the former sites of Camp Papago Park in Arizona, Camp Concordia in Kansas, Camp Tonkawa in Oklahoma, and Camp Hearne in Texas in, respectively, 2019, 2022, 2022, and 2023. I got the information about the re-purposing of parts of Camp Concordia by the Concordia Lutheran Church from Lowell May. I attended the Victory Day celebration at Camp Concordia in 2022. Doris Lutes of the Phoenix Parks and Recreation Department sent me a map showing hundreds of single-family homes superimposed over what once was the Papago Park POW camp.

My information about the enduring appeal of the POW-built Nativity scene from Camp Algona comes from Jerry Yocum at the Camp Algona POW Museum. Former camp commander George H. Lobdell described how the prisoners built the Nativity scene in his book *The Golden Rule Challenge: Command of World War II German POW Camps in the Upper*

Midwest (Classic Day, 2004), pages 320–25. Yocum sent me a copy of Lobdell's book.

Cathy Lazarus, a volunteer with the Camp Hearne Historic Site, took me for a ride in a golf cart through the overgrown sections of the former camp site in 2023 to see "the Scene of the Crime" of Hugo Krauss's murder.

I found the locations of the graves of the POW camp murder victims in the Find-A-Grave feature on www.ancestry.com.

I traveled to Fort Leavenworth in 2023 and visited the graves of the fourteen German POWs who were executed. The tombstones and the grounds of the prison cemetery were immaculately maintained. There were no flowers or other memorials on the Germans' graves.

The most surprising sight in the prison cemetery was a new grave—the first in many decades—holding the remains of a convicted murderer from my home city of Virginia Beach. I remembered the case from my days as a journalist. The occupant of the grave, navy veteran Andrew Chabrol, had been convicted in 1991 of kidnapping and murdering Navy Petty Officer 2nd Cl. Melissa Harrington, and had been executed by lethal injection. A quirk in the law had allowed Chabrol to be buried at Arlington National Cemetery—a place of high military honor. But Harrington's widower and other navy veterans persuaded Congress to change the law, and Chabrol's remains were disinterred from Arlington and reburied with those of the German POWs and other convicted criminals in the prison cemetery at Leavenworth. I refreshed my memory of the Chabrol case and the efforts to remove his remains from Arlington with a *Navy Times* article by Hope Hodge Seck, "Sailor's Killer to Be Removed from Arlington Thanks to New Law," on April 12, 2023, which I found at www.navytimes.com/news/your-navy/2023/04/12/sailors-killer-to -be-removed-from-arlington-thanks-to-new-law/.

My account of Edgar Beyer's visit to his father Walter's grave comes from David Lamb's story in *The Los Angeles Times*, "Prisoners of Silence," on November 30, 1990. Lowell May reported seeing flower arrangements attached to the chain-link fence behind the graves in the 1990s.

Kenneth Knox's personal papers at UC-Davis show that he tried for several years to generate interest in moving the fourteen Germans' remains out of the Leavenworth prison cemetery to Germany. He found support from an organization of former German paratroopers, but nothing ultimately came of the effort.

Truman's commutations of the sentences of Menschner and the seven Germans convicted in the Camp Hearne killing are included in the case files of, respectively, M-GCM and B-GCM at NARA St. Louis.

The former Kansas POW's comments about privations in postwar Germany and his comment that he wished he were still a prisoner in America come from the magazine article "Stalag Sunflower: German Prisoners of War in Kansas," by Patrick G. O'Brien, Thomas D. Isern, and R. Daniel Lumley in the November 1984 issue of *Kansas History*, page 195. I found the article at www.kshs.org/publicat/history/1984autumn_obrien.pdf.

I obtained my information about Gerd Kruse from O'Brien, Isern, and Lumley, "Stalag Sunflower," page 198. I spoke briefly to Kruse's son George by telephone in 2022. My information about the Goedecke family, as well as Freida Goedecke's quote, comes from O'Brien, Isern, and Lumley's "Stalag Sunflower," page 198.

Arnold Krammer offers an excellent summary of the stories of the German POWs who hid in America for years after the war on pages 136–39 of *Nazi Prisoners of War in America* (Scarborough House, 1979). The last of the Germans to remain at large, Georg Gaertner, revealed his true identity to Krammer in a telephone call after reading the latter's book. I read longtime fugitive Reinhold Pabel's book *Enemies Are Human* (John C. Winston, 1955).

Provost Marshal General Lerch explained that thousands of German prisoners surrendered after D-Day because they knew they would be treated well in America in his already-cited March 2, 1945, address to Congress, which I found in the Farrand Collection.

Judith M. Gansberg's book *Stalag: U.S.A.: The Remarkable Story of German POWs in America* (Thomas Y. Crowell, 1977) is the most in-depth study of the POW reeducation program. She renders her verdict on the program on page 199.

The historian Harold Deutsch's take on America's handling of German POWs during World War II comes from Krammer's *Nazi Prisoners of War in America*, page 225.

My description of the increased militancy of America's POWs since World War II is based on my reading of Robert C. Doyle's *The Enemy in Our Hands: America's Treatment of Prisoners of War from the Revolution to the War on Terror* (University Press of Kentucky, 2010), which analyzes the treatment of POWs from the Korean Conflict, the Vietnam War, and the "War on Terror" on pages 247–349. I also consulted Louis Fisher's book *American Military Tribunals and Presidential Power: American Revolution to the War on Terrorism* (University Press of Kansas, 2005).

Doyle quotes Krammer's view that our treatment of enemy prisoners says much about who we are on page 348 of *The Enemy in Our Hands*.

My description of the case of former navy SEAL Edward Gallagher comes from the *New York Times* story "Anguish and Anger from the Navy SEALS Who Turned in Edward Gallagher," on December 27, 2019. My information about a different military jury condemning the torture of a terrorist by interrogators at Guantanamo Bay, Cuba, comes from the *New York Times* story "Military Jury Shows Its Disgust Over C.I.A. Torture," on November 7, 2021. My reference to the ongoing impacts of the torture of 9/11 suspects on their seemingly endless court cases at the U.S. base in Guantanamo Bay, Cuba, comes from an *Associated Press* story published in *The Virginian-Pilot* newspaper of Norfolk, Virginia, on August 11, 2024, under the headline "Torture Muddles 9/11 Gitmo Cases."

My description of Iran's penchant for "hostage diplomacy" comes from the *New York Times* story "A Brief History of Iran's Hostage Swapping," on June 16, 2024. My account of the case involving the Huawei Technologies executive comes from the *Washington Post* column by Amanda Coletta, "China's 'Hostage Diplomacy' Standoff with China is Over. But How Much Damage Was Done?" on September 25, 2021. My account of the Brittney Griner–Victor Bout prisoner exchange comes from various newspaper articles, including a column by Lara Jakes, "Griner Case Draws Attention to 'Wrongful Detentions," in *The New York Times* on July 17, 2022. My information about the mass prisoner exchange in August 2024 comes from the *New York Times* story "Behind the Prisoner Swap: Spies, a Killer, Secret Messages and Unseen Diplomacy" and an editorial, "In This Prisoner Swap, Relief, Joy—But No Moral Equivalence" on August 1, 2024; and the *Washington Post* stories "Three Americans Freed in Major Prisoner Swap with Russia are Welcomed Home" and "Russia Released 16 Prisoners. Hundreds of Others Were Left Behind" on August 2, 2024. The *Times* story includes the State Department's information that even after the big exchange, seventy Americans were still being held in foreign nations on dubious charges. Neither the Huawei, Griner, nor Gershkovich cases had happened when I started researching this book. I would not be surprised if more such cases have made headlines by the time the book is published.

Jaworski's reflections on the German people's responsibility for the horrors of Nazism come from *After Fifty Years,* page 12. So does his warning that no nation, including the United States, is safe from the kind of metamorphosis that took place in Germany in the 1930s and 1940s. Jaworski repeatedly sounded that warning in writings and speeches that I found in his personal papers at Baylor.

For background on Jaworski's actions in the Watergate case, I consulted his book *The Right and the Power: The Prosecution of Watergate* (Gulf,

1976), as well as three already-cited profiles of Jaworski in *Esquire* and *Texas Monthly* magazines: Brock Bower, "The Conscience of Leon Jaworski," *Esquire* magazine, February 1975; Henry Hurt III, "Have Conscience, Will Travel," *Texas Monthly*, November 1977; and Robert Draper, "Colonel of Truth: How My Grandfather, Leon Jaworski, Saved America," *Texas Monthly*, November 2003. I needed only a few reminders about the case, having been captivated by it as a young man.

Jaworski's personal papers at Baylor contain numerous documents and newspaper clippings about his prosecution of the Black GIs at Fort Lawton for rioting and murder. His letter telling his wife about the importance of his case to his career is part of his collection of personal correspondence. Because I consider Jaworski a hero of the Watergate story, it was hard for me to read in Jack Hamann's book, *On American Soil: How Justice Became a Casualty of World War II* (Algonquin Books, 2005), that he had withheld critical evidence in the Fort Lawton case in 1944. The posthumous revelation was a double blow to Jaworski, who once told an interviewer, "I don't give a damn what the bastards say about me, as long as I have a chance to tell my side." He added, "If history wrote that I was trying to be forthright and honest, that's all I want."

The army's 2007 decision to overturn the Fort Lawton convictions was covered by *The New York Times* on October 27, 2007, in a story headlined "1944 Convictions of Black G.I.'s Is Ruled Flawed." It's far from clear to me whether the evidence that Jaworski withheld would have prevented the Black soldiers from being convicted in the racially charged atmosphere of the day. But that does not excuse Jaworski's actions.

I found detailed information about Franklin Coslett's postwar work in Holland in "History of the Holland Office of 6801 MIS-X Detachment," June 10, 1946, on the website Netherlands Escape Lines, at wwiinetherlands escapelines.files.wordpress.com/2014/10/history-holland-office-6801-mis-x.pdf. My information about Coslett's later life as a pioneering TV newsman at WBRE-TV in Wilkes-Barre, Pennsylvania, comes from the already-cited stories in the *Citizens' Voice* and *The Wilkes-Barre Record* of Wilkes-Barre, as well as the obituary "Franklin D.Coslett; Pioneering TV Newsman" in the *Standard-Speaker* of Hazelton, Pennsylvania, on February 14, 1992.

I got my information about Col. Henry Spicer's impressive postwar career from a telephone interview with his son Randy in 2022 and from Spicer's biography on the U.S. Air Force website, "Major General H. R. Spicer," at www.af.mil/About-Us/Biographies/Display/Article/105564/major-general-hr-spicer/.

I learned about Louis Biagioni's postwar life from his son Albert and from Biagioni's OSS personnel file in RG 226. Albert told me his father's story about President John F. Kennedy's cup, and also about Biagioni's later correcting of people at the coffee shop who denied or downplayed the Holocaust. Albert also told me his father had researched the Papago Park murder case and did not think the U-boat men had deserved to die for killing a traitor.

I learned about James Schmitz's life after the war from his nephews John and James Schmitz and his niece Rita Schmitz. Schmitz's nephew James even sent me a grainy photo of a theater marquee in La Salle County in 1945 advertising one of his uncle's upcoming speeches.

William Schaefer described his postwar career in his author's note to *People Too* (Pageant Press, 1971). I found more details in his obituary in the *Columbus (Ga.) Ledger-Inquirer* on September 18, 1979, "Schaefer Dies at 79 in Hospital." I got a glimpse of Schaefer's side career as an author in "Col. William H. Schaefer, U. S. Army, Ret.," a reminiscence about Schaefer by one of his men, Dr. Peter Carl Graffagnino, that was printed in "The Doctor's Lounge," a column in the *Bulletin of the Muscogee County (Georgia) Medical Society* 10, no. 12 (December 1963): 9, www.graffagnino.com /doctorslounge/colwilliamhschaefer.htm.

Page 95 of *People Too* contains Schaefer's comment that "injustice stinks" no matter where it occurs.

Bibliography

Adams, Meredith Lenz. *Murder and Martial Justice: Spying and Retribution in World War II America*. Kent, Ohio: Kent State University Press, 2011.

Aldrich, Edward Farley. *The Partnership: George Marshall, Henry Stimson, and the Extraordinary Collaboration That Won World War II*. Guilford, Conn.: Stackpole Books, 2022.

Atkinson, Rick. *An Army at Dawn*. Vol. 1 of *The Liberation Trilogy*. New York: Henry Holt, 2002.

———. *The Day of Battle*. Vol. 2 of *The Liberation Trilogy*. New York: Henry Holt, 2007.

———. *The Guns at Last Light*. Vol. 3 of *The Liberation Trilogy*. New York: Henry Holt, 2013.

Bacque, James. *Other Losses: An Investigation into the Mass Deaths of German Prisoners at the Hands of the French and Americans After World War II*. Toronto: Stoddart, 1989.

Beevor, Anthony. *The Fall of Berlin 1945*. New York: Penguin Books, 2003.

———. *Ardennes 1944*. New York: Viking, 2015.

Biddle, Francis. *In Brief Authority*. New York: Doubleday, 1962.

Biess, Frank. *Homecomings: Returning POWs and the Legacies of Defeat in Postwar Germany*. Princeton, N.J.: Princeton University Press, 2006.

Billie, George J., and Christine M. Billie. *Merchant Mariners at War: An Oral History of World War II*. Gainesville: University Press of Florida, 2008.

Billinger, Robert D., Jr. *Hitler's Soldiers in the Sunshine State: German POWs in Florida*. Gainesville: University Press of Florida, 2009.

——. *Nazi POWs in the Tar Heel State*. Tallahassee: University Press of Florida, 2008.

Bisnette, Dena, and Joe Gilliam. *Images of America: Concordia (KS)*. Charleston, S.C.: Arcadia, 2015.

Blum, John Morton. *V Was for Victory: Politics and American Culture During World War II*. New York: Harcourt Brace Jovanovich, 1976.

Breuer, William B. *The Air-Raid Warden Was a Spy and Other Tales from Home-Front America in World War II*. Hoboken, N.J.: Castle Books, 2005.

Brickhill, Paul. *The Great Escape*. London: Cassell, 2000.

Burnham, Margaret A. *By Hands Now Known: Jim Crow's Legal Executioners*. New York: W. W. Norton, 2022.

Caddick-Adams, Peter. *Monte Cassino: Ten Armies in Hell*. Oxford: Oxford University Press, 2012.

Carlson, John Roy. *Under Cover: My Four Years in the Nazi Underworld of America*. New York: E. P. Dutton, 1943.

Carlson, Lewis H. *We Were Each Other's Prisoners: An Oral History of World War II American and German Prisoners of War*. New York: Basic Books, 1997.

Chrisinger, David. *The Soldier's Truth: Ernie Pyle and the Story of World War II*. New York: Penguin Press, 2023.

Churchill, Winston. *The Second World War*. Vol. 4, *The Hinge of Fate*. Boston: Houghton Mifflin, 1950.

——. *The Second World War*. Vol. 5, *Closing the Ring*. Boston: Houghton Mifflin, 1951.

——. *The Second World War*. Vol. 6, *Triumph and Tragedy*. Boston: Houghton Mifflin, 1953.

Coen, Ross. *Fu-Go: The Curious History of Japan's Balloon Bomb Attack on America*. Lincoln: University of Nebraska Press, 2014.

Corvo, Max. *Max Corvo: OSS Italy, 1942–1945*. New York: Enigma Books, 1990.

Costelle, Daniel. *Prisonnieres Nazis en Amerique*. New York: Acropole, 2012.

Dando-Collins, Stephen. *The Big Break: The Greatest American WWII POW Escape Story Never Told*. New York: St. Martin's Press, 2017.

Delmont, Matthew F. *Half American: The Epic Story of African Americans Fighting World War II at Home and Abroad*. New York: Viking, 2022.

de Normann, Roderick. *For Fuhrer and Fatherland: SS Murder and Mayhem in Wartime Britain*. Gloucestershire: Wrens Park, 1996.

Diggs, J. Frank. *Americans Behind Barbed Wire: A Gripping World War II Memoir*. New York: ibooks, 2000.

Dobbs, Michael. *Saboteurs: The Nazi Raid on America*. New York: Vintage Books, 2005.

———. *Six Months in 1945: From World War to Cold War*. New York: Alfred A. Knopf, 2012.

Doyle, Robert C. *The Enemy in Our Hands: America's Treatment of Prisoners of War from the Revolution to the War on Terror*. Lexington: University Press of Kentucky, 2010.

Duffy, James P. *Target America: Hitler's Plan to Attack the United States*. Westport, Conn.: Praeger, 2004.

Duke, Florimond. *Name, Rank, and Serial Number*. With Charles M. Swaart. New York: Meredith Press, 1969.

Eppinga, Jane. *Death at Papago Park POW Camp: A Tragic Murder and America's Last Mass Execution*. Charleston, S.C.: History Press, 2017.

Ferguson, Clarence. *Kriegsgefangener (Prisoner of War)*. Waco, Tex: Texian Press, 1983.

Fisher, Louis. *American Military Tribunals and Presidential Power: American Revolution to the War on Terrorism*. Lawrence: University Press of Kansas, 2005.

Gage, Beverly. *G-Man: J. Edgar Hoover and the Making of the American Century*. New York: Viking, 2022.

Gansberg, Judith M. *Stalag: U.S.A.: The Remarkable Story of German POWs in America*. New York: Thomas Y. Crowell, 1977.

Gavin, James. *Stormy Weather: The Life of Lena Horne*. New York: Atria Books, 2009.

Goldhagen, Daniel Jonah. *Hitler's Willing Executioners: Ordinary Germans and the Holocaust*. New York: Vintage Books, 1997.

Gorenberg, Gershom. *War of Shadows: Codebreakers, Spies, and the Secret Struggle to Drive the Nazis from the Middle East*. New York: Public Affairs, 2021.

Grande, Peter J. *Images of America: United States Disciplinary Barracks*. Charleston, S.C.: Arcadia, 2009.

Green, Vincent. *Extreme Justice*. New York: Pocket Books, 1995.

Hamann, Jack. *On American Soil: How Justice Became a Casualty of World War II*. Chapel Hill, N.C.: Algonquin Books, 2005.

Hamilton, Nigel. *The Mantle of Command: FDR at War, 1941–1942*. New York: Mariner Books, 2014.

Heisler, Barbara Schmitter. *From German Prisoner of War to American*

Citizen: A Social History with 35 Interviews. Jefferson, N.C.: McFarland, 2013.

Hinshaw, David. *The Home Front*. New York: G. P. Putnam's Sons, 1943.

Hodgson, Godfrey. *The Colonel: The Life and Wars of Henry Stimson, 1870–1950*. New York: Alfred A. Knopf, 1990.

Houston, Jeanne Wakatsuki, and James D. Houston. *Farewell to Manzanar*. New York: Ember, 1973.

Jähner, Harald. *Aftermath: Life in the Fallout of the Third Reich, 1945–1955*. New York: Vintage Books, 2021.

Jaworski, Leon. *After Fifty Years*. Houston, Tex.: Gulf, 1961.

———. *Confession and Avoidance*. With Mickey Herskowitz. Garden City, N.Y.: Anchor Press / Doubleday, 1979.

———. *Crossroads*. With Dick Schneider. Elgin, Ill.: David C. Cook, 1981.

———. *The Right and the Power: The Prosecution of Watergate*. Houston, Tex.: Gulf, 1976.

Jordan, Jonathan W. *American Warlords: How Roosevelt's High Command Led America to Victory in World War II*. New York: NAL Caliber (Penguin Group), 2015.

Kaufman, Mozart. *Fighter Pilot: Aleutians to Normandy to Stalag Luft I*. San Anselmo, Calif.: M. and A. Kaufman, 1993.

Koop, Allen V. *Stark Decency: German Prisoners of War in a New England Village*. Hanover, N.H.: University Press of New England, 1988.

Krammer, Arnold. *Nazi Prisoners of War in America*. Lanham, Md.: Scarborough House, 1979.

Le Chene, Evelyn. *Mauthausen: The History of a Death Camp*. London: Corgi, 1973.

Lewin, Ronald. *The Life and Death of the Afrika Korps*. New York: Quadrangle / New York Times Book Co., 1977.

Lewis, Lt. Col. George G., and Capt. John Mewha. *History of Prisoner of War Utilization by the United States Army, 1776–1945*. Washington, D.C.: Department of the Army, 1955.

Library of America, ed. *Reporting World War II: Part One, American Journalism, 1938–1944*. New York: Literary Classics of the United States, 1995.

Library of America, ed. *Reporting World War II: Part Two, American Journalism, 1944–1946*. New York: Literary Classics of the United States, 1995.

Littlejohn, Jeffery L., and Charles H. Ford, eds. *The Enemy Within Never Did Without: German and Japanese Prisoners of War at Camp Huntsville, 1942–1945*. Huntsville: Texas Review Press, 2015.

Lobdell, George H. *The Golden Rule Challenge: Command of World War II German POW Camps in the Upper Midwest.* Seattle, Wash.: Classic Day, 2004.

Macintyre, Ben. *Prisoners of the Castle: An Epic Story of Survival and Escape from Colditz, the Nazis' Fortress Prison.* New York: Crown, 2022.

Mallett, Derek R. *Hitler's Generals in America: Nazi POWs and Allied Military Intelligence.* Lexington: University Press of Kentucky, 2013.

Marsh, Melissa Amateis. *Nebraska POW Camps: A History of World War II Prisoners in the Heartland.* Charleston, S.C.: History Press, 2014.

May, Lowell A. *Camp Concordia: German POWs in the Midwest.* Manhattan, Kans.: Sunflower University Press, 1995.

May, Lowell A., and Mark P. Schock. *Prisoners of War in Kansas, 1943–1946.* Manhattan, Kans.: KS Publishing, 2007.

McKay, Sinclair. *The Fire and the Darkness: The Bombing of Dresden, 1945.* New York: St. Martin's Press, 2020.

McNabb, Chris. *The SS: 1923–1935.* London: Amber Books, 2009.

Merridale, Catherine. *Ivan's War: Life and Death in the Red Army, 1939–1945.* New York: Picador, 2006.

Moore, John Hammond. *The Faustball Tunnel: German POWs in America and Their Great Escape.* Annapolis, Md.: Naval Institute Press, 1978.

Morison, Elting. *Turmoil and Tradition: A Study in the Life and Times of Henry L. Stimson.* Boston: Houghton Mifflin, 1960.

Newton, Jim. *Eisenhower: The White House Years.* New York: Anchor Books, 2012.

Overy, Richard. *Russia's War.* New York: Penguin, 1998.

———. *Why the Allies Won.* New York: W. W. Norton, 1995.

Pabel, Reinhold. *Enemies Are Human.* Philadelphia: John C. Winston, 1955.

Parnell, Wilma. *The Killing of Corporal Kunze.* With Robert Taber. Secaucus, N.J.: Lyle Stuart, 1981.

Porter, Cecil. *The Gilded Cage: Gravenhurst German Prisoner-of-War Camp 20, 1940–1946.* Gravenhurst, Ontario: Gravenhurst Book Committee, 2003.

Pyle, Ernie. *Brave Men.* New York: Penguin Books, 2023.

Reeves, Richard. *Infamy: The Shocking Story of the Japanese American Internment in World War II.* New York: Henry Holt, 2015.

Reid, P. R. *The Colditz Story.* London: Coronet Books, 1974.

Richter, Hans Werner. *Beyond Defeat.* Greenwich, Conn.: Fawcett Crest, 1962.

Sage, Jerry. *The Man They Called "Dagger" of the OSS.* New York: Dell, 1985.

Sayers, Michael, and Albert E. Kahn. *Sabotage! The Secret War Against America*. New York: Harper and Brothers, 1942.

Schaefer, William H. *People Too*. New York: Pageant Press, 1971.

Shay, Jack. *The Fort McClellan POW Camp: German Prisoners in Alabama, 1943–1946*. Jefferson, N.C.: McFarland, 2016.

Shirer, William L. *The Rise and Fall of the Third Reich: A History of Nazi Germany*. New York: Fawcett Crest, 1960.

Snyder, Timothy. *Bloodlands: Europe Between Hitler and Stalin*. New York: Basic Books, 2010.

Spicer, Bruce W. *There Was an Eagle Here: The Story of Maj. Gen. Henry R. Spicer and Memories of the 357th Fighter Group in World War II*. Lewiston, Idaho: Steeley, 2012.

Stafford, David. *Endgame, 1945: The Missing Final Chapter of World War II*. New York: Little, Brown, 2007.

Stimson, Henry L., and McGeorge Bundy. *On Active Service in Peace and War*. New York: Harper and Brothers, 1947.

Thompson, Antonio. *Men in German Uniform: POWs in America During World War II*. Knoxville: University of Tennessee Press, 2010.

Tolliver, Raymond F. *The Interrogator: The Story of Hanns Joachim Scharff, Master Interrogator of the Luftwaffe*. Atglen, Penn.: Schiffer Military History, 1997.

Tusa, Ann, and John Tusa. *The Nuremburg Trial*. New York: Skyhorse, 2010.

Vaillant, John. *Fire Weather: A True Story from a Hotter World*. New York: Alfred A. Knopf, 2023.

Vonnegut, Kurt. *Slaughterhouse-Five*. New York: Dial Press, 2005.

Waters, Michael R. *Lone Star Stalag: German Prisoners of War at Camp Hearne*. College Station: Texas A&M University Press, 2004.

Whitlock, Flint. *The Rock of Anzio: From Sicily to Dachau, a History of the U.S. 45th Infantry Division*. New York: Hachette, 2005.

Whittingham, Richard. *Martial Justice: The Last Mass Execution in the United States*. Annapolis, Md.: Naval Institute Press, 1997.

Yeager, Gen. Chuck, and Leo Janos. *Yeager: An Autobiography*. New York: Bantam Books, 1985.

Acknowledgments

One of the first people I contacted when researching this book was Lowell May, a retired army veteran who had helped preserve Camp Concordia in Kansas. May invited me to visit the site of the old camp in north-central Kansas. He not only showed me around but gave me so many documents that I could barely fit them all in my luggage. I read two books May wrote on German POWs in Kansas and contacted him repeatedly with questions and further requests. May and other "amateur" historians have helped preserve the story of the German POW camps and enabled me to write this book. Others include Cathy Lazarus at the Camp Hearne Historic Site in Texas, Jerry Yocum at the Camp Algona POW Museum in Iowa, and Julie Spivey of Virginia Beach, who was instrumental in creating the Camp Ashby historical marker at the Virginia Beach library where my project began. I also relied on excellent books by professional historians, such as the late Arnold Krammer, Michael R. Waters in Texas, and Robert Billinger Jr. in Florida; and authors with a keen eye for details, such as Melissa Amateis Marsh in Nebraska.

At the U.S. National Archives II in College Park, Maryland, archivist Eric Van Slander took an interest in my project and helped me find my way through the tens of thousands of documents relating to the old POW camps. Other archivists at College Park who helped me with documents or photos included Stephanie Haeg, Suzanne Zoumbaris, Vincent Green, William Green, Kaitlyn Crain Enriquez, and Jessica Guerrero. At the National Archives regional office in St. Louis, Holly Rivet, Timothy Rose, Dean Gall, and others made research there easy. At the University of California-Davis, Sara Gunasekara helped me access the Kenneth Knox Collection. At the Hoover Institution Library and Archives at Stanford University in Palo Alto, California, Daniel Keough helped me review the Stephen M. Farrand Collection, as well as several hard-to-find books. At the Baylor University Library in Waco, Texas, archivist Benna Vaughan and others helped me examine Leon Jaworski's personal papers in the library's Texas Collection. Shawn Kent at the Yale University Library in New Haven, Connecticut, provided me with online access to Secretary of War Henry Stimson's wartime diary.

Marilyn Helmers of the Andover (Massachusetts) Center for History & Culture combed through records in an unsuccessful search for James Greyfield of Shawsheen Village. She and I had no more success in finding Greyfield than the army did in 1944–45. Jim Greer of Omaha, Nebraska, told me about his encounters with German POWs while he was a merchant mariner in World War II. Tim Stangell of Concordia, Kansas, described his late father Carl's experiences as a guard at POW Camp Concordia. Rod Williamson, the historian of Camp Chaffee, Arkansas, told me the story of the camp and the surrounding area. Peter Grande, the historian for the U.S. Disciplinary Barracks at Fort Leavenworth, Kansas, offered helpful information about the incarceration and hanging of the Germans at the U.S. Disciplinary Barracks at Leavenworth. Doris Lutes of the Phoenix Parks and Recreation Office told me what became of the former site of POW Camp Papago Park. My thanks also to Alyssa Gueldyeva at the International Red Cross in Geneva, Switzerland; Landa Jacobo at The Texas Collection at the Baylor University Library in Waco, Texas; Lisa Keyes at the Kansas State Historical Society in Topeka, Kansas; and Susie Haver of the Cloud County Tourism office in Concordia, Kansas, for helping me obtain photos for the book.

Most of the American POWs who were caught up in the exchange proposal with Germany had no living relatives who knew their stories. I was lucky to find four of the fifteen whose stories I could tell in detail. One of them, OSS agent Louis Biagioni, had lived just thirty minutes from my home in the last years of his life, and his son Albert still lived nearby. Albert shared Louis's documents and photos and his fond memories of his father. James Schmitz's niece, Rita Schmitz of Texas, and his nephews James Schmitz of Illinois and John Schmitz of Chicago, spoke with me by phone about their beloved uncle. Members of Illinois veterans groups including Jay Less, Dave Mumper, and John Duback also helped me find information about James Schmitz. I'm grateful to Elodie Martin, the administrator of the Oflag 64 "alumni" website, www.oflag64.us/, and to Dave Stewart for helping me obtain a copy of William Schaefer's book about his POW experiences, *People Too*. Claudia Dant, curator of the Wabash County (Illinois) Museum, described for me Schaefer's birthplace of Kitchen's Bridge at the start of the twentieth century. Henry Spicer's sons, Randy Spicer of California and Tony Spicer of North Carolina, told me about their father and directed me to outstanding sources for his part of the story.

I'm grateful to my agent, Farley Chase, for going above and beyond to help me shape the dark and complicated tale of the German POW murders and their repercussions. My editor at Crown, Paul Whitlatch, offered insightful suggestions from our very first Zoom call and kept pressing me to tell the story better. Assistant editor Katie Berry helped me every step of the way. Thanks also to mapmaker Gene Thorp, copy editor Elisabeth Magnus, production editor Patricia Shaw, text designer Aubrey Khan, production manager Heather Williamson, publicist Josie McRoberts, and marketer Chantelle Walker.

My longtime friend the late Paul R. Tyler Jr. of Kansas City accompanied me on a research trip to Concordia, Kansas, and Oklahoma, and noticed things I missed. Tim Sullivan did the same at Fort Leavenworth. Bill Graves of Beaverton, Oregon, and Mark Haas of Fairfax County, Virginia, read early drafts of the manuscript. Lise Olsen and Ron Ulfohn of Houston opened their home to me during my travels in Texas. My wife, Kema Geroux, helped me with research and by reading drafts of the manuscript. I could not have written this book without her support and that of our children, Sarah, Nick, and Cody. My late father, Raymond H. Geroux, lived through some of the combat in Europe described in this book and told me just enough about it to spark my curiosity.

Art Credits

PAGE 5, MIDDLE: Photo courtesy of the Schmitz family

PAGE 5, BOTTOM: Photo courtesy of Randy Spicer

PAGE 6, TOP LEFT: Photo courtesy of Albert Biagioni

PAGE 6, TOP RIGHT: National Archives

PAGE 6, BOTTOM RIGHT: U.S. Department of Defense

PAGE 6, BOTTOM LEFT: National Archives

PAGE 7, TOP: U.S. Army photo courtesy of Fort Leavenworth
Public Affairs

PAGE 7, BOTTOM LEFT: National Archives

PAGE 7, BOTTOM RIGHT: Photo courtesy of Albert Biagioni

PAGE 8, TOP: National Archives

PAGE 8, MIDDLE: Photo by William Geroux

PAGE 8, BOTTOM: Photo by William Geroux

Index

About the Author

WILLIAM GEROUX is the author of *The Ghost Ships of Archangel* and *The Mathews Men*. He spent twenty-five years as a journalist, writing often about the military and winning awards for breaking-news coverage, investigative journalism, and feature writing. A native of Washington, D.C., and graduate of the College of William and Mary, Geroux lives in Virginia Beach, Virginia.